D061424J

INSIGHT GUIDE

ENGLAND

DISCOVERY
CHANNEL

APA PUBLICATIONS
Part of the Langenscheidt Publishing Group

ABOUT THIS BOOK

Editorial

Project Editor
Pam Barrett
Editorial Director
Brian Bell

Distribution

UK & Ireland
GeoCenter International Ltd
The Viables Centre, Harrow Way
Basingstoke, Hants RG22 4BJ
Fax: (44) 1256-817988

United States
Langenscheidt Publishers, Inc.
46–35 54th Road, Maspeth, NY 11378
Fax: (718) 784-0640

Canada
Prologue Inc.
1650 Lionel Bertrand Blvd., Boisbriand
Québec, Canada J7H 1N7
Tel: (450) 434-0306. Fax: (450) 434-2627

Worldwide
Apa Publications GmbH & Co.
Verlag KG (Singapore branch)
38 Joo Koon Road, Singapore 628990
Tel: (65) 865-1600. Fax: (65) 861-6438

Printing

Insight Print Services (Pte) Ltd
38 Joo Koon Road, Singapore 628990
Tel: (65) 865-1600. Fax: (65) 861-6438

CONTACTING THE EDITORS
Although every effort is made to provide accurate information, we live in a fast-changing world and would appreciate it if readers would call our attention to any errors or outdated information that may occur by writing to us: **Insight Guides, P.O. Box 7910, London SE1 1WE, England. Fax: (44 20) 7403-0290. insight@apaguide.demon.co.uk**

This guide book combines the interests and enthusiasms of two of the world's best-known information providers: Insight Guides, whose titles have set the standard for visual travel guides since 1970, and Discovery Channel, the world's premier source of non-fiction television programming.

The editors of Insight Guides provide both practical advice and general understanding about a destination's history, culture, institutions and people.

Discovery Channel and its extensive Web site, www.discovery.com, help millions of viewers explore their world from the comfort of their own homes and also encourage them to explore it first-hand.

This new Insight Guide completes the set covering the United Kingdom. It is apposite that it should appear now, at the start of the third millennium, as Scotland, Wales and Northern Ireland have all launched their own assemblies and the English have begun to cry "What about us?"

Insight Guides provides comprehensive coverage to the disparate parts of the kingdom, with titles on Great Britain (which is the United Kingdom without Northern Ireland), Wales, Ireland, and Scotland, with separate full Insight Guides to Glasgow, Edinburgh, Oxford and London. In addition, 24 Insight Compact Guides cover every major tourist destination, from Cornwall to the Scottish Highlands. These detailed, inexpensive guides would be

EXPLORE YOUR WORLD®
DISCOVERY CHANNEL

handy point of reference for information on travel, hotels, shops, restaurants and more, and there are floor plans to England's top half-dozen sites. A Travel Tips index is on the back cover flap, which also serves as a handy bookmark.

The contributors

Insight: England was edited by **Pam Barrett**, an experienced Insight Guide editor who lives near Sissinghurst in "the Garden of England" in Kent. A history graduate, she wrote the history chapters and compiled the essays on three of the good things in English life: music, theatre and food.

For the Places section she drew on the expertise of the Insight Compact Guide authors who have contributed to the great success of these pocket companions. Particularly useful have been **Susie Boulton** in Cambridge, **Roland Collins** in Cornwall, **Christopher Catling** in the New Forest and the Cotswolds, **Michael Ivory** in Stratford, **W. R Mitchell** in the Lake District, **John Scott** and **Harry Mead** in Yorkshire, **Roly Smith** in Northumbria and the Peak District, **Andrews Eames** in Dorset, **Dorothy Stannard** in Bath, and **Tony Halliday**, the series editor of Compact Guides.

Roger Williams, who wrote the Compact Guide to *The South Downs* and is editor of *Insight Guide: London*, was drafted in to work on *Insight Guide: England*, contributing the essay on landscape painting. The feature on the English character was written by **Brian Bell**, Insight Guides' London-based editorial director.

The Travel Tips were compiled by **Sue Platt**, who cut her Insight Guide teeth on the Travel Tips of the Great Britain title. She also proofread the text and compiled the Index.

ideal companions to the present book if you intend to explore in depth various parts of England.

How to use this book

Insight Guide: England is carefully structured to convey an understanding of this ancient nation and its culture, as well as to guide readers through its sights and activities:

◆ The **Features** section, indicated by a yellow bar at the top of each page, covers the history and culture of the country in a series of brief but informative essays.

◆ The main **Places** section, indicated by a blue bar, is a complete guide to all the sights and areas worth visiting. Places of special interest are coordinated by number with the specially drawn maps.

◆ The **Travel Tips** listings section, with an orange bar, provides a

Map Legend

— ·· —	International Boundary
——	National Boundary
— — —	County/Unitary Authority Boundary
—•—	National Park/Reserve
— — —	Ferry Route
⊖	Underground
✈ ✈	Airport: International/Regional
⛟	Bus Station
■	Parking
❶	Tourist Information
⊠	Post Office
† ✝	Church/Ruins
†	Monastery
☾	Mosque
✡	Synagogue
⌂ ⌂	Castle/Ruins
∴	Archaeological Site
∩	Cave
⚑	Statue/Monument
★	Place of Interest

The main places of interest in the Places section are coordinated by number with a full-colour map (e.g. ❶), and a symbol at the top of every right-hand page tells you where to find the map.

CONTENTS

Summer
afternoon
on the river

Insight on ...

Information panels

Travel Tips

Places

THIS ENGLAND

Its long history has left a legacy of contradictory images.
The fun is in finding out which of them are true

On a dull day in June 1948, a passenger on board the *Empire Windrush* looked out over the grey dock at Tilbury to the fields beyond and said to a *Guardian* newspaper corrrespondent: "If this is England, I like it." He was one of the 492 passengers arriving from the brilliant sunshine lands of Trinidad and Jamaica, lured to England by the promise of work. If his future in a multi-ethnic England turned out to be not quite as rosy as the authorities had painted, he nevertheless arrived on England's shores, like most visitors, with great expectations that were not, at the start, disappointed.

Everybody has their own idea of England, and the country is cliché-ridden: Bobbies and double-decker buses, thatched cottages and country houses, village pubs and cream teas, pearly queens and real queens, cheery Liverpudlians, eccentric aristocrats, Cockney chimney sweeps and people constantly shaking hands and saying "How d'you do?"

Visitors will have fun finding out which of their preconceptions are true, and which false, about "this blessed plot, this earth, this realm, this England" (a Shakespeare quote, inevitably). Some might be surprised to find that there is no longer smog in London, that it doesn't rain as much as they had heard, that strict queueing is no longer expected at bus stops, that Indian restaurants far outnumber fish-and-chip shops, and that the English cricket team is constantly being beaten by the nations it taught how to play the game.

They might be delighted, too, to find that the countryside often does look, as it did to the *Empire Windrush* immigrant, remarkably green and enticing, and that in spite of 21st-century motorway madness and urban sprawl, there are still corners that match up to the most fanciful idyll. The 18th-century poet William Blake imagined Jerusalem being built on England's "green and pleasant land", but perhaps he saw the country through the rose-coloured spectacles of an English mystic. Yet the essence of England is a romantic vision, though not even the most effusive tourist board brochure would attempt to match John of Gaunt's deathbed tribute in Shakespeare's *Richard II*:

> *This royal throne of kings, this scept'red isle,*
> *This earth of majesty, this seat of Mars,*
> *This other Eden, demi-paradise,*
> *This fortress built by Nature for herself*
> *Against infection and the hand of war,*
> *This happy breed of men, this little world,*
> *This precious stone set in a silver sea,*
> *Which serves it in the office of a wall,*
> *Or as a moat defensive to a house,*
> *Against the envy of less happier lands.*   ❑

PRECEDING PAGES: May Morning in Oxford; Judges' Breakfast Parade, London; capturing a photo-finish at an Essex racecourse; celebrating at London's annual Notting Hill Carnival.
LEFT: patriotic balloons for sale – though most buyers are tourists.

THE ENGLISH CHARACTER

Some see this restless island race as tolerant, charming and funny – others find them arrogant, insular and hypocritical. What are they really like?

Given the magpie-like tendency of the English to appropriate and absorb any cultural, political or linguistic invention that takes their fancy, it comes as no surprise that John Bull, the cartoon personification of the English character, was created by a Scotsman. John Arbuthnot, a mathematician and physician, invented him in 1712 as an honest cloth merchant in order to satirise the trading iniquities of the French.

Over the next century John Bull developed into a fat, jovial farmer, frequently sporting a Union Jack waistcoat and accompanied by a no-nonsense bulldog. During World War II, when England faced the threat of military invasion for the first time since 1066, man and dog seemed to merge eerily into the heroic figure of Winston Churchill.

But Churchill differed from the caricature in being a man of ideas as well as a man of action. John Bull had none of the war leader's imagination or eloquence: he was stolid, trustworthy and unreflective, believing in common sense, good manners and fair play. He was, in other words, the epitome of a "good chap", the ultimate accolade that an Englishman can bestow – even when the recipient of the compliment happens to be an Englishwoman.

The view from abroad

Foreigners saw another side to John Bull's character, condemning him as arrogant and prejudiced and regarding his politeness as a cloak for hypocrisy. They still do. A recent French Tourist Office report analysed the English as being "conservative and chauvinistic... profoundly independent and insular, constantly torn between America and Europe".

Historically, such judgments have an uncanny consistency. In the 16th century, a Dutch merchant, Emmanuel van Meteren, declared that the English were "bold, courageous, ardent and cruel in war, but very inconstant, rash, vainglorious, light and deceiving, and very suspicious, especially of foreigners, whom they despise." In 1800, the Prussian statesman Karl August von Hardenberg wrote: "Not only England but every Englishman is an island. He has all the qualities of a poker except its occasional warmth".

Naturally, the English arrogantly ignored such criticisms. "The English delight in Silence more than any other European Nation," explained the essayist Joseph Addison in 1711. Henry James agreed in 1881: "An Englishman is never so natural as when he is holding his tongue." Breaking this silence, Cecil Rhodes, a vicar's son who became an empire builder in southern Africa, suggested that foreigners were simply envious: "Ask any man what nationality he would prefer to be, and 99 out of 100 will tell you they would prefer to be Englishmen." Carrying this belief to its logical conclusion, Rhodes even dreamed of bringing the recalcitrant colonies of the United States back into the British Empire.

LEFT: traditional pubs, though threatened, still exist.
RIGHT: dressed for the weather, and radiating a particular kind of English confidence.

It was the British and not the English Empire, of course, which was only fitting since many of its most ablest administrators were Scots. But, as indisputably the dominant partner in the union between England, Scotland and Wales, the English have seldom made any distinction between the terms "British" and "English", using them interchangeably to the eternal annoyance of their Celtic partners.

This imprecision – "the English never draw a line without blurring it", said Winston Churchill – is certainly a national characteristic. Perhaps it derives from their mongrel make-up. They originated as tribal hunters who arrived from

Jutland and Lower Saxony and were later conquered by the Normans, a coalition of Viking pirates who, having converted to Christianity and adopted the French language, proceeded to impose efficient administration and fiscal competence on England's lax feudal system. In 1867 the writer Matthew Arnold concluded: "The Germanic part, indeed, triumphs in us, we are a Germanic people; but not so wholly as to exclude hauntings of Celtism, which clash with our Germanicism, producing, as I believe, our humour, being neither Germanic nor Celtic, and so affect us that we strike people as odd and singular, not to be referred to by any known type, and like nothing but ourselves."

It was the lax aspect of the English character which most influenced the language. The anarchic nature of the English language and its ability to absorb other people's grammatical constructions and vocabulary like a sponge has helped make it the first or second language used by 650 million people around the world. Unlike more regulated languages, its flexibility allows it to be spoken badly and still be understood.

The obsession with sport

Games such as football and cricket also shook off the country that invented them, and today the English, although devoting a large part of their time to sport, mainly as spectators, routinely expect to be defeated by the countries to which they exported the games. It is, they say, playing the game rather than winning that is important, and, as the writer Vita Sackville-West put it: "The Englishman is seen at his best the moment that another man starts throwing a ball at him." By this token, being a good loser is viewed as a sign

THE ENGLISH AS SEEN BY STATISTICIANS

Although it has the highest proportion of agricultural land in Europe (71.2 percent), England has the lowest proportion of employment in farming (1.9 percent). Most of England's 49 million people live in cities, yet countryside causes win widespread allegiance: the Royal Society for the Protection of Birds has 1 million paid-up members and the National Trust, dedicated to preserving the past, has 2½ million.

Women outnumber men by 782,000 but earn less on average (£433 a week for men, £314 for women). Average working hours are 46.47 for managers, 39.6 for secretaries. For a small country, there are wide discrepancies. In the northwest and southeast, 43 percent of people take at least

one foreign holiday a year, compared with 29 percent in the east, Sixty percent of people in the prosperous southeast say they are in good health, compared with 46 percent in the economically depressed northeast.

Immigrants from the old British Empire did not distribute themselves evenly around the country. One in four residents of London and 1 in 10 people in the West Midlands belongs to an ethnic minority group, but the proportion plummets to 1 in 100 in the southwest. Nationally, the average is 1 in 16, a total of more than 3 million people. Of these, 28 percent are black, 26 percent Indian, and 21 percent Pakistani or Bangladeshi.

of maturity – except by a minority of football hooligans whose robust nationalistic traditions can be traced back to Henry V's 15th-century footsoldiers at Agincourt.

The same casual approach was brought to bear when choosing a national patron saint. St George, a 3rd-century Christian martyr, never set foot in England. Tales of his exploits – most notably, rescuing a maiden from a fire-belching dragon – must have struck a chord in medieval society when related by soldiers returning from the Crusades. St

independence becomes more wide-ranging, the isolated English may for the first time need to define themselves in terms of nationalism. It may be too late now to invent a national dress, and a new national anthem won't be easy to find either. (The closest anyone ever gets is a rousing rendition of William Blake's cryptic *Jerusalem*, whose first lines, "And did those feet in ancient time walk upon England's mountains green", proudly recall the legend that Jesus Christ was one of the country's early tourists.) Nationalism

George's Day, on 23 April, has traditionally passed almost unnoticed and only recently has the English flag (a red cross on a white background) been waved at soccer matches to spur on England's hard-pressed players.

England on its own

Such old apathy may dissolve now that both Scotland and Wales have been granted by the British parliament a limited degree of independence in the form of separate legislative assemblies in Edinburgh and Cardiff. If that

LEFT: putting on the style for a top race meeting.
ABOVE: a different kind of style on a night out.

does not easily take root in such a land, where people lay great emphasis on their individuality ("An Englishman's home is his castle") and distrust institutions ("I know my rights").

The institutions of the European Union are not sympathetic to this philosophy – unlike the ever accommodating Church of England, which accepts, in pragmatic English style, that its social and ceremonial functions are much more important to most of its casual adherents than any spiritual enlightenment it might offer. After all, it has long been accepted that God is an Englishman, most likely educated at Eton College – and even if, by some misfortune, He isn't, He is in all probability still a jolly good chap. ❑

DECISIVE DATES

England's history is coloured by its monarchs, who believed in a divine right to rule

PREHISTORY

500,000 BC: Boxgrove Man, from Sussex, the first known human in England.

5000 BC: Britain becomes an island.

4000 BC: Hill fort at Maiden Castle, Dorset.

3000 BC: Stone-Age people arrive, probably from the Iberian peninsula. Long barrows (tombs) and flint mines.

2000 BC: Stonehenge built. Other stone circles at

Aylesbury, Wiltshire, and at Castlerigg, Cumbria.

700 BC: Celts arrive from central Europe.

ROMAN OCCUPATION (55 BC–AD 410)

55 BC: Julius Caesar heads first Roman invasion.

AD 43: Conquest begins under Emperor Claudius.

AD 61: Rebellion of Boudicca, Queen of the Iceni in East Anglia, crushed.

AD 119: Hadrian's Wall built to keep back Picts and Scots.

circa **AD 200:** Three-mile city wall built around Londinium (London).

AD 360: Constantine, the first Christian Emperor, declared Roman Emperor while in York.

AD 410: Roman troops withdraw to defend Rome.

ANGLO-SAXON & DANISH KINGS (449–1066)

449–550: Arrival of Jutes from Jutland, Angles from south of Denmark, Saxons from Germany. England divided into separate kingdoms.

500: King Arthur takes up struggle against Saxons.

597: St Augustine, sent from Rome to convert the English, becomes first Archbishop of Canterbury.

circa **650:** *Beowulf*, first English (Anglo-Saxon) literature, and first vernacular literature in Europe.

circa **700:** Lindisfarne Gospels are completed.

731: The Venerable Bede completes his invaluable *History of the English People*.

897: Alfred the Great, King of Wessex, founder of the navy, defeats the Vikings at sea. He translates the Bible and Bede's work into English and oversees the compilation of the *Anglo-Saxon Chronicle*.

980–1016: Viking invasions are renewed.

1017: Canute, the first Danish king, chosen by the Witan (Anglo-Saxon national council). He rules as an English king, dividing the country into Northumbria, East Anglia, Mercia and Wessex.

1042: Edward the Confessor, step-son of Canute, moves his court to Westminster

THE NORMANS (1066–1154)

1066: Conquest of England by William, Duke of Normandy. French-speaking Normans are given lands.

1067: The Tower of London is begun.

1080: Harrying of the North: savage destruction of everything north of York by the Normans.

1080–1100: A period of major monastery and cathedral building begins.

1086: The Domesday Book, a complete inventory of England, is made.

THE PLANTAGENETS (1154–1399)

1154: Henry II, descendant of Geoffrey of Anjou, starts the line of Angevin kings.

1167: First scholars study at Oxford.

1170: Archbishop Thomas Becket is murdered.

1171: The conquest of Ireland begins.

PRECEDING PAGES: Wat Tyler is beheaded as Richard II looks on. **LEFT:** William the Conqueror's invasion of Britain, from the 12th-century Bayeaux Tapestry. **RIGHT:** the Tower of London in the 15th century.

1215: Barons force King John to sign Magna Carta (Great Charter) at Runnymede. This is the first document to recognise the people of England as a whole, and gives them constitutional rights.

1264: England's barons defeat Henry III at Lewes, Sussex, which leads to the founding of the first parliamentary House of Commons the following year.

1277–88: English conquest of Wales.

1281: First Cambridge University college founded.

1337–1453: Hundred Years' War with France.

1348–49: The Black Death plague kills nearly half the population.

1362: English is made the official language of Parliament and the Law Courts.

1381: Peasants' Revolt: rebels take London and burn Savoy Palace. The leader, Wat Tyler, is beheaded at Tower Hill by the Lord Mayor of London.

1387: Geoffrey Chaucer's *Canterbury Tales,* the greatest work of medieval English, is published.

HOUSES OF LANCASTER AND YORK (1399–1485)

1455–85: Wars of the Roses between the competing Houses of York and Lancaster, to be dramatised in Shakespeare's *Richard III.*

1472: York Minster is completed.

1476: William Caxton sets up England's first printing press.

THE TUDORS (1485–1603)

1485: Henry VII is crowned king after defeating Richard III. His marriage to Elizabeth of York unites the two houses.

1497: John Cabot sails from Bristol to explore the North American coast.

1509: Henry VIII succeeds to the throne. Papal authority in England is abolished, and the monarch becomes Supreme Head of the Church of England.

1528: Hampton Court is acquired by Henry VIII.

1536: Act of Union joins England and Wales.

1536–40: Destruction or closure of 800 monasteries, nunneries and friaries.

1541: Henry VIII assumes title of King of Ireland.

1558: England's last possession on the Continent, Calais, falls to France. Elizabeth I begins her 45-year reign over the English Renaissance.

1565: Tobacco is introduced to England.

1565: Bottled beer invented by Dean of St Paul's.

1580: Sir Francis Drake completes his circumnavigation of the world.

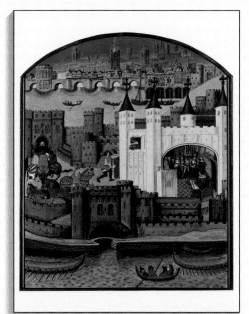

ENGLISH MONARCHS SINCE THE NORMAN CONQUEST

NORMAN	LANCASTER	STUART	HANOVER
William 1066–87	Henry IV 1399–1413	James I 1603–25	George I 1714–27
William II 1087–1100	Henry V 1413–22	Charles I 1625–49	George II 1727–60
Henry I 1100–35	Henry VI 1422–61	[*Commonwealth*	George III 1760–1820
Stephen 1135–54	**YORK**	*1649–53*	George IV 1820–30
PLANTAGENET	Edward IV 1461–83	*Protectorate 1653–60*]	William IV 1830–37
Henry II 1154–89	Edward V 1483	Charles II 1660–85	Victoria 1837–1901
Richard I 1189–99	Richard III 1483–85	James II 1685–89	Edward VII 1901–10
John 1199–1216	**TUDOR**	William and Mary	George V 1910–36
Henry III 1216–72	Henry VII 1485–1509	1689–1702	**WINDSOR** (*from 1917*)
Edward I 1272–1307	Henry VIII 1509–47	Anne 1702–1714	Edward VIII 1936
Edward II 1307–27	Edward VI 1547–53		(*abdicated*)
Edward III 1327–77	Mary 1553–58		George VI 1936–52
Richard II 1377–99	Elizabeth I 1558–1603		Elizabeth II from 1952

1585: William Shakespeare of Stratford-upon-Avon begins his dramatic career in London.
1588: The Spanish Armada is defeated.

THE STUARTS (1603–1714)

1603: James VI of Scotland, son of Mary, Queen of Scots, is crowned James I of England, uniting the two kingdoms.
1605: Guy Fawkes fails to blow up Parliament.
1620: The Pilgrim Fathers set sail for America. The first recorded game of cricket is played at Boxgrove Priory in Sussex.
1642–49: Civil War between Royalists and republican Roundheads. Numerous castles and fortified

houses are razed. The monarchists are defeated and Charles I is beheaded.
1649–53 The Commonwealth: Parliament, under the Puritan leadership of Oliver Cromwell, declares that the office of kings should be declared "useless, burdonesome and dangerous".
1853–60 The Protectorate: Parliament re-formed.
1658: Death of Oliver Cromwell.
1660: Monarchy is reinstated under Charles II.
1665: The Great Plague kills one-fifth of the 500,000 population of London.
1666: The Great Fire of London.
1672–1700: St Paul's Cathedral, London, is rebuilt by Sir Christopher Wren.
1694: The Bank of England is established.
1706: Beau Nash becomes Master of Ceremonies in Bath, making it a fashionable spa resort.
1712: Last execution for witchcraft takes place.

THE HOUSE OF HANOVER (1714–1836)

1714: George I of Hanover, Germany, is invited to take the throne. He speaks no English and shows little interest in his new subjects.
1721: Sir Robert Walpole becomes Britain's first prime minister, a new parliamentary concept, and in 1732 moves into 10 Downing Street.
1739: John and Charles Wesley begin to preach Methodism, which takes hold particularly in the Midlands and the North. England's most notorious highwayman, Dick Turpin, hanged in York.
1769: Captain Cook, from Whitby, Yorkshire, makes first voyage to Australia.
1775: James Watt patents the first steam engine. Thomas Crapper invents the flushing water closet.
1785: *The Times* begins publication.
1791: Thomas Paine's *Rights of Man* is published.

ARCHITECTURAL STYLES

NORMAN
1066–1190 England's "Romanesque". Stout pillars, round arches. White Tower, London, Durham Cathedral.
EARLY ENGLISH GOTHIC
1190–1260 Thin walls, pointed arches, richly moulded. Westminster Abbey, Wells Cathedral.
DECORATED
1270–1350 Carved

bosses and capitals, extravagant tracery. Westminster Hall.
PERPENDICULAR
1350–1550 Last of Gothic styles. Wider arches, extended tracery on windows. St George's Chapel, Windsor.
TUDOR, JACOBEAN
1550–1714 Half-timbered or redbrick

with fancy chimneys. Country manors, Hampton Court, St James's Palace.
ENGLISH BAROQUE
London churches by Christopher Wren (1632–1723) St Paul's Cathedral, Royal Naval College, Greenwich.
GEORGIAN, REGENCY
18th–19th century notable in elegant, plain

facades of terraces. Brighton, Bath, Regent's Park, London.
VICTORIAN
19th century Mostly revivals: Neo-Gothic (Houses of Parliament, Tower Bridge, Manchester Town Hall), neoclassical (British Museum, Birmingham Town Hall), Neo-Tudor (Lincoln's Inn, London).

1799: Marylebone Cricket Club sets down the rules of cricket.
1802: J.M.W. Turner is elected to the Royal Academy aged 27, the same year that John Constable first exhibits at the Academy.
1805: Death of Admiral Lord Nelson at the Battle of Trafalgar. Napoleon's fleet is destroyed.
1807: Abolition of the slave trade.
1815: Duke of Wellington defeats Napoleon Bonaparte at Battle of Waterloo (in modern Belgium).
1819: Peterloo Massacre: parliamentary reform protestors are killed by troops in Manchester.
1823: William Webb Ellis devises the game of rugby.
1829: Sir Robert Peel founds the Metropolitan Police in London, known as "Peelers" or "Bobbies".
1830: The world's first railway, from Stockton to Darlington, in northern England, opens.

THE VICTORIAN AGE (1837–1901)

1837: Victoria becomes Queen, aged 18. She marries Albert of Saxe-Coburg three years later.
1851: The Great Exhibition is held in London.
1865: *Alice's Adventures in Wonderland* published.
1877: William Morris, instigator of the influential Arts and Crafts Movement, founds the Society for the Preservation of Ancient Buildings.
1885: The age of consent is raised to 16.
1891: The first Sherlock Holmes story appears in *Strand* magazine.
1894: Manchester Ship Canal, to Liverpool, opens.
1895: The National Trust is formed to protect the country's heritage property.
1899: Edward Elgar's *Enigma Variations* completed.

THE EDWARDIAN ERA (1901–14)

1907: Rudyard Kipling, author of *The Jungle Book*, receives the Nobel Prize for Literature.
1909: Old age pensions are introduced. England's first department store, Selfridges, opens in London. Louis Blériot flies the English Channel.
1912: The *Titanic*, largest ship ever built, sinks.
1914–18: World War I. More than 1 million Britons and Allies die, mainly in northern France.

HOUSE OF WINDSOR (so named from 1917)

1918: Universal suffrage (except women under 30). Nancy Astor is Britain's first woman MP (1919).
1926: A General Strike paralyses the nation.
1927: The BBC is founded.

LEFT: Sir Walter Raleigh, Elizabethan buccaneer.
RIGHT: Margaret Thatcher, first woman prime minister.

1928: Sir Alexander Fleming discovers penicillin.
1936: Edward VIII abdicates to marry an American divorcée, Mrs Wallis Simpson.
1939–45: World War II. Fewer military casualties than World War I, but many civilians die in heavy bombing of ports and cities.
1946: National Health Service is established.
1951: Festival of Britain is held on London's South Bank, creating the Royal Festival Hall.
1953: Coronation of Queen Elizabeth II.
1959: Opening of the M1, England's first motorway, linking London and Birmingham.
1962: The Beatles, a popular group from Liverpool, enter the pop charts with *Love Me Do*.

1965: Capital punishment is abolished.
1966: England hosts World Cup football and wins.
1973: Britain joins the European Community.
1979: Margaret Thatcher becomes Britain's first woman prime minister.
1994: First trains run through the Channel Tunnel.
1996: Shakespeare's Globe, a replica of the theatre burnt down in 1599, opens in London.
1997: Diana, Princess of Wales, dies in a car crash.
1998: Northern Ireland peace accord signed.
1999: Scottish and Welsh assemblies begin to exercise a limited degree of devolution from Parliament at Westminster. The right of hereditary peers to sit in the House of Lords is abolished.
2000: Celebrations at the Millennium Dome at Greenwich by the River Thames. ❏

CONQUEST AND CONFLICT

The Romans made their mark, Christianity was established, the Normans

conquered the country, and centuries were spent in warfare

Recorded history begins with the successful Roman invasion in AD 43. The Celtic Queen (Boudicca) Boadicea led a failed rebellion in AD 61, and succeeded in destroying their capital, Londinium. Some 60 years later, to repel border raids, a wall was built across the north of England. Much of it remains, running from Carlisle to Newcastle. Roman control lasted nearly 400 years, leaving behind a series of walled towns – London, York and Bath among them – linked by a network of roads so well constructed that they survived for centuries. The remains of Roman baths, amphitheatres and villas can still be seen today. The Romans also introduced Christianity, literacy, and the use of Latin, but when they left, their influence faded surprisingly fast.

Anglo-Saxons and Vikings

The next wave of invaders – Angles and Saxons – pushed the native Celts westward into Wales and north into Scotland, and established their own kingdoms. In the mid-9th century the Danes (Vikings) gave up raiding and decided to settle. Alfred of Wessex, "Alfred the Great" agreed that they would control the north and east ("the Danelaw"), while he ruled the rest.

The Anglo-Saxons introduced their Teutonic religion and Christianity soon disappeared, except among the Celts. At Lindisfarne, in Northumberland, a monk called Columba established a monastery where beautifully illustrated Gospels, now kept in the British Museum, were produced. At the end of the 6th century Augustine was sent on a Christian mission from Rome and became the first archbishop of Canterbury.

The Norman Conquest

After Alfred's death Canute, the Danish leader, became king and ruled well, but left no strong successor. The crown passed to Edward "the

LEFT: Henry VIII, who brought about the Reformation.
RIGHT: a fanciful Victorian depiction of Julius Caesar's arrival in Britain.

Confessor", a pious man who built Westminster Abbey. On his death, in 1066, Harold, his nephew, became king. William of Normandy came to claim the throne allegedly promised him by Edward, and defeated Harold on Senlac Field, near Hastings. The Norman Conquest is the best-known event in English history.

William was crowned in Westminster Abbey and set out to consolidate his kingdom. Faced with rebellion in the north, he took brutal action, devastating the countryside, then building a string of defensive castles. In order to collect taxes, William had a property record compiled; the Domesday Book, now kept in the Public Records Office in London, is a fascinating document of early social history.

After William's son Henry died in 1135, civil war broke out between the followers of his daughter, Matilda, and her husband, Henry Plantagenet, and those of her cousin, Stephen. Eventually the Plantagenet dynasty gained the upper hand and Henry became king in 1154.

Monasteries and myths

During this period the monasteries became centres of power. Canterbury, Westminster and Winchester were the most active in the south, Fountains Abbey and Rievaulx in the north. Benedictine orders were a vital part of the feudal system, while the more spiritual Cistercians founded the wool trade, which became England's main source of wealth. Both provided hospitality to a stream of pilgrims, such as those in Chaucer's *Canterbury Tales*, written in the 14th century.

Chaucer's Knight also demonstrates the medieval courtly tradition that engendered the

Arthurian myth. Arthur probably existed, but it was Geoffrey of Monmouth, a 12th-century historian, who invented the legends, his magical sword, Excalibur, and the wizard Merlin, and designated Tintagel Castle in Cornwall as Arthur's birthplace.

Shakespeare's kings

William Shakespeare drew on the lives of the Plantagenet and Tudor kings who ruled from 1154 to 1547, around whom he wove fanciful plots and heroic tales. But he did not tackle the first Plantagenet king, Henry II: that was left for T.S. Eliot, in *Murder in the Cathedral*. Relations between Church and State became in-

creasingly strained during Henry's reign. Archbishop Thomas Becket resisted the king's interference in clerical matters and when Henry articulated his wish that someone would "rid me of this meddlesome priest", four knights took him literally and murdered Becket on the altar steps of Canterbury Cathedral (1170).

Henry's son Richard I, known as Coeur de Lion (Lionheart), came to the throne in 1189. He spent most of his time in the Holy Land fighting Crusades. At home his prolonged absence and expensive exploits plunged the country into chaos, which, presided over by his brother and successor John, produced the legendary Nottingham outlaw, Robin Hood, who preyed on the rich to give to the poor.

Magna Carta

Every English schoolchild knows that King John was a Bad King. He quarrelled with the Pope, upset the barons and imposed high taxes. The barons presented him with a series of demands on behalf of the people, which became the Magna Carta (Great Charter) signed at Runnymede near Windsor in 1215. Although history sees the Charter as a milestone, it brought no immediate solution.

John's son, Henry III, proved little better, filling his court with foreign favourites and embarking on a disastrous war with France. The barons, under Simon de Montfort, rebelled and in 1265 de Montfort summoned a parliament which has been called the first House of Commons. Under Edward I, Henry's son, Wales was conquered, and Edward's newborn son became Prince of Wales, a title held by the heir to the throne ever since.

THE HUNDRED YEARS' WAR

The Hundred Years' War (1337–1453) began when Edward III claimed the French throne. At the best-known battle, Crécy, more than 30,000 French troops were killed, but by 1371 the English had lost most of their French possessions.

After a peaceful lull, Edward's claim was revived by his great-grandson, Henry V, later immortalised by William Shakespeare as Prince Hal. With very few English casualties, Henry defeated the French at Agincourt, starved Rouen into submission, and made a strategic marriage to a French princess. By the time of his death in 1422, he controlled all northern France.

Plague and poll tax

The reign of Edward II had little to commend it. He lost Gascony, upset his barons, and was deposed by Parliament in 1327. His son, Edward III, spent most of his reign fighting the Hundred Years' War (*see facing page*). On the domestic front, times were hard. The Black Death, which reached England in 1348, killed nearly half the population of 4 million during the next 50 years. By leaving so much land untended and making labour scarce, it gave surviving peasants a better bargaining position. When a Poll Tax was introduced in 1381, the peasants of Kent and East Anglia rose in rebellion. Their revolt was brutally suppressed but it precipitated the end of the feudal system.

The Wars of the Roses

Scarcely had the Hundred Years' War ended when rivalries between the powerful dukes of York and Somerset led to the Wars of the Roses. This name was actually coined by the 19th-century novelist Sir Walter Scott, but it is a convenient shorthand for these battles between the House of York, symbolised by the white rose, and that of Lancaster, symbolised by the red.

During the course of these wars the murders took place of the young princes, Edward and Richard, said to have been smothered while imprisoned in the Tower of London in 1483 – although the guilt of their uncle, Richard III, has never been proved. Richard was killed during the Battle of Bosworth, in Leicestershire, where Shakespeare, portraying him as a hunchback, had him offering his kingdom for a horse.

The wars ended after Richard's defeat with the marriage of Henry VII (1485–1509) to Elizabeth of York. This united the opposing factions and put the country under the rule of the Tudors. Henry refilled the royal coffers, depleted by years of war, but most of the money was squandered by his son, Henry VIII, on a series of French wars.

The break from Rome

Henry VIII is remembered as the gluttonous and licentious ruler who married six times, divorced twice and beheaded two of his wives. He also brought about the Reformation, which

LEFT: bad King John.
RIGHT: the Battle of Agincourt in 1415.

made England a Protestant country, because the Pope refused to annul his marriage to Catherine of Aragon. Other well-known, but ill-fated, characters in this drama include Thomas Wolsey, Archbishop and Lord Chancellor, who had Hampton Court Palace built as an exhibition of his wealth and who was later charged with treason; Sir Thomas More, beheaded for refusing to recognise Henry as the Supreme Head of the Church; and Thomas Cromwell, who carried out the king's wish to destroy the country's monasteries (1536–39) but made the mistake of taking Protestantism too far, and was decapitated on Tower Hill.

"Bloody Mary"

When Henry died in 1547, he was succeeded by his only male heir, Edward, a sickly 10-year-old who died six years later. His half-sister Mary then came to the throne and won the nickname "Bloody Mary". A devout Catholic, she restored the Old Religion and had some 300 Protestants burned as heretics. Mary is also remembered as the monarch who lost the French port of Calais, the last British possession on the Continent, during a renewed war with France. More remorseful about this than the loss of so many lives, she declared that when she died the word "Calais" would be found engraved on her heart. ❏

FROM ELIZABETH TO EMPIRE

*Civil war, industrial revolution, the establishment of a parliamentary system
and the growth of an Empire transformed the country*

The Elizabethan Age has a swashbuckling ring to it: the Virgin Queen and her dashing courtiers, the defeat of the Spanish Armada, and the exploits of the great "sea dogs", Frobisher and Hawkins. Sir Walter Raleigh brought tobacco back from Virginia; Sir Francis Drake circumnavigated the world. Even the great poets Sir Philip Sidney and John Donne spent time before the mast – although William Shakespeare, stayed at home, entertaining crowds at the Globe Theatre in London.

Elizabeth I spent much of her long reign (1558–1603) resisting Catholic attempts to dethrone or assassinate her. She had re-established Protestantism but was constantly challenged by those who wished to put the Catholic Mary Stuart, Queen of Scots, on the throne. The execution of Mary in 1587 removed the conspirators' focal point and the defeat of the Spanish Armada the following year put an end to Catholic conspiracies.

Elizabeth was succeeded by Mary's son, James I, the first of the Stuarts, but his reign, too, was bedevilled by religious controversy. Puritans called for a purer form of worship and Catholics engineered a number of plots, one of which resulted in Sir Walter Raleigh's 13-year imprisonment in the Tower of London.

The most famous of the conspiracies was the Gunpowder Plot of 1605, when Guy Fawkes attempted to blow up the Houses of Parliament, an event still commemorated on 5 November, when Fawkes is burned in effigy throughout the land. Puritan protests were more peaceful, but James had little sympathy. Some left the country: a small group who became known as the Pilgrim Fathers set sail in the *Mayflower* in 1620 and founded New Plymouth in North America.

Civil War

The Stuart period was one of conflict between Crown and Parliament, and under Charles I relations with Parliament went from bad to dreadful. King and Commons were constantly at each other's throats and in 1641 discontented Irish Catholics took advantage of their disarray to attack the settlers who had taken their land during the reign of James I. Thousands were massacred and the subsequent outcry in England precipitated the seven-year Civil War.

Opposition to the royalists was led by Oliver Cromwell, whose troops' short-cropped hair led them to be called Roundheads. Charles's defeat in 1649 led to his execution on a scaffold erected outside Inigo Jones's Banqueting House in Whitehall. He reputedly wore two shirts, so he would not shiver in the January cold, causing people to think he was afraid.

In Scotland, Charles's son and namesake was crowned king. He marched into England where he was defeated at Worcester, and eventually escaped to France. Meanwhile, Cromwell and "the Rump" – the Parliamentary members who had voted for Charles's execution – declared England a Commonwealth. In 1653 Cromwell

LEFT: the Battle of Trafalgar, painted by J.M.W.Turner.
RIGHT: Elizabeth I, the "Virgin Queen".

dissolved Parliament, formed a Protectorate with himself as Lord Protector and ruled alone until his death in 1658. Without him republicanism faltered and in 1660 Charles II was declared king. In 1678 an agitator called Titus Oates disclosed a bogus "Popish Plot" to assassinate the king. Thousands of Catholics were imprisoned and no Catholic was allowed to sit in the House of Commons – a law that was not repealed for more than 150 years.

Whigs and Tories

Fear of the monarchy ever again becoming too powerful led to the emergence of the first polit-

ical parties, both known by nicknames: Whigs, a derogatory name for cattle drivers, Tories, an Irish word meaning thugs. Loosely speaking, Whigs opposed absolute monarchy and supported religious freedom, while Tories were upholders of Church and Crown.

In 1685 Charles was succeeded by his brother, James II (1685–89), who imposed illegal taxation and tried to bring back absolute monarchy and Catholicism. Rebellions were savagely put down, with hundreds hanged and many more sold into slavery. Whigs and Tories allied against him and in 1688 offered the crown to James's daughter, Mary, and her husband, the Dutch prince William of Orange. This move became known as the Glorious Revolution because Parliament had proved more powerful than the Crown – a power spelled out in a Bill of Rights, which severely limited the monarch's freedom of action.

William landed in England and James fled to France. Backed by the French, he arrived in Ireland in 1689 where Irish Catholics lent him support, but with disastrous results for both sides. At Londonderry 30,000 Protestants survived a 15-week siege but were finally defeated. In 1690, William's troops trounced James at the Battle of the Boyne, and he fled to France. Protestant victory was complete.

War with France dragged on, becoming, in Queen Anne's reign, the War of the Spanish Succession. Her commander-in-chief, John Churchill, Duke of Marlborough, won a famous victory at Blenheim in 1704, for which he was rewarded with Blenheim Palace, near Oxford. During Anne's reign the name Great Britain came into being when, in 1707, the Act of Union united England and Scotland.

Hanoverian Britain

On Anne's death, a reliable Protestant monarch was needed. George of Hanover, great-grandson of James I on his mother's side, but with a Hanoverian father, and German in language and outlook, was invited to Britain. He never learned to speak fluent English, and had no great liking for his subjects.

The Hanoverian dynasty, under the four Georges, spanned a period of nearly 115 years. It was a time of wars with France and Spain, of expanding empire, industrialisation and growing demands for political reform.

THE GREAT PRETENDERS

The Hanoverian period saw the last violent attempts to overthrow the monarchy, in the shape of the two Jacobite Rebellions in support of the "Pretenders", descendants of James II. The first rebellion, in 1715, in support of James, the "Old Pretender", was defeated near Stirling and its leaders fled to France. Thirty years later Charles, the "Young Pretender", known as Bonnie Prince Charlie, raised a huge army in Scotland but was savagely defeated in battle at Culloden by the Duke of Cumberland. No more "Pretenders" arose. From then on power struggles would be political ones, for it was with politicians and Parliament that real power lay.

The growth of London

When George and his queen, Sophia, arrived from Hanover in 1714 the city's population stood at 550,000 despite the ravages of the Great Plague of 1665 which killed 100,000 Londoners. This was due largely to migrants from rural areas who came in search of work.

London had been partially rebuilt after the Great Fire of 1666, which started in a baker's shop in Pudding Lane and destroyed two-thirds of the timber-built city. But the subsequent elegant buildings designed by Sir Christopher Wren (1632–1723), such as St Paul's Cathedral, were a far cry from the overcrowded and insanitary slums in which most people lived.

In the more affluent areas, some streets were widened to allow carriages to pass and rudimentary street lighting was introduced in the early 19th century. Westminster Bridge was illuminated by gaslight for the first time in 1813. Theatres, concert halls and newly fashionable coffee houses sprang up.

Royalty spent their time at Buckingham House, Kensington Palace and Hampton Court. George III was the first monarch to live in Buckingham House and George IV had it redesigned by John Nash into a Palace. Parliament met at Westminster, although not in the present building, which was built after a fire destroyed its predecessor in 1834.

Colonial power

The treaty signed at the end of the Seven Years' War with France in 1763 allowed Britain to keep all its overseas colonies, making it the leading world power. The empire had been growing since 1607 when Virginia, the first British colony in America, had been established. In 1620 English Puritans had settled in Massachusetts and other settlements were made later in the century. By 1700 most were governed by a Crown official and incorporated into Britain's Atlantic Empire.

Throughout the 17th century the demand for goods – furs, rice, silk, tobacco, sugar – led to a series of wars with the Dutch and the French from which Britain emerged in control of much of West Africa, Newfoundland and Nova Scotia and some of the Caribbean islands. French and English battled for supremacy in Canada and

India during the 18th century. By 1760 England had proved the clear winner. Colonial trade, unfortunately, went hand in hand with slavery. It was not until 1807 that the tireless efforts of William Wilberforce helped make the trade illegal and another 27 years before slavery was abolished in all British colonies.

Agriculture and industry

Radical changes took place in the English countryside in the late 18th century: the narrow-strip system of farming which had prevailed since Saxon times ended when a series of Enclosure Acts empowered wealthier landowners to seize

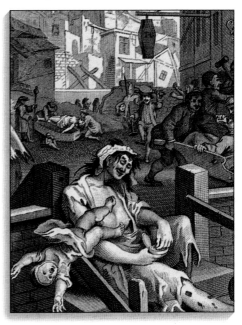

land and divide it into enclosed fields. This explains the patchwork quality of much of Britain's countryside. Arable farming became more efficient and profitable, but for the evicted tenants it was a disaster. The dispossessed farmers left their homes to look for work in the towns, which soon became impossibly overcrowded.

The first steam engine was devised at the end of the 17th century but it was the Scottish inventor James Watt (1736–1819) who modified the design in the 1770s and made steam an efficient source of energy, which would power trains and ships as well as factory machinery. Steam pumps allowed speculators to drain deep

LEFT: John Churchill, Duke of Marlborough.
RIGHT: slums depicted by Hogarth in *Gin Lane*.

coal mines, which vastly increased coal production. Abraham Darby's method of smelting iron with coke instead of charcoal hugely increased the production of iron which was used for machinery, railways and shipping. In 1776, the world's first cast-iron bridge was built in Coalbrookdale, Shropshire, and can still be seen today. Textiles had long been a vital part of Britain's economy and James Hargreaves' invention of the Spinning Jenny and the power loom in the 1770s and 1780s opened the way to mass production. As in agriculture, mechanisation destroyed the livelihood of many.

Goods and materials needed improved trans-

portation to reach a market, and the 18th century saw massive outlay on canal building. By 1830 all the main industrial areas were linked by waterways, although most of these would fall into disuse when the new railways proved faster and more efficient (today, cleared out and cleaned up, they provide thousands of miles of leisure boating, with more miles of canal in Birmingham than there are in Venice). New roads were built, too. By the early 19th century, men such as Thomas Telford and John Macadam, who gave us the road surface called "tarmac", had created a road network totalling some 125,000 miles (200,000 km).

Above all, this was the age of the railways,

when iron and steam combined to change the face of the country, and were romanticised in such paintings as *Rain, Steam and Speed* by J.M.W. Turner. The Stockton and Darlington line, designed by George Stephenson, inventor of the first steam locomotive, the *Rocket*, was the first line to open, in 1825, followed five years later by the first inter-city line, from Liverpool to Manchester. Isambard Kingdom Brunel, who designed the elegant Clifton Suspension Bridge across the Avon Gorge, laid down the Great Western Railway.

The fear of revolution

The two events that most alarmed the British ruling classes in the late 18th century were the American War of Independence and the French Revolution – a fear exacerbated by wars with France and Spain and the dissatisfaction provoked by heavy taxes and the loss of trade they caused. Known as the Napoleonic Wars, these hostilities began in 1793 and rumbled on until 1815, giving Britain two of its greatest heroes, Admiral Lord Nelson (1758–1805) and the Duke of Wellington (1759–1852).

However, political change in England was to come not through revolution but gradual reform. Between 1832 and 1884 three parliamentary Reform Bills were passed, extending the franchise.

The 1829 Emancipation Act, which allowed Catholics to sit in Parliament, was another measure that frightened the old school. And the Repeal of the Corn Laws – heavy taxes on imported corn which were crippling trade and starving the poor – split the ruling Conservative Party. The "Peelite" faction, followers of the pro-repeal Sir Robert Peel, joined with Whigs to form the Liberal Party.

The age of Dickens

In London, the squalor and crime that Charles Dickens (1812–70) portrayed so evocatively in his novels were all too real. But change, although slow, was on the way. After a cholera epidemic in 1832 measures were taken to provide drainage and clean water. The police force that Sir Robert Peel established in 1829, and which took the nickname "Bobbies" from him, was helping combat crime. Peel also abolished the death penalty for many petty crimes, influenced by the ideas of the utilitarian thinker Jeremy Bentham, who founded University College, London where his corpse, fully clothed, still sits in a glass case in the entrance hall.

Working-class people, on the whole, were not attracted by revolutionary struggle and preferred to pursue their aims through trade union organisation and representation in Parliament. The first working-class member of Parliament, in 1892, was John Keir Hardie, the Scottish miners' leader, and 14 years later the British Labour Party won its first parliamentary seats. Although Karl Marx (1818–83) lived and worked in London for much of his life – his tomb can be seen in London's Highgate Cemetery – his ideas were shared only by a relatively

Bernard Shaw (1856–1950), who believed in combining education with entertainment, introduced radical politics into his work; and Oscar Wilde (1854–1900), who was to end his glittering career in a prison cell on charges of homosexuality, poked sophisticated fun at London's high society.

All in all, Britain was feeling quite pleased with itself by the time of Queen Victoria's Diamond Jubilee in 1897. The jubilee celebrated 60 years on the throne for the woman who had spent much of her reign as a black-clad widow, who had given her name to the age, and who ruled over the biggest empire in the world. ❑

small group of middle-class intellectuals.

Middle-class life was comfortable and pleasant. Improved transport – including the world's first underground railway, opened in London in 1863 – enabled people to work in towns but live in leafy suburbs.

Shaw and Wilde

At the theatre, audiences were being entertained by the plays of two Anglo-Irish writers: George

LEFT: bustling trade in the Port of Bristol.
ABOVE LEFT: Admiral Lord Nelson, famous naval hero.
ABOVE RIGHT: four generations of royalty: Victoria with future monarchs George V, Edward VII and Edward VIII.

THE PRE-RAPHAELITES

John Ruskin (1819–1900) was one of the founders of the Pre-Raphaelite Brotherhood of painters and writers which flourished in the final years of the 19th century. William Morris (1834–1906), who devoted himself to the revival of medieval arts and crafts, shared Ruskin's ideals. Examples of his decoration and furnishings can be seen at Kelmscott Place, near Oxford, which was for a time the centre of the Brotherhood's activities. The work of fellow Pre-Raphaelites Edward Burne-Jones, John Millais and Dante Gabriel Rossetti is spread through galleries in London, Birmingham, Manchester and Liverpool.

MODERN TIMES

Following the ravages of two world wars and the end of its imperial adventure,
England was forced to redefine its relationship with the rest of Europe

World War I claimed more than a million British casualties, most of them under the age of 25. The scale of the carnage shocked even such patriots as the writer Rudyard Kipling (1865–1936), who had been firmly committed to the war aims. There were other effects, too: men who had fought in France and been promised a "land fit for heroes" were disillusioned when they found unemployment and poor housing awaiting them. Women who had worked in factories while the men were away were not prepared to give up their independence.

There were strikes on the railways and in the mines and political unrest led to four general elections in just over five years, including one that brought the Labour Party to power for the first time. In 1926 a general strike paralysed the country but demands were not met and the men returned to work worse off than before.

The roaring twenties

There was another side to life. For some, unaffected by gloomy financial reality, these were the Roaring Twenties. Women with cropped hair and short dresses drank cocktails and danced to the new music, jazz, which had arrived from America. Silent films, another US import, were the wonder of the age. Writers like Virginia Woolf and D. H. Lawrence were opening new horizons for the curious and daring.

The effects of the New York Stock Market crash of 1929 spread throughout Europe and by 1931 England was entering the Great Depression. Three million people lost their jobs and suffered real misery with only the "dole", a limited state benefit, to keep them from starvation and homelessness. The depression hit less hard in the south of England and the Midlands where recovery was faster, mainly due to the rapid growth of the motor, electrical and light engineering industries. The bold, geometric designs of Art Deco, which began in Paris in 1925, could soon be seen adorning spanking new factories lining the main roads which were starting to fill with small family cars.

World War II

With memories of the "war to end all wars" still fresh in people's minds, there was great reluc-

LEFT: bathing belles take to the water.
RIGHT: the arrest of suffragette Emmeline Pankhurst.

tance to enter another conflict. But by 1939 appeasement of German aggression was no longer tenable. Britain's island status saved it from invasion, but intensive bombing raids tore the heart out of many ports and cities.

Sir Winston Churchill received massive popular support as a war leader but, when hostilities ended, the electorate, determined not to return to the pre-war class divisions, voted in a Labour government. The basis of the welfare state was laid, with free medical care for all and financial help for the old, the sick and the unemployed. The Bank of England, coal mines, railways and steelworks were nationalised.

The end of empire

One far-reaching consequence of the war was that it hastened the end of empire. India became independent in 1947, the remaining colonies in the next two decades. Jamaica and Trinidad gained autonomy only in 1962, but their people were among the first black immigrants to Britain in the early 1950s, when they were welcomed to fill the labour gap. Newcomers from the Caribbean settled mainly in London, while those from the Indian sub-continent went to the Midlands, where textiles and the car industry offered employment.

The post-war years were ones of uneasy peace. Britain joined the war against North Korea from 1950 to 1954. In 1956, following Egyptian nationalisation of the Suez Canal, British and French forces conspired to attack Egypt. These were also the years of the Cold War, which prompted Britain to become a nuclear power. The first British hydrogen bomb was tested in 1957, two years after the first nuclear power station opened in Cumberland (now Cumbria). The Campaign for Nuclear Disarmament, born in response, organised impressive protest marches.

But all was not gloom and doom. In 1951 the Festival of Britain was held around the newly built Royal Festival Hall on London's South Bank – the National Theatre was added to the concrete complex in 1964. Two years later Elizabeth II was crowned in Westminster Abbey. Britain's Television Age began in earnest that day, as millions watched the coronation on tiny flickering screens.

By the late 1950s unemployment was low and average living standards were rising. Harold Macmillan, the Conservative prime minister, declared in a famous speech that people had "never had it so good".

The pendulum swings

The 1960s saw an explosion of new talent, much of it from the north of England. Alan Sillitoe and Stan Barstow wrote about working-class life in an unprecedented way. Northern actors, such as Albert Finney, achieved huge success and, in the cinema, directors Lindsay Anderson and Karel Reisz made British films big box-office attractions. Pop music, as it was now called, underwent a revolution when the Beatles became world celebrities and turned

---

TIMES OF CHANGE

In the 1950s increasing numbers owned TV sets and labour-saving devices. New universities were built, making higher education a possibility for more than the few. Most people had two weeks' paid holiday and holiday camps blossomed alongside traditional resorts.

Social attitudes were changing too, reflected in the rise of a group of writers known as "angry young men", including John Osborne and Arnold Wesker, whose plays challenged conventional attitudes and values. Their popularity marked the beginning of a move away from the dominance of the middle class in literature and of America in popular culture.

Liverpool into a place of pilgrimage. A relaxation of attitudes and the introduction of the contraceptive pill prompted a sexual revolution. It was a decade of optimism, and national self-confidence was infectious.

During the winter of 1973, when an oil embargo and a miners' strike provoked a State of Emergency and brought down the Conservative government, the self-confidence collapsed. That year Britain finally became a full member of the Common Market (now the European Union). Rising oil prices pushed up the cost of living, inflation took its toll, and unemployment soared. An IRA bombing campaign brought home the seriousness of the situation in Northern Ireland, whose parliament was dissolved in 1972 when the British government imposed direct rule. Oil was discovered in the North Sea but revenues were largely soaked up in welfare payments to the jobless.

The Thatcher years

By 1979, unemployment had reached 3½ million and a wave of strikes plunged the country into disarray. An election returned the Conservatives to office under their new leader, Margaret Thatcher. The impact of the West's first woman prime minister was enormous, but her personal popularity soon faded. It was dramatically revived in 1982 by the Falklands War when an invading Argentinian force was beaten off the South Atlantic islands.

The 1980s became known as the Thatcher decade. For many it was one of increased prosperity, and bright new shopping centres sprang up all over the country. In London, the derelict docklands area was regenerated, with a small airport and light railway system, offices and prestige housing developments.

For others, particularly in the north, where steelworks, shipyards and mines had closed, the 1980s were grim. A long, acrimonious miners' strike in 1984 weakened the unions. Many coal mines were subsequently closed and most of Britain's nationalised industries were privatised.

The nervous Nineties

As the 1990s began, the City was no longer riding so high. Recession returned and after 11 years, people began to tire of the Iron Lady's

---

LEFT: Tube stations became wartime bomb shelters.
RIGHT: Tony Blair, who led New Labour to power.

uncompromising style. She was ousted in 1990, by her own party, and replaced by John Major, a less combative leader.

Britain's technical status as an island was removed in 1994 when the first fare-paying passengers travelled by rail to Paris and Brussels through the Channel Tunnel.

That *fin-de-siècle* feeling

Two events in 1997 shook the nation. In a May general election the Conservatives were swept from power as the Labour Party roared in with an unassailable overall majority of 179 seats in the House of Commons. The second event was the

death of Diana, Princess of Wales, in a car crash in Paris. The wave of grief that swept the country took everyone by surprise. Initially, the tragedy seemed to strengthen the embattled monarchy.

Tony Blair's new government soon disappointed many by promoting unexpectedly conservative economic and social policies with evangelical fervour. But Blair's personal ratings remained high, and inflation low. When, in 1999, Scotland, Wales and even the politically divided Northern Ireland set up regional assemblies with limited powers of self-government, people began to ask where that left England. Perhaps, some suggested, it was time to trade in British patriotism for English nationalism. ❏

HOMES THAT COST A STATELY PILE

England's aristocracy no longer has the money to keep up their stately homes. Ingenuity has been employed to keep them from crumbling to dust

You can't go far in England without stumbling across a stately home, usually set in rolling acres of parkland and carefully tended gardens. Some of the houses are architectural gems; others are a hotch-potch of styles which indicate that their founders possessed more wealth and illusions of grandeur than good taste. What they have in common is that they are too big and too expensive to run, and their 20th-century owners have had to make sacrifices in order to keep them.

This has meant either opening them to the public themselves, or handing them over to the protection of the National Trust or English Heritage, two independent charities dedicated to the protection of historic buildings.

BUSINESS ACUMEN

Of the many who have turned their homes into a family business, the Duke of Bedford (above) has been among the most successful, turning 18th-century Woburn Abbey into one of the most popular visitor attractions in the country. The house and its private art collection are splendid, but it is the safari park in the grounds which has proved the biggest draw.

Beaulieu, in Hampshire, home of the Montagues since the mid-16th century, is another success story. It now contains the most impressive – and most visited – collection of vintage cars in the country, displayed in the National Motor Museum.

Other families help pay the bills by hiring their homes out as film sets. Castle Howard, the splendid Yorkshire home of the Earls of Carlisle, created by architects Sir John Vanbrugh and Nicholas Haksmoor in the early 18th century was the setting for the television version of Evelyn Waugh's novel *Brideshead Revisited*.

△ **BLICKLING HALL**
One of the most impressive Jacobean houses in the country, the 17th-century hall, near Norwich, is cared for by the National Trust.

▽ **LONGLEAT**
Elizabethan Longleat was the first stately home to be opened to the public, in 1948. The safari park in its grounds is a great commercial success.

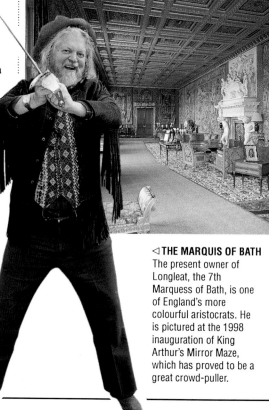

◁ **THE MARQUIS OF BATH**
The present owner of Longleat, the 7th Marquess of Bath, is one of England's more colourful aristocrats. He is pictured at the 1998 inauguration of King Arthur's Mirror Maze, which has proved to be a great crowd-puller.

Running a stately home has never been easy. Georgiana, Duchess of Devonshire, became mistress of Chatsworth House in 1774 when she married at the age of 17. The vast mansion must have been overwhelming for a teenaged bride with a negligent husband. Georgiana began to indulge a weakness for gambling. Over the next few years she lost a fortune, and by 1786 she owed £100,000, the equivalent of £6 million (US$9.6 million) today.

Charismatic and fascinating, Georgiana became a leader of fashionable society, but at home she was drawn into a menage à trois which made her the subject of excited scandal.

But Georgiana had a more serious side: she became involved in politics, campaigning for the Whigs in the 1784 election. Satirists had a field day: the picture above, showing her kissing a trades-man, is captioned "most approved method of securing votes". She died in 1806, much loved, widely mourned, and deeply in debt.

△ CHATSWORTH HOUSE
The Palladian splendour of the "Palace of the Peaks" is maintained by astute marketing. Visitors flock to the opulent state rooms and fine art collection.

▽ LYME PARK
Italianate Lyme Park, one of the biggest houses in Cheshire, is under the protection of the National Trust, its rooms and deer park open to the public.

△ PRIDE AND PROFIT
In the popular BBC TV version of Jane Austen's *Pride and Prejudice*, with Colin Firth and Jennifer Ehle, Lyme Park had a starring role.

THE CULTURAL SCENE

The English may be enthusiastic amateurs, but they know what they like and they love a good show

The English are not overly serious about their culture, nor are they overly exacting in what they expect. But if what is on offer reflects their taste, then England is, by and large, a contented, middle-brow nation which knows what it likes and is wary of intellectuals or anybody who appears to be too clever. Everyone is proud that Shakespeare had the good sense to be English, but only a dedicated minority translates that pride into sitting through his plays.

The arts are offered little government funding. The flagship Royal Opera House in London devours a significant chunk of what there is, leaving little for the provinces. Snobbery is not as obvious as in countries with a large bourgeois class, and even the Minister of the Arts doesn't feel the need to wear evening dress to a major opera performance. The larger cities are proud of their arts centres and resident orchestras, but touring companies often perform to poor houses. The same could be said of sports, at which the English no longer excel. While the major football and cricket matches draw crowds, most clubs are desperate to attract more people.

The film industry, continually dreaming of beating Hollywood at its own game, bowls along in an awkward but often endearing way, well supported by the home crowd who love to root for the underdog. The terrestrial television networks maintain a surprisingly high standard in the face of increasing competition from cable and satellite channels. Fine art has little encouragement by either government or a buying public (who are annually outraged by entries for the avant-garde Turner Prize), but many of the major city galleries, including the National Gallery, are free. And there is an English delight in amateur achievement which makes the Royal Academy's Summer Exhibition a huge crowd puller.

The English love occasions and will turn up in droves to see well-publicised major art exhibitions, queue all day to attend the Last Night of the Proms, and sleep in their cars to obtain a ticket to Wimbledon's Centre Court (and what an outcry there was when Wimbledon stopped being an amateur event).

The English reserve stops people hurling abuse in the theatre at plays that should never have been staged, and it keeps their heads tucked in books and newspapers whenever they have to sit next to strangers on crowded buses or trains. But alongside this there is a tolerance which allows an alternative culture to flourish. This makes a fertile breeding ground for fashion, music and art, which are increasingly inter-related.

Belatedly, the English have discovered the joys of good food and drink, and become more relaxed about when and where they can be consumed, a sure sign that the culture has a certain confidence. ❏

LEFT: Henley-on-Thames boat race is a high-fashion event.

THEATRE

"Plays make mankind no better and no worse," claimed Lord Byron.

But as a tourist attraction they do wonders for London's economy

From the moment you arrive in Stratford-upon-Avon you know you are in The Birthplace of the Bard. From the Shakespeare Tour buses to the T-shirts proclaiming "Will Power", from Ann Hathaway's cottage to the site of New Place, where the great man spent his later years, this pretty little town is dedicated to the Shakespeare industry.

What it is all based on are the plays, performed by the Royal Shakespeare Company in the severe modern theatre beside the Avon, as they are in theatres throughout the world. By some rare gift this 16th-century writer was able to encapsulate emotions, to universalise petty jealousies and major tragedies, in words that still ring fresh and new, with humour that seems to work even translated into Japanese.

Shakespeare is part of the national heritage, revered even by those who rarely, if ever, visit a theatre. Lines from his plays are part of the language, even if their provenance isn't always known. Most actors express a wish to play Hamlet at some time in their career, and there are few classical directors who don't itch to stage their own interpretation of the works. And if it is the cinema, with films like *Shakespeare in Love*, that brings the bard to new young audiences, then that is all to the good.

Outside Stratford, the best places to see Shakespeare productions are at the Barbican in London, where the RSC performs when in town, and on one of the National Theatre's three stages: the Olivier, the Cottesloe and the Lyttelton. But you could probably see a Shakespeare play, professional or amateur, somewhere in the country on most nights of the year.

More than just Shakespeare

Shakespeare worship should not blind prospective audiences to the fact that there are so many other admirable English playwrights. From

---

LEFT: *Cats* on stage: the lyrics came from T. S. Eliot's more playful poetry and his publishers get royalties.

RIGHT: "Will Power" T-shirts: as a commercially minded playwright, Shakespeare would have approved.

Christopher Marlow (1564–93), Shakespeare's contemporary, whose plays (such as *Dr Faustus* and *The Jew of Malta*) are still performed, to William Congreve (1670–1729) the greatest exponent of Restoration comedy; from Richard Sheridan (1751–1816) whose masterly comedies *The Rivals* and *The School for Scandal*,

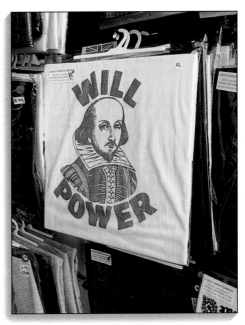

still amuse audiences, to George Bernard Shaw (1856–1950), actually Dublin-born and Anglo-Irish, but often claimed by the English theatre because he spent much of his life in London, where many of his works were first staged. Plays such as *Man and Superman* are usually in production somewhere, and his *Pygmalion*, of course, was the basis for *My Fair Lady*.

In the 18th and 19th centuries the great actor-managers came into their own, specifically David Garrick (1717–79), who managed the Drury Lane Theatre, and Sir Henry Irving (1838–1905) who starred with Ellen Terry (1847–1928) at the Lyceum Theatre in a string of Shakespearian productions.

Twentieth-century successes

But the English theatre doesn't need to live in the past. The 20th century produced a great number of talented playwrights, actors and directors, as diverse as Sir Noël Coward (1899–1973), whose sparkling comedies dominated the 1920s and 1930s, and Joe Orton (1933–67), who brought to the 1960s a new kind of dark humour (*Loot*, *Entertaining Mr Sloane*).

The career of the actor Sir Laurence Olivier (1907–89) spanned much of the century. He first appeared in an all-boys' production of

KNIGHTS AT THE THEATRE
Sir Henry Irving (1838–1905) was the first actor to be knighted for services to the theatres, in 1895.

was Arnold Wesker, whose first plays, *Chicken Soup with Barley* (1958) and *Roots* (1959) premiered in Coventry, then moved to the Royal Court, which became *the* place to see new drama.

Peter Shaffer moved out of the kitchen, with plays such as *Five Finger Exercise*, a drama of middle-class life, and *The Royal Hunt of the Sun*, about the conquest of Peru. Harold Pinter astounded critics and audiences with his early plays – *The Room* and *The Birthday Party* – and went on to become a huge and lasting success. At the turn of the millen-

Taming of the Shrew at the age of 15, and was still acting until shortly before his death. He had a magnetic stage presence, and his performances, in both Shakespearian and contemporary works, were unforgettable.

The 1950s and 1960s were a fertile period for the theatre: Peter Hall was the director to watch, first with his own company, then as director of the Royal Shakespeare Company, before moving to the National Theatre in 1976. John Osborne's *Look Back in Anger* burst on to the stage at the Royal Court in 1956, and initiated the revival of post-war English drama. Expressions such as "angry young men" and "kitchen sink drama" entered the language. One leading proponent

nium, a new play by the 70-year-old writer went into production at the Almeida Theatre in Islington. Pinter's success can be judged by the fact that the term "Pinteresque" became common currency. Tom Stoppard sprang to public attention with *Rosencrantz and Guildenstern are Dead* in 1966, and continued to attract full houses with his witty wordy plays throughout the 1970s. Both he and the prolific Michael Frayn are still producing high-quality work.

Theatre for the new millennium

Theatre today spans the spectrum. There are the big Andrew Lloyd-Webber musicals which fill the West End houses year after year: the performance of *Cats* was in 1980, and the Royal Shakespeare Company's production of *Les Misérables* opened in 1985 (though, in terms of longevity, neither can compete with Agatha Christie's *The Mousetrap*: it opened in early 1952, so has been on the stage for longer than Elizabeth II has been on the throne). Popular pieces from the 1940s and 1950s are continually revived, as well as Shakespearian works and other classics.

The Royal Court, after several years playing in the West End, returned to its refurbished

> **BACK TO ITS ROOTS**
>
> In summer Shakespeare's plays can be seen on the spot where they were first performed, in a replica of the Globe Theatre on the South Bank of the River Thames.

But London isn't the only place to see good theatre. The prolific Alan Ayckbourn tries out all his plays in Scarborough, his home town. Brighton often gets new plays before the West End; and the Nottingham Playhouse and the Opera House in Buxton are both admirable venues. Sir Ian McKellen, one of contemporary theatre's brightest stars, left London for Leeds because he found the audiences more appreciative. Later the same year the Manchester Royal Exchange received an award for Theatre of the Year. ❑

home in Sloane Square in January 2000, where it continues to stage (sometimes controversial) works by new dramatists, and to maintain its high standards. The celebrated Old Vic at Waterloo has seen some difficult years, but soldiers on, staging a mixture of high-quality productions – as does its adventurous younger cousin, the Young Vic, nearby. In the late 1990s the Almeida Theatre in Islington (and the company's productions in the West End) gained a name for excellence and innovation, attracting top writers, director and actors.

LEFT: a performance at Shakespeare's Globe.
ABOVE: if you want to act, you have to learn to fight.

> **DRAMA FESTIVALS**
>
> **Bath Fringe Festival** mid-May to early June, coinciding with the Bath International Music Festival, tel: 01225 463362 for both events.
> **Brighton Festival** mid-May, drama, comedy and music staged in numerous venues, tel: 01273 713875.
> **Buxton International Festival of Music and the Arts**, last week in July, tel: 01298 25106.
> **Cambridge Shakespeare Festival** July to October, open-air productions in college gardens, tel: 01223 322640.
> **Ross-on-Wye International Festival**, last two weeks in August, tel: 01594 544446.

FESTIVALS

The English love a good ceremony. Some of the annual events originated in the pre-Christian era, while others are relatively new inventions

England has dozens of festivals, some ancient, some modern, some zany, most highly colourful, yet none that could truly be called national. St George's Day (23 April), the date that honours the national saint, passes virtually unnoticed in most places; Bank Holidays (so-called because they are the only week

day on which banks close) are national holidays but have no celebrations attached, apart from a widespread desire to get into a car and head for the countryside or the beach.

The day that most unites the nation is Guy Fawkes, 5 November, when bonfires are lit in back gardens, village greens and public parks, and guys – floppy-limbed newspaper-stuffed effigies of the man who tried to blow up the Houses of Parliament in 1605 – are burned, while firework displays light up the skies and keep local fire brigades on the alert. It's a moot point whether people are celebrating his failure to blow up parliament – or his commendable attempt.

In Lewes, Sussex, site of the biggest cele-

brations, unpopular public figures are lampooned and their effigies burned, while Bonfire Boys march noisily through the town rolling tar barrels and throwing fire crackers.

Pagan rites

Real old English festivals are mostly celebrated in spring and early summer, many attached to ancient pagan May Day rituals, welcoming the spring. Cornwall hosts the best known of these: at Padstow the 'Obby 'Oss, a figure vaguely resembling a horse, but wearing a black mask and hooped skirt, is carried through the streets decked out with greenery, accompanied by white-clad dancers, and ending up at Prideaux Place, the local stately home, where the public are allowed into the grounds for the festivities.

At Helston in west Cornwall on Flora Day, a week later, the Furry Dance brings the town to life, as men in morning suits and women in ball dresses whirl through the streets in a day-long dance and the pubs do a roaring trade.

Morris dancers are a feature of May Day celebrations in many towns and villages, and they also pop up at other local fêtes and festivals. Theirs is a strange and ancient dance, in which participants, decked with bells and ribbons, brandishing sticks and waving handkerchiefs ("their handkerchiefs swinging about their heads like madmen", said one scathing 16th-century observer), leap around in circles, often accompanied by a Green Man, who is supposed to symbolise fertility.

Other pagan festivals long ago taken on board by the Christian church are celebrated in the Peak District throughout the summer. "Well dressing" (*see page 283*) believed to originate from thanksgiving for the gift of water, sees tapestries made of flower petals erected over village wells in Wakes Week, held around the feast day of the local saint. A procession and a fair or fête are always part of the celebrations. In Bakewell it's the occasion of a cheerful carnival with satirical and historical tableaux touring the town on decorated floats.

The Garland Ceremony in Castleton is another

ancient ritual, celebrating the return of spring on Oak Apple Day (29 May). A Garland king and queen are chosen, she dressed in a Jacobean outfit, he completely obscured by a huge bell-shaped frame covered in wild flowers. They patrol the village on horseback, accompanied by most of the population.

Rushbearing festivals still take place in the Lake District, dating back to the days when earth-floored churches were covered in fresh rushes in summer. At Ambleside, Grasmere and Warcop there are cheerful processions of children decked in flowers, carrying rushes to the village church.

The Lake District also goes in for some bizarre festivals such as gurning – a competition to see who can pull the funniest face; and the Biggest Liar competition in Wasdale, where participants outdo each other in trying to make their tall stories sound credible.

White Monday (late May) is celebrated in Cooper's Hill, Gloucestershire by the 400-year-old custom of cheese rolling. A master of ceremonies bowls a round cheese down the hill (which has a gradient of 1 in 3), and local lads pursue it, with the winner keeping it as his prize. The ceremony becomes pretty raucous, and was threatened by a ban after a participant was injured in 1999.

In Northumbria, New Year's Eve is marked by a spectacular ceremony, the Fire Festival, believed to date back to Celtic times, which marks the end of the old year and the birth of the new. A group of men, led by a torch-bearer, carry blazing half-barrels around the market square and at the stroke of midnight tip them on to a huge bonfire in the centre which ignites in a ball of flame. A similar smaller ceremony, the Baal Fire, celebrates midsummer in the village of Whalton.

Carnival

Every town of any size once had a carnival, when the traditional pre-Lent celebrations were modified and transposed to June or July when the weather was better. A carnival queen was chosen, inventive decorated floats processed through the streets, and a fun fair kept children amused. Sadly, these occasions have become

---

LEFT: the Castleton Garland Queen rides out.
RIGHT: dressing up for London's Notting Hill Carnival.

MIRACLE PLAYS

The best known of these ancient plays with biblical themes are performed at York, Coventry and Chester. Two plays from the latter cycle were set to music by the composer Benjamin Britten.

diluted in most places and are often little more than an excuse for local businesses to advertise their goods and services.

The biggest and best carnival in the country, and the only one true to the real carnival spirit, is the late-August Bank Holiday celebration in the west London neighbourhood of Notting Hill. It's an event that has grown over a few decades from a local party begun by the area's West Indian residents, to an enormous colourful affair with fantastically costumed

parades, myriad street stalls and endless steel bands, reggae and rock music, which attracts revellers and observers from far and wide.

Celebrating music and drama

Apart from these celebrations, there are music and drama festivals all over the country, from the prestigious and well-known ones in places such as Brighton (mid-May), Bath (late May), Ross-on-Wye (August) and Cheltenham (October), to smaller local ones in numerous towns. There are also the pop and rock and folk festivals, of which Glastonbury (June) and Cambridge (July) are the biggest and best known, attracting leading international bands. ❏

MUSIC

"The English don't like music," said the conductor Malcolm Sargent,
"they just like noise." But some of the noise they make is sublime

Samuel Johnson, eminent 18th-century man of letters, once wrote, "Of all noises I think music the least disagreeable," a sentiment with which many English people would empathise. You don't find music on every street corner; many folk tunes are of Scottish or Irish rather than English origin; and

the only performance of classical music many people ever attend is the Last Night of the Proms, a jolly jingoistic finale to the season of excellent and affordable concerts held in London's Albert Hall in August and September.

Yet England has a strong musical tradition with a loyal following. The early death of Henry Purcell (1658–95), before he could fulfil his potential, has been described as "a national calamity". Purcell was a major influence on the naturalised British subject, George Frederick Handel (1685–1759) whose *Messiah* is still widely performed and much loved. Handel followed his master, the future King George I, to London and spent the rest of his life there.

The quintessentially English composers are Sir Edward Elgar (1857–1934); Ralph Vaughan Williams (1872–1958); Gustav Holst (1874–1934); Benjamin Britten (1913–76) and Sir William Walton (1902–83).

A stream of music

Elgar grew up in a musical household and once said that "a stream of music flowed through our house… and I was all the time bathing in it". Elgar's *Enigma Variations* is played all over the world, as is his romantic cello concerto, although no one has bettered the performance and recording by cellist Jacqueline du Pré, who died tragically young of multiple sclerosis in 1987. Elgar's third and last symphony, commissioned by the BBC, remained unfinished on his death, but was eventually completed, after considerable debate (Elgar had wanted it left alone), by Anthony Payne, and first performed by the BBC Symphony Orchestra in 1997.

Towards the end of the 19th century Vaughan Williams immersed himself in the study and revival of English folk music, but his best-known works are the *Sea Symphony*, a choral-orchestral work based on poems by Walt Whitman, the *Sinfonia Antartica*, and his shorter *Fantasia on a theme by Thomas Tallis*.

Gustav Holst (his un-English name comes from Swedish ancestors) began life as a village organist. He would be revered for his *Planets* suite, even if he had never written another note. In a "best of the millennium" poll the suite came second to Vivaldi's *Four Seasons*.

The name of Benjamin Britten, who began composing at the age of five, is closely connected with the Aldeburgh Festival, in Suffolk, which he initiated in 1948 after his first opera, *Peter Grimes*, was performed at nearby Snape. He later acquired Snape Maltings, which was opened as the festival venue in 1967, and the prestigious event takes place there every June (*see page 173*). Britten wrote numerous operas, including *Billy Budd*, and a widely performed children's opera. His lifetime companion, the tenor Peter Pears (1910–86), interpreted many of his works.

Sir William Walton completes the English quintet. A composer of great originality, his most frequently heard work is the witty *Façade*, in which a parody of various musical styles accompanies poems by Dame Edith Sitwell, recited through a megaphone. Walton also wrote a great deal of music for the cinema, including the score for *Henry V* (1944), directed by and starring Laurence Olivier.

MUSIC BY THE LAKE

A delightful outdoor venue is Kenwood House, where concerts are held by the lake in summer.

Where to hear it

The classical music scene today is a lively one. At London's Royal Festival Hall, adjacent to the National Theatre on the south bank of the Thames, there are performances most nights in the Queen Elizabeth Hall or the Purcell Room. At London's newest auditorium, at the Barbican Centre, you can hear an eclectic range of music interpreted by leading orchestras and conductors. The Royal Albert Hall in South Kensington stages everything from popular classics to opera in the round, plus occasional high-profile pop and folk concerts. Recitals and chamber music can be heard at more intimate venues, such as St John's, Smith Square (close to the Houses of Parliament) and the cosy, Art Nouveau-style Wigmore Hall (near Baker Street), where short Sunday morning concerts, with coffee or sherry after the performance, are a pleasant way to spend the morning.

After massive and controversial rebuilding and renovations the Royal Opera House in Covent Garden reopened in December 1999 and is once more attracting the best names in the business. And the English National Opera performs a wide range of works (in English) at the London Coliseum in the heart of town, at more affordable prices than Covent Garden.

There are several top dance venues in London: the Royal Ballet dances at Covent Garden, the English National Ballet at the Coliseum; and the refurbished Sadler's Wells in Islington plays host to a wide range of classical and contemporary dance groups, as does the Peacock Theatre at the Aldwych.

Although London, of course, has the most venues, the rest of the country is not starved of high-quality music. Birmingham's Symphony Hall has been acclaimed as among the finest modern auditoriums in the world, and under Sir Simon Rattle the Birmingham Symphony Orchestra became one of the most highly regarded in Europe – a reputation that looks set to continue under his successor, Junichi Hirokami. In Manchester, the perfect acoustics of the Bridgwater Hall attract top musicians and conductors from all over the world.

In summer, the gardens of numerous stately homes and castles are settings for outdoor concerts, where audiences bring picnic hampers,

rugs and chairs: idyllic on fine evenings, but you have to take a chance on the weather.

The most stylish musical picnics take place at Glyndebourne, at the foot of the South Downs in Sussex, although the operatic productions themselves are staged indoors in the splendid modern opera house which, in 1994, was built to extend the original.

There are also music festivals held all over the country; some of them attract well-known names, others offer good opportunities to hear talented young musicians who may be the names of the future. All in all, you will find there's no shortage of places to enjoy "the least disagreeable" of noises. ❑

LEFT: Sir Simon Rattle in rehearsal.
RIGHT: waving the flag at the Last Night of the Proms.

PAINTING THE LANDSCAPE

*The English countryside has inspired poets, musicians
and, above all, painters. Two of them possessed genius ahead of their time*

England's major contribution to European art is in landscape painting. And in landscape painting two figures – James Mallord William Turner, the son of a Covent Garden barber in London, and John Constable, whose father was a miller in Suffolk – were supreme.

England did not share Europe's earlier tradition of art based on Christianity. Church property was destroyed or seized under Henry VIII in 1535, and the puritanical Protestants who ousted the monarchy in the mid-17th century rid the church of all signs of idolatry. For longer than any Englishman can remember, paintings and icons in church have been frowned upon.

Back to nature

The English not only turned against what they saw as the vanity and pomp of Rome; they also failed to take much interest in the established Anglican Church of England. "There is no religion in England," noted the French philosopher Montesquieu in 1730. "If anyone mentions religion people begin to laugh." The great religious houses were in ruins, but Shakespeare's "ruined choirs that once so sweetly sang" inspired a piety among Romantics in the back-to-nature Age of Reason.

In England, poets such as William Wordsworth (1770–1850), bard of the Lake District and scourge of the prevailing Industrial Revolution, extolled the simple beauty of nature, an idea that soon became fashionable: walking was a habit taken up by intellectuals, and the "English garden" overturned the convention of formal Italianate gardens in favour of more informal plantings. The word "picturesque" entered the language, meaning a view that resembled a landscape or view that suggested a painting.

William Turner had no education but from time to time he was moved to write poetry, and his early paintings – *Tintern Abbey* (1794) and

Buttermere (1798) – were also subjects of Wordsworth's poems. Turner went on the first of numerous tours of the country when he was 14, in 1789, the same year he entered the Royal Academy. His tireless pens and brushes made him one of England's most prolific painters. He made jottings wherever he went and many parts

of England can lay claim to his attention. "Turner seats" have been put up in the Yorkshire Dales to admire the scenes he painted. Around the south coast, in Hastings and elsewhere, he depicted stormy seas, influenced by Dutch maritime painting. And at Petworth House in Surrey, where he was given a studio, he painted English parklands. The Turner Gallery at the Tate Britain gallery in London holds the best part of his works.

He worked in watercolour (at the time considered merely a medium for colouring prints) and, from 1796, in oils. That same year he had his first exhibited oil painting, *Fisherman at Sea off the Needles*, depicting a small boat on a

---

LEFT: *View of Hampstead Heath, Looking Towards Harrow* (detail), by John Constable, 1821.
RIGHT: William Wordsworth, the inspirational poet of the romantic English landscape.

perilously stormy moonlit night. He always lived near water, never far from the Thames, and he took houses near the sea to watch the effects of the sun on the water. He also toured Europe, exploring the Alps, which benefited from the dramatic nature of his paintings. Scenes painted by Turner are often disappointingly undramatic when viewed in real life.

He was a small, industrious figure, who wished to be left alone to get on with his work. Constable sat at the same dining table at the Royal Academy, but they were not friends and they never spoke to each other about their work. In the 1840s, living with his mistress in Chelsea, Turner was known to his neighbours as Mr Booth and was thought to be a retired admiral. His lack of education and rough manner may have cost him the presidency of the Royal Academy which he deserved.

Turner had been elected a full member of the Academy in 1802, the year John Constable first exhibited there. Four years later, Constable met Wordsworth in the Lake District. They had much in common: a desire for the simple rural life and no time for any luxury or grandeur their fame might have brought. Born six years after the poet, in 1776, Constable never lost sight of his Suffolk roots. "The sound of water escaping

SCHOOLS AND STYLES

Medieval art Confined mainly to illuminated manuscripts, such as the Lindisfarne Gospels, Winchester School.

Renaissance England's Renaissance produced notable portraiture, such as the School of Miniatures.

Baroque Portraiture by Van Dyck, classical scenes, such the Banqueting House ceiling by Rubens in Whitehall.

Grand Manners & Conversation Pieces 18th-century studies of the wealthy. Principally Joshua Reynolds, first president of the Royal Academy, and Thomas Gainsborough. George Stubbs, renowned animal painter, earned more by painting portraits of horses with their owners.

Pre-Raphaelites Started in 1848, with William Morris,

founder of the Arts & Crafts Movement which led to Art Nouveau in Europe. These idealists, including D.G. Rossetti and Edward Burne-Jones, harked back to a golden age of medieval craftsmanship and legends of Camelot. (*See Birmingham and Manchester art galleries.*)

Camden Town Set Walter Sickert and associates respond edto the French Post-Impressionists.

St Ives Not so much a school more a 1920s West Country retreat, for Barbara Hepworth and Ben Nicholson. Now an outpost of the Tate Gallery.

Sensation! Damien Hurst, Rachael Whitehead, Tracey Emin – Tate Prize candidates bring the shock of the new.

from mill dams, willows, old rotting planks, slimy posts and brickwork, I love such things," he said. "These scenes made me a painter." Unlike Turner, Constable never strayed far from home. He never went abroad and all his work was done in the south of England. His father owned Dedham and Flatford mills in the Stour valley which can be identified in his paintings, as can many parts of the river. Even in his day it was known as "Constable country". But pressure of work obliged him to live nearer London, at least for half the year, and

His brush strokes were so fevered, so light and dashing that his works were called "sketches", for they were often more like impressions of what he saw. Later he might work a sketch up into a more formal, composed painting. Critics dismissed the sketches as being lesser works, and complained about his "whitewash" and "snow", the strokes of white that lightened his subjects. Today the sketches are often more appreciated than the finished canvases.

In 1821 his *View on the Stour* won a gold medal at the Paris Salon. Turner's work,

he bought a house in Hampstead, which looks down over the city. The flat Suffolk landscapes had begun his obsession with skies, but it was here that he began to collect and classify them, writing down the time and date he had observed them. Clouds were, he believed, the chief organ of sentiment.

Constable brought a freshness of light and colour to his large canvases, such as *The Hay Wain* (1820, the National Gallery, London), which has become almost a cliché of English art, and still consistently tops popularity polls.

LEFT: Turner's *Rain, Steam and Speed* (1844).
ABOVE: Constable's biggest hit, *The Hay Wain* (1820).

described by Constable as "airy visions, painted with tinted steam", was also an enormous influence abroad.

Turner's impressionistic works such as *The Fighting Tameraire* or *Rain, Steam and Speed*, were as far from mainstream European art in their day as Picasso's *Les Demoiselles d'Avignon* was in his. Turner was to be emulated both in Britain and abroad. In Britain he was never surpassed. And it would be more than 50 years before a French painter, Claude Monet, exhibited in the Salon a painting of a glimpse of a sunrise on water, *Impression: Soleil Levant*, which inspred a French critic to describe him, dismissively, as an *Impressioniste*. ❏

FOOD

A growing interest in food, combined with the influences of a multicultural society, means that eating is England has become much more exciting

Once upon a time English food had a very bad reputation. Charges of overcooked vegetables and stodgy puddings were made. Pub food consisted mainly of shepherd's pie and sausages. Sandwiches were accused of curling at the edges. You couldn't get a glass of wine in many restaurants, or a cup of coffee

in many pubs. And you couldn't get a decent cup of coffee anywhere.

Most of these criticisms were well-deserved, although they didn't take account of the many corners of the country where local produce resulted in regional specialities. The joys of freshly caught crabs in Cromer, shrimps in Morecambe Bay or smoked fish in Craster were often overlooked. The variety of spicy local sausages in Cumbria or new season lamb from the Romney Marshes also went unnoticed.

But recent visitors to England have noticed an enormous change in culinary habits. Whether it's the plethora of television cooks – cooking and gardening programmes flood the TV chan-nels – the availability of ingredients from all over the globe, or the input of new ideas due to foreign travel, both the range and the quality of food are undeniably better.

Of course, it would not be strictly true to say that it is all English food. The lines between national cuisines have become blurred, and as new inputs have arrived, there has been a cor-responding growth of interest in food which is typically English, but produced using the best and freshest ingredients.

Dietary changes have made a difference, too: venison, an old English favourite that had all but disappeared, became popular again because it is so low in fat. Ostrich didn't really catch on, and a lot of entrepreneurs lost money they had invested in the ostrich farms which seemed like the coming thing in the early 1990s. Once it was accepted that overcooking kills vitamins, crunchy vegetables came to stay; while garlic, once an English staple, but for years derided as unsociably smelly, returned to the kitchen in force once its health-giving properties were recognised.

A break with tradition

Traditional eating patterns have undergone a gradual change: few people now eat the "full English breakfast" of fried eggs, sausages, bacon and mushrooms – colloquially known as "the heart attack special". But it is still on offer in most bed-and-breakfast establishments – and often eaten with great appreciation by those who usually breakfast on a bowl of cereal and a piece of wholewheat toast.

The typical English tea – sandwiches, cakes and pots of tea – survives in country tea rooms, where it can be wonderfully welcoming after a long walk – but has disappeared from most households, because people usually aren't at home at "teatime".

Fish and chips are still popular, and, in sea-side towns particularly can be delicious, but over-fishing has made white fish such as cod relatively scarce and expensive, so it is no longer a cheap alternative to meat. In many places fish-and-chip shops have closed down, to be replaced with restaurants selling take-away tandoori or Chinese food.

The huge increase in Chinese and Indian restaurants, ranging from the cheap take-away to the high quality establishment, reflects the influence of England's immigrant communities on the daily diet. Indian food in particular is hugely popular – although much of it is an anglicised version which would be unrecognisable in India or Pakistan.

Italian, food, too, has become so ubiquitous that there is a whole generation of English people who could not imagine a world where pizza or lasagna was not readily available – and may not even realise it is Italian.

The increase in vegetarianism has also been influential. Not so long ago regarded as a rather odd fad, that was probably not very good for you, it is now so acceptable that not only do specialist vegetarian restaurants thrive, but virtually every eating establishment offers vegetarian alternatives, which are frequently more adventurous and tempting than those geared towards carnivores.

The streets of London and other major cities are lined with restaurants and cafés offering a fusion of culinary styles, as might be expected, but what is more surprising is that this wide choice of food has radiated to provincial towns and rural communities. Many village pubs will have menus that range from warm goat's cheese salad to roast beef, from seared sea bass to steak and kidney pie.

Culinary gains and losses

English cheeses have made a comeback in recent years. When soft cheeses from the Continent first became widely available, indigenous varieties such as Cheddar, Wensleydale and Stilton fell out of fashion. But their worth has now been recognised once more – as has that of Somerset-made varieties of soft cheeses such as Brie and Camembert.

Many small grocers' shops and delicatessens sell regional cheeses, and there are specialist shops where the variety is almost overwhelming. At Christmas, Stilton, recognised as the

> ### SMALL IS BEAUTIFUL
> Be wary of small restaurants with long menus: fewer choices usually mean the food is really fresh and home-cooked.

queen of English cheeses, is sold in discreetly decorated gift boxes by superior stores such as Harrods and Fortnum & Mason.

The variety of food available, together with some restrictions imposed by the European Union, has had some unfortunate side effects. Many people complain that the fruit and vegetables available in English supermarkets have been bred for shape and appearance and that taste has been sacrificed. Still more lament the fact that while you can buy kiwi fruit and mangoes, it can be hard to find a true

scrunchy English apple, except in apple-growing areas, where you can buy them at roadside stalls and farm shops. Farmers' markets, where fresh produce is sold direct from the growers, are also making an appearance.

One thing the English are still traditional about is their puddings, also known as desserts. Passion fruit sorbet is all very well, and there are those who think that profiteroles represent the height of French achievement, but a strong body of opinion holds that treacle tart, chocolate mousse or apple pie are the only civilised way to finish a meal. Catering to this demand, many otherwise adventurous restaurants put such comfort foods on their menus. ❏

LEFT: fresh-baked pies sell out fast.
RIGHT: fish and chips are still popular.

COUNTRY PUBS

The English pub is an institution, offering warm beer, good company,
and a welcome to all. That's the tradition. But what's the reality?

Everyone knows what an English country pub looks like. It has roses climbing around its weathered oak door, a smiling landlord and busty barmaid, exposed timbers on the ceiling, a fire in the inglenook in winter, an umbrageous garden heavy with wisteria in the summer. Stuffed foxes, copper pots and

chestnut pans decorate the walls and regulars' pewter and silver mugs hang above the bar. Friendly locals invite visitors to join them in games of skittles or shove ha'penny, while the cricket team, triumphant from its afternoon battle on the village green, has a well-deserved pint or two in the Public Bar. In the Saloon Bar motoring anecdotes and shaggy-dog stories are passed around amid congenial conversation, and lovers plan their wedding in The Snug. Game pie and beef stew are on the menu, the Stilton cheese is perfection, and the creamy ale slides down like Olympian nectar.

You'll be lucky. The conviviality that once existed in the village pub has not entirely gone, but it has diminished. Drink-driving laws, better homes to live in and a growing disparity between the cost of alcohol in supermarkets and the price of drinks in pubs, all contrive to keep pubs fairly empty for much of the week.

Nevertheless, country pubs remain a solid English institution. On weekdays local workers forgather in their lunch hour for inexpensive snacks; on Friday and Saturday night the better catered establishments, often with separate restaurants, are highly popular and at weekends and early evenings children are more welcome than they have ever been – which is not necessarily saying much (under 14 they are not, legally, allowed in at all). In many country areas, pubs are the object of planned walks, an escape from bad weather, and are often the only place to go to find any sustenance.

Real ale

Until Tudor times, the traditional English tipple was ale, made simply with fermented malt from barley. Then, in 1520, "Turkeys, heresies, hops and beer. All came to England in the one year". The dried flowers of hops, plants that spiral up some 20 ft (6 metres) in special hop gardens mainly in Kent (*see page 186*), have been used ever since, for flavouring and preserving ale. With the inclusion of hops, ale becomes beer, though the two names are often used interchangeably these days.

"Real ale" is usually made with hops. The mainstay of all pubs, it is drawn from the barrel alive and fermenting, via a pump on the bar. It is crystal clear, at cellar temperature and, with no added carbon dioxide gas, has not much of a head on it. Served in chunky "jugs" or slim "straight" glasses, its potency is registered in degrees of gravity displayed on the pump label: 3 per cent is weak, 5 per cent strong, 3.4–3.8 per cent average. As well as the pub's regular beer, there are sometimes "guest" ales brought in to make a change. These delight in bizarre and often offensive names.

As pubs and brewing are part of England's heritage, it is not surprising to find some brewers trying to fight the monolithic producers and keep to the old ways. A few publicans brew their own beer and there are scores of micro-breweries across the country. It is always worth enquiring if there is a local beer. Real ale, like wine, has a problem travelling, and even larger brewers often don't stray far from their region: Adnams in Suffolk, Harveys in Sussex, Sam Smiths in Yorkshire.

FROM ALE TO BEER

Turkeys, heresies, hops and beer
All came to England in the one year
– traditional saying

Beer is not the only local drink. Cider is famous in Hereford, the West Country and Kent, though it can be strong, especially Devon's notorious scrumpy, and may be served only in half-pint measures. Local wines, too – generally medium-dry whites – go on sale near wine-producing areas in the south of England.

The word "pub" is merely the shortened form of "public house", an indication that the earliest ale houses were private homes where the occupant brewed beer and sold it at the front door or across the table in the living room. Today most pubs have two separate bars: the Public Bar, which is the basic drinking shop, a bare-board room where games are played; and the Lounge or Saloon Bar, a carpeted front room where wives (if they are really lucky) get taken on a Saturday night, and where notices may warn that anyone in dirty working clothes will not be permitted – being choosy about who they serve is one of the landlords' God-given rights. Often a self-imposed class distinction operates between the two bars.

Oldest and smallest

Many pubs are ancient, some say they are haunted. There are several claimants to being the oldest pub in England, on sites that may date back 1,000 years. The Trip to Jerusalem, carved out of a rock beneath the castle in Nottingham, was in business in the 13th century, catering for Crusaders who were off to the Holy Land – or perhaps that was just a boast when it came to closing time. The smallest is the 17th-century Nutshell in Bury St Edmonds, Suffolk, which measures a cosy 15ft 10in by 7ft 6in (4.8 by 2.3 metres)

When customers were illiterate Anglo-Saxons, poles topped with evergreen boughs were stuck outside public houses to show where they were. From these, pub signs developed. There are more than 15,000 different names for some 50,000 pubs in England, the most common being The Red Lion. A children's car game is to score points for each part of the body represented in a sign: one point for a King's Head, two points for the Queen's Arms, 10 for The Coach and Horses (or 20 if there are four horses). Signs are not, alas, sacrosanct, although it is mainly in the cities that names are changed on corporate instructions, with trendy chains

such as the Slug and Lettuce on the increase, and "traditional" (meaning bogus) Irish bars.

It is hard work running a pub, as any landlord, without being asked twice, will tell you. Apart from the physical exertion and the ability to tolerate bores for hours at a stretch, their days are long, though many keep to traditional closing times, shutting their doors in the afternoon and at 11o'clock at night.

But the real joy of a country pub is finding good beer, good company and a good landlord, who at closing time comes round to the front of the bar (to convince the police, if they arrive, that he is merely drinking with friends), closes the pub door and locks everyone in. ❏

LEFT: sign of a good pub in Derbyshire.
RIGHT: a pub needs a welcoming barmaid.

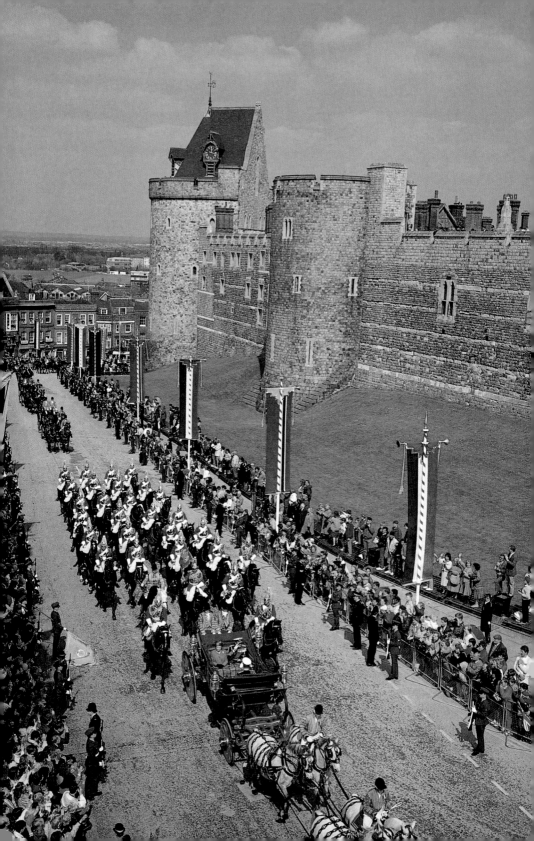

PLACES

*A detailed guide to the country, with principal sites
clearly cross-referenced by number to the maps*

For all the fuss it has made in history, for all the language it has distributed about the world, England is a rather small place. The largest of the four constituent elements that make up the United Kingdom, it covers 50,331 sq miles (130,357 sq km), about the same size as New York State or one of New Zealand's islands. But its population of around 49 million is two and a half times New York State's, 15 times both New Zealand's islands. Heavy traffic on motorways is therefore to be expected; getting a seat on a train, particularly during rush hour, is a rare pleasure.

By far the greater portion of the population lives in the south. The large northern towns, Liverpool, Manchester, Newcastle, which grew vast on the Industrial Revolution, have struggled to catch up with the post-industrial age, while Birmingham, Britain's second city, has benefitted from its more central location. The country is divided into counties, the old English shires, where sheriffs transacted local business. They have provided titles for the nation's nobility and though their names and boundaries have been tinkered with twice in post-war years, they are redolent of the country's past and continue to inspire local pride.

At the start of the third millennium, England, like most countries, is a more homogenised nation than ever before. Local accents and dialects that not long ago were thick on the ground, are now waning, but the fact that they do remain confirms that the country is made up of many constituent parts. Motorways bring visitors close to every corner, but often, not far from the motorway or main road, is an apparently quite rural place: a town or village church spire pointing the way. Everywhere is within relatively easy reach.

What England has to offer most is ever-changing landscape, sparklingly green, often rolling. Its high spots are not particularly high, but they provide incomparable scenery, in the Peak District, in the Pennines, on the South Downs, among the Yorkshire and West Country moors and around the Lake District. And the sea, often blustery and bracing, is never far away. The variety of architecture is extraordinary, and it characterises every part of the country, from West Country thatch to Cotswold stone, weatherboarded Kent to half-timbered East Anglia, red-brick Cheshire, black-slated Cumbria, and the sandstones, red and yellow, of Cumbria and York.

It doesn't take much effort in England, and not many miles, to feel that you have travelled a long way. ❑

PRECEDING PAGES: a carriage in Windsor Great Park; a cluster of cottages in Bickleigh, Devon; the Farne Islands, Northumbria.
LEFT: celebrating a State Visit at Windsor Castle.

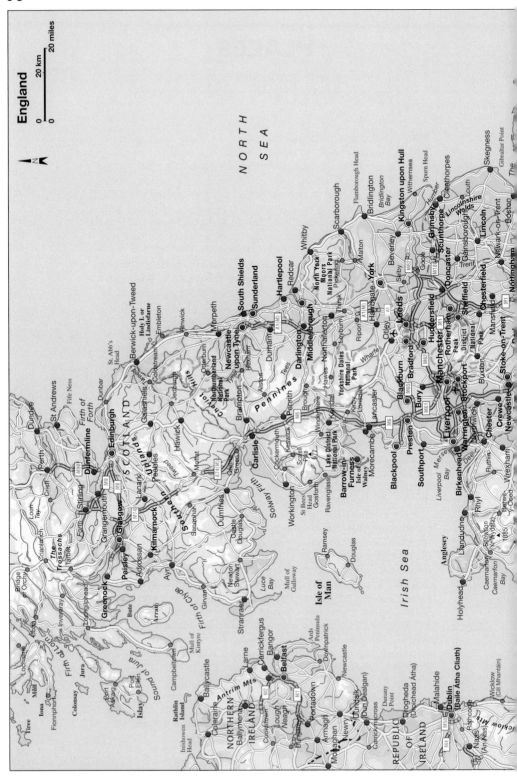

England

N

0   20 km
0   20 miles

N O R T H

S E A

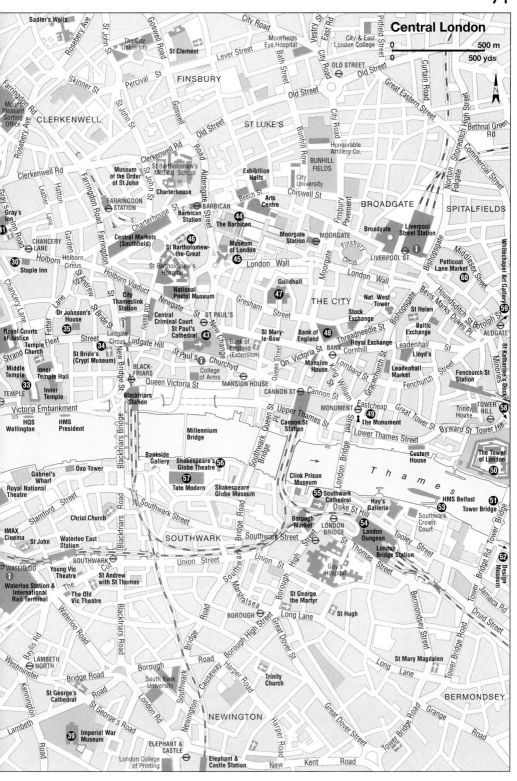

Central London

CENTRAL LONDON

Few cities offer such a variety of sites and experiences: there is something to suit every visitor, to fit every whim. Start with the bright lights in the centre and work outwards

Map on pages 70–71

The centre of London is a small place. The best part of it is taken up by the the West End, which includes Oxford Street, Soho and Covent Garden, as well as the elite areas of Mayfair and St James's. On its south side are the royal and political powerhouses of Whitehall and Westminster, to the east Bloomsbury and the British Museum. Few cities can make a visitor so contentedly footsore from wandering the streets and discovering its secrets. As Samuel Johnson, compiler of the first English dictionary, said, "When a man is tired of London he is tired of life, for there is in London all that life can afford."

The pigeon-filled precinct of **Trafalgar Square ❶** is a good starting point. This is the strategic heart of London and is an impressive, if traffic-clogged, public open space. The square was laid out in the 1830s and 1840s by Sir Charles Barry and dedicated to the memory of Admiral Lord Nelson and his decisive victory over Napoleon's fleet off Cape Trafalgar in 1805. It is a paragon of the classical style, enclosed by graceful white facades and dominated by the 162-ft (50-metre) **Nelson's Column** and four bronze lions. Trafalgar Square acts as a transportation hub, traversed by a dozen bus lines and five different tube lines. It is also the scene of London's riotous annual New Year's Eve celebrations and it has been the site of political demonstrations for more than 100

PRECEDING PAGES: the London Eye, a Ferris wheel built by the Thames for the millennium. **LEFT:** Whitehall Horse Guard. **BELOW:** Trafalgar Square.

FACT FILE

Situation On roughly the same latitude as Berlin and Vancouver, 40 miles (64 km) from the North Sea.
Size 115 sq miles (300 sq km).
Population 6.8 million.
Transport system Underground (tube) and buses. Day tickets can be transferable. Paris is 3 hours by Eurostar train from Waterloo station. Boat trips on the Thames from Charing Cross pier.
Indigenous inhabitants Cockneys (traditionally those born within the sound of Bow Bells in the City).
Tallest building 1 Canada Square, Canary Wharf.
Biggest disappointment You can't go up it.
Biggest nightclub Home, Leicester Square.
Oldest pub Prospect of Whitby (1520), east London.
Biggest attraction Tower of London.
Newest attraction Millennium Dome.
Finest building Westminster Abbey.
Best for roast beef Simpsons in the Strand, Rules in Maiden Lane.
Best view of the city Boat trip from Charing Cross Pier
Ethnic areas *Chinese:* Chinatown, Soho. *Caribbean:* Brixton, southeast. *Asian:* around Brick Lane, east London, and Southall, west London. *Arabic:* Bayswater.

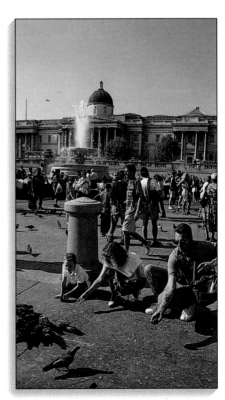

years. Demonstrations here against Margaret Thatcher's poll tax (an unpopular local-government tax) helped precipitate her downfall in 1990. Another famous woman is remembered here: Madame du Barry, the mistress of Louis XV, is said to have brought the French Crown Jewels to London in 1793 and buried them in the grounds of the old Royal Mews, later demolished to make way for Trafalgar Square. Madame du Barry returned to France and lost her head upon the guillotine without disclosing the whereabouts of the missing jewels.

Along the north flank of Trafalgar Square is the **National Gallery** (open daily 10am–6pm, Wed till 8pm, Sun 2–6pm; admission free). Founded in 1824, the gallery has since grown into one of the most outstanding and comprehensive collections in the world, with a list of masters ranging from Leonardo da Vinci and Rembrandt to El Greco and Van Gogh. In 1991 the Sainsbury Wing, designed by Robert Venturi, was opened to house the rich Renaissance collection. Single pictures, or series of pictures, are often highlighted to give great detail of painters' working methods and their times. There are frequent lectures and events, and even music in the Sainsbury Wing foyer.

Around the corner, established in 1856, is the superb **National Portrait Gallery** (opening times as National Gallery). Presenting an illustrated British history, it now contains the faces of more than 9,000 famous Britons, and it often stages important photographic exhibitions.

To the right of the National Gallery is **St Martin-in-the-Fields** church, the oldest-surviving structure on Trafalgar Square, built along simple but elegant lines by James Gibbs in 1722–26. The church became well known during World War II when its crypt was a refuge from the Blitz. St Martin's is still the parish church for Buckingham Palace, with royal boxes at the east end.

BELOW: having
fun in a Trafalgar
Square fountain.
RIGHT: the National
Gallery, London's
finest art collection.

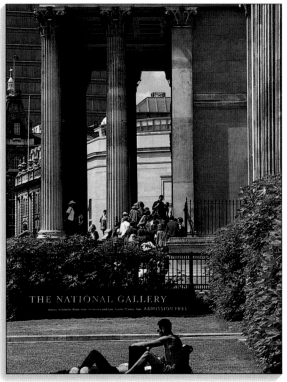

THE NATIONAL GALLERY

Covent Garden and theatreland

Northeast of Trafalgar Square begins the maze of narrow streets and tiny alleys called **Covent Garden ❷**. The name derives from the convent garden that occupied the area until Henry VIII's Dissolution. The present piazza was designed by Charles II's architect, Inigo Jones, and it was a meeting place for society until the royal palace moved from Whitehall, and a market for flowers, fruit and herbs was licenced, in 1670. At the centre of the cobblestoned piazza are the superb steel-and-glass **market pavilions** constructed in the 1830s to house market stalls.

The market was moved to new quarters south of the river at Nine Elms in 1974, and in the early 1980s Covent Garden was refurbished into an area of restaurants, shops and cafés. It is now a showplace for buskers (street entertainers) and a summer mecca both for office workers at lunchtime and for tourists round the clock. Covent Garden is also popular for afternoon shopping, especially cobblestoned **Neal Street** which has a collection of speciality shops.

Candlelit concerts are held in the last two weeks of July each year to celebrate the first Punch and Judy show, staged here in 1662. There is an antiques market on Mondays, and the Jubilee Market at weekends offers arts and crafts, food stalls and puppet shows. But the action really heats up at night. Those with a taste for English tradition might imbibe at the many ancient pubs in the area such as the **Lamb and Flag** (on Rose Street, off Floral Street), a 17th-century pub once frequented by prizefighters and known as the "Bucket of Blood".

In the corner of Covent Garden, helping to complete the collonade, is the majestic refurbished **Royal Opera House ❸**, home of both the Royal Opera and Ballet companies. Part of the building occupies the market's former Floral Hall. On the same side of the square is the **Theatre Museum** (open Tues–Sun 11am–7pm;

Map
on pages
70–71

Punch and Judy, perennial puppet favourites.

BELOW:
Covent Garden for shopping and street entertainment.

Berry Bros, well-established wine merchants in St James's Street.

entrance charge). Numerous actors are memorialised in **St Paul's Church**, also designed by Inigo Jones, in 1631. Covent Garden, the backdrop for the musical *My Fair Lady*, is synonymous with British theatre, particularly Drury Lane to the east, where the **Theatre Royal**, was established in 1663, and where Charles II's mistress, Nell Gywynne (1650–87), first made her name as a comedienne.

Books and movies

Bibliophiles hasten towards **Charing Cross Road** ❹, the western boundary of Covent Garden district with a string of bookshops ranging from old-fashioned Foyle's to giant Borders, but more important are specialist enclaves such as Zwemmer's (art and photography). The secondhand bookshops have a great atmosphere. For a change of scene, stroll through the **Photographers Gallery** (open Mon–Sat 11am–5.30pm; admission free) in Great Newport Street, where there are changing video and photographic exhibitions. The gallery has a café.

Charing Cross Road runs up the east side of **Leicester Square** ❺. This is the domain of tourists, pigeons and buskers, filled with the bright lights of the capital's main cinemas. Traffic free, except for stars' limousines at premieres, it has a central square with a statue of London-born Charlie Chaplin as The Little Tramp, and a Shakespeare fountain. On the north side is London's showpiece nightclub, Home. Leicester Square and Charing Cross Road are the areas for clubbers.

South of Covent Garden, the Strand connects Trafalgar Square with Fleet Street and the City. By Waterloo Bridge is **Somerset House** ❻ (open Mon–Sat 10am–6pm, Sun 2–6pm, entrance charge), Britain's first purpose-built office block in the 1770s. It houses the superb **Courtauld Institute** collection of Impressionist paintings with works by Van Gogh, Gauguin and Cézanne.

BELOW: Theatre Royal, Haymarket.

Gentlemen's clubs and royal London

A much different atmosphere is found in **Pall Mall** ❼, on the west side of Trafalgar Square, a sedate and elegant avenue that runs through the heart of St James's. This is London's "Club Land" – the exclusive gathering place of English gentlemen behind the closed doors of the Athenaeum, White's, the Carlton and a dozen other private enclaves. The street takes its name from *paille maille*, a French lawn game imported to England in the 17th century and played by Charles I on a long green which once occupied this site.

Wedged between the wood-panelled halls of Pall Mall and the leafy landscape of Green Park are a number of stately homes. The most impressive of these is **St James's Palace** ❽, built on the site of a leper hospital, St James the Less, by Henry VIII in the 1530s. A royal residence until the 19th century, St James's is now occupied by Prince Charles and his royal staff. Neighbouring royal mansions include **Marlborough House**, and the residences of **Clarence House** and **Lancaster House** where Chopin played a royal command performance for Queen Victoria.

The Mall is London's impressive ceremonial way, a broad tree-lined avenue that runs from Buckingham Palace to Admiralty Arch. The spectacular Trooping the Colour takes place on the Mall each June, as Queen Elizabeth rides sedately down the avenue in a horse-drawn carriage with an escort of Household Cavalry as part of a 200-year-old ceremony to mark the official birthday of the monarch. The legions mass on **Horse Guards Parade** ❾, a huge open space behind Whitehall, where the various royal units troop their regimental flags to the tune of marching music and thundering drums. The Household Cavalry can also be seen as they ride down the Mall on their way to and from the Changing

Map on pages 70–71

Although St James's Palace is no longer a royal residence, foreign ambassadors are still known as Ambassadors to the Court of St James.

LEFT: riding along The Mall.
BELOW: Horse Guards in Whitehall.

of the Guard at Buckingham Palace (11.30am daily in summer, alternate days in winter). They also mount guard outside the old palace entrance on Whitehall.

Overlooking the Mall is the **Institute of Contemporary Arts ⑩** (open daily, noon–7.30pm, Fri till 9pm; entrance charge), the cutting edge of modern painting, sculpture and the performing arts, housed in the Georgian-style Nash House.

Buckingham Palace

Londoners have a love-hate relationship with **Buckingham Palace ⑪**. To some, the Queen's home is irredeemably ugly, but it's also held in esteem as the symbol of Britain's royalty. The palace arose within a mulberry grove in the early 18th century as a mansion for the powerful Duke of Buckingham. It was purchased in 1762 by George III (who preferred to live in St James's Palace) for £28,000. However, it wasn't grand enough for George IV (the Prince Regent), and soon after the building came under his control in 1820 he commissioned his favourite architect, John Nash, to rebuild it on a more magnificent scale. The improvements led to considerable controversy: Parliament authorised an expenditure that "might not be less than £200,000"; the work actually ended up costing more than £700,000.

Despite all the alterations, the palace wasn't occupied until Victoria became queen in 1837 and made it the official royal residence in London. Visitors gather in front of Buckingham Palace for the Changing of the Guard and perhaps to snatch a glimpse of the Queen, who is in residence when the flag is flying. In summer, the more dedicated may decide to buy a ticket to see the State Rooms (open Aug–Sept, daily 9.30am–4.15pm; tickets at Green Park tube from 9am; entrance charge). Otherwise, only two sections of the palace are open to the public: the **Royal Mews** (stables), and the **Queen's Gallery** (open daily

BELOW: the royal residence, Buckingham Palace.

10am–5pm; entrance charge). The gallery displays a rotating sample of paintings from the fabulous Royal Collection, which includes masterpieces by Vermeer, da Vinci and Titian.

Bounding Buckingham Palace on the north and east are two of London's renowned green spaces – St James's Park and Green Park. **St James's Park** ⑫ in particular has lush vegetation and a tranquil lake. It provides haven for water birds, office workers and civil servants. The wooden footbridge across the lake gives a superb view of Buckingham Palace. **Green Park** ⑬ is a wild and rugged contrast. There are no tidy flower beds or fountains – just expanses of grass where Charles II used to take his daily constitutional.

Westminster's grandeur

A short walk from the southeast corner of St James's Park is **Westminster**, the seat of English government for nearly 1,000 years. Westminster is also a holy place – the burial ground of English monarchs, the site of one of the greatest monasteries of the Middle Ages and the location of the most inspiring Gothic architecture in London. The area used to be a marshy wasteland inhabited only by lepers until the 11th-century reign of Edward the Confessor, who took such a liking to Westminster that he built both a great church and a palace upon the reclaimed land.

Westminster Abbey ⑭ (open Mon–Fri 9.15am, last admission 3.45pm, Sat 1.45–2.45pm; entrance charge, *floorplan at end of book*) was consecrated on 28 December 1065; Edward died nine days later and was buried before the high altar. In December 1066, the ill-fated Harold (soon to lose his throne to William the Conqueror) was crowned as the new king during a special ceremony in the Abbey. Since that day, all but two English monarchs have been crowned in the church.

A floor plan of Westminster Abbey can be found on page 399.

BELOW: the south front of Westminster Abbey.

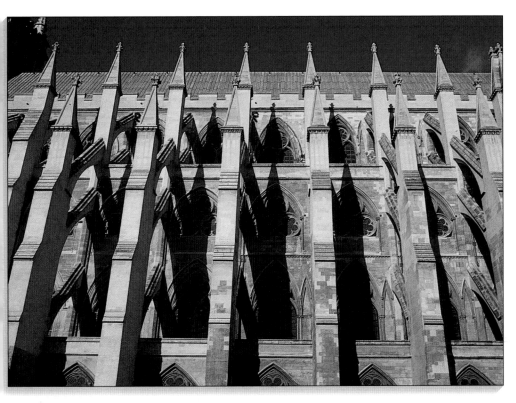

THE MOTHER OF PARLIAMENTS

There are few things that the English like more than a parliamentary scandal. They have not been disappointed

Politicians have long been a source of amusement for the English, who love nothing more than savouring a scandal in high places. Their behaviour has made them the subject of some of the great cartoonists from William Hogarth (1697–1764), James Gillray (1757–1815) and Thomas Rowlandson (1756–1827) to present-day practitioners such as Steve Bell (*The Guardian*) and Peter Brookes (*The Times*).

By and large Members of Parliament this century have not been found to be greedy or corrupt, though the last decade of the 20th century saw a number of back-benchers – MPs without government or opposition (shadow) cabinet positions – caught in some sleazy deals. Most, when found out, do the decent thing and quietly leave office, or the House. A few hang on tenaciously or take accusations to court.

The major scandals of modern Westminster are undoubtedly sexual. This has not always been the case: William Pitt the Younger, prime minister in 1783 and 1804 and satirised below as a windmill unable to make up his mind, was immune, dying a virgin, while the great Victorian prime minister William Gladstone's crusades involving late night wandering through London's seediest streets in the hope of saving fallen women was seen merely as eccentric.

The most dramatic sexual scandal happened in the early 1960s, when Christine Keeler, a good-time girl, bedded both a Soviet diplomat and John Profumo, the Minister of War (though not simultaneously). Profumo had to resign when he lied about the affair, and the scandal helped the Conservatives lose the 1964 election.

Today's Members of Parliament have learned little since, suffering a perennial weakness of the flesh. Many, claiming pressure of work, fall into bed with their secretaries or researchers. Sometimes they are discovered to have a number of mistresses or even, as in the case of one flamboyant Conservative MP, joining a mother and daughter in the same bed, while a Minister for the Arts is reported to have involved his favourite football strip in lovemaking sessions.

More recently homosexuality is stealing the headlines, even though Parliament now gives long-term partners of homosexual MPs the same privileges as wives. Some parliamentarians feel it best to come out before being outed. Often the Press already has files inches deep and is waiting to pounce. Jokes about bottoms and boys make up the subsequent headlines and confirm the English schoolboy sense of humour. ❑

LEFT: William Pitt satirised as an unsettled windmill. **ABOVE:** Christine Keeler and the Profumo affair that helped topple a government.

Little remains of Edward's Saxon abbey; it was rebuilt under the Normans and then redesigned in flamboyant French-Gothic style 200 years later. The abbey's top treasures are the **Royal Chapels**, among them the **Henry VII Chapel**, a 16th-century masterpiece of fan-vaulted ceilings in pure white stone, decked out in the colourful medieval banners of the Knights Grand Cross of the Order of the Bath. Behind lies the Royal Air Force Chapel, with a stained-glass window containing the badges of every squadron that fought in the 1940 Battle of Britain. **Poets' Corner** contains the graves of Chaucer, Tennyson and Dryden, plus monuments to Shakespeare, Milton, Keats and Wilde. The abbey also houses the **English Coronation Chair**, built in 1300 for Edward I and still used for the installation of new monarchs.

Map on pages 70–71

Houses of parliament

On the river side of Westminster Abbey rise the **Houses of Parliament ⓯**, an intrepid Gothic structure designed in the 1830s by Charles Barry and Augustus Pugin after the old Westminster Palace, dating from the reign of Edward the Confessor, caught fire. The building is a triumph of Victorian England: 940 ft (280 metres) long with 2 miles (3 km) of passages and more than 1,000 rooms. At the south end is **Victoria Tower**, from which a Union flag flies whenever Parliament is in session, while on the north side rises the majestic Clock Tower, commonly known as **Big Ben** after the massive bell, cast in 1858, that strikes the hours.

The Jewel Tower, remnant of the old Westminster Palace.

Within Parliament are the two governing bodies of Great Britain, the House of Commons and the House of Lords, which moved into the old Palace of Westminster after Henry VIII vacated the premises in the 16th century. The Commons, comprising the elected representatives of various political parties, is the scene of both lively debate and loutish heckling. You can watch from the safety of the **Visitors' Gallery** when Parliament is in session (queue at St Stephen's entrance from 5pm Mon, Tues and Thur, 9.30am Wed and Fri; entrance charge; or request an entrance permit from your MP, tel: 0207 219 3000) – and wonder, like so many others, how the British government ever gets anything accomplished.

BELOW: the Palace of Westminster, seat of the nation's Parliament.

The lavish State Opening of Parliament takes place in the House of Lords each autumn, as the monarch reads a proclamation from a golden throne at the head of the room. Though now reformed, and no longer a club for the aristocracy, the atmosphere of the chamber retains a hallowed air. One relic of the old Westminster Palace to withstand a fire that all but destroyed the building in 1834 is **Westminster Hall**, a 240-ft (72-metre) long room built in 1099 with a sturdy hammer-beam roof of ancient oak. The hall has witnessed some of the most dramatic moments in English history – from the trial of Sir Thomas More in 1535 to the investiture of Oliver Cromwell as Lord Protector in 1653. An exhibition about Parliament in history is on at the **Jewel Tower** (open daily 10am–5pm, till 4pm in winter; entrance charge), a moated keep beside the Abbey and a last relic of the Palace of Westminster. It held the king's jewels, clothing and furs until the reign of Henry VIII.

Whitehall is the broad and busy avenue that runs north from the Houses of Parliament to Trafalgar Square. Once the fulcrum of British colonial power, it is still home to the Foreign and Commonwealth

Auguste Rodin's "The Kiss".

Offices, the Treasury, Admiralty and Ministry of Defence – and the Prime Minister's 17th-century residence at **No. 10 Downing Street** – but many of the government departments have moved to more modern locations. For a contrast to the drab architecture of modern government take a detour to **Banqueting House** (open Mon–Sat 10am–5pm, Sun 2–5pm; entrance charge), just beyond on the right, a brilliant relic of the old Whitehall Palace and a masterpiece of English baroque. Inigo Jones built the hall for James I in 1622. Peter Paul Rubens added the lovely allegorical ceiling commissioned by Charles I, who stepped on to the scaffold from here for his public beheading in 1649.

Best of British art

Victoria Street shoots southwest from Parliament Square as an unexpected corridor of steel and glass skyscrapers in the heart of neo-Gothic London. Almost hidden between the corporate headquarters and banking houses is the terracotta bulk of **Westminster Cathedral** , England's premier Roman Catholic church. It arose in the 1890s in a bizarre Italo-Byzantine style. Climb the **Campanile Tower** for a superb view of Westminster and Belgravia.

BELOW: Westminster Cathedral.
RIGHT: Rodin's *The Burghers of Calais*, in Victoria Tower Gardens.

   Millbank follows the curve of the Thames to the south of Parliament Square, first passing **Victoria Tower Gardens** (home of Rodin's *The Burghers of Calais*) before sweeping round to the grand neoclassical **Tate Britain** (open Mon–Sat 10am–5.30pm, Sun 2–5.30pm; admission free). This houses British art from the past three centuries, from Hogarth to Hodgkin, Stubbs to Stanley Spencer, as well as contemporary Tate prize winners. The Clore Gallery has the extensive Turner collection. A shuttle bus and river boat provide a connecting service to the Tate Modern Gallery at Bankside (*see page 99*).

Shopping and waxworks

Oxford Circus, the hub of several tube lines, is halfway down **Oxford Street ⑳**, London's busiest shopping street (*see next page*). It marks the boundary between **Marylebone** and the exclusive district of **Mayfair**. The Marylebone (pronounced *marly-bun*) district sprawls along the southern edge of Regent's Park, and was infamous in the 18th century for its taverns, boxing matches and cockfights. Now it is a staid neighbourhood of doctors, dentists and accountants.

You can't miss the long queues outside the **London Planetarium** and the adjacent **Madame Tussaud's Wax Museum ㉑** (both open daily 9.30am–5.30pm; entrance charge; combined tickets available) on Marylebone Road. The waxworks were founded in 1802 by Marie Tussaud, a tiny woman who learned her craft in post-Revolution Paris – making wax effigies of the heads of guillotine victims. Today's effigies, which vary from the breathtakingly lifelike to the barely recognisable, range from pop stars and sports heroes to popes.

Nearby, at a familiar address, 221b Baker Street (actually between Nos 237 and 239), is the **Sherlock Holmes Museum** (open daily 9.30am–6pm; entrance charge), where the fictitious detective's housekeeper shows visitors around his famous home. Hereford House in Manchester Square just off Baker Street, contains the superb **Wallace Collection ㉒** (open Mon–Sun 10am–5pm, Sun 2–5pm; admission free), a treasure chest of 17th- and 18th-century art and ornaments, among which there are Sèvres porcelain, Limoges enamels and antique French furniture. On the walls are works by Titian, Rubens and Holbein.

Classy **Mayfair** is a centre of English wealth, the home of oil barons and property giants, of landed aristocrats and self-made nabobs. Its narrow streets are abuzz by day with the flow of cash, but at night the district slides into an eerie quiet as the

Map on pages 70–71

When Sherlock Holmes met his end in Strand *magazine in 1899, the event was reported in the* Press, *people wore black armbands, 20,000 subscriptions were cancelled and the publishers' shares fell. Arthur Conan Doyle brought him back to life in 1901.*

BELOW: the Beatles in wax at Madame Tussaud's.

Selfridges, the first West End store, opened in 1909.

Bespoke St James's.

Covent Garden stall.

Harrods.

Portobello Road.

CAPITAL SHOPPING

Where you shop depends on what you want — and who you are

West End The principal shopping streets are Oxford Street and Regent Street, which bisect at Oxford Circus. The smarter end is towards Marble Arch, and the bargain shops are to the east. As well as dozens of menswear and and women's fashion shops, **Oxford Street** also has the large department stores, including Marks & Spencer, Selfridges and John Lewis (whose slogan is "never knowingly undersold"). Liberty, purveryors of classic fabrics, is in a half-timbered building in **Regent Street**, near Hamley's giant toy store. Burberry's and the Scotch House have outlets in Regent Street. **Tottenham Court Road** is the place to buy electronic equipment.

Bond Street and St James's New Bond Street and Old Bond Street are the smart end of town. Designer fashion houses mingle with art galleries (including Sotheby's auction house), and nearby **Burlington Arcade** offers bijou gems for the rich. **Savile Row**, parallel to Old Bond Street, is where shirts and suits are elegantly tailored – at a price. On the other side of Piccadilly is **St James's,** designed originally for the court hangers-on, everything here is bespoke. Old-fashioned barbers and unashamed cigarette and cigar shops make this a male preserve. Fortnum and Mason at 181 Piccadilly sells the best of British foods.

Covent Garden One of the first, and one of the most successful, developments from old market to new, London's former fruit and vegetable traders' stalls are now bijou shops. Paul Smith, London's leading men's fashion designer, is in Floral Street. **Long Acre** has Stanford's, the largest travel bookshop, and Dillon's art bookshop. The best shops for books, antiquarian, second-hand and new, are round the corner in **Charing Cross Road**. On the north side of Covent Garden are the intriguing small shops in Earlham Street and Neal Street, where Neal's Yard is a honeypot for vegetarians.

Kensington and Chelsea West London led the fashion stakes in the Swinging Sixties. Now rich patrons remain. In **Knightsbridge** Harvey Nichols and Harrods hold sway. Beauchamp Place near Harrods was a favourite shopping haunt of the late Princess Diana. Sloane Street, with a clutch of elegant furniture designers, leads to Peter Jones department store in **King's Road**, where young fashion shops begin. **High Street Kensington**, where the famous Biba store once flourished, has a number of fashion boutiques. Adjoining it is **Kensington Church Street**, for genuine, and genuinely expensive, antiques.

Markets London has more than 100 street markets, which carry on a tradition going back to the Middle Ages. **Berwick Street** in Soho has classic Cockney fruit and vegetable stalls every day. **Petticoat Lane**'s main market, selling all kinds of items, is a great Sunday morning attraction and has a genuine London heart. **Portobello Road** near Notting Hill Gate is a lively street dealing in antiques, though dedicated hunters will also head to **Bermondsey Antique Market**. Younger browsers visit **Camden Passage Market** which has a rich mixture of stalls and a reputation for good-value antiques. Portobello Road and Camden Market are particularly crowded on Saturday. ❑

financial wizards and fashion models retreat into their terracotta towers. By the mid-18th century, the powerful Grosvenor family had purchased the land and developed Mayfair into an elegant Georgian housing estate. This enticed the wealthy of dreary inner London to move out and settle in one of the city's first suburbs.

Today, Mayfair is known for its stylish shops and lavish auction houses. The names roll off the tongue as a testament to affluence: Cartier, Rolls-Royce, Floris, Gieves & Hawkes, Yardley and Smythson's. **Bond Street** ㉓ is where you can buy something for that person who already has everything. For a quiet walk, try one of Mayfair's elegant Victorian arcades, the tiny covered streets lined with a startling array of unique and interesting shops. The **Royal Opera Arcade** is the oldest, but the **Piccadilly**, **Prince's** and **Royal Arcades** are just as elegant. **Burlington Arcade** with its uniformed doormen is the most famous, only a few doors up from the **Royal Academy of Arts** ㉔. The Academy has changing exhibitions of major artists and its Summer Exhibition of amateur and professional artists provides light entertainment and perhaps the chance to pick up a bargain.

Mayfair antiques and art are world-famous. **Christie's** in King Street auctions more than 150,000 objects a year, while **Sotheby's** in New Bond Street has seen some of the most important deals in art history. Have your photograph taken between Roosevelt and Churchill in a Bond Street pavement sculpture, a reminder of Mayfair's links with Americans.

Piccadilly Circus

Piccadilly Circus ㉕ is the spiritual heart of the West End, once a roundabout and now a meeting place of black cabs, red buses and awe-struck tourists. The bronze statue of Eros stands atop a fountain on the south side of the mêlée, but is outshone by a neon curtain blasting advertising slogans to the masses. Nearby in Coventry Street is the **Trocadero** entertainment centre, whose attractions include **Segaworld**, a huge hi-tech indoor entertainment theme park.

On Piccadilly's north side, John Nash's **Regent Street** divides Mayfair and **Soho** as effectively as if there were an ocean between them. Soho, long known for its low-life bars and sex clubs, has recently returned to being a neighbourhood of foodshops and restaurants, with a cosmopolitan population of East European émigrés and a thriving Chinese community. The sleazy side of Soho has all but gone. Raymond's well-established Revue Bar has terribly tasteful strip shows and a few hole-in-the-wall dens offer "live" entertainment.

In the heart of Soho is **Berwick Street** ㉖, the site of one of the best fruit and vegetable markets in London, excellent for both quality and price, and a place to go to hear genuine Cockney accents. Beyond the sleaze are some historic landmarks: Karl Marx used to live around the corner on **Dean Street** in the building now inhabited by an Italian restaurant, Quo Vadis. John Logie Baird succeeded in transmitting some of the earliest pictures via wireless from a workshop in nearby **Frith Street** in 1926. His was a new-fangled invention that would soon be known as television. **Soho Square**, in the heart of the area, is particularly lively at lunchtime and weekends.

Map on pages 70–71

TIP

For literature and on-line information on where to go and stay in England, visit the In Britain tourist office on the corner of Lower Regent Street and Charles II Street.

BELOW: Eros, Piccadilly Circus.

Art from the Near East in the British Museum.

BELOW: Georgian elegance in Bloomsbury.
RIGHT: the British Museum.

Brainy Bloomsbury

For a change in mood, hop on the tube at Piccadilly Circus and ride four stops to Russell Square. This will deposit you in **Bloomsbury**, the intellectual and scholastic heart of the city, dominated by the **British Museum** ❷ (open Mon–Sat 10am–5.30pm, Sun 2.30–6pm; admission free), one of the largest and best in the world. The museum is both a priceless art collection and a monument to human civilisation, encompassing antiquities from almost every period and every part of the world – Egyptian, Assyrian, Greek, Roman, Indian, Chinese, Islamic and Anglo-Saxon. Among its multiple treasures are the Rosetta Stone from Egypt (the key that unlocked the secrets of hieroglyphic script), the great 7th-century Anglo-Saxon Sutton Hoo treasures, the Nimrud friezes from Mesopotamia and the Elgin Marbles, the remarkable figures that once graced the Parthenon in Athens (and may do so again if insistent Greek demands are met). Don't expect to see everything in one day; a week would not be time enough.

The **British Library** was established within the same 19th-century building. However, the entire library of more than 9 million books – including a Gutenberg Bible, the Magna Carta and original texts by Shakespeare, Dickens and Leonardo da Vinci – has been moved to a £500 million edifice near Euston Station. The Reading Room (once the workshop of Karl Marx) has been redesigned as an education and information centre, linked to the rest of the building by a giant steel and glass roof over the museum's inner courtyard.

The **Thomas Coram Foundation** ❷ (open Mon and Fri 1.30–4.30pm; entrance charge) at No. 40 Brunswick Square is home of the Foundling Hospital Art Treasures and displays the works of Hogarth, Gainsborough and Kneller. Bloomsbury was the address of such intellectual figures as John Maynard

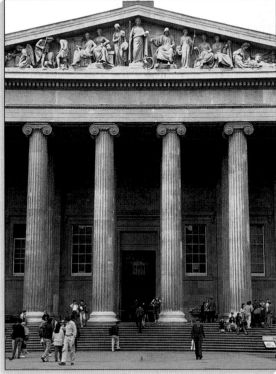

Keynes and Virginia Woolf (*see page 194*). But of all the writers and thinkers who have lived here one stands head and shoulders above the others: Charles Dickens. The **Dickens House Museum** (open Mon–Sat 10am–5pm; entrance charge) at 48 Doughty Street is where he lived with his family from 1837 to 1839 and wrote parts of *Oliver Twist*, *Nicholas Nickleby* and *Pickwick Papers*. The house is filled with portraits, letters, furniture and other personal effects of Victorian England's most famous novelist.

East of Bloomsbury Square is the hardworking district of **Holborn** (pronounced *ho-bun*). A pair of silver griffins on either side of Holborn High Street marks the official boundary of the City of London. Nearby is **Staple Inn** ⟨⟩, a timber-framed Elizabethan structure (the only one left in central London) that once served as a hostel for wool merchants.

Hatton Garden in Holborn is the centre of London's lucrative diamond trade.

Legal London

Lying between Holborn and the Thames are the prestigious **Inns of Court** – the confluence of London's legal world since the Middle Ages. There were originally 12 inns, founded in the 14th century for the lodging and education of lawyers on "neutral" ground between the merchants of the City and the monarchs of Westminster. But today only four remain. Dr Johnson called the inns "the noblest nurseries of humanity and liberty in the Kingdom". Even today, no one can enter the legal profession in London without acceptance into one of the inns – a practice known as "passing the Bar". **Gray's Inn** ⟨⟩ has a garden designed by Francis Bacon in 1606, a haven of plane trees and smooth lawns that provides a tranquil lunchtime retreat away from the hustle of the City. **Lincoln's Inn** ⟨⟩, north of Fleet Street, has a medieval hall and a 17th-century chapel by Inigo Jones. The leafy

BELOW: Sherlock Holmes Museum.

Samuel Johnson, resident of Fleet Street and compiler of the first English dictionary.

expanse called **Lincoln's Inn Fields**, once a notorious venue for duels and executions, is now restricted to peaceful pursuits such as picnics and summer sunbathing. On the north side of the fields at No. 13 is the **Sir John Soane Museum** (open Tues–Sat 10am–5pm; admission free), an outlandish mansion which is a British Museum in miniature. John Soane, a celebrated 19th-century architect, lived here and built up a remarkable collection of antiquities, paintings and architectural designs. Nowhere else in London can you see such an odd assortment of artefacts, including a sarcophagus, under one roof. A highlight of its art gallery is Hogarth's satirical *Rake's Progress*.

The most fascinating of the inns is the twin complex comprising the **Inner** and **Middle Temples ㉝**. The name derives from the Knights Templar, a medieval religious fraternity that occupied this site until the early 14th century. The temple has changed little: it is still a precinct of vaulted chambers, hammer-beam roofs and lush wood panelling. In the 16th-century Middle Temple Hall, Shakespeare's own company once performed *Twelfth Night* for the Elizabethan court.

The 12th-century **Temple Church** is one of only four "round churches" left in England. The lawyers and judges, clad in white wigs and flowing black robes, who now inhabit the Temple look as anachronistic as the buildings.

Fleet Street takes its name from the Fleet River, which once flowed from Hampstead River into the Thames. Until the 1980s, the street was the centre of the national newspaper industry. Then the papers adopted computers, dispensed with unionised typesetters, built new printing works in Docklands and moved their editorial offices to cheaper locations. Not a single national newspaper remains in Fleet Street. **St Bride's ㉞** is the official parish church of the British Press, an impressive 17th-century church built by Christopher Wren.

BELOW:
Lincoln's Inn.

Dr Johnson's House ⑤ (open Mon–Sat 11am–5pm; entrance charge) is at 17 Gough Square, on the north side of Fleet Street. This is where Samuel Johnson lived from 1748 to 1759 assembling the *Complete Works of Shakespeare* and his famous dictionary. Between bouts with pen and ink, he did his drinking nearby at **Ye Olde Cheshire Cheese** in Wine Office Court.

The South Bank

The **South Bank Centre** ㊱ (across Waterloo Bridge), is a controversial concrete landscape and fine arts forum, which started life as a post-war cheering-up exercise for the 1951 Festival of Britain. It continues its funfair role with the 450-ft (135-metre) **London Eye** ferris wheel, erected for the millennium and giving unprecedented views over all London. The **Royal Festival Hall**, a spacious arena famed for its acoustics, plays host to the London Symphony and Philharmonic orchestras. Next door, the **Queen Elizabeth Hall** and the **Purcell Room** are used for a variety of events, from chamber music to poetry readings.

The **National Film Theatre** sits in the shadow of Waterloo Bridge, presenting a repertory of vintage and foreign-language films as well as the London Film Festival each November. Close by, in the middle of a roundabout in front of Waterloo Station, is a huge circular glass building, the British Film Institute's **London IMAX Cinema**, which houses Europe's biggest screen. The Museum of the Moving Image, beside the Film Theatre, has been undergoing restoration.

The bulky **Royal National Theatre** comprises three theatres – the Olivier, Lyttelton and Cottesloe – renowned for the quality of their productions. The **Hayward Gallery** (open daily 10am–6pm, Tues–Wed till 8pm; entrance charge) with changing exhibitions of contemporary art, rounds off the South Bank show.

Map on pages 70–71

TIP

There's always something to see and do free at the South Bank: lunchtime concerts, jazz on Sunday, and the National Theatre pre-performance recitations; plus great views from the restaurants.

BELOW: book market on the South Bank.

*The Imperial
War Museum.*

By Westminster Bridge is the majestic **County Hall ③**, which now contains two hotels, the **London Aquarium**, whose 41 exhibits range from sharks to stingray, and the **FA Premier League Hall of Fame**. Upriver beyond Westminster Bridge is **Lambeth Palace ③**, which has been the London residence of the Archbishop of Canterbury for nearly 800 years. It is seldom open to the public.

Another great landmark south of the river is the **Imperial War Museum ③** (open daily 10am–6pm; entrance charge), situated in Lambeth within the remains of the "Bedlam", the old Bethlehem Hospital for lunatics. Weaponry, vehicles, paintings, uniforms, decorations and scale models have been joined by a Holocaust exhibition. You don't have to be a warmonger to find it fascinating.

Village Hampstead and Regent's Park

To visit one of London's loveliest and most historic "villages", head north on the Northern Line from Waterloo Station. For more than 300 years **Hampstead ④** has attracted men of arts and letters, such as John Keats (1795–1821). **Keats House** is open to the public (Keats Grove; open Mon–Fri 10am–5pm, closed 1–2pm, Sun 2–5pm; admission free), as is the house where Sigmund Freud spent his last year. The famous couch can be seen at the **Freud Museum** (open Wed–Sun noon–5pm; entrance charge) at 20 Maresfield Gardens. Hampstead is home to music, stage and cinema stars who help its trendy flavour, but it also has a village atmosphere, aided by the proximity of 790-acre (310-hectare) **Hampstead Heath**. Hampstead is best viewed on foot, window shopping along the High Street, or exploring the area's elegant Georgian and Regency mansions. An 18th-century decree forbade building on the Heath, thus preserving a tract of dark woods and lush meadows.

Kenwood House (open daily 10am–6pm in summer, 10am–4pm in winter;

BELOW: barges and Chinese delights, in the canal by Regent's Park.

admission free), a magnificent Adam building, is the only large structure. It houses the Iveagh Bequest, a rich collection of English and Dutch paintings with works by Rembrandt, Reynolds and Vermeer.

Haverstock Hill runs from Hampstead into **Camden Town**, a journey that takes you from the literary past into the rag-tag present. Camden became famous in the 1960s as a gathering place for hippies, street artists and various vagrants, who set up small shops and stalls around **Camden Lock ④**. The market is now one of the most popular London weekend attractions, featuring antiques, crafts, old clothes, military surplus goods – and talented buskers (street entertainers).

Local wildlife at London Zoo

Just west of Camden Town is **Regent's Park ④**, a massive green space with a long and chequered history. Henry VIII established a royal hunting ground here on land seized from the Abbess of Barking. In the early 19th century, the park became part of the Prince Regent's (later George IV) great scheme for a huge processional thoroughfare and palace complex to stretch from Pall Mall to Primrose Hill. The Prince commissioned John Nash to design and develop the scheme, but the dream got only as far as the famed Regency terraces on the southern fringe of the park, which represent Nash at his best.

London Zoo (open daily10am–4pm; entrance charge) was established in Regent's Park in 1826 by Sir Stamford Raffles, who also founded Singapore. Tommy, the first chimp, arrived in a stagecoach, while the first giraffes were unloaded at London Docks and carried through the City, startling pedestrians. Among the zoo's features are a walk-through aviary designed by Lord Snowdon and a glass pavilion housing the ecologically oriented Web of Life Exhibition. ❑

Map on pages 70–71

Take a trip on Regent's Canal on a barge: they run regularly from Camden Lock.

BELOW: Camden Market.

THE CITY AND EAST LONDON

The City of London, just a square mile in size, is the financial heart of the capital. But it has been drifting eastwards towards the renovated docklands area

Map on pages 70–71

Fleet Street sweeps from London's theatreland into Ludgate Hill and the **City of London**, the history-packed square mile that sits on the remains of both Roman and medieval towns. The City has long been the domain of merchants and craftsmen, a powerful coalition of men who helped force democracy upon the English monarchy and then built a thriving mercantile empire. Despite wartime destruction and encroachment of modern office blocks and computers, the City retains something of its traditional ways: the square mile is still governed separately from the rest of London, by the ancient City Corporation and its Court of Common Council – relics of the medieval trade and craft guilds. It also has its own police force and Lord Mayor.

Wren's masterpiece

Sitting at the top of Ludgate Hill is **St Paul's Cathedral ⓭**, dominating the skyline of the City like no other structure, the massive dome punching upward through the forest of high-rises that has come to surround it since World War II. After the Norman St Paul's was destroyed in the Great Fire of 1666, Charles II asked Christopher Wren to design a new cathedral to befit the status of London. Wren's first plan was rejected as too radical, but he then responded with a brilliant blend of Italian baroque and classical influences – a huge cruciform building whose stone cupola takes it to a height of 365 ft (111 metres). Only St Peter's in Rome has a bigger dome.

St Paul's arose from 1675 to 1710 as the first cathedral built and dedicated to the Protestant faith, and was the crowning achievement of Wren's career. It played host to Queen Victoria's Diamond Jubilee ceremonies in 1897; Winston Churchill's funeral in 1965; and the wedding of Prince Charles and Lady Diana Spencer in 1981. The cathedral miraculously survived the Blitz, though the neighbourhood around it was destroyed by German bombs and missiles. St Paul's is also a notable burial place; among those entombed within are Wellington, Nelson, Reynolds, Turner and Wren himself. The cathedral's interior displays the work of the finest artists and craftsmen of the late 17th century: iron grillework of Tijou, wooden choir stalls by Grinling Gibbons, and the murals inside the dome by Sir James Thornhill.

Around the inside of the dome stretches the **Whispering Gallery**, where the voices of anyone standing on the opposite side of the void are easily heard. A winding stairway leads to the balcony outside the dome, where there is a panoramic view of London. (*A floor plan of the Cathedral is printed at the back of this book.*)

Pater Noster Square on the north side of St Paul's, is a commercial development that rose from the rub-

LEFT: a Beefeater at the Tower of London.
BELOW: Mansion House, domain of the Lord Mayor.

CITY OF LONDON

*The Coat of Arms of
the City, symbolised
by the mythical
griffin, often seen
in City streets.*

ble of the Blitz, and has now been recognised as such an appalling error that it is being redeveloped again. Another post-war urban development, directly north, is the **Barbican** ⓸ a residential estate with a number of showcases including the **Museum of London** ⓹ (open Tues–Sat 10am–5.50pm, Sun noon–5.50pm; entrance charge), a superb collection devoted to the history of the city from prehistoric to modern times. There are models of old buildings, reconstructed shopfronts, audio-visual shows, a reference library, antique vehicles and a number of historic artefacts such as the Lord Mayor's State Coach. **The Barbican Arts Centre** is the City's major cultural venue, and the London base of both the Royal Shakespeare Company and the London Symphony Orchestra.

Nearby is **St Bartholomew-the-Great** ⓺, a Norman church which has also served as a stable, factory, wine cellar, coal store, and even as Benjamin Franklin's London printworks during its 1,000-year history.

In the shadows of the Barbican's skyscrapers is the **Guildhall** ⓻ (open Mon–Fri 9.30am–4.45pm; admission free), one of the few buildings to survive the Great Fire and home of the government of the City. This ornate Gothic structure was built in 1411 with funds donated by livery companies, the medieval trade and craft guilds. Within the Guildhall is the famous **Great Hall**, decorated with the colourful banners of the 12 livery companies and the shields of all 92 guilds.

Britain's financial heartland

BELOW: the Lloyd's
building, designed
by Richard Rogers.

A short walk east along Gresham Street brings you to the **Bank of England** ⓼, a building of powerful classical design. Though independent of the government, the Bank prints and mints all British money, administers to the national

Map on pages 70–71

debt and protects the country's gold reserves. Nearby stands the old London **Stock Exchange**, founded in 1773. The trading floor is no longer used – shares are now traded electronically in a skyscraper at the junction of Threadneedle and Old Broad Street – but there's an exhibition of stocks and securities.

Directly opposite the Bank are the **Royal Exchange**, trying to look like the Greek Parthenon, and **Mansion House**, the official residence of the Lord Mayor since the 1750s. Many of the City's treasures (the 15th-century Mayoral Chain of Office, the 18th-century Great Mace and a collection of Corporation plates, tapestries and crystal) are housed within this Palladian-style palace, which is generally closed to the public. Historic churches within a short distance, some built by Wren, include **St Stephen Wallbrook**, the Lord Mayor's parish church.

King William Street leads south from the bustling Bank intersection (the Docklands Light Railway starts here) to London Bridge and the Thames. Between the two is a tall, fluted column peering over the rooftops: the 202-ft (60-metre) **Monument** ⓯ (open Mon–Fri 9am–5.30pm, Sat–Sun 2.30–5.30pm, Mon–Sat 9am–3.30pm in winter; entrance charge), Wren's memorial to the Great Fire of 1666. Climb to the summit for a superb panorama.

Miraculously, only half a dozen people died in the Great Fire of London, which destroyed most of the medieval city. Samuel Pepys, the diarist, dug a pit in his garden to save his wine and "Parmazan" cheese.

The Tower of London

Lower Thames Street traces the medieval banks of the river past the old Billingsgate Fish Market and the elegant Custom House. A squat stone building commands this southeast corner of the City, a medieval fortress known as the **Tower of London** ⓾ (open daily 9.30am–5.30pm; entrance charge; *a floor plan is printed at the back of this book*). The Tower has served over the centuries as fortress, palace, prison and museum, as well as arsenal, archive, menagerie and

BELOW: the Tower of London.

MURDER IN THE BLOODY TOWER

For hundreds of years Beauchamp Tower in the Tower of London was England's most prestigious jail, reserved for enemies of the state. Henry VI and Richard II were among royal prisoners, and in 1483 Edward IV's heirs, Prince Edward, aged 12, and Prince Richard, 10, were murdered in what came to be called the Bloody Tower (they are done to death off-stage in Shakespeare's *Richard III*). The executioner's axe came down on Tower Hill behind the castle, but the privileged lost their lives on the block inside the Tower's grounds, among them two wives of Henry VIII: Anne Boleyn and Catherine Howard.

The Duke of Orleans, captured at the battle of Agincourt in 1485, composed verse and contemplated his fate here for 25 years. The most eloquent prisoners were Sir Thomas More and Sir Walter Raleigh. More, author of *Utopia*, refused to recognise Henry VIII as head of the church, and before his execution he wrote *Dialogue of Comfort against Tribulation*. Raleigh, the Elizabethan buccaneer, wrote *The History of the World* during his 12-year incarceration with his family. One of Shakespeare's patrons, the Earl of Southampton, was painted with his cat which is said to have climbed into the Tower and down a chimney to find him.

The Tower's greatest treasure is the Imperial State Crown, encrusted with 2,800 diamonds, and topped with Edward the Confessor's sapphire. It was made for George VI's coronation in 1937.

BELOW:
Southwark Cathedral.

treasure chest. It is the most alluring of London's many monuments, attracting millions of tourists a year, so expect queues. William the Conqueror built the inner keep, the **White Tower**, as both a military stronghold and a means of impressing his new subjects in England. Constructed between 1078 and 1098, it was the largest building in Britain and soon symbolised royal domination. It remained a royal residence until the 16th century, when the court moved to more comfortable quarters in Westminster. The Tower then became the storehouse for the Crown Jewels and the most infamous prison and execution ground in London. After 1747 the Tower served as the Royal Mint, Archive and Menagerie – until the elephants, lions and bears were moved to Regent's Park Zoo a century later. German spies were executed here in both world wars.

The White Tower contains the diminutive **St John's Chapel**, built in 1080 and now the oldest church in London. Beneath Waterloo Barracks is a vault containing the **Crown Jewels**, including the Imperial State Crown, which sparkles with 3,000 stones and the Royal Sceptre, and which centres around a 530-carat diamond called the Star of Africa. Also worth seeing are the **Crowns and Diamonds** exhibition in the Martin Tower, the **Regimental Museum**'s permanent display of weapons from the mid-17th to mid-19th centuries, and the **New Armouries**, which is given over to temporary exhibitions. The Tower is protected by the Yeomen Wardens or Beefeaters, so-called not because of their carnivorous habits, but because they were founded in the 16th century as the *boufitiers* or guardians of the king's buffet. An authentic chopping block sits upon Tower Green – you may place your head on it for photographs.

The most spectacular of the Thames's many spans is **Tower Bridge** ❺, a striking Gothic edifice opened in 1894. The Tower Bridge Experience shows how the mechanisms work (open daily 10am–6.30pm, 9.30am–5.15pm in winter; entrance charge). The view from the bridge's Catwalk is magnificent.

Southern ways

Downstream on the south side of Tower Bridge is the restaurant-lined **Butler's Wharf** and the Conran Foundation's **Design Museum** ❺, which has changing exhibitions (open Mon–Fri 11am–6pm, Sat–Sun noon–6pm; entrance charge). Heading upstream again, the riverside walk between Tower Bridge and London Bridge passes by *HMS Belfast* ❺. Commissioned in 1939 as the largest cruiser in the British Navy, it is now a museum (open daily 10am–6pm; entrance charge).

Towards London Bridge, the **London Dungeon** ❺ (open daily 10am–6.30pm; entrance charge) provides a gruesome account of life in medieval London – most children love it .

Beyond London Bridge rises the imposing **Southwark Cathedral** ❺. Augustinian canons erected the original church in the 13th century, but the cathedral has been much altered since then. Adjacent, in the St Mary Overie Dock, is a replica of Sir Francis Drake's galleon, the *Golden Hinde*. A few metres away, the **Clink Prison Museum** (open daily 10am–6pm; entrance charge) features old armour and torture instruments. Close to Southwark Bridge is a replica of

Map on pages 70–71

the 1599 **Shakespeare's Globe** ⑤ (performances in summer; guided tours daily from 9.15am, Tue–Sat till 12.45pm, Sun till 2.45pm, Mon till 3.45pm; entrance charge), a theatre-in-the-round which stages the Bard's plays where they were first performed. **Tate Modern** ⑤ is the Tate gallery's 20th-century collection, housed in the seven-storey Bankside Power Station, showing works by all the mainstream artists, from Picasso to Monet, Mondrian and Cézanne.

Back on the north bank of the river, downstream from Tower Bridge, lies **St Katharine's Dock** ⑤. Built in 1828 as a shipment point for wool and wine, the docks were renovated in the early 1980s and have become a posh residential and commercial district. They are the most successful of the docklands developments which extend east from here to the Isle of Dogs where the **Canary Wharf** tower (Britain's tallest office block) marks their modern ambitions.

Mansell Street leads north from the tower into the warren of narrow streets that marks the start of London's **East End**, traditionally the City's working-class district. **Whitechapel** and **Spitalfields** – both at the north end of Mansell Street – are where 19th- and early 20th-century European immigrants settled.

The **Whitechapel Art Gallery** ⑤ (open Tues–Sun 11am–6pm, Wed 11am–8pm; admission free)in Whitechapel High Street (by Aldgate East tube) is a beautiful piece of *fin-de-siècle* architecture, and is one of London's most exciting galleries, hosting regular exhibitions by living artists.

Petticoat Lane ⑥, once the domain of old clothes dealers, is the most famous East End market. Today, the traders – a mixed bag of Cockneys, West Indians and Asians – prove every Sunday morning that racial harmony is indeed possible. The stalls along Middlesex Street are a chromatic jumble of clothes, antiques, food and just about everything else you can think of. ❑

Jack the Ripper, London's most notorious murderer, chose Whitechapel prostitutes for his victims. Guided tours follow in his gruesome footsteps.

BELOW: *HMS Belfast* and Tower Bridge.

WEST LONDON

*The Royal Borough of Kensington and Chelsea
is home to London's affluent. Harrods is the local grocer's store,
Kensington Gardens is the back yard*

Map
on page
102

In the 19th century Chelsea was an avant-garde "village" just outside the sprawl of central London. Among its more famous residents were Oscar Wilde, John Singer Sargent, Thomas Carlyle, Mark Twain and T. S. Eliot. Cheyne Walk, a row of elegant Georgian terraced houses just off the river, has long been Chelsea's most prestigious residential street. George Eliot, J. M. W. Turner and Thomas Carlyle lived there in the 19th century; J. Paul Getty and Mick Jagger in the 20th. Chelsea is where England swung in the 1960s, with boutiques such as Mary Quant's Bazaar, and where punk began in the 1970s with Vivienne Westwood and Malcolm McLaren's boutique, called Sex.

King's Road ❶ is Chelsea's famous thoroughfare and one of London's most curious. Once a tranquil country lane, it was widened into a private carriage road from St James's Palace to Hampton Court on the order of King Charles II. Down on the riverfront is **Chelsea Royal Hospital ❷**, Sir Christopher Wren's masterpiece of the English baroque style, opened as a home for invalid and veteran soldiers in 1682 to match his hospital for sailors at Greenwich. A few hundred army pensioners still reside there, and parade in their famous scarlet frockcoats on Oak Apple Day (29 May). Nearby, tracing the history of the British military from the 15th century, is the **National Army Museum** (open daily 10am–5.30pm; admission free). **Ranelagh Gardens** stands adjacent to the Royal Hospital, the site of the Chelsea Flower Show each spring.

On Royal Hospital Road is the strange little **Chelsea Physic Garden** (open April–Oct, Wed and Sun 2–5pm; entrance charge), a botanical laboratory from which cotton seeds were taken to the American South in 1732. Walk across Albert or Chelsea Bridge and enjoy the lush expanse of **Battersea Park ❸** on the south bank, with gardens designed as part of the Festival of Britain in 1951 and the Buddhist Peace Pagoda, commemorating the 1985 Year of Peace.

Belgravia for the seriously rich

Having crossed the Thames again and returned to King's Road, leave Chelsea by proceeding east, crossing Sloane Square and entering the elegant district of **Belgravia**. The area was used for grazing until Thomas Cubitt developed it as a town estate for aristocrats in the early 19th century. The district retains this exclusive quality as the home of diplomats, senior civil servants, celebrities and the occasional duke or lord. Belgravia is littered with grand Regency terraces and squares, bound by cream-coloured mansions and carefully tended gardens. Behind these grand facades lie the diminutive mews and tiny cobblestoned alleys that once served as stables. This is London's most expensive residential district.

LEFT: looking across the Albert Hall towards Kensington Gardens.
BELOW: croquet player at the Hurlingham Club in Fulham.

Peter Pan in Kensington Gardens.

North of Belgravia via Sloane Street is the bustling neighbourhood of luxury shops and hotels at **Knightsbridge**. This is the home of **Harrods ❹**, London's most famous department store. At night, its light-spangled facade resembles an enormous Victorian birthday cake. As in the British Museum, you could spend days wandering the aisles of Harrods and still not see everything. But be sure to visit the food halls, which display more than 500 varieties of cheese, 140 different breads and 160 brands of whisky. The Victorian tiles underfoot are under a preservation order, which means they cannot be removed or altered without government permission.

Museums of the arts, natural history and science

South Kensington tube station (one stop after Knightsbridge) is the jumping-off point for Exhibition Road's cluster of fine museums. The **Victoria & Albert Museum ❺** (open Tues–Sun 10am–5pm, Mon noon–5.50pm; donations encouraged) is the most famous of these. It houses a marvellous collection of

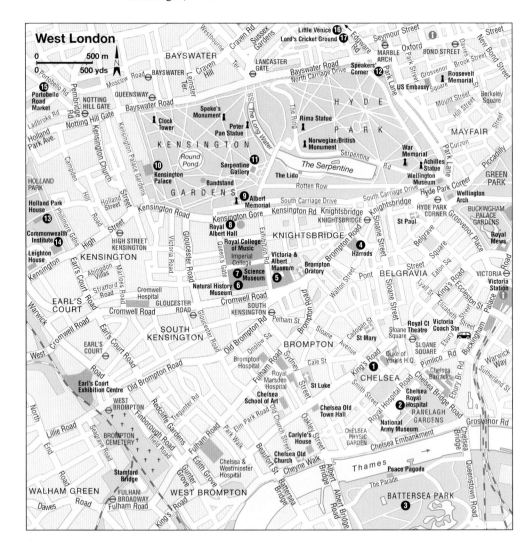

Map on page 102

millions of items dedicated to the fine and applied arts of all nations, eras and styles. It has been called a vast box of delights and indeed there must be something for everyone within its brick walls. The maze-like interior includes 7 miles (11 km) of galleries, with exhibits that range from furniture and paintings to textiles and armour. Highlights include the Raphael "Cartoons", the Great Bed of Ware from 1590 and the TT Tsui Gallery of Chinese Art.

For pterodactyls, try the **Natural History Museum** ❻ in Cromwell Road (open Mon–Sat 10am–5.50pm, Sun 1–5.50pm; entrance charge). It has one of the best dinosaur and prehistoric lizard collections anywhere. The Life Galleries also have fascinating exhibits on early man, Darwin's theory of evolution, human biology, birth and whales (including a life-sized model of a blue whale). In the Earth Galleries (geology section) you can experience a simulated earthquake, or examine a piece of the moon. The Discovery Centre is popular among children, as is the adjacent **Science Museum** ❼ (open daily 10am–6pm; free after 4.30pm), which has items ranging from Puffing Billy, one of the oldest surviving locomotives, to spacecraft and satellites.

One of Victorian England's greatest monuments also lies within South Kensington. Queen Victoria laid the foundation stone for the **Royal Albert Hall** ❽ in 1867 in memory of her late husband, Prince Albert, who was responsible for many of the South Kensington institutions. The circular 7,000-seat auditorium is still one of the largest theatres in London, and stages a varied programme from pop concerts to brass band competitions. However, the Albert Hall is most famous for the BBC-sponsored summer Promenade Concerts – the Proms – a marvellous showcase of both classical and more modern music. The final concert is traditionally a playful combination of serious music-making and boisterous audience participation. This Last Night of the Proms is broadcast live on BBC television, and millions across the nation tune in for their annual dose of flag-waving and old-fashioned sing-along.

Across Kensington Gore the **Albert Memorial** ❾, a flamboyant – even vulgar – Gothic monument, rises suddenly from the plane trees of Kensington Gardens and Hyde Park. Prince Albert sits under a lavish canopy, forever reading the catalogue from the 1851 Great Exhibition held in Hyde Park. Marble figures on the lower corners of the steps depict America, Asia, Africa and Europe.

Prince Albert of Saxe-Coburg, the consort of Queen Victoria, introduced to England the custom of putting up Christmas trees.

BELOW: Hyde Park.

Palaces and gardens

A short walk away through prolific and tranquil gardens is **Kensington Palace** ❿ (open Mon–Sat 9am–5pm, Sun 11am–5pm; entrance charge). Sir Christopher Wren refurbished the mansion for William and Mary in the late 17th century, and for nearly 100 years it served as the principal private royal residence in London. Queen Victoria was born here in 1819. Today it is the London residence of Princess Margaret, and was, until her death, the home of Diana, Princess of Wales. Another popular spot in the park is the **Serpentine Gallery** ⓫, a tiny museum with changing exhibitions of cutting-edge art. Rowing boats can be taken out on the the Serpentine lake and a there is a lido for swimmers in summer. In the northeast corner

TIP

Look out for concerts
and plays in Holland
Park in summer –
an incomparable
outdoor setting.

of Hyde Park is **Speakers' Corner** ⑫ where, particularly on Sundays, it is traditional for orators to defend passionately all manner of causes and beliefs.

Holland Park House ⑬, just west of Kensington Palace via Kensington High Street, gives its name to leafy Holland Park, one of the more interesting green spaces in London. Sir Walter Cope, James I's Chancellor of the Exchequer, built the lavish Jacobean manor on the site in 1606; through his daughter's marriage, it became the property of the Earl of Holland, who surrounded the house with 55 acres (22 hectares) of exotic gardens. Only the east wing of the house survived World War II bombing.

By the park in Kensington High Street, the **Commonwealth Institute** ⑭ (open Mon–Sat 10am–5pm, Sun 2–5pm; entrance charge) marks a complete contrast in style and mood, for this futuristic building is dedicated to the resources, culture and economies of former British Empire outposts. The Institute includes a reference library, cinema and several exhibition galleries such as the Commonwealth Experience with a "heliride" over Malaysia.

Notting Hill's Carnival

North of Holland Park is **Notting Hill**, one of London's most highly sought-after residential districts with handsome white stucco Victorian terraces and villas. However, the relative calm that prevails throughout the year is shattered every August Bank Holiday when the streets explode with music and colour as the city's huge West Indian population stages the largest street carnival in Europe. The atmosphere is electric as thousands flock to see the wild and exciting costumes of the procession which moves to the rhythmic beat of steel bands and reggae music. The district's other famous attraction is the **Portobello Road**

BELOW:
Portobello Road
antiques market.

Market **⓯**. On Saturday the whole street becomes jammed: at the top end with tourists in search of antique treasures, whilst, at the far end, those with an eye for a bargain rummage through the second-hand clothes and bric-a-brac stalls. Fine *objets d'art* do exist, but at a price. Here, in Blenheim Crescent, you can find the travel bookshop where Hugh Grant met Julia Roberts in the 1999 romantic comedy *Notting Hill*.

East of Notting Hill, on the north side of Hyde Park is **Bayswater**, a district that is both trendy and posh, a transport hub and a shopping mall. The area stretches up to **Paddington Station**, the mainline terminal for trains to the west of England and with a direct rail link to Heathrow Airport. To the north of Paddington begins a network of man-made waterways that once linked north London with Oxford and the Midlands. The posh residential district of **Little Venice ⓰** lies at the junction of the Grand Union, Regent's and Paddington Canals and residential moorings for barges here are much sought after.

Refurbished canal barges operated by the **London Waterbus Company** (April–Oct daily, Nov–Mar Sat and Sun) run east from Little Venice to Regent's Park through another exclusive neighbourhood, **St John's Wood**. The Rolling Stones sang about it; the Beatles crossed Abbey Road in the middle of it. Now St John's Wood is populated by an offbeat collection of diplomats, record company executives, pop stars and Porsche-driving businessmen.

Lord's Cricket Ground ⓱ is tucked away in the heart of the Wood. Lord's is the grand shrine of cricket *(see page 310)*, the home of the famous Marylebone Cricket Club (MCC), the governing body of the sport for more than a century. The club was founded by Thomas Lord, the groundsman in 1787, who moved the field here in 1816 ❑

Map on page 102

BELOW: Notting Hill Carnival.

LONDON'S RIVER

Of the many day trips to be taken around London, some of the best can be made by boat along the River Thames, from Royal Greenwich downstream, to Hampton Court upstream

Map on page 108–9

A trip along the River Thames, the main artery around which the city grew, is an instructive and a thoroughly enjoyable way to get to know London. There is a calm, almost rural feel to the journey, which passes well-known landmarks to put history into perspective. From Greenwich to Richmond, every suburb along the river has its own personality, and each can be reached by local London transport, as well as by riverboats. Eastwards, London's Docklands have been greatly renovated, but beyond a few remaining local pubs, it will be a long time before they find any real character.

To the west, however, the river is a focus of pleasure: in the summer, oarsmen and yachtsmen pit their wits against its tides, people stroll along its towpaths and the pubs are wet with warm beer and enlivened by warm company. Regular boat services run from **Westminster** (tel: 020 7930 4097) and **Charing Cross Piers ❶** (tel: 020 7987 1185).

LEFT:
St Paul's Cathedral from the South Bank.
BELOW:
the Millennium Dome, Greenwich.

Downstream: martitime Greenwich

Greenwich ❷ can be reached by train from Cannon Street or London Bridge train stations, on the Jubilee line, or on the Docklands Light Railway. Boats leave from Charing Cross Pier every 30 minutes in peak season and take about an hour. A good time to visit is on Sunday, when there is a crafts market.

There have long been settlements in Greenwich. In the 11th century Vikings pulled their longboats ashore here, killed Archbishop St Alfege and ravaged London. In 1427 Bella Court Palace was built on the riverside and it became a royal retreat. Henry VI made it his favourite residence and subsequent Tudor monarchs – Henry VIII, Elizabeth I and Mary – were all born at Greenwich. It was here, too, that Sir Walter Raleigh is supposed to have laid his cloak over a pool of mud to prevent Elizabeth I getting her feet wet.

James I had the old palace demolished and commissioned Inigo Jones to build a new private residence for Queen Anne. The result was the **Queen's House**, completed in 1637, a masterpiece of the Palladian style and perhaps the finest piece of Stuart architecture in England. Next door is the **National Maritime Museum**, an excellent seafaring collection, swelled with Millennium funds. Here the 1805 Battle of Trafalgar is relived and the glory of the nation's maritime tradition unfolds, with boats, paintings and memorabilia from heroic voyages. A short distance up the hill (by foot or shuttle bus) is the **Old Royal Observatory**, constructed at Greenwich by Charles II in 1675 in order to perfect the arts of navigation and astronomy. Since that time, the globe's longitude and time zones have been measured from the Greenwich Meridian, which cuts right through the middle of

The Cutty Sark, last of the great China clippers, Greenwich.

Flamsteed House, now a museum displaying astronomical instruments including the award-winning 18th-century clocks of John Harrison, whose story was told in Dava Sobel's best-selling *Longtitude*. (The Royal Observatory, Maritime Museum and Queen's House are open daily 10am– 5pm; combination tickets available.)

Greenwich sits on the Meridian: 1 January 2000 began here. The **Millennium Dome ❸** was sited directly north of the Park on an abandoned gas storage site (underground to Greenwich North). The great white "tent" contains 14 themed zones celebrating British ideas and technology.

Greenwich has been associated with British sea power for 500 years (the Royal Naval Dockyards were built downstream at Chatham, *see page 181*). In the late 17th century Sir Christopher Wren built the **Royal Hospital for Seamen** at Greenwich, an elegant, baroque complex that became the **Royal Naval College**. Its chapel and Painted Hall, decorated in the early 18th century by Sir James Thornhill, are open to the public (open daily 2.30–4.45pm daily; admission free). On the waterfront are anchored two of England's most famous ships. The *Cutty Sark* (open Mon–Sat 10am–6pm; entrance charge), built in 1869, was the last of the great China clippers, a speedy square-rigger that once ran tea from the Orient to Europe. It has been superbly preserved and now contains a small museum and a collection of ship figureheads. Its own figurehead is of the hag who pursued Tam O'Shanter in the Robert Burns poem, getting so close she pulled off his horse's tale: she is wearing a "cutty sark" – a cut-down shift. Nearby sits the tiny *Gipsy Moth IV*, the yacht in which Sir Francis Chichester sailed solo round the world in 1966.

Take the riverboat further downstream to catch a glimpse of the **Thames Barrier ❹**. This great shining steel wall, which stretches 1,700 ft (520 metres) across the width of the River Thames, protects London from flooding.

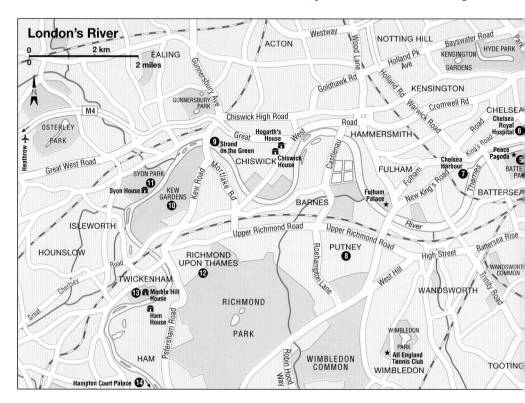

Upstream: gardens and grand houses

Riverboats go upriver from Charing Cross, too, past Westminster and Lambeth to Battersea and Chelsea, followed, on the north bank, by the District tube line, and on the south bank by the overground train line from Waterloo. Opposite the Peace Pagoda in **Battersea Park ❺**, erected for the 1985 Year of Peace by Japanese Buddhists, is Sir Christopher Wren's **Chelsea Royal Hospital ❻**, a home for old soldiers, and beyond, the upmarket housing and office development at **Chelsea Harbour ❼**. But the leafy riverbank does not really begin until **Putney ❽**, where the celebrated University Boat Race between Oxford and Cambridge begins each March. Putney, a residential area, can be reached by riverboat, or by taking the District Line to Putney Bridge.

The next crossing point is Hammersmith Bridge. The Piccadilly and District Underground lines go to Hammersmith, the starting point of a riverside walk that leads to Chiswick and has a number of popular riverside pubs, such as the Dove on Upper Mall. This historic 18th-century tavern is where the patriotic *Rule, Britannia* is supposed to have been written by Thomas Arne. **Strand on the Green ❾**, just beyond, has lively Georgian houses and charming fishermen's cottages. After your walk, try one of the good riverside pubs, including the Bull's Head and City Barge, both nearly 400 years old.

A further diversion at Chiswick is **Hogarth's House** (open Wed–Mon 11am–6pm, Sun 2–6pm; entrance charge), a 17th-century mansion now filled with engravings and personal relics of one of England's most famous artists. **Chiswick House**, an early 18th-century Palladian villa designed by the third Earl of Burlington, is even more delightful. (Train from Waterloo to Chiswick, or District or Piccadilly tube lines to Turnham Green; open daily 10am–6pm; entrance charge).

Map on page 108–9

The Peace Pagoda in Battersea Park.

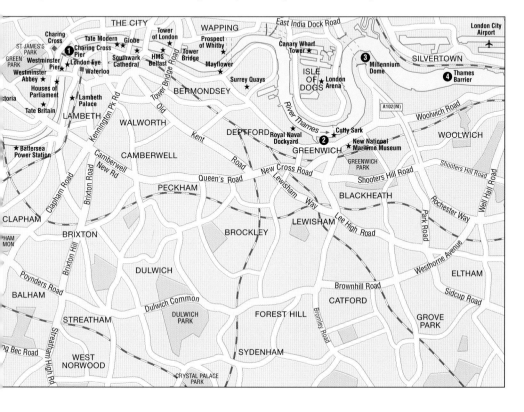

Tropical house in Kew

Kew, a quiet suburb upstream and across the Thames from Chiswick, plays host to the Royal Botanic Gardens, often called simply **Kew Gardens** ❿ (open daily 9.30am–dusk; entrance charge). The gardens, with 300 acres (120 hectares) of exotic plants from around the world, were first planted in 1759 under the direction of Princess Augusta, who was then living on the site. In 1772, George III put Kew in the hands of botanist Sir Joseph Banks, who had just returned from a round-the-world expedition to collect plant specimens with Captain Cook, and the collection grew. Today there are special areas given over to redwoods, orchids, roses, rhododendrons, alpine and desert plants.

The most famous of Kew's nurseries is the **Palm House**, a vast Victorian pavilion of steel and glass containing hundreds of tropical plants. It was restored following storm damage in 1987 when many of Kew's old and rare species of trees were damaged or lost, but it is once again open to the public. The latest addition to the greenhouses is the ecologically correct and energy-saving **Princess of Wales Conservatory**, opened in the same year.

Across the Thames from Kew is another famous botanical centre – **Syon Park** ⓫ (house open April–Sept, Wed–Sun and public holidays, 10am–5pm entrance charge; gardens daily 10am–dusk). The Dukes of Northumberland built a great mansion on the site in the 16th century, while the lush gardens were added later by the great English landscape gardener, "Capability" Brown. Syon offers a number of interesting attractions: the **National Gardening Centre**, the **Living Butterfly Museum** and **Syon House** itself, which has a lavish baroque interior and vivid conservatory. To reach Syon Park from central London, take the District Line to Gunnersbury, then the 237 or 267 bus to Brent Lea Gate. From Kew, cross Kew Bridge and take the bus.

The largest and smelliest flower in Kew Gardens is the "Rafflesia Arnoldi", named after Sir Stamford Raffles, the founder of Singapore. It flowers every five years

BELOW: running by the river at Richmond.

Richmond ⓬ (train from Waterloo, District tube line, or on foot along the towpath from Kew) retains its village atmosphere with a cluster of book and antiques shops, tea salons and charming riverside pubs (The Three Pigeons and the White Cross are two of the most popular). The Victorian-style **Richmond Theatre** sits on the edge of the green and is an important showcase for big-name productions on their way to the West End. **Richmond Park** was enclosed by Charles I as a hunting estate and is now the only royal park that keeps a large stock of deer. The walk to it up Richmond Hill from the centre of town leads to a magnificent view west over the Thames.

Bus 65 or 371 from Richmond will take you to the flamboyant 17th-century **Ham House** (open Mon–Sat 1–5pm, Sun noon–5.30pm; entrance charge), an annex of the Victoria & Albert Museum. It has a rich collection of period paintings (notably Reynolds and Van Dyck), tapestries, furniture, carpets and clothing. Cavaliers and Roundheads do fierce battle each spring as part of a three-week Richmond Festival.

Richmond Bridge leads across to **Twickenham**, known for its many mansions. It is also the home of English rugby (international games are staged in winter at the huge Twickenham Rugby Football Ground).

The 18th-century **Marble Hill House** ⓭ (open May–Sept, daily 10am–6pm, Oct–April, 10am–4pm;

entrance charge) on Richmond Road is a Palladian-style dwelling that provided a retreat for the secret affairs: George II and George IV kept mistresses here. The kings' house contains a fine picture gallery and a lovely garden, the scene of outdoor Shakespeare productions and concerts in summer. Riverside Twickenham offers such worthy pubs as the White Swan, the Eel Pie and the Barmy Arms.

King Henry's Tudor palace

Above Twickenham is Teddington and the first lock, which marks the end of the tidal Thames, and then **Hampton Court Palace** ⓮ (open April–Oct, daily 10am–6pm, Nov–Mar till 4pm, last ticket 45 minutes before closing; entrance charge; tickets can be bought with train tickets at Victoria Station). Its two distinctive architectural styles make it both the paragon of the Tudor style and the self-proclaimed English version of Versailles. In the early 16th century, Hampton Court was built by Cardinal Wolsey as the finest and most flamboyant residence in the realm. When Wolsey fell from grace, he gave the palace to Henry VIII in a futile attempt to regain favour. The king fell in love with it and moved there with Anne Boleyn. He ordered the construction of the Great Hall, the Clock Court and the Library, and enlarged the gardens. Elizabeth I is supposed to have used Hampton Court as an illicit love nest away from the prying eyes of London. She also planted the gardens with exotic trees and flowers brought to England from the New World by Sir Francis Drake and Sir Walter Raleigh.

In the 1690s, the sumptuous **State Apartments** were designed by Sir Christopher Wren for William and Mary, who also commissioned during their reign the famous **Maze** and the Tijou grillework atop the entrance gates. Today the 1,000 rooms are filled with paintings, tapestries and furnishings from the past 450 years. ❑

A Tudor welcome to Hampton Court.

BELOW: the palace's famous maze.

THE THAMES VALLEY

Rural serenity can be found close to the capital. Between London and Oxford, the Thames flows by affluent and picturesque towns and villages. Highlights include the imposing Windsor Castle

Map on page 116

London

The Thames wends its way west through the so-called Home Counties, a name that encapsulates a romanticised idea of England, neat, safe and civilised. The Thames Valley is quintessentially English: lush, leafy and pretty, with half-timbered houses, stately homes and a few Roman and medieval remains, yet only a short distance from the capital and the southeast via the M25, the ever-crowded orbital motorway, and regular train services.

Start the tour by taking Exit 13 off the M25 for a visit to **Runnymede ❶** (open summer 8.30am–5.30pm, winter 9.30am–4.30pm; National Trust; parking fee). This pleasant riverside meadowland is where, in 1215, King John, under pressure from his barons, signed the Magna Carta, the document that is said to contain the basis of English freedoms, although it brought little immediate benefit. According to tradition, the king's men camped on one side of the river, the barons on the other, and they met on the neutral ground now called Magna Carta Island. Above the meadows stands Cooper's Hill, which has glorious views of Windsor Castle, and which inspired the 18th-century poet Alexander Pope to garland it with "eternal wreaths". At the foot of the hill lies the not-very-impressive Magna Carta Memorial, presented by the American Bar Association, and the John F. Kennedy Memorial. Runnymede has a great diver-

PRECEDING PAGES: party time at the Henley boat race. **LEFT:** Eton student celebrating 4 July. **BELOW:** lazy days on the river.

FACT FILE

Largest town Reading.
Communications Accessible via the M25 orbital motorway; Windsor is a 50-minute train journey from London Waterloo (direct) and Paddington (change at Slough). There are also river boat services in summer between Runnymede, Windsor, Henley-on-Thames and Marlow.
Historical data Dorchester began as a Roman fortress, known as Durocina; Windsor Castle was founded in the 12th century by Henry I; Magna Carta was signed at Runnymede in 1215.
Major attractions Windsor Castle – main residence of the Royal Family; Cliveden – once the home of the Astor family; Cookham – picturesque village and birthplace of artist Stanley Spencer; Henley-on-Thames – famous for the July regatta; Sonning – the prettiest of the Thames villages; Dorchester – an ancient Roman town.
For the children Legoland at Windsor, a 150-acre (60-hectare) theme park. Direct train and/or bus connections from London.
Interesting diversions: St Albans, with a medieval cathedral and the remains of the Roman city of Verulamium The Garden of the Rose, which grows the white rose of York and the red rose of Lancaster.

TIP

Madame Tussaud's
Royalty and Empire
Wax Exhibition is
housed in Windsor's
railway station. It
includes the detailed
scene of Queen
Victoria's 1897
Diamond Jubilee
celebrations (open
daily in summer
9.30am–5.30pm; till
4.30pm in winter).

sity of flora and fauna, and parts of it have been designated a Site of Special Scientific Interest (SSSI). There is a well-designed programme of guided walks available (tel: 01784 432891 for details).

Residence of sovereigns

From Runnymede you can take the riverside road from **Staines** to **Datchet**, just across the river from which towers **Windsor Castle ❷** (open summer 10am–5.30pm, winter 10am–4pm; various closing days, tel: 01753 831118 for details; entrance charge). Since the reign of Henry I in the 12th century, Windsor, England's most famous castle, has been the chief residence of English and British sovereigns. William the Conqueror founded the original structure, a wooden building that probably consisted of a motte and two large baileys enclosed by palisades. The stone fortifications were built in the 12th and 13th centuries. Rising dramatically on a chalk cliff above the Thames, the castle you see today incorporates additions by nearly every sovereign since. In the 19th century, George IV and Queen Victoria spent almost £1 million on improvements. The 20th century saw great restorations of the interior, in particular of **St George's Chapel** (closed Sun), the worst casualty of a disastrous fire in 1992. The chapel, begun in 1477, is one of the finest examples of Perpendicular architecture in England (rivalled only by King's College Chapel, Cambridge and the Henry VII Chapel at Westminster). Henry VIII, Jane Seymour and Charles I are buried in the choir, while the tombs of Henry VI and VII, William IV and three of the Georges lie in the crypt.

In the Upper Ward are the **State Apartments**, accommodation for visiting foreign sovereigns, which are closed when occupied and when the Queen is in

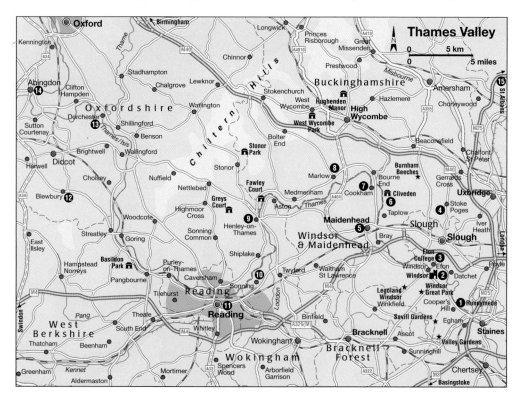

residence. Lavishly furnished, they include many important paintings from the royal collection, including works by Rubens, Van Dyck, Canaletto and Reynolds, and drawings by Holbein, Michelangelo, Leonardo and Raphael. **Queen Mary's Dolls' House** can also be seen and is one of the most popular parts in the castle.

Climb the 220 steps for the wide valley view from the Round Tower, and venture south of the castle to the **Great Park**, more than 2,000 acres (800 hectares) of lush greenery. The **Savill and Valley Gardens** have the world's biggest collection of rhododendrons.

As a complete contrast, **Legoland Windsor**, 2 miles (3 km) from the town centre on the B3022 Bracknell/Ascot road, is a theme park based around the children's building blocks – millions of them. Its 150 acres (60 hectares) of wooded landscape include, among other things, a roller coaster dragon ride, a space tower, a flying school, and Miniland – a miniature Europe made of millions of Lego pieces. There are also workshops and a learning centre: Lego is a contraction of two Danish words, *Leg Godt*, meaning "Play well", and the park puts a suitably worthy emphasis on learning as well as having fun (open mid-Mar–end Oct, daily 10am–6pm; mid-Jul–early Sept, till 8pm; tel: 0990 04 04 04). Shuttle buses run from near Windsor station; Green Line buses run from London Victoria, tel: 020 8668 7261.

From Eton to Henley

Across the river from Windsor is **Eton College** ❸ (open Mar–Oct; tel: 01753 671000 for details), the most famous of English public schools, founded in 1440 by 18-year-old Henry VI. The original set of buildings included a collegiate church, a grammar school and an almshouse. Henry intended that the church and school

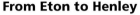 **TIP**

Weather permitting, the Changing of the Guard at Windsor takes place at 11am every day except Sunday, and many find it more splendid than the Buckingham Palace ceremony.

BELOW:
Windsor Castle.

should become a place of pilgrimage and devotion to the Virgin, but the Wars of the Roses intervened. He was murdered in the Tower of London and every year on the anniversary of his death an Etonian lays a wreath of lilies in the cell in which he died.

Beyond Eton's cloisters stretch the playing fields on which, the Duke of Wellington is said to have remarked, the Battle of Waterloo was won.

Eton is a cluster of red-brick Tudor buildings with small towers and hulking chimneys. The **School Yard** (outer quadrangle), the **Long Chamber** and the **Lower School** all date from the 15th century. The chapel, in Perpendicular style, has 15th-century wall paintings depicting miracles and legends of the Virgin. Most of the windows were damaged in World War II, but some of the modern ones are interesting. The cloisters, dating from the 1440s, are stunning.

Stoke Poges ❹, north of Eton and on the far side of **Slough**, was the inspiration for Thomas Gray's most famous poem, *Elegy Written in a Country Churchyard*. A statue erected in 1799 commemorates him with a somewhat maudlin inscription, but the sheer beauty of the churchyard – its old lich-gates, its rose bushes and its garden of remembrance – enchant most visitors.

Picturesque towns and villages

About 6 miles (10 km) upriver from Eton lies **Maidenhead ❺**, the starting point for some of the most beautiful countryside in the valley. Known in medieval times as Maydenhythe, meaning maidens' landing place, its bridges are its most interesting feature: the 128-ft (38-metre) arches of Brunel's railway bridge are the largest brick spans ever constructed. From Maidenhead the A4130 goes 8 miles (13 km) direct to Henley, but there are several picturesque villages and towns clustered on either side of the river nearby. **Bray**, nestled in a bend in the Thames just south of Maidenhead, has a lovely church that dates from 1293. The **Jesus Hospital**, founded in 1627, still cares for 26 elderly people.

BELOW:
the Shell Fountain
in the grounds
of Cliveden.

Taplow is another pretty village on the north side of the Thames opposite Maidenhead. From here a road leads through Burnham to **Burnham Beeches**, a pastoral stretch of 375 wooded acres (150 hectares).

Upstream from Maidenhead, poised dramatically above cliffs, is **Cliveden ❻** (main rooms and temple open April–Oct, Thurs and Sun 3–6pm; woodlands and estate Mar–end Oct, 11am–6pm; entrance charge; tel: 01628 605069). This Italianate house was built for the Duke of Sutherland in the 1850s and was once the home of the Astor family. Before World War II Nancy Astor, the first woman to be elected to parliament, turned it into a meeting place for politicians and celebrities. Today, Cliveden is owned by the National Trust, but is run as a luxury hotel. The gardens are decorated with Roman fountains, temples and topiary. Maps, available at the entrance, show suggested walks through the **Cliveden Reach**, a stretch of woodland with spectacular views of the Thames.

Cookham ❼ is yet another picturesque riverside village, but it's best known as the home of the artist Stanley Spencer (1891–1959). Spencer's portrait, *Cookham Bridge*, hangs in London's Tate Britain gallery. A gallery dedicated to his work is housed in the King's Hall on Cookham High Street (open Easter–Oct, daily, Nov–Easter, Sat–Sun). A copy of his painting of the *Last Supper* hangs in the church, parts of which date from the 12th century. The 15th-century tower is unusual, as it is one of the few church towers with both a clock and a sundial.

Marlow ❽ lies 6 miles (9 km) upriver. In Saxon times it was called Merelaw, but what you see today is comparatively new: a broad high street, several pleasing 18th-century buildings, a graceful suspension bridge and **All Saints' Church** (the latter both date from the 1830s). Walks along the river below Marlow Lock are refreshing, as is the 25,000 acres (10,000 hectares) of **Quarry Wood**.

Map on page 116

The ornate clock tower at Cliveden.

BELOW: the *George and Dragon*, a well-known watering hole at Marlow.

Taking to the water at Henley.

BELOW: in Henley for the regatta.

Crew capital of the world

Henley-on-Thames ❾, a small market town with numerous Georgian buildings, has been known for its races since 1839, when it hosted the world's first river regatta. The four-day **Henley Regatta**, usually held in the first week of July (*see page 122–23*), attracts rowers from all over the globe. It also attracts a champagne-drinking crowd decked out in Edwardian elegance – white linen dresses, striped blazers and straw hats. A strict dress codes operates in the stewards' enclosure. Less celebrated regattas are held on other summer weekends. As its name implies, the **River & Rowing Museum** in Mill Meadows (open summer Mon–Sat 10am–6.30pm, Sun 11am–6.30pm, winter till 5.30pm; entrance charge; tel: 01491-415610) casts its net wider than the world of rowing.

There are several stately homes around Henley, but the most exquisite is **Greys Court**. West of Henley on the road to Peppard, this well-preserved Tudor house includes the remains of a 14th-century manor house (open Mar–Sept, Mon, Wed, Fri 2–6pm; entrance charge; tel: 01491 628529). There is a crenellated tower, a huge donkey wheel once used for drawing water and a garden maze.

Shiplake is a sprawling village notable for its church, rebuilt in 1689, but housing excellent 15th-century stained glass from the abbey church of Saint-Bertin in Saint-Omer, France. Shiplake is best visited en route to **Sonning** ❿, often considered the prettiest of the Thames villages. The little islands that rise here in the river make the views especially pastoral. In Saxon times, Sonning was the centre of a large diocese, with a cathedral, a Bishop's Palace and a Deanery. Today, only parts of the Deanery garden walls remain, though the present church incorporates fragments of Saxon work. The old houses in the village are well preserved. The half-timbered **White Hart Inn** is 500 years old and has a lovely rose garden, and the 11-arched bridge is one of the oldest on the river.

Reading ⓫ is the single industrial town in the lower valley, an important traffic hub and retail centre but a somewhat dreary place, capitalising on the Thames Valley's aspiration to be Silicon Valley. The playwright Oscar Wilde (1854–1900) was broken by two years' hard labour in the red-brick prison.

Streatley and **Goring**, 10 miles (16 km) north on the A329, face each other on either side of the river. Streatley is the prettier of the two, situated at the foot of the Berkshire Downs. Five miles (8 km) northwest is **Blewbury** ⓬, a lovely little town with thatched cottages, orchards, watercress beds and winding lanes.

Upriver about 8 miles (13 km) is **Dorchester** ⓭ (backtrack to Streatley and look for signs to the A4074). This ancient town was once a Roman fort (then known as Durocina) and, during the 7th century, a cathedral city. The 13th-century abbey church was spared demolition during the Dissolution of the Monasteries (1536–40) by a local resident who bought it from the Crown for £140. The stained glass in the nave dates from the 14th century. In the chancel is a fine example of a Jesse window in which Jesse, Christ's ancestor, lies on the sill with a fruit vine springing from his belly. Dorchester's High Street, which follows the line of the Roman road to Silchester, is lined with period timber-framed buildings.

Map on page 116

Abbeys, roses and Romans

From Dorchester, the road leads to **Abingdon** ⓮ on the doorstep of Oxford. The town sprang up in the 7th century around a powerful Benedictine abbey. In the 14th century the townspeople, aided by the mayor and students of Oxford, rose up against the monks, though it was not until the Dissolution that the abbey lost its power. Most of the ecclesiastical buildings were destroyed (don't be fooled by the 19th-century artificial ruins in the abbey grounds), but there are some authentic remains. These include the abbey **Gateway**, the 13th-century **Checker** (Counting House) with its idiosyncratic chimney, and the 15th-century **Long Gallery**. In the **Guildhall** is a grammar school dating from 1563. East Saint Helen's Street, with the church at the foot, is perhaps the prettiest street, but many others have houses dating from the 17th and 18th centuries.

A short detour will take you to two places that should not be missed. Get back on the M25 and travel north to Exit 21A. At Chiswell Green you will find the **Gardens of the Rose** (open June–late Sept, Mon–Sat 9am–5pm, Sun 10am–6pm; entrance charge), a glorious garden run by the Royal National Rose Society. From here it's only a few miles north-east to **St Albans** ⓯ (or take the next exit on the M25). A pleasing market town, this was once the Roman settlement of Verulamium, and remains of its walls are still visible. The **Verulamium Museum** (open Mon–Sat 10am–5.30pm, Sun 2–5.30pm; entrance charge) has a wonderful collection of mosaics and remains of a Roman bath house and theatre can also be seen. **St Alban's Cathedral** (open daily; donations welcomed) was founded in 793 and, while nothing of that abbey remains, there are 11th-century Norman arches and windows, as well as some magnificent Early English and Decorated arches from the 13th and 14th centuries. ❑

St Alban was the first English Christian martyr, beheaded by the Romans early in the 3rd century.

BELOW:
blossoming in the Gardens of the Rose.

LITERARY CONNECTIONS

For a relatively small area, the Thames Valley has a surprisingly high number of literary connections.

● Alfred, Lord Tennyson was married in Shiplake church in 1850. There are rumours that he delayed his marriage for so long (he was 41 and had been engaged for many years) because he was worried about the mental instability which ran in his family.

● Oscar Wilde spent two years in Reading Prison, convicted of homosexual offences. On his release in 1897 he went into exile in France, where he wrote *The Ballad of Reading Gaol*. He never recovered his health or spirits, and died a broken man in 1900.

● Eric Blair (1903–50), better known as George Orwell, author of *1984* and *Animal Farm*, is buried in the graveyard at Sutton Courtenay.

● In Marlow's West Street, commonly known as Poets' Row, Mary Wollstonecraft wrote *Frankenstein*. In 1817 she and her husband, the poet Percy Bysshe Shelley, settled here for a short time. While here he wrote a series of pamphlets entitled *The Hermit of Marlow*, and composed and published the poem *The Revolt of Islam*.

● Thomas Gray completed his *Elegy Written in a Country Churchyard* while living in Stoke Poges in 1751.

THE ENGLISH SEASON

The Season is when high society is on display. The events are mostly sporting, but a sense of style is far more important than a sense of fair play

The English Season was an invention of upper-crust Londoners as a series of mid-summer amusements. This was the time when young girls "came out" at society balls, at which eligible young men would be waiting to make a suitable match. Mission accomplished, the families would repair to their country homes. The presence of royalty is an important ingredient, and the royal family has long taken a keen interest in the sports highlighted by the Season.

The events are completely insignificant compared to their importance as social gatherings. People who care nothing for rowing attend Henley Regatta in the first week of July; philistine amateurs flock to the Royal Academy's Summer Exhibition; the musically challenged die for a ticket to Glyndebourne's opera season on the south coast; and ill-informed people queueing for tickets to Wimbledon often seem to think it's the only tennis tournament in the world.

Eliza Dolittle, played by Audrey Hepburn in *My Fair Lady* (right), summed it up when, beautifully dressed by Cecil Beaton for the Royal Enclosure at Ascot, she forgot she was supposed to be a lady and urged a horse to "move yer bloomin' arse!". Such working-class passion is not welcome at an event where decorum, good breeding and a fancy hat take precedence over anything as vulgar as sporting enthusiasms.

▷ **HENLEY REGATTA**
Striped blazers and boaters are *de rigueur* at this Edwardian, public-school outing among the beer and Pimm's tents on the banks of the Thames in Oxfordshire.

▽ **ROYAL ASCOT**
Hats feature strongly at Royal Ascot in June, not least in the Royal Enclosure. This famous race course is near Windsor.

△ **POLO IN THE PARK**
International Polo Day at the Guards Polo Club, Windsor Great Park, is the height of this sport of kings (Prince Charles is a keen player) and rich South Americans. The pitch here – and the one in Richmond Park – is usally lined by Range Rovers and Rolls-Royces.

△ GLYNDEBOURNE
Charmingly set on the South Downs near Brighton, this summer opera location is renowned as much for its lavish picnic hampers as it is for its star performances, which are now staged in a new, enlarged building.

▽ CROQUET
The Hurlingham Club, by the river in Fulham, is host to the national championships of England's eccentric and surprisingly vicious game of croquet, otherwise played on country-house lawns.

THE ALTERNATIVE SEASON

Muddy fields and dripping camp sites don't dampen the spirits of those attending the "alternative" season – the annual round of music festivals. The larger ones attract the best bands from around the world and you don't have to be a hippy, crustie or a member of a youth tribe to attend. Many people take a tent to the large weekend events, some come only for one day.

The largest rock event, the Glastonbury Festival in Somerset, takes place at the end of June. More than 1,000 performances are given on 17 stages by more than 500 bands. It's fast becoming *the* place to be seen, and therefore tickets sell out quickly.

If you can't get to Glastonbury, try the four-day Phoenix festival which takes place in mid-July at Stratford-upon-Avon. This is a family-oriented event, with a crèche and seven music stages vying with comedy, circus and funfairs.

The best world music festival is Womad, held in Reading in mid-July. There are workshops and arts and crafts, with good facilities for families. The Reading Festival in late August attracts some of the best US rock groups. Smaller events are the July Cambridge Folk Festival and the Irish Fleadh, in Finsbury Park, north London, in June.

▽ CHELSEA FLOWERS
The Chelsea Flower Show in the grounds of the Royal Hospital Chelsea in May is an early taste of the Season. It can be a terrible crush but thousands find it rewarding.

▽ WIMBLEDON FORTNIGHT
The tennis tournament still attracts worldwide attention. Even the royal family gets involved: this is the trophy presented to the champion by HRH the Duchess of Kent.

OXFORD

England's first mass-production car factory was built here but now traffic is a major headache. The town has had better luck with its university, which justifiably draws the tourists

Maps:
Area 140
City 128

The seat of England's oldest university, **Oxford**, "the city of dreaming spires", was also the site of the first Morris Motors car factory and since World War II has been an industrial city as much as an academic one – something that is easy to forget when touring the colleges and museums. A good starting point is **Carfax** (the name derives from the French *Quatre Voies*, "four ways"), where the four main streets – Cornmarket, High Street, Queen Street and St Aldate's – meet. **Carfax Tower **, all that remains of St Martin's Church, dates from the 14th century, and from the top you get a good view of the city (open Easter–Oct, daily 10am–5.30pm, Sun 2–5.30pm; Nov–Easter, 10am– 3.30pm; entrance charge).

From Carfax, walk south along St Aldate's (passing the impressive, neo-Jacobite Town Hall on the left) and turn left into Blue Boar Lane and the entrance to the **Museum of Oxford** (open Tues–Sat 10am–5pm; entrance charge). Displays inside highlight the history of the city from prehistoric times to the industrial age. The most macabre exhibit is the skeleton of Giles Covington, an Oxford Freeman who was convicted of murder and executed in 1791. Afterwards, carry on down St Aldate's to **Christ Church**, the grandest of the colleges (open Mon–Sat 9am–5pm, Sun 12.45–5.30pm) founded in 1525 by

PRECEDING PAGES:
pedal power around the colleges.
LEFT: the dreaming spires.
BELOW: the Encaenia parade.

FACT FILE

Location At the confluence of the Thames (here called the Isis) and the Cherwell.
By air Heathrow (40 miles/64 km) connected by CityLink X70 coach service every half-hour, journey time 1 hour 10 minutes; Gatwick (70 miles/112 km) CityLink X80 service every two hours, journey time 2 hours 10 minutes; Birmingham International (65 miles/104 km, six National Express coach services a day, journey time 90 minutes).
By road M40 motorway from London (Junction 8) and the Midlands (Junction 9); journey time about 90 minutes from central London except during rush hour.
By bus Oxford Tube from London Victoria 9am–8pm every 12 minutes (tel: 01865 772250); CityLink X90 from Victoria Coach Station (tel: 01865 785400) every 20 minutes. Journey time approx. 1 hour 40 minutes.
By train Every hour from London Paddington, tel: 0345 484950, journey time approx. 1 hour.
Guided tours Walking tours start at Carfax Tower, tel: 01865 792653, or Tourist Office, tel: 01865 726871; open-top bus tours, tel: 01865 790522 or 01865 819393
Bike hire Tel: 01865 249368.
Tourist information The Old School, Gloucester Green, tel: 01865 726871.

Cardinal Wolsey, Henry VIII's chancellor, on the site of an earlier priory. **Tom Tower**, built by Sir Christopher Wren in 1681, looms over the main entrance (visitors enter through the **War Memorial Gardens**).

It was in the pool known as Mercury in the centre of Tom Quad that Anthony Blanche was dunked in Evelyn Waugh's novel "Brideshead Revisited".

Christ Church chapel is also the city **Cathedral**; the 13th-century spire is one of the earliest in England, and the building contains some exquisite stained glass, including the St Catherine Window and other works by Pre-Raphaelite artist, Edward Burne-Jones. Lining the south side of the vast **Tom Quad** is the enormous **Hall**, with a magnificent hammerbeam ceiling. To the north is the neo-classical **Peckwater Quad** and the smaller Canterbury Quad, where the **Picture Gallery** (open Mon–Sat 10.30am–5.30pm, Sun 2–5.30pm) has a fine collection of Renaissance paintings.

If you continue a short way down St Aldgate's you'll come to **Alice's Shop**, drawn by Sir John Tenniel as "the old sheep shop" in *Alice Through the Looking Glass*. Needless to say, it sells every imaginable Alice-related souvenir.

South of Christ Church, extending to the confluence of the Thames and Cherwell, is the glorious **Meadow**. Along the Thames are the university boathouses and it's here, in Eights Week in late May, that the college races take place. The Broad Walk runs east–west across the Meadow, and from it a path cuts north to **Merton College ⓓ** (open daily 2–4pm), founded in 1264. The **library** in **Mob Quad** (the oldest complete quadrangle in Oxford) was built in the 1370s (guided tours Mon–Fri 2–4pm). Much of the medieval structure remains, and the 16th-century bookshelves make it the first of its kind in England, where the books were set upright instead of being kept in presses. The **Max Beerbohm Room** in the Mob Quad's west wing is devoted to drawings by the writer and caricaturist (1872–1956), one of Merton's illustrious graduates.

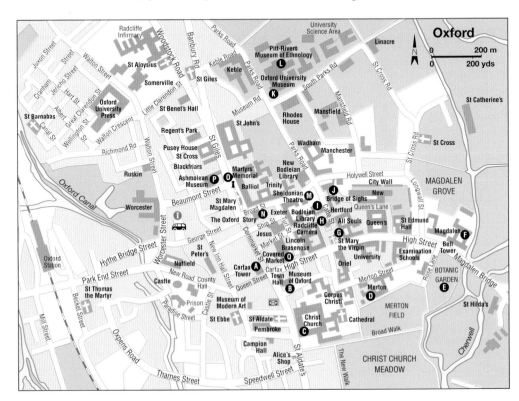

From botany to books

From Merton make your way to Rose Lane and the **Botanic Garden** Ⓔ (open daily 9am–5pm, till 4pm in winter). Founded in 1621 by Henry Danvers, Earl of Danby, as a physic garden for the School of Medicine, this is the oldest Botanic Garden in Britain. From the central pond, the view through the arch to Magdalen Bell Tower is magnificent. A great variety of roses are grown, and there's a wide range of tropical plants in the massive **glasshouses** (open daily 2–4pm) next to the Cherwell. Leaving the gardens you arrive at the High Street, just opposite **Magdalen College** Ⓕ (open daily 11am–6pm), founded in 1458 by William of Waynflete. The chapel is a fine example of Perpendicular architecture, and the cloisters, the heart of the college, are stunning. The **Bell Tower** (1505) was used as a vantage point by Royalist forces during the Civil War (1642–46) and is famous for the Latin grace sung from the top by choristers on May Morning. Behind the college's New Buildings is the deer park, **Magdalen Grove**, and the lovely **Water Walks**, a maze of stream-side paths.

From Magdalen, follow the High Street to **St Mary the Virgin** Ⓖ, the original hub of the university, where all ceremonies were held and documents kept. The main entrance is the baroque **South Porch**: built in 1637, it was directly inspired by the canopy that Bernini had just built over the high altar of St Peter's in Rome. The 15th-century nave is a fine example of the Perpendicular style, with slender columns and large windows. It was here, in 1556, that Archbishop Thomas Cranmer faced his persecutors for the last time. Refusing to denounce the Reformation, and retracting all previous recantations, he was dragged from the church and burned at the stake in Broad Street. The **tower** (open daily 9am–5pm; entrance charge) offers a magnificent view of the city.

Map on page 128

You can tour the town on an open-top bus.

LEFT: punts by Magdalen Bridge.
BELOW: Merton College courtyard.

*Students make
good tour guides.*

BELOW: the lovely
Bridge of Sighs.

On the north side of Radcliffe Square stands the **Radcliffe Camera** , one of Oxford's most familiar symbols, founded as a library in 1749 and absorbed into the Bodleian as a reading room in 1860. The **Bodleian Library** ❶ itself dominates the scene: it is one of the world's largest libraries, founded in 1602 and now housing over 6 million volumes, including 50,000 precious manuscripts. The serene and magnificent **Old Schools Quadrangle**, in Jacobean-Gothic style, is the centrepiece, and beyond the main entrance of the library lies the old **Divinity School**. Begun in 1426, it is regarded as one of the finest interiors in Oxford, and has a fine vaulted ceiling. (The library is closed to the public but guided tours of the Divinity School, Quadrangle and Exhibition buildings start at the Divinity School, 10.30am, 11.30am, 2pm, 3pm.)

Unmissable museums

Nearby, the **Bridge of Sighs** ❶ marks the beginning of New College Lane and links the two parts of Hertford College. This pretty bridge is an anglicised version of the Venice original. From here you could follow the lane to **New College** (not new at all, it was founded in 1379 and has lovely original cloisters), but our tour goes north, up Parks Road to the **Oxford University Museum** ❻ (open daily 12–5pm; admission free), a splendid neo-Gothic structure begun in 1855, with slender iron columns and wrought-iron vaulting in the glass roof. It is a treasure house of zoological, entomological and geological exhibits, among them the skeleton of an iguanodon dominating the main hall, and a model of a dodo (plus a few remains of the real thing) brought to England in 1638.

Through the doors to the rear is the **Pitt-Rivers Museum of Ethnology** ❶ (open Mon–Sat 1–4.30pm; admission free), an exotic collections of artefacts

from all corners of the world, begun by Lt-General Pitt-Rivers (1827–1900) when serving abroad with the Grenadier Guards. A cabinet containing the shrunken heads of Ecuadorian Indians, along with shrinking instructions, is one of the more ghoulish exhibits in this temple to Victorian scientific curiosity.

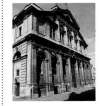

Map on page 128

Retrace your steps down Parks Road now to the **Sheldonian Theatre** (open Mon–Sat 10am–12.45pm, 2–4pm; entrance charge), the first architectural scheme of the young Christopher Wren, which he designed in 1669 at the age of 30 while still a professor of astronomy. The bestowal of honorary degrees takes place here each June but for most of the year the Sheldonian is used for concerts and lectures. The ceiling is held up by huge wooden trusses in the roof, details of which can be seen on the climb up to the cupola, which provides fine views over central Oxford.

Sir Christopher Wren's Sheldonian Theatre.

Adjacent to the theatre is the **Museum of the History of Science** (open Mon–Fri 10.30am–1pm, 2.30–4pm), which displays the apparatus used during World War II to prepare penicillin for mass production. Opposite the Sheldonian, on the aptly named **Broad Street**, stands **Trinity College** (open daily 10.30am–noon, 2–5pm), founded by monks from Durham Abbey in 1286. Unlike most Oxford colleges, the Front Quad is not closed off from the street, and its lawn almost invites visitors to enter. Apart from the baroque chapel, with its splendidly carved wooden panelling, stalls, screen and reredos, the principal attraction of Trinity is its fine gardens, entered through a wrought-iron screen from the Garden Quad.

Next to Trinity is **Blackwell's**, one of the world's most famous academic bookshops. Opened in 1879, the original shop was tiny, and even today the initial impression is of an average-sized provincial bookstore. Downstairs,

BELOW: Morris's early production line at Cowley.

THE CAR CAPITAL

In 1901, young William Richard Morris, who had begun his working life at the age of 14 repairing bicycles, set up his own cycle shop in Oxford High Street. An ambitious and talented young man, he saw that the future lay with the horseless carriage, and by 1912 had progressed to building the prototype of the "Bullnose" Morris Oxford car in a garage in Longwall Street, a project that set Morris on the road to fame and fortune, and launched Oxford into the industrial era. Just one year later he established his automobile plant at nearby Cowley, Britain's first mass-production line for affordable cars. He sold 393 cars in his first year; by the end of the 1920s he was producing 100,000 annually, and had built a separate factory for his successful MG Super Sports model.

Knighted in 1928, Morris became Viscount Nuffield a decade later, partly through his generosity to hospitals and other medical projects. In 1937 he donated the site and funds to build Nuffield College. He had always had a prickly relationship with the university and city authorities, and was anxious that the new college should help build a bridge between the academic and non-academic worlds. He would be proud of the research developments that have taken place there in recent decades.

however, is the underground Norrington Room, an enormous space stacked with shelves devoted to every topic under the sun.

On the other side of Trinity is **Balliol College** (open daily in term time), renowned for having produced a greater number of politicians and statesmen than any other college in Oxford. They include Lord Jenkins of Hillhead (present Chancellor of the University) as well as former prime ministers Harold Macmillan and Edward Heath. Together with University College and Merton, Balliol claims to be the oldest college in Oxford, founded in 1263. In 1361 John Wycliffe, Master of the college, spoke out against corruption and worldliness within the established church, and his teachings resonated through Europe. Little of the original college remains; what we see today is mostly Victorian.

Peddling an audio-visual experience.

Continuing the Oxford Story

Much of the southern side of Broad Street is distinctive for its colourful facades above shops selling antiquarian books and artists' materials. Here, too, is **The Oxford Story** (open April–Oct, 9.30am–5pm, July–Aug, 9am–6.30pm, Nov–Mar, 10am–4pm; entrance charge), a museum primarily devoted to the history of the university. Visitors are propelled through the ages aboard a motorised medieval desk, experiencing the sights, sounds, smells and personalities of this 800-year-old institution, accompanied by Magnus Magnusson's taped commentary (children's and foreign-language versions are available).

Opposite Balliol a cross in the road marks the point where the Protestant Martyrs, bishops Thomas Cranmer, Hugh Latimer and Nicholas Ridley, were burnt at the stake. Around the corner at the southern end of broad St Giles, they are further commemorated by the **Martyrs' Memorial** **O**, which was erected

BELOW: Broad Street and Balliol.

in 1841. Before Latimer and Ridley were consumed by the flames in 1555 (Cranmer followed a year later) Latimer offered these words to his colleague: "Be of good comfort, Master Ridley, and play the man. We shall this day light such a candle, by God's grace, in England, as I trust shall never be put out."

Map on page 128

Ashmole's great collection

The neo-classical building opposite the Martyrs' Memorial is the **Ashmolean Museum** ❷ (open Tues–Sat 10am– 5pm, Sun 2–5pm; admission free) whose main facade stretches along the north side of Beaumont Street (entrance through the west wing). Built from 1841 to 1845, the Ashmolean is the oldest museum in the country, and one of the greatest in the world. Set up by Elias Ashmole in 1683, its first home was in purpose-built premises on Broad Street (now the Museum of the History of Science). The origin of the collection goes back to Lambeth, London. There, in a pub called The Ark, the 17th-century naturalist and royal gardener John Tradescant displayed the extensive collection of rarities and curiosities gathered on his trips to Europe or given to him by sea captains. After his death in 1638, Tradescant's son, also called John, added numerous items from the New World. The collection was bequeathed to Ashmole, who presented it to the university. Items from The Ark can still be seen in the **Tradescant Room** on the first floor. They include a rhinoceros-horn cup from China, Henry VIII's stirrups and hawking gear, and, as the star attraction, **Powhattan's Mantle**. Powhattan was a Virginian Native American chief and, as any American child will tell you, the father of Pocahontas.

The **Antiquities Department** has a fine Egyptian section, and extensive displays covering Ancient Greece, Rome and the Near East, as well as Dark-Age

Bicycle rickshaws are a novel way to get around.

BELOW: the Ashmolean Museum.

Map on page 128

TIP

There is a pleasant café in the vaulted basement of the Ashmolean, which can also be reached directly from outside.

Europe and Anglo-Saxon Britain. It is in the latter section that the museum's most famous artefact, the **Alfred Jewel**, is kept. Found in Somerset in 1693, it is regarded as the finest piece of Saxon art ever discovered. It bears the inscription *Aelfred mec heht gewyrcan* ("[King] Alfred had me made").

The other main attraction is the **Department of Western Art** on the first floor, which includes drawings by Michelangelo and Raphael, as well as *The Hunt in the Forest*, painted by the Florentine artist Paolo Uccello in 1466.

Continue south down noisy Cornmarket Street, and turn left into Market Street for the **Covered Market** ❻. Established by the Paving Commission in 1774 as a permanent home for the stall holders cluttering the streets, this is an Oxford institution that can't be missed. The central range is dominated by the butchers, whose fronts are hung with a variety of carcasses. There are also a high-class delicatessen and a pasta shop; shops selling sausages and meat pies; as well as tea shops and cafés – including the traditional "greasy spoon" – all vying for custom alongside smart boutiques and florists.

You can leave by an arcade via the tastefully restored **Golden Cross Yard**. Now equipped with a pizzeria, boutiques and shops selling organic products, this stands on the site of one of Oxford's oldest inns, where Shakespeare's plays are said to have been performed in the cobbled yard. Leaving the yard, you'll find yourself back at Carfax, where the tour began, but if you still have any energy left you could take a right turn on to Pembroke Street to the **Museum of Modern Art** (open Tues–Sat 10am–6pm, Sun 2–6pm; entrance charge) which occupies an old brewery warehouse, and mounts some interesting changing exhibitions. The nearby Moma Café is a good place to rest your legs after all your exertions, and have something to eat and drink. ❑

BELOW: the colourful Covered Market.

ANNUAL EVENTS

May Morning the choir of Magdalen College sings a Latin grace from the Magdalen Bell Tower at 6am – an unforgettable sound. This is followed by Morris dancing in Radcliffe Square and Broad Street, and by the unorthodox but equally traditional practice of students jumping from Magdalen Bridge into the River Cherwell.

Ascension Day the ancient ceremony of Beating the Bounds starts at St Michael's Church in Northgate, and reconfirms the limits of the parish.

Eights Week held in May, in the fifth week of the Trinity (summer) term, when eight-oared crews from all colleges compete for the distinction of "head of the river". The boat that crosses the finishing line first without being bumped is the winner.

Spring Bank Holiday Monday the Lord Mayor's Parade of splendidly decorated floats and tableaux runs from St Giles to South Park.

Encaenia in the week following the end of the summer term (in June), this is the main honorary degree ceremony, when dignitaries process to the Sheldonian Theatre.

St Giles' Fair (9–10 September) is the date of this colourful and much-loved local fair, which has been taking place since 1624.

THE GREAT PALACE OF BLENHEIM

Blenheim Palace, near Woodstock, is a baroque masterpiece, a place of pilgrimage and a good day out for children

Some 8 miles (13 km) northwest of Oxford, its main street flanked by Georgian houses, is the attractive little town of **Woodstock** which grew prosperous through glove making. Pleasant though it is, it is overshadowed by its grand neighbour, **Blenheim Palace** (open Mar–Oct, daily 10.30am–5.30pm; park open all year, 9am–4.45pm; entrance charge). In the early 18th century the great palace, designed by Sir John Vanbrugh and his assistant Nicholas Hawksmoor, was given by a grateful nation to John Churchill, 1st Duke of Marlborough, after his victory over the French at the Battle of Blenheim in 1704. Although recognised as a masterpiece of English baroque, its sheer ostentation made it an object of controversy right from the start.

The gilded **State Rooms** are the most impressive, decorated with tapestries, paintings and sculpture; and the beautiful **Long Library** contains more than 10,000 volumes. Many visitors are most interested in Blenheim as the birthplace and home of Sir Winston Churchill (1874–1965), and they will be delighted with the large collection of his manuscripts, paintings, books and letters.

It is quite possible to spend an enjoyable day at Blenheim without even going into the house. The huge park in which it stands, covering some 2,100 acres (800 hectares), was landscaped by "Capability" Brown (1715–83). Its centrepiece is the **lake**, spanned by Vanbrugh's Grand Bridge. The shallow side of the lake, called the Queen Pool, is home to a variety of water fowl, which makes it particularly popular with birdwatchers.

ABOVE LEFT: Blenheim gardens and the lake.
RIGHT: Sir Winston Churchill; the palace facade.

It was in the little Temple of Diana overlooking the lake that Sir Winston proposed to Clementine Hozier in August 1908. The young couple made their home in London, but spent a lot of time at Blenheim.

One of the great attractions of the grounds is the **Marlborough Maze**, the largest in the world. It occupies the Walled Garden at the south side of the estate, an area known as the **Pleasure Gardens**, which includes putting greens, giant chess and draughts boards, and some bouncy castles for children, as

well as a herb garden, butterfly house, tearoom and adventure playground. The area can be reached on a miniature railway which trundles through the grounds, but if you have the energy its nicer to walk, admiring the ancient oak trees as you go.

The 1st Duke is has a large monument in the palace chapel, but Sir Winston and his wife are buried in Bladon parish churchyard, just outside the walls of the park. ❏

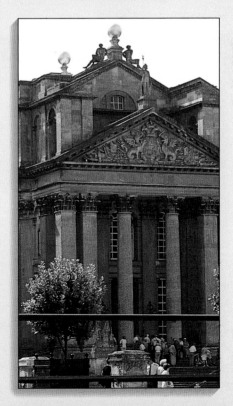

THE COTSWOLDS

Map on page 140

To many people, this area, with its Roman remains and ancient castles, its picturesque villages and leafy lanes, its lush river valleys and riverside pubs, represents the essence of England

London

The creamy white limestone of the Cotswold Hills defines the boundaries of the region and gives it its character, a harmonious landscape of fields bordered by drystone walls, churches with majestic towers, opulent town houses and snug cottages with roofs of limestone tiles. Most people start a visit to the Cotswolds at **Oxford ❶**, usually combined with a trip to **Blenheim Palace ❷** (*see pages 127–35*). From Oxford, go west on the A40 and make a short detour off to the right to the romantic ruins of 15th-century **Minster Lovell Hall** with its interesting dovecote (open May–Sept, Thurs–Sun 10am–6pm; admission free). Then it's back on the road again to **Burford ❸** which has one of the region's finest high streets, lined with 17th- and 18th-century cottages and descending sharply to a packhorse bridge over the River Windrush. A massive church stands beside the bridge, with a splendid Renaissance monument to Henry VIII's barber and surgeon, Edward Harman.

West of Burford the Windrush flows through a series of unspoiled villages, but we are heading a short way south on the A361 to **Lechlade**, where Percy Bysshe Shelley (1792–1822) was inspired to write *A Summer Evening Churchyard*. You can follow his footsteps on a path inevitably called Shelley's Walk, to **St John Bridge**, at the highest navigable point on the Thames. Beside the bridge

PRECEDING PAGES: the idyllic village of Lower Slaughter. **LEFT:** willow trees and willowy spires. **BELOW:** a group of Morris dancers.

FACT FILE

By car The M40 and M4 motorways provide easy access to the Cotswolds from London, as does the M5 from the Midlands and the north.

By bus National Express from London Victoria to Oxford, Cheltenham, Cirencester, Gloucester and Stow-on-the-Wold, tel: 0990 808080.

By train Every hour from London Paddington to Oxford, tel: 0345 484950; services to Cheltenham and Gloucester from Wales, the Midlands and south-west England, tel: 01222 430400.

Major towns Cheltenham, Cirencester, Gloucester, Oxford.

Main festivals Cheltenham Festival of Music (July), tel: 01242 227979; Cheltenham Festival of Literature (October), tel: 01242 521621; Gloucestershire Guild of Craftsmen, Painswick (July–Sept), local painting and sculpture, tel: 01684 773417.

Outdoor activities Cotswold Walking Holidays, tel: 01242 254343; Cotswold Country Cycles (cycle hire), tel: 01386 438706; Cotswold Gliding Club, tel: 01285 760473.

For children Broadway Country Park, tel: 01386 852390.

Tourist information Broadway, tel: 01386 852937; Cheltenham, tel: 01242 552878; Gloucester, tel: 014522 421188; Oxford, tel: 01865 726871.

*A memorial to
William Morris in the
churchyard.*

TIP

If you would like a
leaflet on suggested
walks around
Sherborne, contact the
estate office, tel:
01451 844257.

is the **Trout Inn** (very pretty, but so popular that it's often crowded) and a minor road to **Kelmscott Manor ④** (open April–Sept, Wed 11am–1pm, 2–5pm; entrance charge), famous as the summer residence of the Pre-Raphaelite poet and craftsman William Morris (1834–96). There is a comprehensive account of Morris's life and the Arts and Crafts Movement which he co-founded, and works by several members of the movement. He and his wife, Jane, are buried beside the rustic and unspoiled village church – the kind he loved most.

A circular route: Fairford to Cirencester

Some 5 miles (8km) west in **Fairford ⑤** is the finest of Cotswold churches with an extraordinary 15th-century stained-glass window which depicts the biblical story from the Creation to the Crucifixion. The Last Judgment window, with its fiery red devils and grim details of eternal punishment, is a masterpiece.

Continue along the A417 to Ampney Crucis – which also has a fine church – then take a right turn on the B4425 to **Barnsley ⑥** where you skirt Barnsley Park before entering the main street of a village where, until recently, overhead cables and television aerials were banned in an attempt to preserve its timeless tranquillity. The village is best known for the lovely 4-acre (1.6-hectare) garden of **Barnsley House** (open Mon–Thurs and Sat 10am–5.30pm; book in advance; tel: 01285 740281). Gazebos, statuary and various stone structures form the framework of this unusual garden, created by the late David Verey.

The B4425 joins the A40. Turn left here, then look for a right turn signposted to **Sherborne ⑦** where 18th-century **water meadows** are being restored to working order by the National Trust, complete with sluice gates and flood channels. Sherborne was built as a model estate village in the mid-19th century and

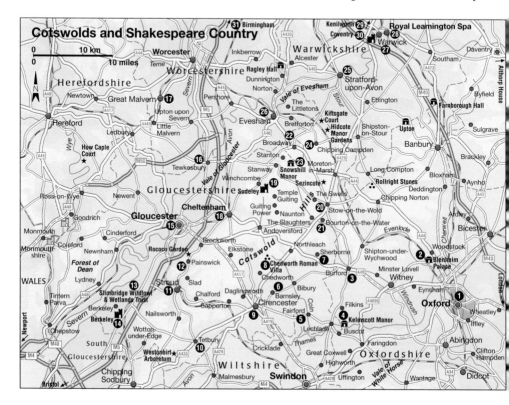

consists of rows of attractive identical stone cottages. The main house has a flamboyant facade and there are good monuments in the church alongside.

Turn left when the A429 joins the A40, and just south of Northleach you'll see signs to **Chedworth Roman Villa** ❽, in a delightful woodland setting overlooking the Coln Valley. Mosaics here include a wonderful depiction of the seasons, with winter personified as a peasant in a billowing hooded cloak bringing home a hare for the pot. In one corner of the site is a *nymphaeum*, a small sanctuary to the goddess of the spring who supplied the villa with water. The Romans introduced the edible snails that are found around the villa and inhabit the railway cuttings which are now a nature reserve. Chedworth village has a handsome Norman church with a fine stone-carved 15th-century pulpit, and a good pub, the Seven Tuns, in which to relax after your sightseeing.

Capital of the Cotswolds

Whether you pronounce it "Cissiter", as purists suggest, or "Siren", as the locals say, **Cirencester** ❾ used to be Corinium, the hub of a network of Roman roads, and it retains the rectilinear street plan of a Roman town. Gardeners are used to turning up lumps of mosaic, and any building project must be preceded by an archaeological investigation, the fruits of which are displayed in the excellent **Corinium Museum** (open Mon–Sat 10am–5pm, except Mon in winter, Sun 2–5pm; entrance charge), where life-sized tableaux depict Roman daily life.

Cirencester also has an interesting parish church, **St John the Baptist**, with a fine wine-glass pulpit, one of the few to survive the Reformation. If the magnificent tower is open (times vary) climb to the top for a view of **Cirencester Mansion**, otherwise hidden from view by what is said to be the world's tallest

Map
on page
140

The Cotswolds towns grew prosperous through wool.

LEFT: Cirencester's Wool Market.
BELOW: the magnificent tower of St John the Baptist.

yew hedge. Beyond the mansion the broad tree-lined avenues of **Cirencester Park** are open to the public. An early example of English landscape gardening, it was laid out by the first Earl of Bathurst in the early 18th century, with some help from his friend, the poet Alexander Pope (1688–1744). The walk to the park takes you through some of the town's most handsome streets, lined with the houses of wealthy wool merchants.

Tetbury to Gloucester

The poet Laurie Lee, born in the Slad Valley near Stroud, celebrated the region in his popular 1959 novel, "Cider with Rosie".

We are going a little way south now, to **Tetbury** ❿, which was a quiet backwater until Prince Charles moved to nearby Highgrove. It's an attractive little place, with a 17th-century market hall and a wonderfully theatrical church, a rare example of Georgian Gothic.

Just south of the town lies the **Westonbirt Arboretum** (open daily 10am–8pm or sunset if earlier; tel: 01666 880220), a glorious estate, its trees interplanted with camellias, azaleas, rhododendrons, cherries and maples which bring thousands of visitors during May and October for the spring and autumn colour.

Next we head for **Stroud** ⓫, which is back on the A419. The steep-sided valleys around the town provided it with fast-running streams, ideal conditions for woollen mills in the 18th century, when Stroud was the capital of this industry. A few of the grand mills continue to produce high-quality cloth but most have been converted to other uses.

BELOW:
The Clothier's Arms at Stroud.

Some 3 miles (5 km) up the A46 is **Painswick** ⓬, known for its elegant stone houses; a churchyard with 99 topiaried yews forming a series of avenues to the church; and some elaborately carved "table top" and "tea caddy" tombs. North of town, Painswick Rococo Garden (open Wed–Sun 11am–5pm, daily

July–Aug; entrance charge). Dotted with temples and gazebos and surrounded by woodland, the garden is at its most impressive at snowdrop time, when the flowers carpet the ground.

Those interested in wildlife could make a slight detour here (take the A419 which crosses the motorway, then turn left on the A38) to the **Slimbridge Wildfowl and Wetlands Trust** ⓭ (open daily 9.30am–5pm; entrance charge), founded by artist and naturalist Sir Peter Scott in 1946 on a marshy site beside the River Severn. The ponds are home to an array of wildfowl from around the world, and viewing hides are dotted around at strategic points.

While you're on this side of the motorway, you might wish to visit a splendid castle just south of Slimbridge. At **Berkeley Castle** ⓮ (open May–Sept, Tues–Sat 11am–5pm, Sun 2–5pm; entrance charge; tel: 01453 810332 for winter hours), with its massive Norman keep, you can see the Great Hall, where the barons met before riding to Runnymede to force King John to sign the Magna Carta in 1215; and the cell where Edward II spent his last days before he was murdered in 1327. Despite this regicide, the castle has remained in the hands of the same family from 1153 to the present.

Back on the A38, we are now heading for **Gloucester** ⓯, not one of the most beautiful cities but one of great historical interest and full of unusual and fascinating museums (*see below*), making it a good place for a rainy day. Founded by the Romans, it became an important Saxon town, and later one of the country's busiest ports. From the renovated docklands area you can take a short cruise through the port and along the canal on the *Queen Boadicea II* (tel: 01452 318054 for details and bookings). Gloucester's Norman **Cathedral** (open daily, daylight hours; donation requested), small by cathedral standards, has two fine

Bagpipes at Berkeley Castle.

BELOW: narrow boats in Gloucester docks.

GLOUCESTER'S BEST MUSEUMS

The National Waterways Museum (open daily 10am–5pm; entrance charge) interactive displays and hands-on activities which children love.

Museum of Advertising and Packaging (open Mar–Sept, daily 10am–6pm, Oct–Feb, Tues–Sun 10am–5pm; entrance charge) a fascinating, nostalgic collection amassed by Robert Opie, whose parents chronicled playground games, folklore and songs.

Soldiers of Gloucester Museum (open Tues–Sun 10am–5pm; entrance charge) the history of local regiments, with a section on women at war.

Gloucester Folk Museum (open Mon–Sat 10am–5pm and Sun 10am–4pm in July–Sept; entrance charge) working model railways and exhibits on traditional methods of salmon and elver fishing.

Tailor of Gloucester Museum (open Mon–Sat 9.30am–5.30pm; entrance charge) reveals the real-life tale behind the Beatrix Potter story of the mayor's magic waistcoat.

City Museum and Art Gallery (open Mon–Sat 10am–5pm & Sun 10am–4pm in July–Sept; entrance charge): houses a surprisingly wide collection, from dinosaurs to local flora, Saxon sculpture and Celtic bronze and medieval metalwork.

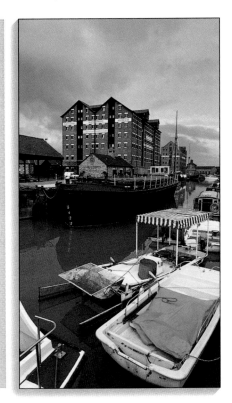

tombs: that of Robert, Duke of Normandy, William the Conqueror's eldest son, and of Edward II, murdered at nearby Berkeley Castle (*see page 143*).

You may now decide to go north to Tewkesbury and Great Malvern, or east to Cheltenham. For **Tewkesbury** ⑯ take the A417/B4211. It's a pretty little town on the confluence of the Severn and Avon rivers, and a number of its half-timbered buildings now serve as pubs – the 17th-century Bell Inn is worth a stop. There's also a fine Norman abbey church, with splendid views of the Malvern Hills from the top of its square tower.

Twelve miles (20 km) north is **Great Malvern** ⑰ once a spa town and still known for Malvern water which gushes from the spectacular surrounding hills. The town's other claim to fame is the **Malvern Festival**, held in late May, which specialises in the music of Sir Edward Elgar (1857–1934) who lived at nearby Little Malvern.

Royal connections

If you opted for this short diversion you could now return on the motorway to **Cheltenham** ⑱, the gracious Regency spa town which became popular as a summer resort after George II visited to "take the waters" in 1788. To get the feel of the town, stroll along the broad leafy avenue known as The Prom, where a splendid fountain is dominated by a statue of Neptune. To one end of The Prom lie the Imperial Gardens and elegant Montpellier Walk; to the other, **Cheltenham Art Gallery and Museum** (open Mon–Sat 10am–5pm; entrance charge), which combines local history and colonial trappings with furniture made by members of the Arts and Crafts Movement. Nearby, in Clarence Road, the **Holst Birthplace Museum** (open Tues–Sat 10am–4pm; entrance charge) celebrates

GUSTAV HOLST
COMPOSER
WAS BORN HERE
21st SEPT. 1874

Welcome to the Holst Birthplace Museum in Cheltenham.

BELOW: the broad and leafy Prom at Cheltenham .

Gustav Holst (1874–1934) who spent his early life here. The **Museum of Costume** (open Wed–Mon 11am–4pm; entrance charge) shows what the fashion-conscious have been wearing over the past two centuries.

Cheltenham is very lively in March, when members of the racing fraternity descend for the Cheltenham Gold Cup and the Champion Hurdle; and again in July, when its highly rated Festival of Music is held (tel: 01242 227979 for details), and in October, for the Festival of Literature (tel: 01242 521621).

North of Cheltenham on the B4632 is a place with royal connections of a different kind: **Sudeley Castle** ⓳ (open April–Oct, 10.30am–5pm; entrance charge) was briefly the home of Catherine Parr (1512–48), the only one of Henry VIII's wives to survive him. Only six weeks after becoming a widow she married Lord Admiral Seymour, Sudeley's owner, but died a year later and was buried in the chapel. The castle was ruined during the Civil War which erupted in 1642, but restored during the 19th century. Among its glories are some fine furnishings, paintings by Rubens and Van Dyck, and lovely romantic gardens.

Continue north for a short way on the B4632 then turn right on the B4077 for **Stow-on-the-Wold** ⓴, the Cotswolds' highest town ("Stow-on-the-Wold where the wind blows cold", as the local rhyme has it). Here, royal connections were nothing to boast about: the church was used as a prison for Royalists during the Civil War and suffered considerable damage. The unusual north porch, with two yew trees growing out of the masonry, was added as part of the 1680 restoration. The enormous market square was in use until the 1980s, and the wooden stocks on the green were used to punish those who looked on market days as an opportunity for pilfering. Stow now has a reputation as an antiques centre, and you will find numerous interesting shops and galleries.

Map on page 140

TIP

If the kids don't want to leave Sudeley's adventure playground, promise them a ride on the Gloucester to Warwick Steam Railway (daily in school holidays and on summer weekends; tel: 01242 621405).

LEFT: players at Sudeley Castle.
BELOW: stocks at Stow-on-the-Wold.

Flamingos live in natural surroundings at Birdland.

Models and manors

Around Stow are some of the Cotswolds' most attractive villages, among them **Upper** and **Lower Slaughter**, and **Bourton-on-the-Water ㉑**. The latter has far too many gift shops and cafés, but it remains a pretty little place, with elegant 18th-century bridges spanning the Windrush as it flows through the centre. The **Model Village** (open April–Sept, daily 9am–6pm, Oct–Mar, 10am–4pm; entrance charge) is a delightful miniature reconstruction of Bourton; and the **Model Railway** (open April–Sept, daily 9am–5pm, Oct–Mar weekends; entrance charge) will delight anyone who is nostalgic about train sets.

Close by is **Birdland** (open April–Sept, daily 10am–6pm, Oct–Mar, 10am–4pm; entrance charge) where most of the 500 or so birds were bred and can wander freely in natural surroundings. The best time to visit is at feeding time, around 2.30pm.

Backtrack now to the A424/A44 to visit **Broadway ㉒**, a manicured and mellow village, crammed with antique shops, art galleries and tea shops. The church, about a mile away, has ancient topiaried yew trees, rustic monuments and a sense of tranquillity. In the village itself, the imposing Lygon Arms Hotel is a Renaissance building restored by members of the Arts and Crafts Movement in the early 20th century and now celebrated for its restaurant.

William Morris, co-founder of the movement, spent holidays at Broadway Tower, now contained in nearby **Broadway Country Park** (open April–Oct, daily 10am–6pm; tel: 01386 852390), where there is a rare-breeds enclosure, a Country Life in Wartime exhibition, and an adventure playground.

Close to Morris's tower (and reached by a turning off the A44 at Broadway Green just before you enter the village) is **Snowshill Manor ㉓** (open

BELOW: a shop in mellow Broadway.
RIGHT: Tudor Snowshill Manor.

Map on page 140

April–Oct, Wed–Mon 1–5pm; National Trust), an attractive Tudor manor house, restored by the eccentric Charles Paget Wade from 1919 to 1951. The Arts and Crafts influence is obvious in his work. He also assembled an eclectic range of objects, ranging from musical instruments to toys, tools and Japanese armour. For some, Snowshill's greatest appeal is the garden, conceived as a series of rooms enclosed by walls and hedges which forms a maze around the house.

Chipping Campden

Chipping Campden ❷ is an idyllic Cotswolds town, kept in a state of perfect preservation by the Campden Trust, which ensures that power cables are hidden and modern shopfronts banished. The sheer variety of buildings here is unusual, from the flamboyant Jacobean gatehouse of Campden Manor, to the Perpendicular-style church of St James, the 14th-century house of a wealthy merchant, William Grevel, and the Renaissance-style Market Hall, built in 1670.

Three miles (5km) outside town are two delights for garden lovers. **Hidcote Manor Gardens** (National Trust; tel: 01386 438333 for hours), created at the beginning of the 20th century by Lawrence "Johnnie" Johnstone, is a highly architectural garden, known for its rare shrubs and trees and for some outstanding herbaceous borders. Even those who prefer a more naturalistic style of gardening are usually won over by Hidcote.

Just down the road is another stunning garden **Kiftsgate Court** (open April–Sept, Wed, Thurs, Sun 2–6pm, and Jun–July, Sat; entrance charge), an informal terraced garden famous for its roses, especially the *rosa filipes* which grows at will and flowers profusely in June. If you are visiting at this time, it makes a lovely last stop on your tour of the Cotswolds. ❑

Roses at Kiftsgate Court are at their best in June.

BELOW:
a mellow corner in Chipping Camden.

CONSERVING THE COTSWOLDS

The whole of the Cotswolds has officially been declared an Area of Outstanding Natural Beauty, a designation that restricts development and provides government funds to encourage traditional low-intensity farming. Just about every town and village centre is now a Conservation Area, which means that development is kept to a minimum. Where new buildings are permitted they have to conform to strict criteria, using recycled Cotswold stone, lime mortar and wooden-framed windows.

Disused barns may no longer be converted to dwellings, as they were for some years after changes in farming methods made them redundant, although they may now be used for small-scale industrial activities which do not change the rural character of the building or surroundings.

As in many other parts of the country, local authorities tread a tightrope: they must maintain the life of the area and provide employment and housing, but also try to preserve the essential character of the region, which attracts vital tourism and makes the area such a desirable place to live. Above all, they must avoid making museum pieces out of the villages; while preserving their beauty is important, they are living communities and must be allowed some degree of change.

SHAKESPEARE COUNTRY

You may go to Warwickshire to see Stratford, Shakespeare's town, but it has many other treasures – great castles, cathedrals, and the art galleries of Birmingham, England's second city

Maps:
Area 140
City 152

The novelist Henry James (1843–1916) described his much-loved county of Warwickshire as "mid-most England, unmitigated England..." and this is the region we shall cover in this tour. It is an area of patchwork fields, mellow brick houses and country lanes, with the River Avon running through it. But it is also a region which contains Birmingham, England's second-largest city, and Coventry, which was once synonymous with the British car industry.

A tour of Shakespeare Country must begin in **Stratford-upon-Avon ㉕** where the Bard was born on 23 April 1564. Stratford is a pleasant town, set on an attractive stretch of the Avon where it is joined by the Stratford Canal. Start your tour at the point where the two bridges over the Avon funnel pedestrians and traffic into town, and where there is a large car park and the ever-busy Tourist Information Centre. Beyond the traffic, in **Bancroft Gardens**, overlooking the canal basin, is the **Gower Memorial Ⓐ**, on which Shakespeare sits, surrounded by Hamlet, Prince Hal, Falstaff and Lady Macbeth.

Follow Bridge Street now to Henley Street where the informative **Shakespeare Centre** (tel: 01789 204016) stands next door to **Shakespeare's Birthplace Ⓑ** (open Mar–Oct, daily 9am–5pm, Nov–Feb, 9.30–4pm; entrance charge). This timber-framed building was the Shakespeare family home and

PRECEDING PAGES:
the nine-arched
bridge at Stratford.
LEFT: Anne
Hathaway's Cottage.
BELOW:
the man himself.

FACT FILE

By car The area is fringed with motorways: the M5 to the west, and the M1 and M6 to the north and east; the M42 orbits Birmingham from the south; the M40 from London and Oxford gives direct access to Stratford, Warwick and Leamington Spa.

By coach There are National Express services from London Victoria and London Heathrow as well as between major towns in the area; tel: 0990 808080.

By rail Direct services run from London Paddington to Evesham, Stratford and Leamington; from London Marylebone to Warwick; and from London Euston to Birmingham and Coventry; tel: 0345 484950.

By air From Birmingham International there are flights to and from New York and Chicago, plus internal flights and scheduled and charter flights to 40 European cities; tel: 0121 7677145.

Tourist information Birmingham, tel: 0121 6432514/ 0121 7804321; Coventry, tel: 024 7683 2303; Evesham, tel: 01386 446944; Leamington, tel: 01926 311470; Stratford, tel: 01789 293127.

Guided tours Shakespeare's Life in Stratford, tel: 01789 412602, Thurs and Sat, 10.30am; Guide Friday, open-top bus tours to Shakespeare sites, tel: 01789 294466.

business premises – his father was a glove maker, wool merchant and money lender, and became mayor in 1568. The building has been authentically restored and furnished (it served as a pub before it was bought for the nation in 1847).

In the nearby High Street is a building not associated with Shakespeare: the **Harvard House ⓒ** (open May–Sept, daily 10am–4pm; entrance charge). Covered with ornate carved heads and friezes, this was the childhood home of Katherine Roberts, who married Robert Harvard and whose son John emigrated to America in the 17th century and became the principal benefactor of the university that bears his name.

Continue to Chapel Street, where **Nash House ⓓ** (open Mar–Oct, daily 9.30am–5pm, Nov–Feb, 9.30am–4pm; entrance charge), home of Shakespeare's grand-daughter Elizabeth, is a fine building stocked with 17th-century tapestries, ceramics and furnishings, and which now houses a small archaeological museum. It adjoins the site of **New Place**, which Shakespeare bought as a retreat from London. All that remains of New Place are two wells and some foundations but beyond lies a lovely Tudor-style **knot garden** and the **Great Garden** where two mulberry trees stand, one supposedly a cutting from the original planted by Shakespeare, the other planted by the actress Peggy Ashcroft in 1969.

Opposite the site of New Place stands the **Guild Chapel**, mostly 15th-century but originally founded in 1269. Over the chancel arch are the remains of what must have been a spectacular wall painting of the Last Judgment. Continue along Church Street, past the wonderfully intact **Almshouses**, and turn into the street appropriately named Old Town where stands Hall's Croft, home of Shakespeare's daughter, Susanna. At the bottom, go right into Trinity Street to **Holy Trinity Church ⓔ** (open Mar–Oct, Mon–Sat 8.30am–6pm, Sun 2–7pm,

A tour bus outside Nash House.

BELOW: the Knot Garden on the site of New Place.

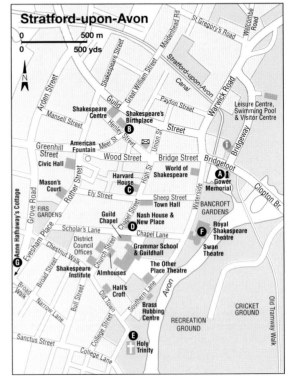

Stratford-upon-Avon

Nov–Feb, Mon–Sat 8.30am–4pm, Sun 2–5pm) dating mostly from the 14th century. It is worth a visit for its own sake, but most people come to pay homage at **Shakespeare's grave** beneath a simple stone in the chancel.

The riverside park can be entered through Old Town. Dominating the far end is the **Royal Shakespeare Theatre** and the **Swan Theatre** ❻ (for backstage tours, tel: 01789 412602). Built in the early 1930s, after the previous building was destroyed by fire, the theatre, which has some marvellous Art Deco interior fittings, is the home of the Royal Shakespeare Company (RSC), which also performs at **The Other Place** in Southern Lane.

We are now back at Bancroft Gardens and the nine-arched bridge, where we began, but there is one more pilgrimage to make: **Anne Hathaway's Cottage** ❼ (open Mar–Oct, daily 9am–5pm, Nov–Feb, 9.30am–4pm; entrance charge) is in **Shottery**, about 1 mile (2 km) west of town. It can be reached on foot, of course, but there are plenty of tour buses heading that way. It's a delightful timber-framed thatched cottage, with an idyllic cottage garden (not the working farmyard it would have been in Anne's day). The house remained in the Hathaway family until 1892, when it was bought by the Birthplace Trust, and many original items of furniture add to the atmosphere.

Beyond the house is the recently laid out **Shakespeare Tree Garden**, planted with most of the trees mentioned in the plays.

The Vale of Evesham

Follow the River Avon now for a bit of a detour, crossing into Worcestershire to the Vale of Evesham, with its orchards and market gardens. The river swings in a great bend around the town of **Evesham** ㉖, the site of one of the most

Map on page 152

Relaxing over a pint outside the Royal Shakespeare Company's theatre.

BELOW: the Royal Shakespeare Theatre.

The Bell Tower is Evesham's best-known landmark.

important abbeys in the Midlands, founded in 714. The abbey's wealth funded the great Perpendicular **Bell Tower**, still the town's most important landmark. Attractive parkland, popular with picnickers, drops gently towards the river.

In the town museum housed in the **Almonry** (open Mon–Sat 10am–5pm, Sun 2–5pm; entrance charge) you can learn about the great Battle of Evesham in 1265, which ended the rebellion of Simon de Montfort against Henry III. De Montfort's mutilated remains were buried in the abbey church, but such was the veneration shown them by pilgrims that they were removed to a secret resting place.

Warwick and Royal Leamington Spa

Now we're going north again, past Stratford to **Warwick ㉗**, the county town, built on a rise above the Avon, and dominated by the majestic tower of **St Mary's Church**, which can be climbed for a splendid view over the town and surrounding countryside. The tower and nave were rebuilt after a great fire in 1694, but the 15th-century **Beauchamp Chapel** was spared the flames. The gilded brass effigy of Richard Beauchamp, Earl of Warwick, is splendid.

Warwick is a delightful town, with a wealth of Georgian buildings and a few medieval ones which survived the fire. Chief among these is **Lord Leycester's Hospital** (open April–Sept, Tues–Sat 10am–5.30pm, Oct–Mar, 10am–4pm; entrance charge). Timbered and gabled, and founded in 1571 by Robert Dudley, favourite of Queen Elizabeth I, it has always been a home for old soldiers.

Most people come here, however, to see **Warwick Castle** (open April–Oct, daily 10am–6pm, Nov–Mar, 10am–5pm; entrance charge), described as "the most perfect piece of castellated antiquity in the kingdom". It has everything you

BELOW: guarding Warwick Castle.

expect of a castle: a wonderful site, great towers and walls, grim dungeons, sumptuous state rooms and glorious grounds, re-landscaped during the 18th century by "Capability" Brown. There are also convincing historical tableaux, recreated sieges, and Madame Tussaud's waxworks. The entrance fee is quite steep, but it makes a wonderful day's outing.

Royal Leamington Spa ㉘, close by, has recently been declared the most favoured place to live in Britain. It began as a spa town in the late 18th century, and the focal point is still the **Pump Room** by the bridge over the River Leam. To the east are the showpiece Jephson Gardens, named after the 19th-century physician and philanthropist who contributed so much to the town. Some of the finest buildings are to be found along Newbold Terrace opposite the Pump Room; in The Parade, an elegant thoroughfare running northwards; and in the superb curve of Lansdowne Crescent.

Kenilworth and Coventry

Some 4 miles (7 km) north is another splendid castle, **Kenilworth** ㉙ (open Mar–Oct, daily 10am–6pm, Nov–Feb, 10am–4pm; English Heritage). Despite years of neglect and deliberate destruction after the Civil War (1642–49), it remains an evocative place, full of the echoes of history which are brought to life during the summer months by a lively programme of events. The 14th-century Great Hall is one of the many additions made by John of Gaunt (1340–99), which turned the grim Norman stronghold into a fine palace. In 1563 Elizabeth I granted the castle to her favourite, Robert Dudley, who added the gatehouse and apartments. When the queen came to visit she was entertained by a "lady of the lake" floating with her nymphs on a torchlit vessel.

Map on page 140

Among Warwick Castle's most famous lords were Richard Neville, known as "The Kingmaker" for his role in the Wars of the Roses; and the Duke of Clarence, accused of high treason and said to have "drowned in a butt of malmsey".

BELOW: the elegant Pump Room at Leamington Spa.

A medieval doorway at Ford's Hospital.

Coventry ㉚ is known principally for three things: for the destruction it suffered during World War II and the Cathedral which sprang phoenix-like from the ashes; for the story of 11th-century Lady Godiva who rode naked through the streets, protected only by her long hair, in protest against her husband's imposition of taxes; and as the birthplace of the British car industry.

All three are celebrated in the city: the first (*see below*) is the reason many people come to Coventry. The second is commemorated more light-heartedly in the **Godiva City Exhibition** in the **Herbert Art Gallery and Museum** (open Mon–Sat 10am–5.30pm, Sun 2–5pm; entrance charge), where there is a lively presentation of the city's history, and Victorian portraits of the lady. And the third, which began with Daimler in 1896, can be explored in the **Museum of British Road Transport** (open daily 10am–5pm; entrance charge), where hundred of cars, bikes and motorcycles evoke Coventry's special contribution to the industry. There is more to see, of course: although much of the city was, necessarily, redeveloped after the war, some historic buildings remain – **St Mary's Guildhall** with its spectacular Arras tapestry is a reminder of Coventry's wool-trading past; and **Ford's Hospital** is an outstanding medieval building which has functioned as an almshouse since 1509.

England's second city

Birmingham ㉛ was in the forefront of the early 19th-century Industrial Revolution, and has tried to stay at the cutting edge ever since. Still one of the major manufacturing centres, its history is studded with the names of industrial greats, like James Watt, inventor of the steam engine, Matthew Boulton, who pioneered gas lighting, and Sir Joseph Chamberlain, public works innovator.

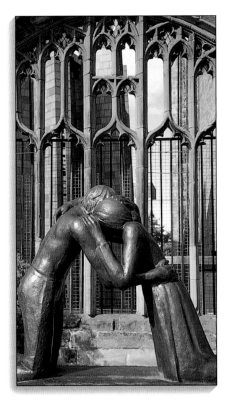

COVENTRY CATHEDRAL

The ruins of the old Cathedral, which form a poignant introduction to the city, are now a place of contemplation, and the venue for Mystery Plays, held every two years, as a symbol of peace and reconciliation.

The new Cathedral, designed by Sir Basil Spence and built from 1955 to 1962, stands at right angles to the old. The broad steps leading to the entrance on the university side are guarded by a striking bronze figure by Sir Joseph Epstein of St Michael triumphing over the devil, while the vast glazed screen is engraved with saints and angels.

Inside, the eye is led past slender supporting columns to Graham Sutherland's celebrated tapestry showing Christ in Glory surrounded by symbols of the Evangelists. The Baptistry is dominated by a window of equal scale and renown, the abstract stained glass the work of John Piper and Patrick Reyntiens; and by a font consisting of a rugged boulder brought from Bethlehem. The small Chapel of Gethsemane is protected by a screen in the form of the crown of thorns, designed by Spence himself.

For further information about the building, call at the Visitors' Centre, where there is a spectacular audio-visual show, treasures from the old Cathedral and gifts from well-wishers round the world.

Whether you approach via the ever-busy road network, or by rail you will be struck by the vivacity, if not by the beauty, of the city affectionately known as Brum. From New Street, Cannon Street climbs to **St Philip's Cathedral**, an outstanding example of English baroque, with the glorious stained-glass windows designed by Edward Burne-Jones (1833–98). Other members of the Pre-Raphaelite Brotherhood are also represented in the city: in Chamberlain Square the **Museum and Art Gallery** (open Mon–Sat 10am–5pm, Sun 12.30–5pm; entrance charge) has a matchless collection of their work.

A pedestrianised area makes a link on one side with **Victoria Square**, where a grandiose 19th-century Town Hall and Council House contrast with some monumental contemporary sculptures. On the other side of Centenary Square, a bridge crosses a section of Queensway to the Hall of Memory, and the city's newest public space, **Centenary Square**, setting for the huge new **International Convention Centre**, whose Symphony Hall has been acclaimed as one of the world's finest auditoriums, its orchestra directed for several years by Sir Simon Rattle. The pedestrianised area leads on to **Gas Street Basin**, once the hub of a transport network on Birmingham's canals – whose mileage is greater than that of Venice – now converted into a lively development of shops, bars and restaurants, and site of the **National Sea Life Centre** (open daily 10am–5pm; entrance charge) which has a completely transparent underwater tunnel – another development from innovative Brum.

A short bus or train journey from the city centre is the University of Birmingham at Edgbaston, home of the **Barber Institute of Fine Arts** (open Mon–Sat 10am–5pm, Sun 2–5pm; admission free) which has an unmissable collection of paintings, from the Renaissance artists to the Impressionists. ❏

Map on page 140

TIP

South of Birmingham is the garden village of **Bournville**, laid out in the late 19th century by the Cadbury cocoa family. **Cadbury's World** (tel: 0121 4514180) tells the story, and offers chocolate tastings.

BELOW: Birmingham is proud of the grand Council House.

CAMBRIDGE

Like Oxford, Cambridge isn't car-friendly. But, with most of its architectural glories concentrated along a short stretch of the River Cam, it's an easy place to find your way around on foot

Maps:
Area 168
City 162

I n 1209, when riots in Oxford resulted in the hanging of three students, a group of scholars settled in the little market town of **Cambridge**, and the seeds of England's second university were sown, although the first college was not founded until 1286. Feuds between townspeople and students ("town and gown") soon erupted and continued for six centuries, although the university's dominant role was established in the 1440s by the demolition of a large tract of the medieval centre to make way for the construction of King's College. Today there are 31 colleges in Cambridge, and most of them are open to the public; some of the more famous ones – King's, Queens', St John's, Trinity and Clare (which is open only at restricted times) – charge an admission fee.

Start your walk at **King's College Ⓐ**, which was founded in 1441 by Henry VI, although the pinnacled gatehouse was added nearly 400 years later by Gothic revivalist William Wilkins and the classical Fellows' Building on the west side is an 18th-century structure. To the right soars the beautiful Perpendicular **King's College Chapel** (open Mon–Sat 9.30am–4.30pm, Sun 10am–5pm, with some variations) with the largest fan-vaulted stone ceiling in the world, its only apparent support the slender columns of the nave. There are also some exquisite stained-glass windows, the work of 16th-century Flemish and

PRECEDING PAGES: punting on the River Cam. **LEFT:** a custodian of King's College. **BELOW:** students at a graduation ceremony.

FACT FILE

By car 60 miles/100 km from London on the M11 (approximately 1½ hours).
By coach National Express services from London Victoria, tel: 0990 808080.
By rail 50 minutes by train from London King's Cross; 1 hour from London Liverpool Street, tel: 0345 484950.
Nearest airport Stansted, 39 miles/48 km (direct hourly train service to Cambridge).
Nearest port Harwich, 68 miles/110km.
Parking The city centre is closed to traffic Mon–Sat 10am–4pm; park in multi-storey car parks: Lion's Yard, Park Street, Gonville Place, Grafton Centre; or look for Park and Ride signs as you enter the city. From these, bus services run to the centre every 15–30 minutes.
Major colleges King's, Queens', Trinity, St John's.
Best museums Fitzwilliam; Museum of Zoology; Kettle's Yard.
Outdoor attractions The Backs; Botanic Gardens; Jesus Green.
Activities Punting on the Cam; tel: 01223 359750 for boat hire, or go to the Quayside, Bridge Street, or the Mill Pond.
Annual events May Week; Folk Festival (July).
Tourist Information Wheeler Street, tel: 01223 322640.

An angel on King's College Chapel.

The statue of Henry VIII in Trinity College has a chair leg in his hand because a student took the sceptre he used to hold.

English craftsmen. The intricately carved rood screen, donated by Henry VIII, is a magnificent example of Early Renaissance woodwork. The renowned **King's College Choir** sings here daily during term time and visitors are welcome to attend services.

Leave the chapel by the north gate to visit **Clare College**, founded in 1326 and resembling an elegant palace. From Clare Bridge, the oldest of the college bridges, there are good views of the river where punts drift sleepily past. Exit into Trinity Lane and turn left to Trinity Hall "the lawyers' college", one of the smaller, more intimate colleges, with a delightful Tudor brick library which has survived almost intact – it can only be admired from outside. From the main entrance, go down Senate House Passage, where you'll pass the domed Gate of Honour of Gonville and Caius College, one of the earliest Renaissance stone structures in the city, before reaching the **Church of Great St Mary ❸**, where the great 16th-century Protestant martyrs – Hugh Latimer and Archbishop Thomas Cranmer – preached. From the tower (123 steps) there is a wonderful view of the town. This church is regarded as the very centre of Cambridge, the point from which all distances are measured.

Go north on Trinity Street, to the **Cambridge University Press Bookshop ❹**, the oldest bookshop in Britain, dating from the 16th century. On your left you will see the Great Gate of **Trinity College ❺**, the largest and richest college, founded by Henry VIII just before his death in 1547. Trinity has produced more than 20 Nobel Prize winners, six prime ministers and numerous poets and philosophers – Lord Byron and Bertrand Russell among them. You can visit the **Elizabethan Dining Hall** (open daily 3–5pm) with an intricately carved minstrels' gallery; and the **Wren Library** (open term time, Mon–Fri noon–2pm, Sat

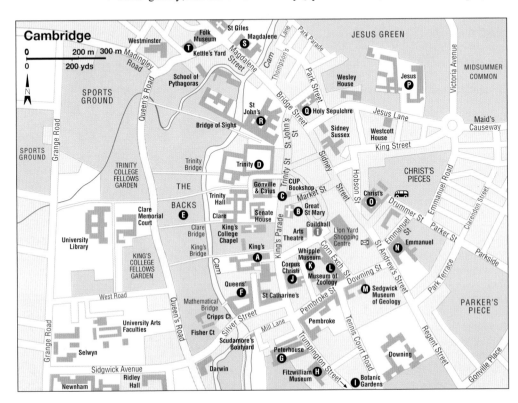

10.30am–12.30pm), one of the finest classical buildings in the country, designed by Sir Christopher Wren as a gift to the college. The 16th-century Great Court is the site of the Great Court Run, in which students must try to run round the perimeter (380 yds/348 metres) within the time it takes the clock to strike 12 (43 seconds). The Olympic runner, Lord Burghley, has been the only successful contestant (in 1927).

Leaving the college, cross **Trinity Bridge** to visit **The Backs E**, the lawns, meadows and gardens that back on to the Cam and are particularly beautiful in spring. The view of the colleges from the rear illustrates the wide variety of architectural styles employed. Beyond the back entrance to King's, turn left into Queens' Green to reach **Queens' College F** (open daily 10.15am–12.45pm, 1.45–4.30pm). The Old Court is a fine example of a medieval quadrangle, and Cloister Court, flanked by the president's lodge, a half-timbered building, makes a delightful setting for summer-evening performances of Shakespearean plays. The Cam divides the college in two and is spanned by the **Mathematical Bridge**, an early 20th-century copy of the one designed by Isaac Newton in 1749. The original was constructed without bolts.

From Queens', head south down Trumpington Street to **Pembroke College**, best known for its chapel, the first work to be completed (1663–65) by Sir Christopher Wren. Almost opposite stands **Peterhouse College G**, the oldest and most traditional of the colleges, founded in 1286 by the Bishop of Ely. The Gothic chapel on the east side is its most outstanding building. Sir Frank Whittle, inventor of the jet engine, was a student here.

To the right of Peterhouse is the **Fitzwilliam Museum H** (open Tues–Sat 10am–5pm, Sun 2.15–5pm; admission free), comprising 46 galleries. Some

Map on page 162

William Pitt the Younger (1759–1806), an early starter, came up to Pembroke at the age of 14, and became England's youngest prime minister only 10 years later.

BELOW: the Great Courts at Trinity.
BELOW: the Mathematical Bridge.

*The atmospheric
Eagle Pub.*

Below: students
past and present at
Christ's College.

contain a priceless collection of paintings, books and manuscripts belonging
to the museum's 19th-century founder, Viscount Fitzwilliam; the lower galleries house antiquities, sculpture, sarcophagi, ceramics and jewellery from
Egypt, Asia, Greece and Rome; the upper rooms display masterpieces by Italian Renaissance artists, Flemish masters, and French Impressionists.

After this you might like to walk down Trumpington Road to the **Botanic
Gardens ❶** (open daily in summer 10am–6pm; winter 10am–4pm; glasshouses
10am–3.45pm all year; entrance charge), one of the finest in the country. A
huge variety of plants provide all-year colour; there are also a Water Garden, a
Winter Garden, an Ecological Area and glasshouses full of tropical plants.

Retracing your steps past Pembroke College you come to **Corpus Christi ❶**,
the only college founded by trade guilds. Its Old Court has resisted 18th-century
refurbishment and looks much as it would have done in the 14th century. At the
back of Corpus, on the other side of School Lane, lies the **Whipple Museum of
the History of Science ❻** (open Mon–Fri 1.30–4.30pm; admission free) housing a selection of scientific and navigational instruments dating from the 14th
century. Close by is the **Museum of Zoology ❶** (open in vacations Mon–Fri
10am–1pm, 2–4.45pm, term time 2–4.45pm; admission free); among its exhibits
are items discovered by Charles Darwin on his 1831 voyage on the *Beagle*.

Cross Downing Street to the **Sedgwick Museum of Geology ❿** (open
Mon–Fri 9am–1pm, 2–5pm; Sat 10am–1pm; admission free), which houses
Britain's oldest intact geological collection. The adjacent **Museum of Archaeology and Anthropology** (open Tues–Sat 2–4.30pm; admission free) is devoted
to pre-history. Downing Street leads east into St Andrew's Street where you
will find the imposing **Emmanuel College ❶**, the first Protestant college,
founded in 1584. The chapel was designed by
Christopher Wren and the garden known as The Paddock has a large pool where Dominican monks used
to fish, before Henry VIII dissolved their friary.

Going north up St Andrew's Street brings you to
Christ's College ❶. The Fellows' Building is attrib-
uted to Inigo Jones; some have their doubts, but it is
a splendid piece of 17th-century classicism. **Fellows'
Garden** (open Mon–Fri 10.30am–12.30pm, 2–4pm)
is a magical oasis in the city centre. Milton's Mulberry Tree (said to have shaded the poet John Milton
as he worked) was one of several planted by James I
in 1608 to stimulate the silk industry.

Head north up Sidney Street and turn right on Jesus
Lane to **Jesus College ❶**, founded by the Bishop of
Ely on the site of a Norman nunnery, to which the
lovely **Cloister Court** belonged. The exquisite Early
English arches, part of the Chapter House, were found
under plasterwork in 1893. The chapel dates from
1200 but was restored by the Victorian Gothicist
Augustus Pugin, and the new ceilings designed by
William Morris' firm. Behind the college lies **Jesus
Green**, a pleasant spot with an open-air swimming
pool, tennis courts and bowling green; on the other
side of Victoria Avenue is **Midsummer Common**.

Now retrace your steps to Bridge Street and turn
right towards the 12th-century **Church of the Holy
Sepulchre ❶** (open daily 10am–5pm), one of only

Map on page 162

five surviving English churches with a round nave. Take St John's Street opposite to visit **St John's College** ❸, entered through an ornate 16th-century Gate Tower. The neo-Gothic chapel, inspired by Sainte-Chapelle in Paris, can be visited (open Mon–Fri 9am–4pm, Sat 9am–noon). The college was founded by Lady Margaret Beaufort, mother of Henry VII, and her statue surmounts the finely carved doorway of the Dining Hall.

The delicate **Bridge of Sighs**, modelled on its Venetian namesake (and best viewed from the Kitchen Bridge), was built in the 19th century to link the older buildings of the college with New Court. From St John's, continue up Bridge Street where, on your right, you will see **The Quayside**, a popular spot in summer, when café tables are set out beside the river and punts can be hired for trips on the Cam.

Crossing the river, you come to **Magdalene College** ❺ on your right. The college showpiece is the **Pepys Library** (open summer, Mon–Sat 11.30am–12.30pm, 2.30–3.30pm; winter, 2.30–3.30pm; admission free). Samuel Pepys bequeathed his 3,000-volume collection to the college in 1703. The library's greatest treasure is the original manuscript of the great man's diary, recording daily life in the 1660s.

Continue up Magdalene Street and you come to the **Folk Museum** (open Mon–Sat 10.30–5pm, Sun 2–5pm, closed Mon in winter; entrance charge), with displays of Fenland paraphernalia. Almost next door is **Kettle's Yard** ❼ (house open Tues–Sun 2–4pm; gallery Tues–Sat 12.30–5.30pm, Sun 2–5.30pm; entrance charge), an unusual museum in four cottages restored by Tate Gallery curator Jim Ede in the 1950s, and filled with works by Ben Nicholson, Henry Moore, Barbara Hepworth and many other artists and sculptors. ❏

St John's Dining Hall is hung with portraits of illustrious college members, including the poet William Wordsworth, and Lord Palmerston, the 19th-century prime minister.

BELOW: the Bridge of Sighs links old and new.

THE HIDDEN HEAD

Sidney Sussex College in Sidney Street is one of the smallest colleges, founded in 1596 on the site of a dissolved Franciscan friary. It is not the most interesting college visually (although it does have attractive shady cloisters), but it is the last resting place of the head of Oliver Cromwell, leader of the Roundheads in the English Civil War. He had briefly been a student here, until his father's death obliged him to return home and take on family responsibilities. In 1643 he returned as military leader and looted the colleges, which supported King Charles I, and requisitioned their courts as barracks.

Cromwell was buried in Westminster Abbey in 1658, but after the restoration of the monarchy two years later his relics were exhumed and his body hung up at Tyburn Gallows, while his head was impaled on a spike at Westminster Hall for 20 years. When the skull eventually blew down it was spirited away and passed through various hands over the centuries before being offered to the college in 1960. It is buried somewhere under the ante-chapel floor, although the exact position remains a secret. Cromwell's portrait hangs in the dining hall but tradition has it that it must be covered by a curtain when loyal toasts are drunk to the Queen at college feasts.

EAST ANGLIA

*The main attractions include boating on the Norfolk Broads,
exploring the Fenlands, discovering medieval churches and
following in the footsteps of John Constable*

Map on page 168

E ast Anglia, in medieval times, was one of the most densely populated and commercialised regions of England. Hard to believe now, when driving through the empty landscapes and sleepy villages of Suffolk and Norfolk. The broad acres of chalk and grassland provided ideal grazing for sheep, and huge quantities of wool were exported, boosted by the arrival of expert Flemish weavers in the mid-14th century. The main evidence of this era of wealth and prosperity is the region's medieval churches – more than 1,000 of them – from Saxon and Norman to Gothic Perpendicular. The great timber-framed houses you will see were also built on the proceeds of wool.

Our tour will begin in **Cambridge ❶** (*see pages 161–65*) and first go some 15 miles (24 km) south on the A1301 to **Saffron Walden ❷**, which gets its name from the orange crocus dye that made the town wealthy. Today it's a delightfully unspoiled market town with a number of timber-framed buildings, several of them decorated with ornamental plasterwork called pargetting. The huge church that dominates the town is a fine example of Perpendicular style.

About 1 mile (1.5 km) west is **Audley End House** (open April–Sept, Wed–Sun noon–6pm, grounds 10am–6pm; entrance charge). The biggest house in England at the time, it was built in grandiose Jacobean style in 1614 for Thomas

LEFT: detail of the mellow Little Hall in Lavenham.
BELOW: fresh crabs at Cromer.

FACT FILE

Location The counties of Essex, Suffolk and Norfolk between the Thames Estuary and The Wash
By car Cambridge is about 60 miles (100 km) from London on the M11/A10; journey time from Cambridge to Norwich about 80 minutes; to King's Lynn 1 hour; to Bury St Edmunds 30 minutes
By bus National Express from London Victoria to Cambridge, about 1 hour 30 minutes; tel: 0990 808080
By rail 50 minutes by train from London King's Cross to Cambridge; 1 hour from London Liverpool Street; 1 hour 50 minutes Liverpool Street to Norwich; tel: 0345 484950
Nearest airport Stansted; direct hourly train service to Cambridge; journey time about 1 hour
Nearest port Harwich (to Hook of Holland and Hamburg)
Major towns Colchester, Ipswich, King's Lynn, Norwich
Attractions The Broads; medieval churches; wool towns
Outdoor activities Birdwatching; boating
For children Pleasurewood Hills, Lowestoft, tel: 01502 508200, one of the largest theme parks in England; Dinosaur Natural History Park, Weston Longville, Norfolk
Tourist information Bury, tel: 01284 764667; Colchester, tel: 01206 282920; Ipswich, tel: 01473 258070; King's Lynn, tel: 01553 763044; Norwich, tel: 01603 666071

Howard, the Lord Treasurer to James I who described it as "too large for a king, but it might do for a Lord Treasurer". Substantial changes were made in the 18th century when Robert Adam (1728–92) remodelled the Great Drawing Room and many other parts, although the Great Hall retains its hammer-beam roof and Jacobean oak screen. Lancelot "Capability" Brown landscaped the grounds at the same time.

When Ely was an inaccessible island the surrounding marshland seethed with fish and eels, and it's the latter that gave the city its name: elge was the Saxon word for "eel district".

The Fens

We are going in the opposite direction now, to the flat Fenland of north Cambridgeshire, which was marshland until it was drained in the 17th century. About 16 miles (25 km) north of Cambridge on the A10 stands **Ely ❸**. Rising shiplike above the city and surrounding fenlands is the great **Cathedral of Ely** (open April–Oct, daily 7am–7pm, Nov–Mar, Mon–Fri 7.30am–6pm, Sun 7.30am–5pm; donations welcomed). The magnificent interior reflects various architectural styles, from Norman to early Renaissance. The crowning glory is the timber octagon, supported by eight columns and crowned by the tower lantern. The **Lady Chapel** is the largest in the country. A museum in the south triforium traces the history of stained glass and demonstrates techniques.

Follow the A10, and the River Ouse, to the north, and branch off on the A1122 towards **Wisbech ❹**, a market town which styles itself the capital of the fens. The two imposing Georgian streets – South Brink and North Brink – illustrate the prosperity that marsh drainage brought. The eccentric **Fenland Museum** (open Tues–Sat 10am–4pm; admission free) has pictures of the town in its heyday, and the complete furnishings of a Victorian post office. **Peckover House** (open April–Oct, Sat, Sun and Wed 12.30–5.30pm; garden

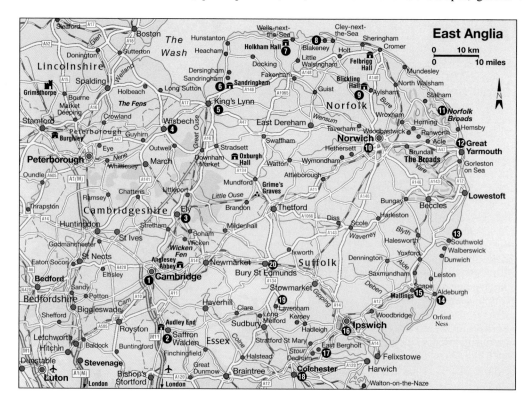

Sat–Thurs 12.30–5.30pm; National Trust), built in 1722, is an interesting town house on North Brink, with an outstanding Victorian garden. Opposite stands the newly restored **Octavia Hill Birthplace Museum** (open April–Oct, Sat, Sun and Wed 2–5.30pm; National Trust). Hill (1838–1912) was a Victorian reformer; she was also one of the founders of the National Trust

Take the A47 for about 12 miles (20 km) to the next stop, **King's Lynn ❺**, a port and market town on the Great Ouse, south of the Wash. Its port is still active and the heart of the town has retained its character with some fine Georgian houses and medieval monuments. Worth seeing are the elegant Customs House; St Margaret's church on the Market Place; and the 15th-century Trinity Guildhall, where, in the Old Gaol House, you could take an audio-visual tour through some of the more gruesome aspects of the town's history.

Take the A149 now, and turn right for **Sandringham ❻** (open April–Oct, daily 11am–4.45pm, except last week in July–first in Aug; entrance charge), bought in 1862 by the Prince of Wales, who later reigned as Edward VII. Largely 18th-century, it has many Edwardian embellishments, and it is now the Queen's country retreat. There are extensive grounds, with lakes and nature trails, and a museum of royal motor cars.

Royal limousines at Sandringham.

A coastal route

A coastal route now, past **Hunstanton**, a popular resort with broad sandy beaches and 60-ft (18-metre) cliffs with distinctive strips of carrstone and red and white chalk. It's the only East Anglian resort facing west, and you get some glorious sunsets over the Wash. The A149 follows the coast east through a series of small villages, seven of which have "Burnham" in their names. At

Map on page 168

LEFT: the River Ouse at King's Lynn
BELOW: Sandringham, the royal retreat.

Holkham is one of Norfolk's finest stately homes, **Holkham Hall**  (open May–Sept, Sun–Thurs 1–5pm; gardens daily 10am–5pm; entrance charge to house, grounds free). Set in magnificent parkland, the sombre Palladian facade hides a grandiose hall and state rooms with paintings by Van Dyck, Rubens and Gainsborough.

East of Holkham lies **Wells-next-the-Sea**, a genuine working port with coasters along the quay and fishing boats bringing in crabs and shrimps. It's also a popular holiday spot and there's a huge caravan park on the dunes behind the beach, and masses of amusements and fast-food outlets by the quay.

A little further on, **Blakeney** ❽ is a pretty coastal village of flint-cobbled cottages, known for its sand-and-shingle spit. **Blakeney Point** at its tip is the summer home for a dozen species of seabirds, including terns, oyster catchers, plovers and redshank. Common and grey seals bask on the sands when the tide is low, and in summer they can be spotted on a ferry trip from Morston Quay.

The last coastal stop for the moment is at **Cromer**, a pleasantly old-fashioned resort with a long sand and shingle beach and a town centre dominated by the soaring church tower. There's a Victorian pier, too, on which stands the Pavilion Theatre, still putting on shows. Fishing boats bring in the famous Cromer crabs, which you can buy throughout Norfolk in the summer months.

Inland to Norwich

Inland now on the A140 to Aylsham and **Blickling Hall** ❾ (open Wed–Sun 1–4.30pm, plus Tues in Aug; garden 10.30am–5.30pm; National Trust), one of England's greatest Jacobean houses. Covered with turrets and gables, bordered by lawns and huge yew hedges, it is also known for its spectacular Long Gallery,

Blickling Hall was the childhood home of Anne Boleyn, Henry VIII's second wife, but little of that house remains. Most of what you see today is 17th century.

BELOW: children crabbing at Blakeney.
RIGHT: the approach to Blicking Hall.

fine furniture and tapestries. The gardens are colourful throughout the year and there are splendid walks to be had in the park.

Continue south on the A140 now to **Norwich** ❿. Before the Industrial Revolution this was one of the most prosperous cities in England. Set amid rich agricultural land it rose to prominence in the Middle Ages as a market and trading centre. There is plenty of evidence of this prosperity: 32 medieval churches and a host of historic houses. There's also a large and colourful market, inviting cafés and pubs, and a pleasantly relaxed atmosphere. The **Castle** (open Mon–Sat 10am–5pm, Sun 2–5pm; entrance charge) has a museum in the keep (which served as a prison until the late 19th century), showing works by the Norwich School of landscape painters, as well as archaeology and natural history.

Down in the town there's an elegant Art Nouveau thoroughfare, the **Royal Arcade**, and the lively **market** in the sloping square. In Bridewell Alley, one of the oldest shopping streets in the city, is the **Mustard Shop**. For nearly 200 years regional farmers have been growing mustard for the firm of Colmans, and this specialist shop-cum-museum stocks products and souvenirs. The magnificent **Cathedral** (open daily 7.30am–6pm; donations welcomed) was founded in 1096 by Bishop Losinga. There are over 1,000 carved and painted bosses throughout the building. The cloisters are the largest in England and the flying buttresses are impressive. You can admire the spire of the Cathedral from **Pull's Ferry**, a medieval flint-and-stone watergate on the River Wensum.

The **Sainsbury Arts Centre** should not be overlooked. Founded by the supermarket family and designed by innovative architect Sir Norman Foster, the building has won several awards. It houses a splendid European collection, including works by Picasso and Modigliani, Henry Moore and Giacometti.

A town crier in Elm Hill, Norwich.

LEFT:
Norwich Cathedral.
BELOW:
antiques at Elm Hill.

TIP

The Broads Authority (tel: 01603 610734) provides information about boat hire, and Broads Tours at Wroxham (tel: 01603 782207) offers all-weather trips.

BELOW: restored sailing ship at Snape.
RIGHT: Aldeburgh's most popular shop.

From the Broads to the Maltings

You can take the A1151 northeast, or the A47 or B1140 east from Norwich to reach the **Norfolk Broads** , a network of navigable rivers and lakes formed by the flooding of medieval peat diggings. Catering for every type of craft, and uninterrupted by locks, these 200 miles (320 km) of quiet waterways are a haven for boating enthusiasts. Many people spend their holidays on the water in a narrow boat, but you can also hire a sailing boat or motor cruiser, by the hour or by the day. There are also trips to see the wildlife of the area. The floating **Broadland Conversation Centre** (open April–Oct, daily; tel: 01603 270479) at Ranworth offers a wealth of information.

If you're doing your navigating through the Broads by road the A47 will take you to **Great Yarmouth** ⑫, where Charles Dickens (1812–70) set part of *David Copperfield*. The town once flourished on its herring catch, but over-fishing killed the industry and now, as the most popular resort on the Norfolk coast, it relies mainly on tourism. Golden sands are hidden from view behind helter-skelters and roller-coasters. The nicest area of town is the historical part around **South Quay**, where the **Old Merchant's House** (open April–Sept, Sun–Thurs; entrance charge; guided tours, tel: 01493 857900) is worth a visit.

Some 10 miles (16 km) south is **Lowestoft**, England's most easterly town, which still retains a small fishing fleet. About 15 miles (24 km) down the coast lies **Southwold** ⑬, a remarkably unspoilt and rather old-fashioned little place. Set on a cliff top it is distinguished by its open greens, created after a fire destroyed much of the town in the 17th century. Victorian seafront terraces, Georgian houses and fishermen's cottages blend smoothly together, and colourful beach huts face the sea across a sand-and-shingle beach. The **Southwold**

Museum (open Easter–Sept, daily 2.30–4.30pm; admission free) is largely devoted to the Battle of Sole Bay, fought against the Dutch in 1672. The church of **St Edmund** is said to be the finest medieval seaside church in England.

You have to go around the estuary of the **River Blyth** to pick up the B1125 to **Aldeburgh** , the birthplace of the international music festival which now takes place at Snape. But Aldeburgh – an unspoilt and pleasant town which has been a port since Roman times – is still very much a festival centre and its hotels and restaurants cater well for visitors to nearby Snape Maltings. The High Street, lined with galleries and bookshops as well as food shops, runs parallel to a steeply shelving shingle beach where fresh fish is sold straight from the boats. The brick and timber-framed **Moot Hall**, which houses a small museum, stands near the promenade, but used to be some way inland, until erosion ate away the land.

Take the A1094 inland, then turn left to reach the well-signposted **Snape Maltings** on the River Alde, the 19th-century red-brick granaries and malthouses converted by Benjamin Britten (1913–76) into a concert hall in 1967. Born in Lowestoft, Britten moved to Snape in 1937 and his opera *Peter Grimes* was performed here eight years later. The main **Aldeburgh Festival** takes place in June (tel: 01728 453543) but other events are held throughout the summer, and riverside galleries and craft and antique shops are open all year.

Constable and Camulodunum

Get on the A12 now for **Ipswich** , the county town of Suffolk. The centre is mostly modern, but there's an atmospheric Victorian dockland on the River Orwell, and a local museum and gallery in the **Christchurch Mansion** (open

TIP

Left-hand turns off the B1125 between Southwold and Aldeburgh take you variously to Dunwich (*see below*); to the Sizewell Nuclear Power Station; and to Thorpeness, with its well-preserved windmill.

BELOW: Aldeburgh's Moot Hall.

DISAPPEARING DUNWICH

Dunwich is best known as the town that isn't. It was once the capital of medieval East Anglia, a prosperous town with eight churches, two monasteries, two hospitals, major shipyards and a population half the size of London. But coastal erosion changed all that. It was kept at bay for two centuries but a terrible storm in 1286 deposited a million tonnes of sand and shingle in the harbour and ended its role as a port. Constant erosion over the centuries has reduced the village to a handful of cottages, a pub, one church, and a beach with a café and a few fishing boats. All that remains of medieval Dunwich are the ruins of Grey Friars monastery and those of the Leper Chapel by the church. A solitary tombstone is sole testimony to All Saints', the last of the medieval churches, which collapsed into the sea in 1921. Local people say that when a storm is threatening, the sound of the bells tolling can still be heard from beneath the waves. Dunwich Museum (open April–Sept, daily 11.30am–4.30pm; entrance charge) charts the history of the town from Roman times to the present day, showing all the buildings lost to the sea. At the present rate of erosion, with recent storms scooping up more of the steeply shelving beach, the museum has about 75 years to go.

John Constable's childhood home. A circular route through Constable Country starts at the car park near Flatford Mill and takes in East Bergholt and Dedham. Guided walks visit the scenes of paintings (National Trust Bridge Cottage Information Centre, tel: 01206 298260).

BELOW:
Colchester Castle.

Tues–Sun; tel: 01473 253246 for details) which has a splendid collection of Constable's paintings (*see below*). There's also 15th-century St Margaret's Church, with a wonderful hammerbeam roof and a Tudor gateway.

East Bergholt ⑰, birthplace of John Constable, lies to the left of the A12 between Ipswich and Colchester. A plaque on railings just before the church marks the painter's birthplace, and the graves of his parents lie in **St Mary's Churchyard**, where a large wooden cage houses the heaviest ring of five bells in England. From the church, follow the signs for **Flatford**, which take you to a car park from where a path leads down to the River Stour, and to **Flatford Mill**, and **Willy Lott's Cottage**, both recognisable as subjects of *The Hay Wain*. Approaching **Dedham** on the B1029, you could visit the **Dedham Rare Breeds Centre** (open Mar–Sept, daily 10.30am–5.30pm; entrance charge). In the village itself you'll see the soaring tower of the **Church of St Mary** (early 16th century) which features in several of Constable's paintings.

Now we're back on the road for **Colchester** ⑱. Set on the River Colne, this was Camulodunum, the first capital of Roman Britain, and a long section of Roman wall and a large gateway still stand. In 1076 William the Conqueror began his castle on the ruins of a Roman temple to Claudius. The great **Norman Keep** is all that remains: it houses the **Castle Museum** (open Mon–Sat 10am–5pm, plus Sun–5pm in summer; entrance charge), which features Roman, Norman and medieval artefacts, a display on the siege of Colchester during the Civil War, and a medieval prison.

From Colchester our route goes northwest on the A134 towards **Sudbury**, just north of which the village of **Long Melford** makes an interesting diversion, to see the mellow Tudor mansion **Melford Hall** (open May–Sept, Wed–Sat

YOUNG CONSTABLE

John Constable was born on 11 June 1776 in East Bergholt House, at the heart of the 12 sq. mile (30 sq. km) valley of the Stour, which he was to paint for the rest of his life. His father, Golding, owned Flatford and Dedham mills, two corn-carrying vessels and some rich farmland. Two of his sisters, Ann and Mary, devoted their lives to horses and dogs, a third sister, Martha, was the only one to marry. An older brother, Golding, was retarded and so the youngest, Abram, eventually took over the family's affairs. At the age of seven, John was sent to boarding school 15 miles (24 km) away, but eventually he returned to attend Dedham grammar school, to which he walked each day. His talent was recognised at school, and in his free time he went on drawing expeditions with a friend, a plumber named John Dunthorne.

Local girls had their eye on the young painter. One, Anne Taylor, wrote: "So finished a model of what is reckoned to be manly beauty I never met with, while the report in the neighbourhood of his excellence in taste and character rendered him interesting in no small degree."

He finally married a local girl, Maria Bicknell, grandchild of the local rector, whom he painted when she was 12, and he was 24.

2–5.30pm, weekends in April and Oct; National Trust); and the village church, which is one of the best examples of Perpendicular architecture in Suffolk.

Map on page 168

Lavenham and Bury St Edmunds

Lavenham ⑲ (reached via the B1071) is one of the finest of the wealthy wool towns, with a huge number of medieval buildings, many half-timbered and tilting at alarming angles. Best known is the lovely ochre-coloured **Little Hall** (open April–Oct, Wed, Thurs, Sat, Sun 2–5pm; entrance charge) in the market place. The Perpendicular-style church has a magnificent tower, bearing the coats of arms of local cloth merchants; and the late 15th-century **Guildhall** (open April–Oct, daily 11am–5pm; National Trust), meeting place of the Guild of Corpus Christi, now houses a museum on 700 years of the wool trade.

North of Lavenham is the last stop on our route, the ancient market town of **Bury St Edmunds** ⑳, aptly named to honour Edmund, the last Saxon king of East Anglia, who was canonised and buried here. In *The Pickwick Papers*, Charles Dickens, who stayed here at the Angel Hotel, called Bury "a handsome little town of thriving and cleanly appearance". The town is now a mixture of architectural styles, but retains much of its original layout; there are no fewer than 980 listed buildings, including the 12th-century **Moyse Hall**, the oldest merchant's house in East Anglia, which now serves as the local museum.

The **Cathedral of St James** stands guard over the ruins of **St Edmunds Abbey**, one of the richest Benedictine foundations in England. It was here in 1214 that a group of barons swore to take up arms against King John if he did not sign the Magna Carta. The **Gate Tower**, the best-preserved feature, gives an idea of the abbey's former splendour. ❏

En route from Bury back to Cambridge you'll pass Newmarket, heart of English horse racing and home to the National Stud (tel: 01638 663464 for tours) and the National Horse Racing Museum (tel: 01638 667333).

LEFT: the ruins of St Edmunds Abbey.
BELOW: Lavenham Guildhall.

CANTERBURY AND THE SOUTHEAST

The county of Kent is known for its fruit and fair women.
It is also the cradle of Christianity in Britain,
a land of castles, moated manors and delightful gardens

Hops, apples, cherries and fair women are the traditional crop from the country's most southeastern county of Kent, known as "the Garden of England". Market forces and agricultural policies have driven all but the fair women to the wall, but the agriculture of the past has shaped the countryside, giving it distinctive hop kilns, while an abundance of wood has led to white weatherboard buildings that can look like New England's. The High Weald is a lovely, rolling landscape, and at Dover the chalk Downs spill dramatically into the sea, giving England its ancient name, Albion, from the Latin *alba* (meaning white).

This is the nearest England gets to the Continent, and it was here that the invaders came: Julius Caesar in 55BC, Angles, Saxons and Jutes in the Dark Ages, William of Normandy in 1066. And it was in the skies over Kent that the ferocious dogfights of the Battle of Britain took place in 1940. Christianity also arrived here with St Augustine in 597, establishing the Church at Canterbury. Today England is linked to the Continent through the Channel Tunnel near Folkestone, bringing hundreds of weekend tourists. They are fortunate to have

PRECEDING PAGES:
fishing boats
at Hastings.
LEFT: Canterbury
Cathedral entrance.
BELOW: Hastings
old town seen
from the castle.

FACT FILE

Main town Canterbury.
By car M2 and A2 from London, 50 miles (80km).
By train From London Charing Cross.
By sea Dover is the principal ferry port to France; the Channel Tunnel is outside nearby Folkestone (from Dover on the M20, London is 75 miles/120km, Canterbury 20 miles/32km on the A2).
Inhabitants Kentish Men (born on the London side of the River Medway, descended from Saxons from the Rhine) and Men of Kent (born on the east and south of the river, descended from Jutes from Jutland).
Big attraction Canterbury Cathedral.
Best garden Sissinghurst Castle.
Best train ride Romney, Hythe and Dymchurch Railway.
What to eat and drink English wines from Lamberhurst, Tenterden; hundreds of types of fruit at Brogdale Orchard; lamb from Romney Marsh.
Annual events Summer concerts at Leeds Castle; opera and theatre companies tour historic buildings in summer, particularly National Trust properties.
Tourist information Canterbury, St Margaret's Street, tel: 01227 766567; Dover, Town Wall Street, tel: 01304 205108.

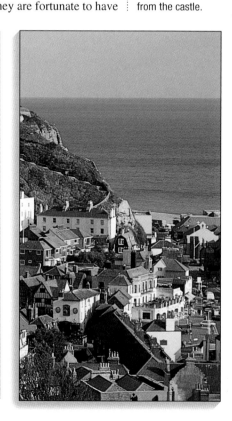

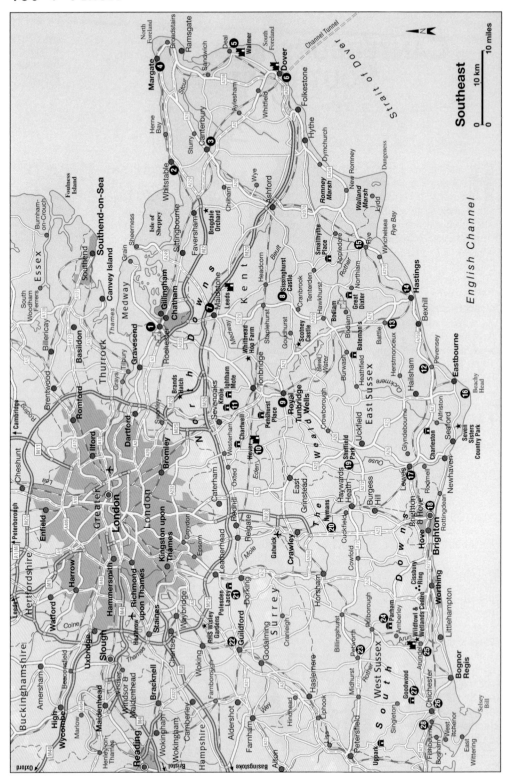

Southeast

Kent as their point of arrival, for within striking distance are many castles, manors, gardens and country pubs to explore.

Map on page 180

Charles Dickens country

The south, Kent side of the Thames estuary is Charles Dickens country. He drew inspiration from the bleak marshes, and the conditions of people who lived by the tidal river. Some marshlands remain, still bleak, but ideal for waders and sea birds. Dickens lived at Gad's Hill in **Rochester ❶**, and the **Charles Dickens Centre** (open daily 10am–4.45pm; entrance charge) in the middle of the old town is a required visit. This ancient town on the River Medway has always been of strategic importance: Watling Street, the Roman road from Canterbury to London, passes through it and the Normans built a fine **castle** with the tallest keep in England (113 ft/32 metres). On the site of a bishopric founded by Augustine, the Normans also built an exemplary **Cathedral** here, which is sturdy, simple and reminiscent of their churches in France.

Charles Dickens, tireless writer and social campaigner.

Chatham is a neighbour in this seamless clutter of Medway towns. Its famous Royal Navy dockyards, established by Henry VIII, were closed by the Admiralty in 1984 with a loss of 8,000 jobs but they found a new lease of life as a museum. **The Historic Dockyard** (open daily 10am–5pm; Wed, Sat–Sun only in winter, entrance charge) covers 80 acres (32 hectares) and has the largest concentration of listed buildings in Britain. Visitors can see the shipbuilding sheds, the sail lofts and the impressive 1,140-ft (350-metre) Ropery, built in 1792.

More of a backwater is **Faversham,** a pretty town also on Watling Street and on the River Swale. Among its ancient quays is a pervading smell of the local brewery, Shepherd Neame. Apples are prolific at nearby **Brogdale Orchard**

BELOW: Dickens's Bleak House in Broadstairs.

CANTERBURY CATHEDRAL

The Church of England's spiritual home is a delightful hotchpotch of styles. For a detailed ground plan, see page 398

Canterbury, the birthplace of Christianity in England, is the mother church of the Anglican Communion, its archbishop the Primate of England. In AD597 Pope Gregory the Great sent St Augustin to England to convert the English, whose religion had lapsed after the Romans had departed. He converted King Ethelbert of Kent, who gave him land on which he founded a monastery (outside the city walls) and the cathedral (within).

In 1170 four knights, thinking they were doing King Henry II a favour, murdered the "turbulent priest", Archbishop Thomas Becket, in the northwest transept. Becket

was promptly canonised and in 1174 Henry performed a penance at his tomb. From then until the Reformation, the cathedral was a place of pilgrimage, not just in England, but throughout Europe. The 14th-century poet Geoffrey Chaucer gives a vivid account of the characters who joined the pilgrimages in the prologue to *The Canterbury Tales*. In 1220 Becket's bones were transferred to a shrine in the Trinity Chapel and in 1935 T. S. Eliot's play about Becket, *Murder in the Cathedral*, was first performed in the Chapter House leading off the Great Cloister.

The cathedral is a hotchpotch of styles, rambling the length of the building, but they manage a worldly grace. The oldest part is the well-lit crypt, from 1100, and there are traces of earlier work; some of its fine carved capitals are unfinished. Four years after Becket's death a fire resulted in the building of the Trinity Chapel to contain his tomb and remodelling by William of Sens of the Choir, which was used by the monks of the adjoining monastery for singing daily psalms.

The glorious, soaring, Perpendicular nave, rebuilt by Henry Yevele in 1400, is the longest medieval nave in Europe, and above the central crossing rises the main Bell Harry Tower (249 ft/90 metres), added a century later. Among the many noble tombs perhaps the finest is that of the Black Prince in the Trinity Chapel, a copper effigy encumbered in full armour.

The Cathedral's stunning stained glass dates from the 12th and 13th centuries and rivals the best in France. The windows in the Trinity Chapel portray the life of Jesus and a noted window of Adam, formerly part of a series showing the ancestors of Jesus in the Choir and Trinity Chapel, is now in the west end of the cathedral.

During World War II a 24-hour watch for enemy planes was kept on the cathedral roof. The town was badly bombed, but the Cathedral remained miraculously unscathed. ❏

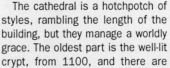

ABOVE LEFT: memorial to the assassination of Thomas Becket. **LEFT:** Henry II and Becket.
ABOVE RIGHT: Chaucer's Canterbury pilgrims.

(open daily 9.30am–5.30pm; entrance charge) which holds the national fruit collection. It grows some 2,000 varieties of apples as well as hundreds of species of other fruits, and produce and plants are for sale. Back on the coast, another attractive town is **Whitstable ❷**, known since Roman times for its oysters. Buy them in the old harbour or try them at the seafront Whitstable Oyster House, which has a delightful small cinema above it, or at Pearsons, the pub opposite. In 1830 George Stephenson built one of the first passenger railway lines to run the half dozen miles from here to Canterbury.

Map on page 180

Canterbury ❸ is the cradle of English Christianity. Its main attraction is, of course, the **Cathedral** (*see left*), which is steeped in history and redolent of its glorious and infamous past. As a place of pilgrimage for Christians from all over Europe, it provided the setting for one of the first great works of English literature, Geoffrey Chaucer's *Canterbury Tales* (1387). In St Margaret's Street the **Canterbury Tales** (open daily 10am–5pm; entrance charge) promises a "medieval adventure" with the sights, sounds and even the smells of the journey made by five of Chaucer's characters.

Visitors still come from all over Europe, and French often seems the *lingua franca* of the reastaurants and pubs in the pedestrianised streets around the cathedral. Despite German aerial bomb attacks in 1942, much of Canterbury's medieval character remains. The town's delights include parts of the original Roman wall which once enclosed it. Also worth visiting are the excavated ruins of **St Augustine's Abbey** near the grounds of **St Augustine's College** where Anglican clergy are trained. Farther east along Longport is **St Martin's Church** which was used for Christian services even before the arrival of Augustine. In the 4th century this area was selected by rich Romans for their villas, and

In "The Canterbury Tales", which runs to 17,000 lines of prose and verse, 29 characters meet up in London to make the pilgrimage to Canterbury, and on the journey most of them tell the stories of their often rather bawdy lives.

BELOW: Canterbury Cathedral cloisters.

*The Roman pharos,
or lighthouse,
at Dover Castle.*

BELOW:
Walmer Castle.
RIGHT: Sandwich.

remains can still be seen. The town's **Heritage Museum** (open June–Oct Mon–Sat 10am–5pm, Sun 1.30–5pm; entrance charge) is located in Stour Street.

Farther east lies **Margate** ❹ which, once opened up to London's East Enders by the railway, became one of the capital's most popular seaside resorts. Bathing machines were invented here by a local Quaker and though rather run down it still has a breezy holiday air. A couple of miles away is **North Foreland**, the tip of the duck's tail of Kent and Britain's most easterly spot. Immediately below is **Broadstairs**, a more up-market resort with a sandy bay and landscaped cliffs, which Dickens described as being "left high and dry by the tide of years". When he knew it, the clifftop **Bleak House** (open mid-Mar–Nov, daily 10am–5pm, June–Aug till 9pm, entrance charge) was called Fort House. He spent his summer holidays there in the 1850s and 1860s.

Sandwich lies along the River Stour, 2 miles (3 km) from the sea. In the 9th century it was an important port, but by the 17th century progressive silting of the estuary left it high and dry, and it is now surrounded by a 500-acre (200-hectare) coastal bird sanctuary. In the 11th century, Sandwich became one of the original Cinque (pronounce "sank") Ports, a string of harbours from here to Hastings with special trading privileges granted in return for maintaining vessels to defend the English Channel from the French – there were regular incursions by both sides. **Walmer Castle** (open daily Easter–Oct, 10am–5pm, Nov–Easter, Wed–Sun, closed Jan; entrance charge) in **Deal** ❺ is still the official residence of the Lord Warden of the Cinque Ports, a post long held by the Queen Mother. Here, too, is the simple camp bed where the great Duke of Wellington, who vanquished Napoleon at Waterloo, chose to die like a simple soldier. On the beach of this small resort Julius Caesar landed in 55BC and on

the shingle beach, from which there is good fishing, there is a plaque that commemorates the event.

Sandwich, Deal and **Dover** ❻ are now billed as "White Cliffs Country", and at Dover, Britain's busiest passenger port, the chalk massif of the South Downs dramatically drops into the sea. On these cliffs the Romans built a lighthouse, the Normans a **castle** (open daily 10am–5pm, entrance charge), and from here Calais can be seen. In the town, the **White Cliffs Experience** (open Mar–Nov 10am–5pm, Nov–Mar 10am–3pm; entrance charge) brings to life the story of Dover, from Roman times to the present day, with a vivid re-creation of the dark days of World War II. The neighbouring Channel port of **Folkestone** is also built beside steep cliffs. The town has a large market by the sea on Sundays where you can buy, among many things, dried dogfish called "Folkestone beef". The nearby **Channel Tunnel** provides fast train and car shuttle services between England and France. The only stop this side of the tunnel before London is **Ashford**, not a town to dwell in, but a jumping-off point for the rest of Kent.

Maidstone ❼ is the county town of Kent, built alongside the River Medway. Places to visit are just out of town: the **Museum of Kent Life** (open Easter–Nov, daily 10am–5.30pm; entrance charge), in Sandling on the north side of the town, has Britain's last working oast house and hop-pickers' huts, and tells the story of how Kent was once filled with seasonal workers from the East End of London who formed great communities in the hop gardens. Southwest at Yalding, near Paddock Wood, is the **Whitbread Hop Farm** (open daily 10am–6pm, 10am–4pm in winter; entrance charge) based around a large collection of hop houses, which also tells the story of hops; shire horses, which once pulled the brewers' drays, are on display. Six miles (10 km) to the south of Maidstone lies

Map
on page
180

Between Dover and Calais the English Channel is just 19.6 miles (31.5 km) wide. The Romans built a lighthouse on the cliffs to guide ships across, and in World War II the town was shelled by German guns France.

BELOW:
Dover beach and ferries to France.

There are a number of good vineyards between Tenterden and Penshurst. Look out for signs offering winery and cellar tours.

BELOW: hop kilns.

Leeds Castle (open daily 10am–5pm, 10am–3pm in winter; entrance charge), residence of the queens of medieval England. This fairytale place, built on islands in a lake, is one of England's finest castles in a lovely setting among 500 acres (200 hectares) of parkland. Grand open-air concerts and *son-et-lumière* shows are put on in the grounds in summer.

Sissinghurst Castle ❶ (open April–mid-Oct, Tues–Fri 1–6.30pm, Sat–Sun 10am–5.30pm; National Trust) is not a castle at all, but the ruins of a 16th-century manor house and a perfect backdrop for one of the most popular gardens in England. During the Seven Years' War it served as a prison for captured French soldiers and for a while it was a work farm for the poor. It was bought by Vita Sackville-West (1892–1962), poet, novelist and gardener extraordinary, and her politician husband Harold Nicolson in 1930. The beautiful gardens arranged as "outdoor rooms" are delightful, though belated revelations about Vita's love life no doubt have helped to bring the curious. The White Garden, has a stunning array of white foliage and blooms and is particularly appealing.

Weavers and the Weald

The surrounding white weatherboarded High Weald towns of **Tenterden**, **Cranbrook** and **Goudhurst** are peaceful country places. In 1747 the villagers of Goudhurst locked themselves in the church while a gang of smugglers from nearby **Hawkhurst** fought the local militia in the churchyard. From this half-timbered town there are wonderful views south over hop and fruit country. These Wealden towns grew rich on wool and weaving. Large, half-timbered hall houses remain, among the most interesting are **Smallhythe Place**, near Tenterden (open Easter–Nov, Sat–Wed 1.30–6pm; National Trust), where the

THE HOP GARDENS OF KENT

Adistinctive feature of the landscape of Kent is the white painted wooden cowls of the round (and earlier square) hop-drying kilns. These once turned with the wind to act as chimneys above the slatted wooden floors over which hop flowers were scattered above some form of heating. There are only a handful of hop farms left in Kent and most kilns have been converted for residential use, though hop bines, which have a pleasant smell, often decorate pubs and kitchens. There was a time, however, when hops, a principal ingredient of English ale, were a mainstay of the local agriculture. They were also an integral part of the lives of the working-class families from the East End of London, who every September would come down to Kent in their thousands, living in special hopper huts and harvesting the bines, the long plants that spiral clockwise around taut twine attached to wires supported by hop poles. Much of it is aching, overhead work, and after the shout of "Pull no more bines" the evening's rewards were singsongs and gatherings on the farms or in the local pubs. For many, this week or two would be the only holiday they had, and there are many East Enders still alive who look back on those working holidays as among the best times in their lives.

actress Ellen Terry lived, and **Great Dixter** (open April–Oct, Mon–Sat 2–5pm; entrance charge) in Northiam, a rival of Sissinghurst and home of the horticulturalist Christopher Lloyd, who has set major trends in gardening in recent years. Nearby is **Bodiam Castle** (open Feb–Oct, daily 10am–6pm, Nov–Dec, closed Mon; National Trust), a classic medieval fort, dating from 1385, set in a generous moat; while **Scotney Castle** (open Mar–Oct, Wed–Fri 11am–6pm, Sat–Sun 2–6pm; National Trust), 5 miles (8 km) southwest, is a thoroughly romantic spot with gardens landscaped in the 18th-century pictorial tradition.

Taking the waters in Tunbridge Wells

To the west, halfway down the A21 between London and Hastings, lies **Royal Tunbridge Wells ❾**, a place supposedly full of blimpish retired colonels who write letters to the *Daily Telegraph* and sign themselves "Disgusted". Dudley, Lord North, a hypochondriac, brought fame and fortune to the town in 1606 when he discovered the health-giving properties of a spring on the common. Court and fashion followed, and the waters, rich in iron salts, were, and still are, taken at the Pantiles. This terraced walk, with shops behind a colonnade, is named after the tilework laid in 1638, some of which is still there. Eight years earlier, Henrietta Maria, wife of Charles I, came here after the birth of Prince Charles; she was obliged to camp in a tent on the common. The former home of the novelist William Thackeray in London Road (known simply as Thackeray's House) is now a restaurant and wine bar with a good reputation. There are several tempting second-hand bookshops in the old part of town.

   Penshurst Place (open April–Sept, daily noon–5.30pm, Oct–Mar, Sat–Sun only; entrance charge), just to the northwest of Tunbridge Wells, is one of Kent's

Map on page 180

TIP

The Kent and East Sussex Railway (tel: 01580 765155) starts its journey to Bodiam from Tenterden. Full-sized steam trains run daily in July and August and weekends the rest of the year. Try Sunday lunch in the restaurant car.

BELOW:
Bodiam Castle.

William Waldorf,
who was made Baron
of Hever Castle in
1896, bought the
"Observer"
newspaper in 1911
and a son was an
owner of "The
Times". His
daughter-in-law,
Nancy, was Britain's
first woman MP.

finest mansions, dating from 1340. Home of the Viscount de L'Isle, it was for two centuries the seat of the Sidney family, notably Sir Philip Sidney, the Elizabethan soldier and poet. A few miles to the west lies **Hever Castle**  (open Mar and Nov, noon–4pm, Apr–Oct, noon–5pm; entrance charge). Henry VIII, who first met Anne Boleyn in this, her father's house, seized Hever after her execution and murdered her brother. William Waldorf, first Viscount Astor, (1848–1919) applied his American millions to make massive and sympathetic improvements to the moated castle, 35-acre (15-hectare) lake and gardens where flowerbeds are laid out exactly as they were in Tudor times 400 years ago.

Some 10 miles (16 km) to the north on the B2026 is **Westerham**, where General James Wolfe, who decisively drove the French from Canada in 1759, was born. His birthplace, **Quebec House** (open Mar–Oct, Tues and Thurs 2–6pm; National Trust), has memorabilia. South of the village is **Chartwell**, (open end April–Oct, Wed–Sun 11am–4.30pm; National Trust) where Winston Churchill lived from 1924 until his death in 1965. There is often quite a queue to see his home and studio where many of his paintings are on display.

Sevenoaks is 5 miles (8 km) to the east on the far side of the A21 and on its outskirts is **Knole** ⑪ (open April–Nov, Wed–Sat, noon–3.30pm, Sun 11am–5pm; National Trust), one of the largest private houses in the country. It was the Archbishop of Canterbury's residence until confiscated by Henry VIII, and Elizabeth I gave it to Thomas Sackville who greatly extended it. It has 365 rooms, 52 stairways and seven courtyards. There are exceptionally fine portraits of the Sackville family by Gainsborough and Van Dyck (though protective low lighting makes some hard to see), as well as some rare furniture. In the 1,000-acre (400-hectare) deer park there is a fascinating Gothic folly birdhouse.

BELOW: Tunbridge Wells' Pantiles.

William the Conqueror's country

In the levels to the east, **Pevensey** has the most considerable Roman monument in Sussex, but the Roman fort was incomplete and could not withstand the landing in 1066 of William, Duke of Normandy, the last man successfully to invade Britain. The Norman Conqueror did not meet up with Harold of England until some 10 miles (16 km) inland; the spot where Harold fell, his eye pierced by an arrow, was marked by William, who built upon it the high altar of the abbey church at **Battle** ⓫ as a thanksgiving. An imposing 14th-century gatehouse leads to the grounds and ruins of the abbey.

The place where William prepared for battle is just 6 miles (9 km) southeast of Battle. The hilltop Norman castle at **Hastings** ⓮ which stands above a warren of caves where smugglers' adventures are re-enacted, is now a ruin, though a siege tent inside tells the battle story on which the town has thrived. The fishermen's boats in the old town are attractive and on the Stade tall, tar-black sheds used by the fishermen for storing nets are architectural fantasies.

To the east is **Winchelsea**, which, like neighbouring **Rye** ⓯, has suffered from floods and the French and now lies high and dry. Edward III (1327–77) gave Rye its walls and gates. The **Landgate** and **Ypres Tower** survive, as well as much half-timbering. Today Rye is a pottery town and there is an active artists' colony whose work can be seen at the Stormont Studio in East Street (open Wed–Sat 10am–5pm; admission free), and the Easton Rooms in the High Street (open daily 10am–5pm; admission free).

From Rye the land lies flat across the great expanse of **Romney Marsh**, a strange, haunted area of a special breed of sheep, of water weeds and wading birds such as the Kentish plover. ❑

Map on page 180

Sheds for drying fishing nets, on the shore at Hastings.

BELOW: fishing boats in Rye.

BRIGHTON AND THE DOWNS

Londoners do like to be beside the seaside and its resorts have a raffish air. Around about are the bracing hills of the Downs with hill forts, horse racing and welcoming pubs

Map on page 180

London
Brighton

The Downs, a parallel chalk range that stripes the south of England, gives the region a distinctive outdoor flavour. Here are the famous horse-racing tracks of Epsom, Goodwood, Fontwell and Kemp Town, the fine golf course at Wentworth, the parklands of Petworth, Glyndebourne and Sheffield Park, tennis at Eastbourne, polo at Cowdray, as well as many fine flowering gardens. Close to the capital, the whole area is well explored and much of the northern "home county" of Surrey is suburban. A few people commute to the city from as far away as the Sussex coast, which has long been a favourite place for a day's outing (5 million visit each year), particularly Brighton, one of the world's first bathing resorts.

The **South Downs** were a highway into Britain for early settlers who started clearing land for farming here 6,000 years ago, leaving it crew-cut by sheep and striated by plough shares. Today in the high spots where Iron-Age forts and flint mines flourished, the wind whispers through copses, windmill sails and woodland clumps which rise over voluptuous gullies and coombs, remnants of the last Ice Age which scooped out devils' dykes and punchbowls. Along the crest runs the white streamer of the South Downs Way, Britain's first designated long-distance bridleway, and a popular path for walkers of all abilities.

PRECEDING PAGES: The Pavilion, Brighton. **LEFT:** Seven Sisters, the end of the South Downs. **BELOW:** a face of Sussex.

FACT FILE: THE SOUTH

County towns Lewes (East Sussex), Chichester (West Sussex), Guildford (Surrey).
By car Brighton is 50 miles (80km) from London, and the journey takes about 75 minutes depending on traffic.
By train Trains go from Victoria to Chichester, Worthing, Brighton and Eastbourne.
By air Gatwick, London's second airport, is half way between Brighton and London: trains from Gatwick to Brighton and Worthing take about 30 minutes. Shoreham is a delightful small airport with 1930s decor.
By sea Ferries from Newhaven to Dieppe, about 4 hours .
Best sandy beach Climping, near Littlehampton.
Best family day out Weald and Downland Museum.
Local words Twitten (passages between streets), cat-creeps (steps between streets on different levels).
The cultural year Brighton Festival (major, multifarious events, three weeks in May), Glyndebourne opera (July).
The sporting year Eastbourne Women's Lawn Tennis Championship (June), Glorious Goodwood horse racing (August), National Bowls Championship, Worthing (August).
Tourist information Brighton, tel: 01273 323755; Chichester tel: 01243 775888.

LITERARY FRIENDS IN THE SOUTH

The Bloomsbury Set, which started in London, ended up in the country, where its cultural traces can still be seen

In his 1903 *Principia Ethica* the philosopher G. E. Moore stated that "By far the most valuable things are the pleasures of human intercourse and the enjoyment of beautiful objects. It is they that form the rational ultimate end of social progress." This served as a springboard from old, stern Victorian values, into a new spirit of freedom. It was a spirit that infused a group of friends who began to meet two years later at 46 Gordon Square in Bloomsbury near the British Museum. Among them were the writers Virginia Woolf and Vanessa Bell (then the Stephen sisters), Lytton Strachey and E. M. Forster, the economist John Maynard Keynes,

and the artists Duncan Grant and Roger Fry.

Little evidence of their creative spirit remains in London, but a visit to a number of sites in the south gives a clue of this intimate and influential group. Virginia and Leonard Woolf bought Monk's House in Rodmell in 1919, seven years after they married. Virginia's sister, Vanessa Bell, took over Charleston near Firle, a delightful small house and garden, now fully restored with their hand-painted cupboards and doors.

Woolf also found a good friend in Vita Sackville-West, who was born at Knole in Kent and, with her husband Harold Nicolson, bought Sissinghurst Castle (*see page 186*). Woolf's 1928 novel *Orlando* is based on their friendship; a copy of the manuscript is displayed at Knole (*see page 188*).

Part of the interest in these literary figures was their private lives. Duncan Grant, though homosexual, was Vanessa Bell's lover and father of her daughter Angelica; Angelica later married David "Bunny" Garnett, who had been Duncan's lover; Vita Sackville-West, whose husband was homosexual, had a long relationship with Violet Treyfusis, daughter of the mistress of Edward VII.

World War II ended the good times. The south of England was a dangerous place. Virginia Woolf, who had suffered from mental illness for most of her life, found her sensitivity tried by the incessant drone of fighters and bombers overhead. Finally one day she walked across the meadows from her house to the River Ouse, filled her pockets with stones, walked into the water and drowned. The 12th-century church of St Michael and All Angels at nearby Berwick suffered bomb damage and after the war Angelica and Quentin Bell painted it in the bright country colours they had grown up with at Charleston.

In 1999–2000 a retrospective of the group's works at London's Tate Gallery confirmed their popular appeal – and many critics' belief that they were merely dilettantes. ❑

CLOCKWISE, FROM TOP LEFT: Woolf's room at Monk's House, Vita Sackville-West, Virginia Woolf, the garden at Charleston.

The South Downs make their final majestic bow at **Beachy Head** , where chalk cliffs reach 530 ft (160 metres) and yearly crumble into the sea. The light-house has recently had to be moved further inland, and the steps down the cliff at Birling Gap are only temporary. From the clifftop there is a view down on **Eastbourne**, a pristine resort which in sunshine can gleam like a slice of the French Riviera. The town was well planned from the start, around the middle of the 19th century, by the 7th Duke of Devonshire: shops are banned from the seafront and there are 200 acres (80 hectares) of public parks. Each year 1.8 million visitors come to see the pier, fortress, and other attractions, including lawn tennis courts in Devonshire Park where women's championships are held prior to Wimbledon each year. West of Eastbourne, Beachy Head is the highest of seven undulating waves of chalk hills known as the **Seven Sisters**. Behind them the **Seven Sisters Country Park** leads into the the **Cuckmere Valley**, a good place for walks, especially starting around the pleasant village of **Alfriston** where the **Clergy House** (open April–Oct, Sat–Mon, Wed –Thurs 10am–5pm; National Trust), a 14th-century thatched hall house, by the village green, was the first property to be acquired by the National Trust, in 1896.

Bloomsbury on Sea

Between the two world wars, this corner of England was a favourite spot of London's literary Bloomsbury set (*see left*). At **Charleston** (pre-booked visits only, tel: 01273 709709)), an 18th-century farmhouse, Vanessa Bell and Duncan Grant drew the literary crowd, and their enthusiastic painting and decoration gives the house great charm. The family's handiwork can also be seen at the nearby church at **Berwick**. In 1919 Vanessa Bell's sister, the writer Virginia Woolf and her husband Leonard bought **Monk's House**, a weatherboarded building among thatched houses in **Rodmell** (open Easter–Nov, Wed and Sat 2–5pm; entrance charge). The village lies in the meadowlands around the River Ouse, where Virginia Woolf drowned in 1941.

Nearby **Firle Place** in West Firle, was refashioned in the 18th-century Georgian style from the Tudor original (open May–Sept, Wed, Thurs, Sat 2–5pm; entrance charge). Firle has been in the Gage family for more than 500 years; Sir Thomas Gage was Commander-in-Chief of the British forces in America during the skirmish of Lexington that began the American War of Independence in 1775. In the Great Hall are paintings by Reynolds, Gainsborough and Van Dyck and a 17th-century map of New York shows Wall Street running behind the city wall.

On the other side of the A27 is **Glynde Place**, an Elizabethan manor belonging to Viscount Hampden with portraits of a family that goes back 800 years (open May–Sept, Wed, Thurs, Sat, Easter day and bank holidays 2–5pm; entrance charge). A mile to the north is **Glyndebourne**, where John Christie and his wife, the opera singer Audrey Mildmay, built an opera house in their Elizabethan home. In 1994 this classic opera venue was modernised, but people still bring their picnic hampers for summer performances in the time-honoured way.

Map on page 180

BELOW: picnic at the opera, Glyndeborne.

TIP

South of Lewes is the
port of Newhaven
where ferries run to
Dieppe in France. Look
out for traders from
Dieppe who regularly
come and set up their
stalls in Brighton,
selling French cheeses
and other produce.

BELOW: Lewes's
celebrated bonfire
night, 5 November,
is England's firiest.

The county town of Lewes

Lewes , the county town of East Sussex, has been the scene of battles since Saxon times and today it is best known for its explosive Guy Fawkes celebrations on 5 November. Lewes is also an antiques and antiquarian book centre. Thomas Paine, author of *The Rights of Man*, which helped to fuel American Independence, lived at Bull House in the High Street from 1768 to 1774. The Barbican in the High Street is the entrance to the **Norman castle** (open 10am–5.30pm, Sun and bank holidays 11am–5.30pm; English Heritage), the high point of the town, built by William de Warrene in the wake of the Norman Conquest. From here there are views over Harry Hill where in 1264 Simon de Montfort and England's barons defeated Henry III, forcing him to sign the Mise of Lewes, which brought about parliamentary government to England. The castle also contains the **Museum of Sussex Archaeology**.

From 1890 the anglophile New England art collector Edward Perry Warren lived with a "male brotherhood" in Lewes House, now occupied by the local council. He commissioned from the French sculptor Auguste Rodin a version of *The Kiss*, with instructions that the man's genitals should be "seen in their entirety". The result horrified the town council and it was only briefly displayed; today it is in the Tate Britain gallery in London. The High Street drops steeply to the River Ouse and over the bridge is Harvey's, brewers of one of the best Sussex beers, and **Anne of Cleve's House** (open daily in summer, 10am–5.30pm, winter Tues and Thurs; entrance charge), a 16th-century timber-framed hall house given to Anne of Cleves in her divorce settlement with Henry VIII.

Beyond it are the outline foundations of **Lewes Priory**, once one of the greatest Cluniac priories in Europe.

Raffish Brighton

London's favourite resort is an hour's train journey from the capital. The story of **Brighton** ⓲ begins with a local doctor, Richard Russell, who in a tract in 1750 extolled the efficacy of sea water, both to drink and to bathe in. The practice became so sociably desirable that when Russell opened an establishment with attendants called "bathers" (for men) and "dippers" (for women), he could count on the patronage of the Prince Regent (later George IV). It became the favourite haunt of "Prinny" and in 1784 he drove a coach from London on a new, direct road from London in 4 hours, 30 minutes. Today the journey is accomplished in less than a quarter of that time. At weekends in summer day trippers arrive at **Brighton station** where a vast market fills its car park on Sundays. From there it's a short walk down Queen's Road and West Street to the promenade, the stony beach and sparkling sea.

Map on page 198

The town has a raffish air, attracting artists, street performers and alternative lifestylers, who are catered for in a variety of good, inexpensive restaurants and bars. Much of the enjoyment in the town is simply in walking the streets. From the station, heading into the old town, the first encounter is with an area called **North Laine** Ⓐ. Here there is something of a time warp back to the 1960s, with candle and craft shops, Third-World traders, vegan specialists, healers, therapists and tattoo parlours. The town also has a reputation for antiques. The more respectable shops are in **The Lanes** Ⓑ, a warren of alleys between North Laine and the sea. The Lanes have various etymologies, but they follow an agricultural pattern, possibly from former fields where hemp was grown to make fishermen's nets. They are the best place to head for when it's time for something to eat: visitors are spoilt for choice.

Bric-à-brac shop in North Laine

BELOW: one of many places to take a break.

The Volks Electric Railway.

North Laine and the Lanes are divided by Church Street where the excellent **Brighton Museum and Art Gallery** ◉ (open Mon–Tues, Thurs–Sat 10am–5pm, Sun 2–5pm; admission free) fills a sturdy Victorian building. Its eclectic contents includes Brighton's last cork shop, an imaginative costume collection, some fine Victorian paintings and an extensive collection of Art Deco furniture and artefacts. The museum is part of an interesting assortment of buildings, which includes the **Dome Theatre** in the old Royal Stables, the **Corn Exchange** in the old riding house, and **The Pavilion Theatre**.

These all lie on the north side of the town's great attraction, the **Royal Pavilion** ◉ (open Jun–Sept, 10am–6pm, Oct–Mar, 10am–6pm; entrance charge). In 1785 the Prince Regent rented a small farm on the Old Steine, and on this site Henry Holland and John Nash, inspired by the architecture of Mughal India, built his lavish Pavilion. The brilliant oriental interiors, designed by Frederick Grace and Robert Jones, are decorated with golden dragons, chinoiserie, burnished palms and coloured glass. The opulent Banqueting Room is laid ready for a feast from the ballroom-sized Great Kitchen which has 500 copper pieces in its *batterie de cuisine*. Concerts are sometimes held in the lovely Music Room. On the first floor Queen Victoria's bed has six mattresses.

Across the Old Steine down by the seafront is the **Sea Life Centre** ◉ (open daily 9am–7pm, 10am–6pm in winter; entrance charge), which has a modern walk-through aquarium, and the **Palace Pier** ◉ With pubs, fish-and-chip shops and amusements arcades, this 1,700-ft (500-metre) protuberance is an English institution. The town's other pier, the **West Pier**, is a listed building, but lack of funds have left it in a sorry and perilous state for many years. On the east side of the Palace Pier is Madeira Drive, where the London to Brighton Veteran Car

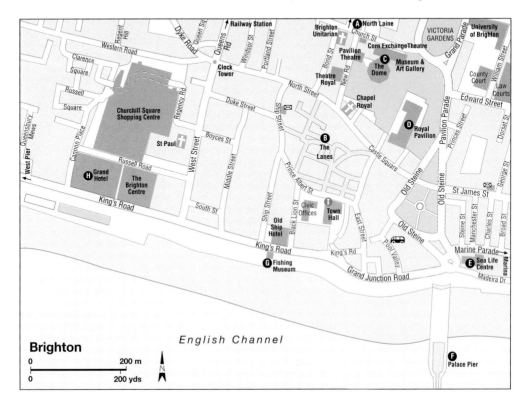

Brighton

0 ———— 200 m

0 ———— 200 yds

N

English Channel

Run ends up every November. The Volks Railway goes more than a mile (2 km) from here along the sea front, passing the nudist beach. Built in 1883, this is the oldest electric railway in the country.

The road above, Marine Parade, leads to **Brighton Marina**, a man-made harbour said to be the largest in Europe, with attendant boutiques, shopping arcades, supermarkets and cut-price cinemas.

Most of the seafront action takes place on the other side of the pier, along the lower promenade, where impromptu bands and dancing can break out at any time. By the small **Brighton Fishing Museum Ⓖ**, barely bigger than the clinker-built fishing "punt" inside it, stalls sell cockles and whelks and other delights of the deep. Behind it is the historic Old Ship Hotel, from where Charles II escaped to France: every year the dash is re-enacted in a small boat race.

The best known hotel is the **Grand Hotel Ⓗ**, the ritzy joint on the seafront that became synonymous with naughty weekends. But the dramatic IRA bomb attack on the building the during the 1984 Conservative Party Conference, which left two dead and more than 30 injured, gave it a more embattled air.

Four miles (6.5 km) east of Brighton is **Rottingdean**, a pleasant village by the sea, though rather cut off from it by the the A259 coastal road. From 1897 to 1902 Rudyard Kipling, the great literary figure of Britain's Empire days, lived at The Elms where he wrote *Kim*, *The Just So Stories* and *Stalky & Co*. His 18th-century house cannot be visited but its walled garden on The Green is open to be enjoyed. He was related to the pre-Raphaelite painter Edward Burne-Jones (1833–98) who lived in North End House on the west side of The Green. He had one of its rooms decorated to look like a country pub and he designed the windows in the church of St Margaret's where his ashes were scattered.

Map on page 198

Nobody can be altogether good in Brighton and that is the great charm of it.
– RICHARD JEFFRIES
(1848–87)

BELOW: Brighton's stony beach and Palace Pier.

WE DO LIKE TO BE BESIDE THE SEASIDE

England's coastal resorts have long attracted a holiday crowd in search of bracing air and a little fun

THIS IS TO ADVISE YOU THAT NATURISTS MAY BE USING THE BEACH AHEAD

The Brighton Parish register of 12 November, 1641 records the burial of a woman who "came for cure". This is thought to be the earliest record in England of anyone using the sea for its curative properties. Within a century, before Dr Russell made the sea cure fashionable, bathing in the sea had become a pastime for visitors to this fishing village and elsewhere. A 1735 print from Scarborough, on the Yorkshire coast, shows bathing machines on the beach. These wooden huts on wheels, used as changing rooms, were drawn by horses into the sea where men were attended by "bathers", women by "dippers". At Margate "Modesty

hoods" were fitted over the steps of these machines, designed by a local Quaker. Male bathers did not always wear costumes at first and, though there are instances of female bathers also swimming naked in Brighton and Scarborough, they generally wore long flannel gowns. An 18th-century writer records how telescopes were used to inspect female bathers "as they kick and sprawl and flounder like so many mad Naiads in flannel smocks". But some actually learned to swim, Dr Samuel Johnson, who came to Brighton in the 1760s, among them.

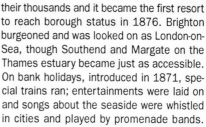

The fashionable arrived, and the populace followed just as soon as there were railways to take them there. Wakes Week in Lancashire took cotton workers to Blackpool in their thousands and it became the first resort to reach borough status in 1876. Brighton burgeoned and was looked on as London-on-Sea, though Southend and Margate on the Thames estuary became just as accessible. On bank holidays, introduced in 1871, special trains ran; entertainments were laid on and songs about the seaside were whistled in cities and played by promenade bands.

A hero of the hour was Captain Webb. In 1875 this dashing former captain of the Cunard line, covered in porpoise oil and wearing a scarlet costume, swam the English Channel in 21 hours 41 minutes. It was the world's first marathon aquatic event.

England's seaside resorts manage to retain a Victorian air: seafront promenades with deck-chairs and bandstands; rusting piers in need of repair. An aroma of vinegar may mingle with the ozone: fish and chips was England's first fast food. Even nudist enclaves (Brighton's was the first, in 1981) have an innocence that makes them seem a million miles from the fleshpots of the world.

Some resorts – Bournemouth, Eastbourne – are smart addresses. But even their airs and graces cannot hide the breezy cheerines that earlier generations of holidaymakers brought to the English seaside. ❏

LEFT: Victorian bathers. **TOP RIGHT:** Capt. Webb.
ABOVE RIGHT: bathing machines, Scarborough.

To the west of Brighton urban ribbon development connects the Sussex resorts of **Worthing**, **Littlehampton** (there is a good sandy beach at **Climping**, on the west side of Littlehampton) and **Bognor Regis**. Worthing is perhaps the most amiable of these resorts. Shaking off its image as a place for retired gentlefolk, it has recently become a popular centre for hi-tech industries. Oscar Wilde took its name for his main character, John Worthing, in his 1895 play *The Importance of Being Earnest*, which he wrote while staying here, and every year he is remembered in the town's August festival.

Just inland from Worthing is the fine church at **Sompting**, visible from the main A27. Dating from 960AD, it is the only Saxon church in the country with a Rhenish helm roof. Faithful parishioners have embroidered views of the Downs on the hassocks.

Iron-Age forts

Behind Worthing are **Chanctonbury** and **Cissbury Ring**s, sites of Iron-Age hill forts. There is little actually to see, but they are atmospheric places and make excellent walks. Cissbury was named after the Saxon leader Cissa, but the hill fort was built long before him, in 240BC. It covers 650 acres (260 hectares), making it the second largest in the country after Maiden Castle in Dorset. For the ramparts a wooden wall was constructed to contain 60,000 tons of chalk excavated from the ditch. The site had already been occupied for around 4,000 years when some 300 flint mine shafts were dug, to a depth of up to 40 ft (12 metres) using deers' antlers as digging tools. The thick grass is springy underfoot; it has never been ploughed, and the rich and ancient flora includes eight kinds of orchids and fleawort, used in bedding to fend off fleas.

Map on page 180

TIP

Picnics can be taken to the large gardens, such as Nymans and Polesden Lacey, (which also has a croquet lawn with mallets for hire).

BELOW: Ditchling Beacon on the South Downs Way.

Chanctonbury, just to the north, is privately owned by the Goring family. In 1760 Charles Goring planted a beech copse around the hill fort, and it maintains mythical properties: run round it seven times on a moonless night to evoke the Devil. Chanctonbury can be reached from **Steyning** (pronounced Stenning), a pleasing small town of 61 listed buildings. Its church of St Andrews has the most impressive Norman nave in Sussex and it gives an idea of the importance that this town, formerly on a navigable river and with its own mint, once had.

Gardens

There are a number of outstanding gardens in Sussex and Surrey, all in the hands of the National Trust. **Bateman's** (open daily Apr–Oct, 11am–5pm) in Burwash was home of the writer and Nobel laureate Rudyard Kipling from 1902 to 1936. This lovely Jacobean building is full of mementoes of Empire Kipling so powerfully evoked, and there is a romantic garden where plays and music are put on in summer. North of the Downs, between East Grinstead and Lewes, is **Sheffield Park** ⓳ (open April–Nov, Tues–Sun 11am–6pm), laid out in the 18th century by "Capability" Brown with lakes, waterfalls and cascades. There is a generous show of bluebells in spring and the Bluebell Railway, steam train runs along a 10-mile (16-km) track from here. **Nymans Garden** ⓴ near Hayward's Heath (open Mar–Nov, Wed–Sun 11am–6pm) is a fine Wealden garden with an historic collection of flora. The best of the North Downs flora can be seen at **Polesden Lacey** ㉑ (open April–Nov, daily 1.30–5.30pm; gardens open all year) near Great Bookham, Dorking. This large Regency villa, where George VI and Queen Elizabeth spent their honeymoon in 1923, was the home of an Edwardian society hostess who gave celebrated parties.

BELOW: Sheffield Park gardens.

The Royal Horticultural Society has its showpiece at **Wisley Gardens**, just north of **Guildford** ㉒ (open daily 10am–4.30pm; entrance charge) on the A3 and England's many serious gardeners make regular visits. Surrey's county town, Guildford, has a castle with Norman walls and a modern cathedral. There are a number of attractive small towns nearby, including **Farnham**, **Godalming**, **Haselmere** and **Shere**.

A trio of stately homes lies to the south of Guildford. **Uppark** near Petersfield (open April–Oct, Sun–Thurs 1–5pm; gardens 1.30am–5pm; National Trust), magnificently restored by the National Trust and reopened in 1995 after a serious fire, dates from the 17th century. Looking like a fabulous dolls' house, it has an art and decorative arts collection and a grand view from its high point 350 ft (106 metres) on the top of the South Downs. **Petworth** ㉓ is a town of myriad antique shops overshadowed by by the great wall of **Petworth House** (open Mar–Nov, Sat–Wed 1–4.30pm; National Trust). This has been home to the Percy family since 1150 and it contains the National Trust's largest painting collection, with works by Van Dyck, Gainsborough, Reynolds, Blake and Turner who had a studio here and executed many paintings of the house and extensive deer park, landscaped by "Capability" Brown. **Parham House** ㉔ (open Easter–Oct, Wed, Thurs, Sun 2–5.30pm; entrance charge) between Petworth and Arundel, is one of the finest Elizabethan buildings in England, and its gardens include a 4-acre (1.6-hectare) walled garden, orchard, maze and heronry.

Due west of Parham, on a high point of the Downs by Bury Hill, is **Bignor Roman Villa** (Easter–Nov, Tues–Sun 10am–5pm, entrance charge). The site dates from the first century and covers more than 4 acres (1.8 hectares) where, beneath thatched buildings, there are mosaics depicting gladiators, Venus and

Map on page 180

Emma Hart, 17, danced on the dining table at Uppark to entertain its reprobate owner, Harry Featherstonhaugh. She later married his nephew, Lord Hamilton, and became Horatio Nelson's mistress.

BELOW:
Arundel Castle.

Map on page 180

TIP

Chichester Harbour is a safe place to learn to sail. Sailing courses are offered at Chichester Marina, tel: 01243 512557. If you just want a 90-minute trip round the harbour, boats leave from Itchenor.

BELOW: Chichester Cathedral.
RIGHT: Bosham Harbour.

Medusa. Nearby is the delightful village of Amberley, with mellow, robust thatched, flint stone houses. The castle ruins are all that remains of the palace of the bishops of Chichester.

To the south of Amberley the River Arun cuts through the South Downs to reach **Arundel ㉕**, home of the Dukes of Norfolk. Its fairytale **castle** (open Easter–Nov, Sun–Fri noon–5pm; entrance charge), which had a Victorian make-over and provided the backdrop for the film *The Madness of King George*, dates from 1070. The Norfolks are the premier Catholic family in England, and though the Catholic Cathedral, built in 1870, is a disappointment, the parish church opposite is intriguingly divided between Anglican and Catholic, the latter part accessible only from the castle. The castle is surrounded by 2 sq. miles (5 sq. km) of parklands which contain a lake and a **Wildfowl and Wetlands Centre**. The Black Rabbit is a popular pub by the River Arun here.

Cathedral of modern masters

The Cathedral town of Sussex is **Chichester ㉖**, a small market town centred on a traditional Market Cross with many Georgian buildings. The modern Festival Theatre, a theatre in the round, has a reputation for excellence. It lies in Priory Park by the old Norman motte and bailey and the remains of the city wall. **Chichester Cathedral** is light and graceful and full of interest. Construction was begun in 1091 and its mixture of Gothic and Norman is enhanced by works of modern art from Marc Chagall, Graham Sutherland, Patrick Procktor and, most notably, John Piper who created the altar tapestry in 1966. Pallant House in West Pallant has further works collected by Walter Hussey, Dean of the Cathedral from 1955 to 1977. Together with Bishop Bell, he was instrumental in giving modern art a place in the cathedral.

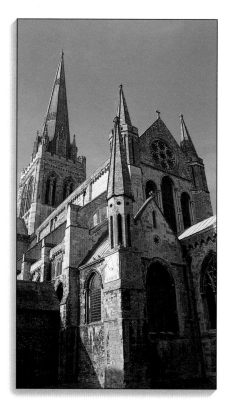

North of Chichester, on the top of the Downs, is **Goodwood ㉗** where the racecourse has a wonderful Downland setting. "Glorious Goodwood" is an annual meeting at the beginning of August. Just beyond it is **The Weald and Downland Open-air Museum** (open Easter–Nov, daily 11am–5pm, in winter Wed, Sat–Sun 11am–4pm; entrance charge). Some three dozen 13th-century timber-framed Weald and Downland buildings have been brought to this 45-acre (18-hectare) site. They include shops and sheds, mills and barns as well as domestic houses and a farmhouse uprooted in the building of the Channel Tunnel.

Chichester grew up as a port, and the sea is not far away. In 1960 the largest Roman domestic building north of the Alps was found at **Fishbourne ㉘** (open daily 10am–5pm; entrance charge). It covers 5.6 acres (2.3 hectares) and may have belonged to the Celtic client king Tiberius Claudius Cogidubnus. Begun in AD 75, it had a quayside and 100 rooms, with impressive mosaic floors, but it was burnt down some 200 years later. In the extensive grounds hedges have been planted following the original pattern.

Among **Chichester Harbour**'s tidal estuaries, which provide the largest stretch of navigable water in the south, **Bosham** stands out as the most timeless, attractive backwater. Its Saxon church, claims to be the oldest site of Christian worship in Sussex. ❏

THE ENGLISH GARDEN

England's temperate climate encourages a great diversity of gardens which blend the grand and the homely in a cosmopolitan range of styles

The formal gardens of great houses have both followed fashion and set the style for the nation's favourite hobby. In medieval times, fruit trees, roses and herbs were grown in walled enclosures: Elvaston Country Park in Derbyshire is a good example. In the 16th century, aromatic plantswere incorporated in "knots" (carpet-like patterns). Tudor Gardens (like those at Hatfield House in Hertfordshire and Packwood House in Warwickshire were enclosed squares of flowers in geometric patterns bordered by low hedges and gravel paths.

The Renaissance gardener also liked snipping hedges into shapes: the most inventive examples are at Hever Castle in Kent. A taste for small flower beds persisted through the 17th and 18th centuries when fountains and canals began to be introduced.

THE ART OF THE LANDSCAPE

In the 1740s a rich banker, Henry Hoare, inspired by Continental art during his Grand Tour, employed William Kent (1685–1748) to turn his gardens at Stourhead in Wiltshire into a series of lakes dotted with grottoes and buildings in the classical style. This was the birth of the landscape garden, known as *le jardin anglais*, that was an entirely English invention. The style was a direct reaction to the formal gardens made in France for Louis XIV at Versailles. Nature instead of geometry was the inspiration, and the idylls of landscape painters became the idylls of gardeners too.

"Capability" Brown (*see panel, right*) rejected formal plantings in favour of natural parkland and restricted flowers to small kitchen gardens. But Humphry Repton (1752–1815) reintroduced the formal pleasure garden. The Victorians put the emphasis on plants and Gertrude Jekyll (1843–1932) promoted the idea of planting cycles to ensure that colour lasted through the year.

△ COTTAGE GARDENS
Such gardens are the pride and joy of thousands of people all over Britain. They're labour-intensive: perennials need to be planned, borders restocked, plants deadheaded and weeds removed. But it's a labour of love.

▷ TRESCO ABBEY GARDENS
Thanks to the influence of the Gulf Stream, sub-tropical flora can flourish at England's south-western tip. These gardens, on the Isles of Scilly, were laid out on the site of a Benedictine priory and contain many rare plants.

◁ GARDEN STATUES
The classicists favoured populating gardens with assorted Greek goddesses and coy nymphs, and the trend gradually evolved to include strikingly modern sculpture. At a more demotic level, brightly painted garden gnomes have their adherents.

THEY CHAMPIONED CHANGING STYLES

△ **HIDCOTE MANOR**
This 17th-century Cotswold house at Mickleton in Gloucestershire, has one of the most beautiful English gardens, mixing different types of plot within various species of hedges. Although covering 10 acres (4 hectares), it resembles a series of cottage gardens on a grand scale, conveying an impression of what Vita Sackville-West called "haphazard luxuriance".

Lancelot Brown (1715–83) was nicknamed "Capability Brown" when he rode from one aristocratic client to the next pointing out "capabilities to improvement". His forte was presenting gardens in the natural state, and his lasting influence lay in his talent for combining quite simple elements to create harmonious effects.

Brown liked to create elegant lakes for his parks, as at Blenheim Palace in Oxfordshire. He was also involved with the gardens at Stowe in Buckinghamshire, which the National Trust today describes as "Britain's largest work of art", and with the gardens at Kew, Britain's main botanical establishment, just outside London.

One of the 20th century's most influential gardeners was Vita Sackville-West (1892–1962), below, who developed her gardens at Sissinghurst Castle in Kent. She revived the 16th-century idea of dividing a garden into separate sections, combining a formal overall style with an informal choice of flowers.

◁ **STOURHEAD**
This Wiltshire garden, birthplace of England's landscape movement, is dotted with lakes and temples and has many rare trees and shrubs. The artful vistas were created in the 1740s, and their magnificence contrasts with the severe restraint of the Palladian house (1721–24).

△ **THE KNOT GARDEN**
This example at Henry VIII's Hampton Court Palace outside London showes the Tudor liking for knots – small beds of dwarf plants or sand and gravel laid out in patterns resembling embroidery. Topiary, statues and mazes provided a counterpoint to the mathematical order.

THE NEW FOREST

The area's highlights include the busy ports of Portsmouth and Southampton, the serene New Forest, the splendid cathedral town of Salisbury, and the ancient stone circle of Stonehenge

Map on pages 212–13

This tour offers plenty of variety, as it includes the ports of Portsmouth and Southampton, the offshore Isle of Wight, the cathedral city of Winchester and the monument of Stonehenge, as well as the New Forest itself.

Portsmouth ❶ is a good place to start: it's a large and confusing city, due to post-war reconstruction, but the main sites are clearly signed. "Historic Ships" signs lead you to the *Mary Rose*, HMS *Victory* and HMS *Warrior*. An inclusive ticket allows you to visit all three and to explore a number of museums and sites dotted around the **Historic Dockyard** (open daily 10am–4. 30pm plus extended hours in summer). The **Mary Rose Exhibition** details the history of Henry VIII's flagship, sunk in 1545, and the **Mary Rose Ship Hall** displays the recovered ship itself. The tour of HMS **Victory**, on which Lord Nelson died at the Battle of Trafalgar in 1805, gives a good idea of life for an 18th-century sailor. On HMS **Warrior**, the first iron-clad warship, you can take a tour or explore alone. With a separate ticket you can also take a tour of the harbour.

Just outside Portsmouth, at Southsea, the **Portsmouth Sea Life Centre** (open daily 10am–5pm; entrance charge) is a great place for children on a rainy day. They can feed stingrays, handle live crabs and watch newly hatched baby sharks and other under-sea life from a walk-through tunnel.

PRECEDING PAGES: summer solstice at Stonehenge. **LEFT:** ponies grazing in the forest. **BELOW:** HMS *Victory* in Portsmouth Dockyard.

FACT FILE

By car The region is easily accessible from most parts of England, although the A3, M3 and M27 are very busy with commuter traffic during rush hours
By coach National Express services to Portsmouth, Salisbury, Southampton and Winchester, tel: 0990 808080
By rail Southampton, Salisbury and Winchester are on main Intercity lines; from Southampton there are local trains to the heart of the New Forest; tel: 0345 484950
By ferry Daily car and passenger ferries operate from Portsmouth and Southampton to Caen, Cherbourg, Le Havre and St Malo; contact Brittany Ferries (Portsmouth), tel: 023 9282 7701, P&O Ferries (Portsmouth), tel: 023 9277 2244; Sealink Stena Line (Southampton), tel: 023 8023 3973; Red Tunnel Ferries, tel: 023 80330333 operate hourly services to East and West Cowes.
Forestry Commission Tel: 023 8028 3771 (for accidents involving animals); tel: 023 8028 2813 (to report animals injured or in distress)
Tourist information Portsmouth, tel: 023 92826722; Southampton, tel: 023 8022 1106; Salisbury, tel: 01722 334956; Winchester, tel: 01962 840500; Lyndhurst New Forest Museum & Visitor Centre, tel: 023 8028 2269; Isle of Wight (Yarmouth), tel: 01983 760015

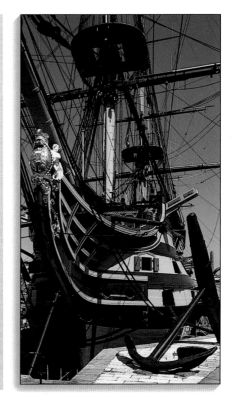

The Medieval Merchant's House in Southampton.

Queen Victoria described her palatial residence as "dear, modest, unpretentious Osborne".

Southampton and "the island"

The M27 motorway will take you the short distance to **Southampton ②**, the port from which the *Mayflower* sailed to America in 1620, and the *Titanic* set out on its ill-fated voyage in 1912. It is still a busy port which, like Portsmouth, suffered badly in World War II. Post-war planning left much to be desired, but it makes the most of its heritage. The **Maritime Museum** (open Tues–Sat 10am–1pm, 2–5pm, Sun 2–5pm; entrance charge) on the Town Quay is a magnificent building with interesting exhibits; the nearby **Museum of Archaeology** (same hours; entrance charge) packs a huge amount of information into a small space; and the **Medieval Merchant's House** (open April–Oct, daily 10am–6pm; entrance charge) has been furnished in keeping with its 13th-century origins.

From Southampton you can take a ferry or hydrofoil to the **Isle of Wight ③**. It's a pretty little place with an old-fashioned feel. **Osborne House** (open April–Oct, daily 10am–5pm; English Heritage) at **East Cowes**, designed by Prince Albert in 1845, was Queen Victoria's private residence. She died here in 1901 and the richly furnished Italianate house remains much as it was then.

Just outside **Newport**, in the centre of the island, is **Carisbrooke Castle** (open April–Oct 10am–6pm, Nov–Mar 10am–4pm; English Heritage). A 12th-century keep survives but most of the rest is 16th-century. Charles I was imprisoned here in 1647 before being taken to London for trial and execution. The star attraction is the 18th-century treadmill, still operated by donkey-power.

Winchester, a cathedral city

Back in Southampton, it's a brief journey on the M3 to **Winchester ④**, which once shared with London the honours of joint capital of England. Start your tour

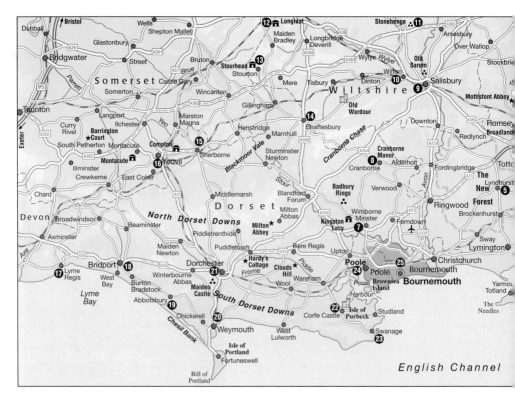

at the **Cathedral** (open daily 7.30am–6.30pm; donations welcomed; pre-booked tour tickets from the information desk, tel: 01962 853137). All architectural styles are represented, from the 11th-century Romanesque north transept to the glorious Perpendicular-style nave. Look out for the oldest choir stalls in England (*circa* 1305); the grave of Jane Austen (1775–1817) in the north aisle; the Edward Burne-Jones windows in the Epiphany Chapel; and contemporary sculptor Anthony Gormley's bronze in the crypt. The precious 12th-century Winchester Bible is displayed in the library.

There's much else to be seen in the town: the **Great Hall** (open daily 10am–5pm; entrance charge) which houses the **Round Table**, improbably linked with King Arthur and his knights, is all that remains of William the Conqueror's castle. **Winchester College** (1382) (open Mon–Sat 10am–1pm, 2–5pm, Sun 2–5pm; for guided tours tel: 01962 621209) has a chapel rich enough to rival the Cathedral; and the ruined **Wolvesey Castle** (open April–Oct, 10am–5pm; English Heritage) was the former home of the Bishops of Winchester.

The New Forest

Head southwest now on the M3/M27 motorways to **Lyndhurst ❺**, capital of the **New Forest**. You can learn about the area at the excellent **New Forest Museum and Visitor Centre** (open daily 10am–5pm; tel: 023 80283914). Also featured in the museum is Alice Liddell, the girl for whom Lewis Carroll (1832–98) wrote *Alice in Wonderland*. She became Mrs Reginald Hargreaves and it is under that name that you'll find her tomb in **Lyndhurst Church**, an exuberant building full of stained glass by William Morris and Edward Burne-Jones, with life-sized angels supporting the timber roof.

Map
on pages
212–13

*A new foal
finds its feet.*

BELOW: Winchester
pupil in the quad.

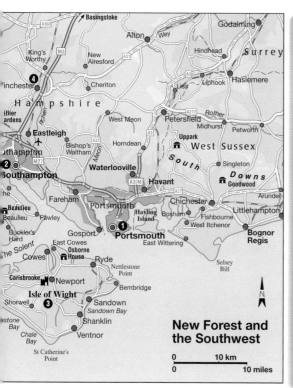

**New Forest and
the Southwest**

0   10 km
0   10 miles

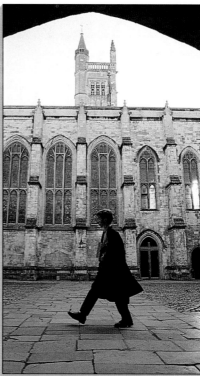

The National Motor Museum at Beaulieu.

Many people come to the New Forest especially to visit **Beaulieu** ❻ (open April–Sept, 10am–6pm, Oct–Mar, 10am–5pm; entrance charge), one of the first stately homes to open its doors to the public. The magnificent **Cistercian abbey** (now a ruin) was built in the 13th century. The cloister, the best-preserved part, is now planted with herbs, and the monks' refectory has been converted into a parish church. The abbey was confiscated and sold by Henry VIII during the 1530s Dissolution and in the 19th century the abbey gatehouse was turned into the baronial-style **Palace House**; beautifully vaulted ceilings survive and the walls are hung with portraits.

From here you can walk through attractive gardens to the ugly building that houses the **National Motor Museum**; hop on an open-topped bus for a tour of the grounds; or queue for a ride on the monorail that encircles them, and gives a fine aerial view. The museum holds a huge collection covering more than a century of motoring, concentrating more on the social history of the car than the mechanical aspects. There are also displays of cars that have broken the land-speed record; and trams, buses and fire engines for children to clamber on.

West to Wimborne

Leave the forest on the A31 for **Wimborne Minster** ❼, where the imposing twin towers of the church rise above Georgian houses. The original minster was built in 705, then destroyed by the Danes; the present one is Norman. Opposite stands the **Priest's House Museum** (open April–Oct, Mon–Sat 10.30am–5pm, Sun 2–5pm; entrance charge), an interesting little place whose attractions include a Victorian kitchen and stationer's shop, an archaeology gallery, a fine garden and a tea shop.

BELOW: relaxing outside the church.

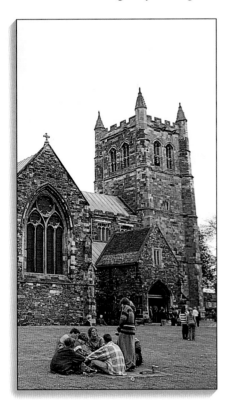

A FOREST TRAIL

An exploration of the forest could begin at Lyndhurst, going south to Brockenhurst where one of England's oldest trees, a 1,000-year-old yew, stands in the churchyard. Stock up with picnic provisions in the village, then follow Rhinefield signs to three beauty spots. The first, Ober Water, is a forest stream alive with minnows where boggy margins support such flowers as the bog asphodel and insect-eating sundew plant. Information boards at the car park indicate a choice of walks.

About 1 mile (2 km) on, you come to Rhinefield Drive, an arboretum planted with rhododendrons, azaleas and giant conifers. Again, there is a choice of marked walks. A right turn off the A35 will take you to Bolderwood Drive, another 19th-century arboretum where you can follow marked walks, keeping an eye out for red, fallow and roe deer.

Heading towards Ashurst you'll find the New Forest Nature Quest (open daily 10am–5pm, tel: 023 8029 2408) where an array of birds and small mammals live in old farm buildings and forest enclosures that approximate to their natural habitat. There is also a reptilary and a butterfly tunnel, and knowledgeable staff give short talks throughout the day. Most people go there to please the children then find themselves fascinated by the place.

West of town is **Kingston Lacy** (open April–Oct, Sat–Wed noon–5.30pm; National Trust), a 17th-century mansion containing works by Rubens, Titian and Van Dyck, and set in grounds farmed by traditional organic methods. North now on the B3078 to **Cranborne Manor** ❽ (open Mar–Sept, Wed 9am–5pm only; entrance charge) where, set around the Jacobean house, is one of England's most appealing gardens, originally planted with roses, clematis and topiary hedges by John Tradescant in the 17th century. The village is pretty, too.

Map
on pages
212–13

Salisbury to Stonehenge

The best place to begin a visit to **Salisbury** ❾ is on a windswept hill just outside it, **Old Sarum**, where extensive ruins of the earlier town are set within the ramparts of an Iron-Age hill fort. Salisbury itself is dominated by the creamy-white limestone **Cathedral** with its wonderful spire, timber roof and Decorated-style cloister. In the Chapter House is displayed one of the four original copies of the Magna Carta (1215). The Cathedral is not the only attraction; stroll around the town enjoying the gracious Queen Anne buildings, or stop for tea or a light lunch at one of them, the National Trust-run **Mompesson House**.

Only 3 miles (5 km) west of Salisbury is **Wilton** ❿, dominated by **Wilton House** (open April–Oct, daily 10.30am–5.30pm; entrance charge), the estate of the Earl of Pembroke. The 17th-century house was designed by Inigo Jones and the grounds – which can be visited separately – have a marvellous adventure playground. Wilton is best known for its carpet manufacture. The original **Wilton Weaving Works** (open Mon–Sat 9am–5pm, Sun 11am–5pm) arranges tours to show you how carpets are produced today. You can also buy quality carpets at factory prices, or bargain-priced seconds.

Between Wilton and Salisbury, the A360 leads about 11 miles (16 km) north to **Stonehenge** ⓫ (open April–Sept, daily 9.30am–6pm, Oct–Mar, 9.30am–4pm; entrance charge), which stands on **Salisbury Plain**. England's most famous ancient monument, it has been declared a UNESCO World Heritage Site. Spanning the period 3,000–1,000 BC (the central ring of stones dates from *circa* 2,000 BC), it comprises 123 bluestones, hauled here from the Preseli Mountains in Pembrokeshire, 200 miles (320 km) away, and larger sarsen stones which outcrop locally.

Its purpose has baffled archaeologists and other experts for centuries and engendered many myths. Inigo Jones, one of the first to investigate the monument, at the behest of James I in the 17th century, concluded it was a Roman temple to Uranus. Though the alignment of the major axis with the midsummer sunrise suggests a religious significance, no firm evidence has been found, and theories about it range from the practical – that it was some kind of calendar – to the extraterrestrial. Whatever its purpose, it seems that its builders must have had some knowledge of mathematics and astrology. It is popularly associated with the Druids, but in fact predated them by about 1,000 years. Regardless of this, present-day Druids and many other people regard it as a place of ritual and worship on Midsummer Eve, and the police regard it as a priority to stop them trespassing. ❏

TIP

Near Stonehenge look for signs to the Hawk Conservancy (open Feb–Oct, daily 10.30am–5.30pm; entrance charge; tel: 10264 772252), which has one of the largest collections of raptors in the world.

BELOW: the graceful arches of Salisbury Cathedral.

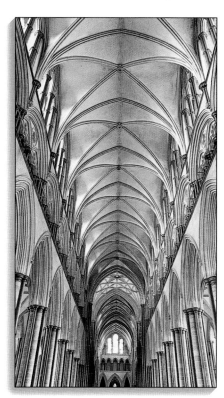

THE SOUTHWEST

Once the ancient Kingdom of Wessex, the region includes the county town of Dorchester, Stourhead's stunning gardens, magnificent Corfe Castle, and some of the best beaches in England

Map on pages 212–13

T he Southwest is a loose title which covers the whole area between the New Forest and the borders of the West Country, returning along the Dorset coast as far as Bournemouth. It picks up where we left off in the previous chapter by making a short detour on the A303/A36 (northwest of Stonehenge) to **Warminster** and **Longleat** ⓬ (house open April–Oct, daily 10am–6pm, Nov–Mar, 10am–4pm; safari park April–Oct, 10am–6pm; entrance charge). The property of the Marquess of Bath, this was the first stately home to be opened to the public (in 1948). The house, Elizabethan in origin and with an eclectic mixture of styles spanning the past four centuries, is splendid, but it is the safari park, where animals roam freely in grounds originally landscaped by "Capability" Brown, which is now the greatest draw.

After your safari, return to the A303 then take a right turn at **Mere** to visit **Stourhead** ⓭ (house open Mar–Oct, Sat–Wed noon–5.30pm, garden 9am–7pm; entrance charge). The Palladian-style house, built for banker Henry Hoare in the 18th century is surrounded by one of the loveliest landscaped gardens in England. Classical temples dedicated to Flora and Apollo stand beside the dark waters of the lake, while tunnels lead to a grotto which houses a life-sized statue. In spring the walks are vivid with azaleas and rhododendrons.

LEFT: The Cobb at Lyme Regis.
BELOW: Siberian tiger at Longleat.

FACT FILE

By car Our starting points are easily accessible via the M3/A303 from London and the east, or via the A4/A36 from Bristol and Bath.

By rail Regular services from London Waterloo to Warminster, about 1 hour 30 minutes; Sherborne and Bournemouth, about 2 hours, tel: 0345 484950.

By coach: There are regular National Express services to Dorchester, Bournemouth and other main towns; for details, tel: 0990 808080.

By ferry Easy access from Portsmouth and Southampton which are served by ferries from Cherbourg, Caen, Le Havre and St Malo. Britanny Ferries (Portsmouth), tel: 023 9282 7701, Sealink Stena Line (Southampton), tel: 023 8023 3973.

Special attractions Cerne Abbas Giant; Corfe Castle; Hardy monuments; Longleat Safari Park; Maiden Castle; Sherborne Abbey Church; Studland Beach and Nature Reserve; Brownsea Island.

Best-known products Portland stone, Purbeck marble

Most famous son Thomas Hardy (1840–1928).

Tourist information Bournemouth, tel: 0906 8020234; Dorchester, tel: 01305 267992; Lyme Regis, tel: 01297 442138; Weymouth, tel: 01305 785747.

Returning to the A303, retrace your route a short way and take the A350 to **Shaftesbury** , one of southern England's few hill towns. Climbing cobbled **Gold Hill**, lined with 18th-century cottages and the remaining wall of a demolished abbey, is like stepping back into a picturesque version of the past. Thomas Hardy (1840–1928) used Shaftesbury, renamed Shaston, as the setting for his 1896 novel *Jude the Obscure*.

Heading west on the A30, our next destination is **Sherborne** ⓮, the burial place of two Saxon kings. There is a wealth of medieval buildings, including the Abbey Church and Almshouse. **Sherborne Castle** (open April–Sept, Tues, Thurs, Sat and Sun 12.30–5pm; entrance charge) is an interestingly eccentric pile, built for Sir Walter Raleigh (1552–1618).

At **Yeovil** ⓰, 5 miles (8 km) west, is the Elizabethan **Montacute House** (open Mar–Oct, Wed–Mon noon–5pm; entrance charge), built in golden stone with ornamental gazebos for the lawyer who prosecuted Guy Fawkes, who tried to blow up the Houses of Parliament in 1605. In the church at **East Coker**, 3 miles (5 km) south, are the ashes of T. S. Eliot (1888–1965), whose ancestors emigrated to America. "In my beginning is my end" he wrote in the poem named after the village.

The Dorset coast

Continue west on the A30 and drop down to the coast at **Lyme Regis** ⓱ just east of the Devon border. This old fishing town was once as fashionable as Bath. Regency bow windows and trellised verandas on Victorian villas line The Parade on the way to the tiny harbour and the projecting arm called **The Cobb**. It was here that the Duke of Monmouth landed in 1685, aspiring to the crown, and here on the steps called Granny's Teeth that Jane Austen's Louisa Musgrave tumbled

BELOW: Gold Hill conjures up a golden age.

in *Persuasion*. **Bay Cottage** at the harbour's end, now a café, is where Austen (1775–1817) lived while writing much of the novel. More recently, the sea-lashed walls formed a backdrop for Meryl Streep in the 1981 film of John Fowles's novel *The French Lieutenant's Woman*.

The road east takes you to **Bridport ⓲**. It is 2 miles (3 km) from the sea, yet there is no denying its marine character. **West Bay** is Bridport's improbable harbour, a narrow channel dug in the shingle bank and flanked by two high piers only feet apart. In the old days, coasters had to be hauled in with ropes.

The next town is **Burton Bradstock**, a pretty spot with thatched cottages, smoky stone and bright window boxes, and a stream that used to drive the flax mills until the last one closed in 1931. Here the **Chesil Bank** begins, curving away eastwards until it becomes the slender link that means the Isle of Portland is not really an island at all, but a peninsula. Chesil Bank has no mercy: to bring a boat in here spells almost certain disaster.

Portland is a place apart: Hardy called it "the Gibraltar of Wessex" and claimed the people had customs of their own. Everything is made of Portland stone, the material used for many of London's best-known buildings. The lighthouse on the southern tip overlooks the water of the treacherous Portland Race.

St Catherine's Chapel on a green hill above the bank at **Abbotsbury ⓳** is a vital mark for sailors and fishermen, as well as a place of prayer. On the land side it overlooks a surprising sub-tropical garden, the ruins of a substantial 15th-century monastic barn, built as a wheat store, and a swan sanctuary, founded in the 14th century.

George III put **Weymouth ⓴** on the map when he went there to convalesce in 1789, and much of the character of an 18th-century watering place remains.

Map on pages 212–13

Thomas Hardy, who used Dorset locations for most of his novels, called Bridport Port Bredy.

BELOW: the harbour at Weymouth.

English Heritage looks after Maiden Castle.

The king's statue stands at the end of the Esplanade, which is lined on one side with stuccoed terraces, on the other by an expanse of golden sands. From Brewers' Quay take a trip through history, the **Timewalk Journey** (daily 10am–5.30pm, till 9.30pm in Aug; entrance charge) which includes entrance to the **Weymouth Museum**, where George III's bathing machine can be seen. A regular ferry service from the jetty runs to the Channel Islands. Another good museum is **Custom House Quay** (open April–Sept, daily 9.30am–8pm, Oct–Mar till 7pm; entrance charge) where interactive displays highlight three centuries of underwater exploration.

Turn inland now and take the A354 some 8 miles (13 km) towards Dorchester. Just outside the town you will come to **Maiden Castle**, a massive Iron-Age hill fort: excavations show that it was occupied some 4,000 years ago. The name has nothing to do with maidens, but derives from "mai dun" meaning great hill; the fort is believed to be the world's largest earthworks.

Dorchester

Dorchester ㉑ is the county town of Dorset, a place well aware of its past. It was the setting for Thomas Hardy's *Mayor of Casterbridge*, and there is a collection devoted to him, including the original manuscript of the 1886 novel, in the **Dorset County Museum** (open April–Oct, daily 10am–5pm, Nov–Mar, Mon–Sat; entrance charge). **Hardy's Cottage** (open April–Oct, Sun–Thurs 11am–5pm; National Trust), the writer's birthplace, is 3 miles (5 km) northeast of the town (*see below for more Hardy memorials*).

BELOW: Hardy's Monument.

But Dorchester isn't all Hardy: it's a pleasant town in its own right, where the pace of life is a little slower than elsewhere. It has another claim to fame (or

THOMAS HARDY

Thomas Hardy (1840–1928) was born at Higher Bockhampton, near Dorchester, the son of a stonemason, and although he spent considerable periods of time in London and travelled in Europe, all his major novels are set in the region. He trained as an architect, but after the success of *Far From the Madding Crowd* in 1874 he was able to concentrate on writing.

A recurrent theme in Hardy's work is the indifference of fate and the arbitrary nature of the suffering it inflicts on mankind. In his own time he was widely criticised for his pessimism, and it must be said that many of his novels, particularly the later ones such as *Jude the Obscure*, are extremely gloomy. In his later years Hardy turned to poetry, which he considered a superior art form, but it is for his novels that he is remembered.

Hardy sites that can be visited, as well as the Dorset County Museum and the Hardy Cottage, mentioned above, are Max Gate, in Alington Avenue, Dorchester (open April–Sept, Mon, Wed, Sun 2–5pm; National Trust), which he designed himself and inhabited from 1885 until his death; and the churchyard at Stinsford, just east of town, where his heart was buried alongside his family, although his body was interred at Westminster Abbey.

infamy) in the **Shire Hall** (open Mon–Fri 10am–noon, 2–5pm; entrance charge), the courtroom where six farmworkers, who became known as the **Tolpuddle Martyrs**, were sentenced to transportation in 1834 for the crime of forming a branch of the Labourers' Union. Such was the public outcry that the men were returned to England after serving two years in Australia, rather than the seven their sentence demanded. The village of Tolpuddle lies just off the A35 to the east of Dorchester, and there is a monument to the men, who became heroes of the later union movement.

To the north of town, on the A352, is the village of **Cerne Abbas**, which has a magnificent tithe barn but is best known for the **Cerne Abbas Giant**, the 180-ft (55-metre) tall priapic club-wealding figure carved into the chalk downs nearby. He is believed to date from the time of the Roman occupation and is obviously a fertility figure.

Also worth a stop as you head east from Dorchester on the A35 is **Athelhampton House** (open Mar–Oct, Sun–Fri 10.30am–5pm, Nov–Feb, Sun only; entrance charge), a fine medieval hall surrounded by impressive Victorian gardens adorned with fountains, statuary and topiaried pyramids.

Corfe Castle and the Isle of Purbeck

Turn off the A35 on to the A351 for **Corfe Castle** ㉒ (open Mar–Oct, daily 10am–5.30pm, Nov–Feb, 11am–3.30pm; National Trust) at Wareham. Sitting on a rocky pinnacle, this is one of England's most impressive ruins and has been an important stronghold since the time of the Norman Conquest. Its finest hour was during the Civil War when the owner, Lady Bankes, defended it against a six-week siege by Parliamentary troops, who later dynamited it to prevent any

Map on pages 212–13

TIP

An alternative route from Dorchester to Corfe Castle is on the A352, but this cuts out several of the Hardy sites, as well as Athelhampton House.

LEFT: the impressive ruins of Corfe Castle.
BELOW: the Cerne Abbas Giant.

repetition. Corfe Common nearby is rich in wildlife and there are splendid views from the folly of Crech Grange Arch.

Head for the coast now (staying on the A351) to **Swanage** ㉓, between Durlston and Swanage bays, "lying snugly between two headlands as between a finger and a thumb", as Hardy put it when he fictionalised the village as Knollsea. Look out for a stone globe 10 ft (3 metres) in diameter, flanked by panels giving sobering information on the nature of the universe; and for the ornate 17th-century town hall facade, made from the famous local marble.

This region is the **Isle of Purbeck** (although it is not an island at all) and is famous both for its marble and for its wonderful white sandy beaches. A whole swathe of the coast is National Trust land, designated the **Studland Beach and Nature Reserve**. As well as one of the best beaches in England, the area supports a variety of rare birds and plants, butterfly habitats and other wildlife. There are a number of public paths and nature trails, plus car parks and the usual National Trust facilities. There is also a clifftop walk westwards to lovely **Lulworth Cove** and the strangely eroded rock formation of **Durdle Door**.

At **Studland Heath**, the eastern tip of the area, a car ferry goes from Shell Bay to Sandbanks, giving access to Poole. Alternatively, take the A351/A350 via Wareham. **Poole** ㉔ is a thriving port sitting on a huge harbour and has a delightful quayside. Curving steps meet under the portico of the **Customs House** with its coat of arms representing an authority the Dorset smugglers never acknowledged. The **Waterfront Museum** (open daily 10am–5pm; entrance charge) has good displays on local history, and a section devoted to the Boy Scout movement, founded by Sir Robert Baden-Powell in 1908 after running the first Scout camp on nearby Brownsea Island.

A nautical welcome to the port of Poole.

BELOW:
Studland Beach on the Isle of Purbeck.

From the quay ferries run regularly to **Brownsea Island** (April–Oct, daily 10am–5pm; entrance charge), which is now National Trust-owned although part of it is leased to the Dorset Wildlife Trust as a nature reserve. A lovely area of heath and woodland, the island is a haven for the now-rare red squirrel, and has a waterfowl sanctuary and a number of good walks that give you great views over Poole Harbour. The island is also accessible by ferry from Swanage, Sandbanks and Bournemouth.

Map on pages 212–13

Bournemouth

Sedate and elegant **Bournemouth** ㉕ was established as a resort at the end of the 19th century and has remained popular ever since, largely due to a great sweep of sandy beach and the attractive parks and gardens that cover its surrounding cliffs. It now has all the accoutrements of a modern seaside resort: amusement arcades, clubs and discos, and a jolly little train which runs along the seafront. If you are there during the summer months, it's worth getting tickets for a performance by the Bournemouth Symphony Orchestra at the Winter Gardens Theatre. Bournemouth's best museum is the **Russell-Cotes Art Gallery** (open Tues–Sun 10am–5pm; entrance charge) which has good Oriental exhibits.

East of town, next to a ruined Norman castle, stands **Christchurch Priory**, which has an impressive Norman nave, although most of the remainder dates from the 13th to 16th centuries. If you've seen enough churches and castles for a while, you might just like to climb nearby **Hengistbury Head**, for splendid views over the Channel, or go a little farther to **Mudeford**, where bright beach huts line the shore and windsurfers whizzing across the bay provide entertainment on windy days. ❏

Ferries leave from Poole for the islands.

LEFT: nature's architecture formed Durdle Door.
BELOW: Bournemouth's sedate Town Hall.

BATH

Visitors no longer come to Bath to take the curative waters, but most go away feeling a lot better after even a short stay in this lively and beautiful city

Maps:
Area 236
City 226

Cradled in the folds of the Mendip Hills and dissected by the River Avon, **Bath** has a long history. The Romans built the baths which give it its name – they are among the most impressive Roman remains in the country – and after years as a popular spa it was transformed, early in the 18th century, into one of the most beautiful cities in Europe. In 1988 Bath was designated a UNESCO World Heritage Site. The transformation of the city was largely thanks to three men: Richard "Beau" Nash, a dandy and gambler and the town's master of ceremonies; Ralph Allen, a far-sighted businessman; and John Wood, an innovative architect. Their influence will be seen everywhere on this tour.

Our tour of Bath begins at the **Pump Room** Ⓐ (open April–Sept, daily 9am–6pm, Oct–Mar, Mon–Sat 9.30am–5pm) which was built in the 1790s. Here the therapeutic waters could be sampled in comfort but it was also a social arena complete with musical entertainment, a place to see and be seen. Admire the room from one of the elegant tables, entertained by the Pump Room Trio (Mon–Sat 10am–12.30pm, Sun 3–5pm), with a Bath bun and coffee to hand. At the far end of the room, a statue of Beau Nash presides over the scene, and in an alcove on the south side, overlooking the King's Bath, spa water is dispensed from a lovely late 19th-century drinking fountain graced by four stone trout.

LEFT: seeing Bath by balloon. **BELOW:** drinking fountain in the Pump Room.

FACT FILE

Location Set in the Mendip Hills, on the River Avon, some 110 miles (175 km) from London.
By car Easily accessible from London and the Midlands on the M4 and M5 motorways.
By coach National Express service from London Victoria Coach Station every 2hours; journey time approx. 3 hours 45 minutes; tel: 0990 808080.
By train First Great Western rail service from London Paddington to Bath Spa, journey time 1 hour 20 minutes; tel: 0345 484950.
By air Bristol Airport, near the M4/M5 junction; tel: 01275 474444.
Major attractions The Roman Baths, the Pump Room, the Abbey, the Assembly Rooms, Pulteney Bridge.
Guided walks From the Abbey Churchyard, Mon–Sat at 10.30am and 2pm, Sun 2.30pm, tel: 01225 477000.
For children The Puppet Theatre at Pulteney Bridge.
River and canal trips Tel: 0891 360396.
Excursions The American Museum at Claverton Manor.
Tourist Information Abbey Chambers, Abbey Churchyard, tel: 01225 477101; free publications such as *This Month in Bath* and *Bath Guide* provide detailed listings of what's on where.

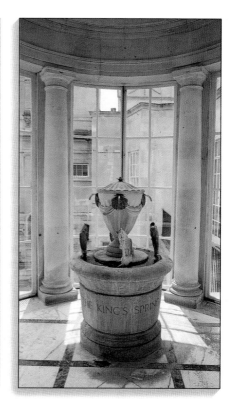

Pass through the Sun Room to the **Roman Baths** ❸ (open April–Sept, 9am–6pm, Aug 9am–6pm and 8–10pm, Oct–Mar 9.30am–5pm; entrance charge). The Great Bath, seen below on entering, was discovered in the 1880s during investigations into a leak in the King's Bath that was causing hot-water floods in local cellars. The Victorians were excited by archaeology and the past and the discovery was greeted with enormous interest throughout Britain.

From here the route leads down to the heart of the baths, the **Temple Precinct**, excavated in the early 1980s. The temple was built around AD60, on the site of the native Sanctuary of Sulis, a Celtic goddess associated with healing whom the Romans identified with their own goddess of healing, Minerva. Finds from the period include coins, votive offerings and petitions to the goddess. There are also curses inscribed on pewter or lead sheets, some written backwards. Other high-lights include the gilded bronze head of Minerva, discovered in 1727 by work-men, the first intimation of the marvellous Roman ruins below, the Gorgon's head which would have adorned the main Temple's pediment, the corner blocks of a sacrificial altar, and the Sea Beast mosaic.

The museum emerges next to the **Great Bath**, from where free guided tours leave every 15–20 minutes, taking in the East and West baths, and the medieval King's Bath. The Great Bath is the best place to see the water at close quarters, bubbling up at a temperature of 115°F (45°C) and laden with 43 minerals, including iron which stains the stone red. Its green colour is caused by light reacting with algae: when the baths were roofed over in Roman times, the water would have been clear. The **King's Bath**, overlooked by the Pump Room, is named after King Bladud, mythical founder of Bath, who, as a prince, suffered from leprosy and roamed the countryside as a swineherd. According to legend

In the ticket foyer of the baths stands a bath chair, invented in the early 19th century to replace the sedan chair. Requiring only one operator, the bath chair was cheap to run, but it could not provide the same bath-to-bed service as the sedan.

Bath's mythical founder, Bladud, is commemorated everywhere. Even the acorns topping the pediment of the Circus allude to his swineherd past.

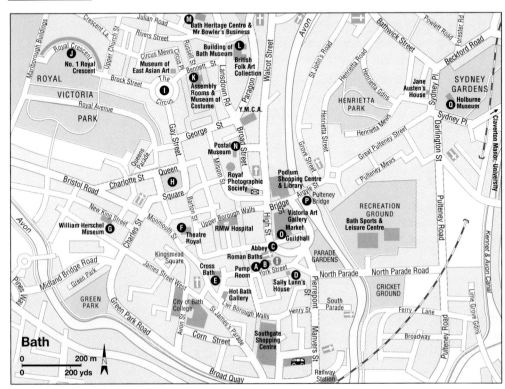

he was miraculously cured when he stumbled upon some hot springs. Duly rehabilitated, he went on to found the city on the site of the curative waters.

Map on page 226

The ancient abbey

From the Baths it is a short hop across Abbey Churchyard to **Bath Abbey** ❻ (open Mon–Sat 10am–4pm; donations welcomed; group tours by arrangement, tel: 01225 422462), the heart of medieval Bath. In 675 a Convent of Holy Virgins was founded here, and although there is no further record of the convent, there is evidence that a Saxon abbey existed by 781. Edgar, the first king of all England, was crowned in the abbey church in 973. He introduced the Benedictine monks who were to control the abbey and the town for the next 500 years.

In 1107, in the wake of the Norman conquest, the Bishop of Somerset moved the seat of the bishopric from Wells to Bath and built a Norman church on the site of the Saxon one. This lasted until 1499, when Bishop Oliver King rebuilt the church in the Perpendicular style characterised by flying buttresses, wide windows and fan vaulting. The Dissolution of the Monasteries by Henry VIII in 1539 brought the work to a halt, leaving the nave without a roof for many years.

Entertainment in the Abbey Churchyard.

The entrance to the abbey is through the **West Front**, with its Jacob's Ladder ("the angels of God ascending and descending on it": *Genesis 28: 12–17*). Inside, the vast windows fill the abbey with light. The east window depicts 56 scenes from the life of Christ in brilliant stained glass. Overhead stretches the lovely fan vaulting. One of the delights of the abbey are the memorials to famous residents and guests who died in Bath for want of the desired cure. Don't miss the one dedicated to Beau Nash ("Ricardi Nash, Elegantiae Arbiter"), who died at the age of 86, impoverished and enfeebled. A door on the south side

LEFT: Bath Abbey.
BELOW:
the Great Bath.

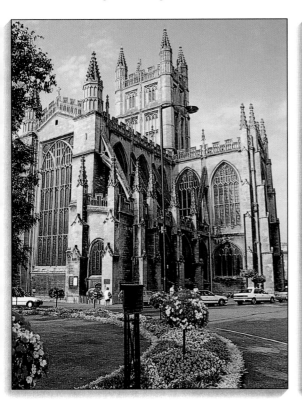

Home of the famous Sally Lunn bun.

In the 1770s Richard Sheridan set his satire, "The Rivals", in Bath, although he made his name with it on the London stage.

BELOW: the glorious sweep of Royal Crescent.

leads to the **Heritage Vaults** (open Mon–Sat 10am–4pm) tracing the history of the abbey from Saxon times to the present day.

From the abbey, take North Parade Passage to **Sally Lunn's House** (open daily from 10am; evening restaurant from 6pm), a restaurant-cum-museum in the oldest house in Bath (15th-century, with a prettified 17th-century facade). It is famous for a highly versatile kind of bun, made on the premises since the 1680s. Its Cellar Museum contains the ancient kitchen with a 17th-century oven and archaeological finds excavated on the site.

West of the Pump Room, along colonnaded Bath Street, is the **Cross Bath** , an oasis of tranquillity with its curvaceous lines and delicate carvings. During the 17th century the bath had a reputation for curing sterility. Mary of Modena, the wife of James II, conceived a much-needed heir after bathing here. A succession of baths have been built on this spot, below which the coolest of Bath's three hot springs rises. The current building was begun by Thomas Baldwin in 1791. Both this and the nearby **Hot Bath** are due for restoration in the year 2000. The latter was fed by the hottest spring, which also served an adjacent "lepers' bath" for people with skin diseases.

Georgian elegance

Head now to Sawclose and the **Theatre Royal** one of the oldest and loveliest theatres in England, which attracted some of the best-known actors of the late 18th century – such as David Garrick and Sarah Siddons. The Royal presents a year-round programme of plays, opera, dance and concerts (tel: 01225 448844) and there are backstage tours on Wednesday and Saturday. From the theatre, go up Monmouth Street and turn left for the **William Herschel Museum** (open

Mar–Oct, daily 2–5pm, Nov–Feb, Sat–Sun 2–5pm; entrance charge), the home and observatory of Herschel, who came here from Hanover in 1761 as an organist, and became musical director of the Assembly Rooms. From this garden, with the aid of a home-made telescope, he discovered Uranus in 1781. He was subsequently appointed Director of the Royal Astronomical Society.

Queen Square ❶ is our next stop. It was built in the 1730s by John Wood the Elder, the architect credited with introducing the Palladian style to Bath. The north side, with Roman portico, is particularly striking. Up Gay Street now to **The Circus ❶**, again designed by John Wood, although completed after his death by his son. This was England's first circular street and there is a wealth of architectural detail, not least the three types of column on the facades: Doric at the bottom, Ionic in the middle, and Corinthian at the top.

John Wood the Younger designed another architectural first: the **Royal Crescent ❶**, built from 1767–74, a short walk west of The Circus. This is Bath's star turn, set in a dramatic position above Royal Victoria Park, and comprising 30 separate properties. **No. 1 Royal Crescent** has become a museum (open Feb–end Oct, Tues–Sun 10.30am–5pm; entrance charge), restored and furnished by the Bath Preservation Trust as it would have been in the 18th century. The Crescent had its share of famous residents: Isaac Pitman, inventor of shorthand, lived at No. 17; and Elizabeth Linley, who was painted by Gainsborough and who eloped with playwright Richard Sheridan, lived at No. 11.

Retrace your steps now past The Circus to the **Assembly Rooms and Museum of Costume ❶** (open daily 10am–5pm, except when booked for functions; admission free to rooms, entrance charge to museum). The magnificent ballroom is lit by cut-glass chandeliers, and there are separate rooms for

Bikes and rickshaws can be hired in Bath.

BELOW: flirtatious performers in the Assembly Rooms.

THE SEASON

The elegant environment created by Nash, Allen and Wood drew the cream of fashionable society during the 18th century. The main "season" was September to May, with most visitors staying from six weeks to three months. From the moment the Abbey bells pealed out to welcome the new arrivals, days were a round of bathing, visiting, play-going and dancing, so finely captured by Jane Austen (1775–1817) in her novels.

Mornings began with a dip in the baths followed by a turn around the Pump Room and breakfast in the Assembly Rooms; afternoons were divided between shops, coffee houses and gaming tables. Twice a week a ball was held at one of the assembly rooms; other nights might be spent at the theatre, where Sarah Siddons held audiences spellbound during the 1770s, or at a concert by the *castrato* Venanzio Rauzzini, for whom Mozart wrote *Exultate Jubilate* in 1774.

At the end of the century Bath began to lose its lustre, as the upper classes deserted it for Tunbridge Wells, Cheltenham and, later, Brighton, where George IV had built the flamboyant Pavilion. Bath turned into a residential city favoured by the professional classes in search of a comfortable but relatively inexpensive living.

Samba dancers at Bath's annual festival.

gambling and taking tea. The Museum of Costume is dedicated to the fickleness of fashion over the past four centuries, with the exhibits on the Georgian period being the most fascinating.

Building, business and banquets

Go north from here, up Paragon, to the **Building of Bath Museum** ⓛ (open mid-Feb–1 Dec, Tues–Sun 10.30am–5pm; entrance charge) which offers an illuminating account of the talents and techniques that created the facades of the city. Across the courtyard is the **British Folk Art Collection** (open Tues–Sat 10.30am–5pm, April–Oct, also Sun 2–5pm; entrance charge), devoted to 18th- and 19th-century arts and crafts and with a shop selling unusual gifts.

The next stop, in nearby Julian Road, is the **Bath Heritage Centre and Mr Bowler's Business** ⓜ (open Easter–31 Oct, daily 10am–5pm, Nov–Easter, Sat–Sun 10am–5pm; entrance charge). The museum relates the story of a 19th-century family firm which operated for 100 years without, it seems, ever throwing anything away. You can wander through the workshop, storeroom, office and factory and imagine yourself back in a less-fashionable part of Bath.

Retrace your steps down Paragon to Broad Street and the **Bath Postal Museum** ⓝ (open Mon–Sat 11am–5pm; entrance charge), from where the world's first postage stamp, the Penny Black, was sent in May 1840. Exhibits track the history of the postal service and touch on some delightful peripheral topics, such as a collection of cupid-covered Victorian Valentine cards.

It's not far now to the **Guildhall** ⓞ, designed in the Adam style in the 1770s by the young Thomas Baldwin who went on to become the city architect. The **Banqueting Hall** (open Mon–Fri 8.30am–5.30pm when it is not booked for

BELOW: Mr Bowler conducting his business.

functions; admission free) is splendid, lined with portraits of of city notables and lit by the finest chandeliers in the city.

Next door is a covered market, a lively cut-through to **Grand Parade**, and then the **Victoria Art Gallery** (open Tues–Sun 2–5pm; entrance charge; entrance on Bridge Street). Several Sickerts and a Whistler are on display along with Gainsborough portraits and J. M. W. Turner's *West Front of Bath Abbey*.

Bridge Street leads to **Pulteney Bridge** ❷, designed by Robert Adam from 1770 to 1774 and lined, like the Pontevecchio in Florence, with tiny shops on either side. On the right side of the bridge steps lead down to the Avon, from where river cruises depart every hour or so, and there are riverside walks to North Parade Bridge. There's also a little café below the bridge which doubles as a puppet theatre and is a big hit with children.

At the east end of imposing **Great Pulteney Street** (another Thomas Baldwin design) is the **Holburne Museum** ❿ (open mid-Feb–mid-Dec, Mon–Sat 11am–5pm, Sun 2.30–5.30pm; entrance charge), housed in an elegant 18th-century mansion which was originally the Sydney Hotel. Among many fine works on display are paintings by Turner, Stubbs, Reynolds and Gainsborough. The latter made his name in Bath, portraying the rich and famous.

The museum stands on the edge of **Sydney Gardens**, which are frequently mentioned in the letters of Jane Austen, who lived nearby at No. 4 Sydney Place from 1801 to 1804, as the scene of public galas and fireworks displays. In the 19th century they were the site of daring balloon ascents The gardens are dissected by Brunel's Great Western Railway (1840–41) and the Kennet and Avon Canal (1810), elegantly incorporated by means of landscaped cuttings and pretty stone and cast-iron bridges. ❑

Map on page 226

TIP

Bath International Music Festival, late May to early June, presents 17 days of music featuring well-known orchestras, ensembles and soloists; tel: 01225 463362 for details.

BELOW: Pulteney Bridge by night.

THE AMERICAN MUSEUM

Visiting an American Museum in a city with a Roman and Georgian heritage may seem odd, but this one is rather special. It is housed in Claverton Manor, set in grounds based on George Washington's garden at Mount Vernon, overlooking a beautiful wooded valley, yet barely 3 miles (5 km) from the city.

A series of rooms have been furnished in different styles: there's the 18th-century Deer Park Parlor from Maryland; the Greek Revival Room, based on a mid-19th century New York dining room; and the New Orleans Bedroom which, with blood-red wallpaper and ornate Louis XV-style bed, evokes the ante-bellum world of Scarlett O'Hara.

There are also galleries devoted to the history of Native Americans, to westward expansion, to whaling, and to American crafts such as quilting and Shaker furniture. A programme of special events features re-enactments of Civil War camp life and Independence Day displays. Opening hours: mid-Mar–early Nov, Tues–Sun 2–5pm; garden open from 1pm weekdays, noon at weekends; entrance charge; tel: 01225 460503. You can reach the museum by bus to the university then 10 minutes' walk; or by car via the A36 towards Bradford-on-Avon.

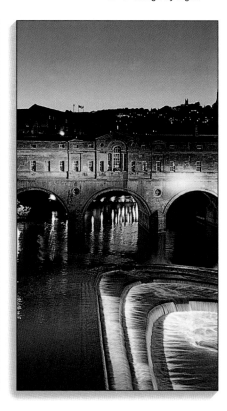

THE WEST COUNTRY

A tour around England's southwestern corner offers a wide variety of scenery, architecture and activities, and the best climate in the country in which to enjoy them

Map on page 236

The West Country is many things to many people. For some it's the bleak moorlands of Bodmin, Dartmoor and Exmoor; for others it is quaint fishing villages and artists' colonies, or the gardens for which Cornwall is famous. This chapter will attempt to offer a little of everything.

The tour starts at **Bath ❶** (*see page 225*) then goes 8 miles (13 km) east to the former mill town of **Bradford-on-Avon ❷**, which focuses on the picturesque main bridge, has one of the best Saxon churches in the country – St Laurence's, founded in 700 – a collection of weavers' cottages and Georgian townhouses, and an impressive 14th-century tithe barn on the edge of town. Bikes can be hired to cycle along the towpath to the nearby village of Avoncliff.

Bristol to Exmouth

After this we go northwest of Bath on the A4 to **Bristol ❸**, a major port since the time of the Phoenicians. Among many sites of interest are the **Cathedral**, founded in 1140: the Eastern Lady Chapel with its rich colouring is especially interesting. From here, Park Street rises to Bristol University, the City Museum and Art Gallery, and Clifton Village, where Isambard Kingdom Brunel's **Suspension Bridge** spans the Avon gorge. Back in the centre, the **Watershed** is a

PRECEDING PAGES: stark cliffs at Botallak.
LEFT: riding the waves.
BELOW: bridge at Bradford-on-Avon .

FACT FILE

The gateways to the West Country are Bath, Bristol, Exeter and Plymouth

By rail Westbound trains leave from London Paddington about every half hour for all the above destinations. Journey times: about 1 hour 30 minutes to Bath and Bristol; 2 hours 30 minutes to Exeter; 3 hours to Plymouth. For all rail information, tel: 0345 484950.

By coach National Express coaches from London Victoria; journey times: about 3 hours 15 minutes to Bath; 3 hours 30 minutes to Bristol; 4 hours 45 minutes to Exeter; 5 hours to Plymouth. For information, tel: 0990 808080.

By car Bath and Bristol are easily accessible from London via the M4, Exeter via the M5, fed from London by the M4, from the north by the M6, Plymouth via the M5/A38.

Some major attractions Wells Cathedral, Dartmoor, Exmoor, Bodmin Moor, Tintagel Castle, St Michael's Mount.

Best museum Tate Gallery, St Ives, tel: 01736 796226.

Walking trails Devon Tourist Information Service, P.O.Box 55, Barnstaple, EX32 8YR; guided walks around Dartmoor, tel: 01626 832093; for Exmoor: tel: 01398 323841.

Tourist Information Exeter, tel: 01392 265700; Plymouth, tel: 01752 264849; Penzance, tel: 01736 62207; St Ives, tel: 01736 796297.

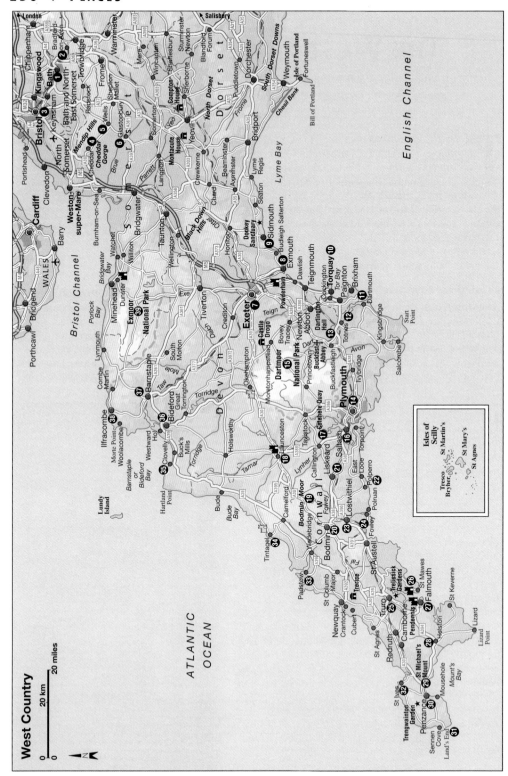

West Country

Map on page 236

pleasant complex of shops, bars and restaurants on the Floating Harbour, and you can visit the *SS Great Britain* (open summer, daily 10am–6pm, winter till 5pm; entrance charge). Designed by Brunel (1806–59), the ship represents Bristol's heyday as a shipbuilding centre. The nearby **Maritime Heritage Museum** (same hours as ship) tells you more about Bristol's seagoing history, and the excellent **Industrial Museum** (open Tues–Sun 10am–5pm; entrance charge), on the quay, presents another aspect of the town's development.

From Bristol take the A38 towards **Cheddar Gorge ❹**, at 3 miles (5 km) long the biggest gorge in England, carved out of karst limestone by the River Yeo. **Gough's Caves** (open summer, daily 10am–5pm, winter, 10.30am–4.30pm; entrance charge) were discovered by Richard Gough in 1890, and 13 years later the skeleton of the 9,000-year-old Cheddar Man was found here. A walkway leads through a series of stalactite-encrusted chambers. In the main village street the **Cheddar Gorge Cheese Co** (open April–Sept, daily 10am–6pm) has a working dairy which documents the history of England's most popular cheese.

The A371 leads southeast from Cheddar to **Wells ❺** a sleepy market town centred on the stunning **Cathedral Church of St Andrew** (open daily 8am–7pm; donations welcomed; *floorplan, see page 398*). Among the many highlights of this early-English Gothic building are the intricately carved West Front, the Choir, with England's oldest Jesse Window, the honey-coloured stone Chapter House, and the extraordinary 14th-century scissor arches. Also well worth a visit is the **Bishop's Palace** (open Easter–end Oct, Tues–Fri 10am–6pm, Sun 2–6pm, daily in Aug; entrance charge), approached over a drawbridge spanning the moat. The ruins of the 13th-century Great Hall stand in tranquil grounds, where you will also see the springs which gave the town its name.

TIP

Admission to Gough's Caves includes entrance to the nearby Cox's Cave, where the Crystal Quest presents a subterranean battle between good and evil, which children usually love.

BELOW: Glastonbury's ancient abbey.

GLASTONBURY

Glastonbury ❻ is best known these days as the site of a hugely popular rock festival held over the summer solstice, its profits donated to charity. But Glastonbury is also the site of the oldest Christian foundation in Britain. The ruined abbey is built on the site of an earlier church, founded in the 1st century when Joseph of Arimethea is believed to have brought here either the Holy Grail or the Blood of the Cross. The winter-flowering hawthorns in the abbey grounds are said to have sprung up when Joseph dug his staff into the ground. Three early kings – Edmund I (died 946), Edgar (died 975) and Edmund Ironside (died 1016) – are buried here.

The existing buildings date from 1184–1303, when Glastonbury was the richest abbey in England, after Westminster. They fell into ruin after the Dissolution of the Monasteries in the 1530s. The remains of a warrior and his female companion interred in front of the high altar are identified by local legend as those of King Arthur and Queen Guinevere.

Glastonbury Tor, high above the little town, offers views as far as the Bristol Channel. On this spot the last abbot and his treasurer were executed in 1539 for opposing Henry VIII.

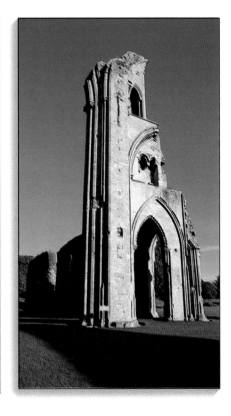

Mol's Coffee House.

Now it's time to get on the M5 motorway and go straight to the university town of **Exeter** ❼. The Roman city wall was completed in AD 200: much of it still stands and most main sites are within its circumference. The focal point is the **Cathedral Church of St Peter** ❶, largely 14th-century but with two Norman towers. The most significant feature is the fan vaulting of the world's longest Gothic vault. In the elegant Cathedral Close the most eye-catching building is 16th-century **Mol's Coffee House** ❷, sadly a coffee house no longer, where Sir Francis Drake (1540–96) is said to have met his sea captains.

Beneath the pavements of the nearby pedestrianised High Street are the **Underground Passages** ❸ (open Jul–Sept and school holidays, Mon–Sat 10am–5.30pm; Oct–June, Tues–Fri 2–5pm, Sat 10am–5pm; entrance charge), 14th-century subterranean aqueducts through which you can take an entertaining guided tour. At the top end of Gandy Street (enlivened with murals) is the **Exeter & Devon Arts Centre** ❹, which has a popular café and a heavy schedule of events. Straight ahead stands the **Royal Albert Memorial Museum** ❺ (open Mon–Sat 10am–5pm; admission free), an imposing edifice with local and natural history, archaeology and fine arts on display in its galleries. Descending to the River Exe and the cobbled **Quayside** ❻ you'll find shops and cafés, plus boats for hire. Visit the **Quay House Visitor Centre** (open April–Oct daily 10am–5pm; admission free) for an audio-visual local history presentation.

Sand, sea and sanctuary

BELOW: Exeter's Maritime Museum.

South of the city, where the estuary meets the sea, is **Exmouth** ❽ (take the A376). Its 2 miles (3 km) of golden sand are the finest in East Devon, and made it the county's first beach resort, in the 18th century. To the east (A3052) is

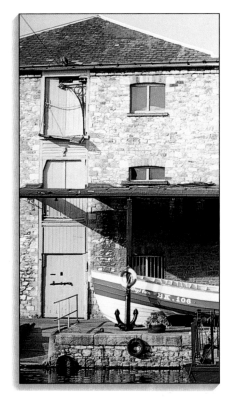

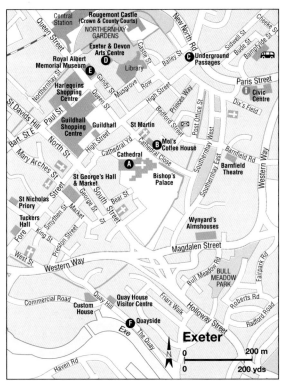

Sidmouth **⑨**, the most attractive and best preserved of East Devon's resorts. Narrow lanes back on to a grand seafront dominated by Regency houses and the shingle beach is framed by cliffs. Just east of the town is the **Donkey Sanctuary** (open daily 9am–dusk; admission free; tel: 01395 578222), a rest home for abused and abandoned donkeys which incorporates nine farms and 160 staff.

Head west after this short diversion, via the A379, down the west side of the estuary, to **Powderham Castle** (open April–end Oct, Sun–Fri 10am–5.30pm; entrance charge; guided tours). This dramatic medieval fortress is set in a deer park, and has a lakeside picnic area and a Children's Secret Garden.

The English Riviera

The road continues via **Teignmouth**, to the great sweep of Tor Bay, and **Torquay ⑩**, a town which likes to emphasise its Mediterranean influences. At night, with the illuminations on, palm trees rustling and people promenading, it could almost be part of the French Riviera. The **Pavilion** on the seafront is a wonderful example of Edwardian wedding-cake architecture.

On the north side of town, reached by the **Oddicombe Cliff Railway** (April–Oct), an attraction in itself, is the **Babbacombe Model Village** (open Easter–Sept, daily 9am–10pm, Oct–Easter, till dusk; ; entrance charge) a microcosm of contemporary England that is particularly inviting when the lights go on at dusk. A couple of miles east is **Kent's Cavern** (open daily 10am–5pm; entrance charge) a network of limestone caves with a massive bear fossilised in a chamber roof. The guided tour is good, but many of the best remains are in the **Torquay Museum** (open Mon–Sat 10am–4.45pm; entrance charge) at the foot of Babbacombe Road.

Maps:
Area 236
City 238

Safe at the Donkey Sanctuary.

BELOW: luxury mooring for sailors in Torquay harbour.

TIP

Dart Pleasure Craft,
tel: 01803 834488,
have daily sailings
from Dartmouth to
Totnes in summer, and
various other cruises
all year round.

Torquay blends seamlessly into Paignton, which has little of the former's elegance, but does have two of the region's best stretches of sand, one off the promenade, the other at **Goodrington**, reached by the **Paignton & Dartmouth Steam Railway** (April–Oct), which chugs through attractive scenery. Behind Goodrington is **Paignton Zoo** (open daily 10am–6pm; entrance charge; tel: 01803 697500) where a number of recreated environments provide a home for some 1,000 animals, many of them endangered species on international breeding programmes.

Brixham is the third town in Torbay, a pretty resort where tourism and fishing harmoniously co-exist. The harbour area, with its active fish market, has real character, and there's a replica here of the *Golden Hind*, the ship that took Sir Francis Drake around the world.

Maritime towns

Take the A379 south now to Kingswear, clinging to the steep banks of the Dart Estuary, from where it is a short ferry ride to **Dartmouth ⓫**, where the waters are thick with boats in one of England's best anchorages. Dartmouth has a long maritime history and a strong naval presence, with the Britannia Royal Naval College on the hill. The town focuses on the **Boat Fleet** (an inner harbour) and the streets running off it, crowded with historic buildings with fine frontages. Duke Street, with a 17th-century Butterwalk, leads to pretty Foss Street and a solid old market, built round a cobbled square.

Just outside town, clamped to a shoulder of rock, is the formidable **Dartmouth Castle** (open April–Oct, daily 10am–6pm, Nov–Mar, Wed–Sun till 4pm; entrance charge). It comprises the original 14th-century castle, a Victorian fort and 17th-century St Petrock's Church.

From Dartmouth you can take the coastal route past **Blackpool Sands**, a lovely golden curve of beach, and **Slapton Ley**, where an inland lake is thick with freshwater birds, on to **Kingsbridge** and **Salcombe**, the latter a fishing village which has become a popular yachting centre, and then on to Plymouth. However, this tour takes you inland to **Totnes ⓬**, an elegant town often described as Elizabethan although its history goes back much further than that. Its face has not changed for centuries, the castle concealed from view by a tumble of houses and the arch of the East Gate spanning the main street.

The **Guildhall** is a lovely building with a pillared portico, and 15th-century St Mary's Church has a delicate Saxon rood screen. In the granite-pillared Butterwalk an Elizabethan market is held on summer Tuesdays, with traders in period dress. Turn right, and **Totnes Castle** (open April–Oct, daily 10am–5pm; entrance fee) soon comes into view, a perfectly preserved Norman motte and bailey structure.

Just off the A384, 2 miles (3 km) north of Totnes, is the gracious 14th-century **Dartington Hall ⓭**, the nerve centre of the Dartington Estate, run by philanthropists Leonard and Dorothy Elmhirst. The hall has a cobbled quad and magnificent hammer-beamed Great Hall; outside, sculptures and a grassy-banked amphitheatre are set in mature woodland. Most visited

BELOW: a steep street in Dartmouth.

is the **Dartington Cider Press Centre** (open Mon–Sat 9.30am–5.30pm, Easter–Christmas also Sun 10.30am–5.30pm), a group of shops and workshops, whose high-quality products reflect the Dartington emphasis on local crafts.

Follow the road to the A38, where you will find **Buckfast Abbey** (open daily 9am–5.30pm; entrance charge), an 11th-century foundation bought in 1882 by a group of French Benedictines who dedicated their lives to its restoration. There are 38 monks there now, keeping bees and making and selling tonic wine.

Now take the A38 straight to **Plymouth ⑭**, the largest conurbation in Devon. Being a naval base, it was a strategic target and badly bombed during World War II. Subsequent building leaves much to be desired. The **Hoe** survived, a broad grassy shoulder between town and sea, where Francis Drake was playing bowls when the Spanish Armada was sighted (1588). **Smeaton's Tower** (the current lighthouse) stands on the Hoe, not far from the formidable walls of the **Royal Citadel** (guided tours in summer, noon and 2pm). A short walk north is the **Barbican**, a corner of old Plymouth preserved, and Sutton Harbour, where fishing and leisure boats mingle.

Sir Francis Drake looks out to sea.

Dartmoor National Park

Dartmoor National Park ⑮ covers some 365 sq. miles (945 sq. km). Reaching 2,000 ft (600 metres), the moor is the highest land in southern England: around half is open moorland, the rest steep wooded valleys with secluded villages. We enter from **Tavistock** on the B3357, which leads to the **High Moorland Visitor Centre** – with well-presented displays, and information on guided walks – and **Princetown**, the highest, bleakest settlement, with Dartmoor Prison looming nearby. The road continues to **Widecombe-in-the-Moor**, a captivating

BELOW: Buckfast Abbey after its restoration.

WEST DEVON HIGHLIGHTS

Saltram House (open April–Oct, Sun–Thurs 12.30–5.30pm; National Trust) set in 470 acres (190 hectares) of grounds in Plymouth's eastern suburbs. Virtually all the furnishings are original, which is rare; there are portraits by Sir Joshua Reynolds and a magnificent salon, reworked by Robert Adam in the 1770s.

Buckland Abbey (open April–Oct, Nov–Dec Fri–Wed 10.30am–5.30pm, mid-Feb–March, Sat–Sun 2–5pm; National Trust), 11 miles (16 km) north of Plymouth, was a 13th-century Cistercian monastery, and the vast barn and abbey church are original. Sir Francis Drake (1540–96), the first Englishman to navigate the globe, and the man who brought potatoes and tobacco from Virginia to England, bought it in 1580, and the rooms house an exhibition devoted to his life.

Morwelham Quay (open daily 10am–5.30pm; tel: 01822 832766 for winter closing times; entrance charge), a few miles north, set in a Designated Area of Natural Beauty at the highest navigable point on the Tamar, is a superbly presented reconstruction of industry and transport in Victorian times. A small railway takes visitors into the disused copper mine, and there are a variety of trails, museums, workshops and children's activities.

little place with two claims to fame: the well-known song which advertises its annual fair in September (*see left*), and its church, known as the cathedral of the moor, because of the height of its tower. Narrow lanes south lead to two pretty villages, **Buckland-in-the-Moor**, with some of the most photographed thatched cottages in Devon; and **Holne**, birthplace in 1819 of writer Charles Kingsley, where you'll find the 14th-century Church House Inn.

Back on the B3357 you will soon reach **Hay Tor** (1,490 ft/450 metres), with far-reaching views; and **Becky Falls** (open March–Oct, daily 10am–6pm, or dusk if earlier; entrance charge), where there are nature trails and woodland walks through pleasant woodland, plus a restaurant, gift shop and picnic area surrounding the waterfalls. Nearby the little granite-built town of **Bovey Tracey** is worth a stop for the **Devon Guild of Craftsmen** (open daily 10am–5.30pm; tel: 01626 832223), housed in an historic riverside mill. You will find a high-quality selection of ceramics, glass and textiles on display and for sale.

Take the A382 towards Okehampton, where a right turn leads to Drewsteignton and **Castle Drogo** (open April–Oct, Sat–Thurs 11am–5.30pm; National Trust), the last castle to be built in England, begun in 1910, and designed by Sir Edwin Lutyens. The formal terraced gardens are open all year.

Now join the A30 to visit the market town of **Okehampton**, where the **Museum of Dartmoor Life** (open daily 10am–5pm; entrance charge) offers detailed visitor-friendly insights into life on the moor. Okehampton's **Castle** (open daily 10am–6pm; entrance charge) has been a ruin since seized by Henry VIII in 1538 but its hilltop setting, with a riverside picnic area below, is delightful. You could go north from here, but our tour follows the road south past lovely **Lydford Gorge** (National Trust) back to Plymouth and into Cornwall.

Across the Tamar

It is said that nothing has done more to keep Cornwall Cornish than the River Tamar. To get a sense of how different from Devon it is, cross via Brunel's **Royal Albert Bridge** (toll payable) at **Saltash** , where there are some interesting things to see: 18th-century houses cluster on the quayside and the home of Drake's first wife, **Mary Newman's Cottage**, can be visited in summer. Outside town stands the imposing Norman church of **St Germans**, and there are several stately homes in the vicinity: **Trematon Castle** (also Norman) can only be glimpsed from the road, but **Antony House** (tel: 01752 812191; National Trust) and **Mount Edgcumbe House** (tel: 01752 822236) are open to the public. Our route takes you north, leaving the main road to visit **Cotehele Quay** (open April–Oct 11am–5pm; National Trust; tel: 01579 351346), perched above the wooded river banks, where there's a medieval house, remarkably unchanged, and a collection of wharf buildings, with a watermill, forge and cider press.

Rejoin the main road now (A388) to **Launceston**, Cornwall's only walled town, founded in the 11th century. **Launceston Castle** (open April–Oct, daily 10am–6pm; English Heritage) sits in immaculate grounds, with views across Bodmin and Dartmoor. The 16th-century parish church, **St Mary Magdalene**, covered with decorative motifs, is the town's other most interesting building. The **Launceston Steam Railway** (Whitsun–end Sept, daily; tel: 01566 775665) with a museum, workshop and buffet, will take you on a trip down memory lane.

Broody Bodmin

Pick up the A30 here and follow it through the brooding, magnificent **Bodmin Moor**. The road enters the moorland at Altarnun, where you can visit the

Brunel's bridge at Saltash.

LEFT: Launceston, from the castle
BELOW: rock formations on Bodmin Moor.

Jamaica Inn, where mysterious things happened.

BELOW: sunset over Lostwithiel's Castle.

Wesley Cottage (open daily 9am–dusk; admission free) where John Wesley (1703–91), founder of Methodism, stayed when preaching in Cornwall. At Bolventor you can visit the **Jamaica Inn** (open April–Oct, daily 10am–5pm; entrance charge) for a theatrical presentation of Daphne du Maurier's story and a collection of smuggling relics. In the courtyard **Mr Potter's Museum of Curiosity** (open Feb–Dec, daily 10am–5pm; entrance charge) is one of the last real Victorian museums, notable for its anthropomorphic stuffed animals.

A minor road follows the River Fowey passing, on your right, **Dozmary Pool**, in the wildest part of the moor. Fed by underground springs it is the stuff of legend: according to Alfred Lord Tennyson, it was here that King Arthur's sword was consigned to the waters after his death. Next you come to **Siblyback Lake**, where there are watersports and you can obtain a day ticket to fish for trout; and, a little further south, **St Cleer's Holy Well**, whose waters were reputed to cure madness.

You are close to Liskeard here, and roads to the coast, but an exploration of the moor is best rounded off by a visit to **Bodmin ⑳**, the western gateway, an old trade route from Ireland which attracted early saints. St Petroc, Cornwall's senior saint, founded a priory here in the 6th century (only fragments remain), and the 15th-century **Church of St Petroc** houses a cask containing his remains. This is the county's largest church and its Norman font is probably the best.

Bodmin Museum (open Easter–Sept, Mon–Fri 10.30am–4.30pm; for other times tel: 01208 77067; admission free) has good exhibitions on local life through the ages. There's a nostalgic taste of sulphur on the **Bodmin & Wenford Steam Railway** (Easter–Oct and Dec, daily; tel: 01208 77963 for special events). Bodmin's bypass skirts the grounds of **Lanhydrock House** (open

April–Oct, Tues–Sun 11am–5.30pm; National Trust), a place with a pleasing lived-in atmosphere. Highlights are the long gallery with a splendid plaster-work ceiling, and extensive grounds planted with rare shrubs. Double back now to **Liskeard** ㉑ on the A 38. Its tin mining heyday is long gone, but there's still a wealth of Georgian buildings, a Regency Market Hall and the **Stuart House**, where Charles I spent several nights during the Civil War (1642–46). In Well Lane, water from the 16th-century **Pipe Well** is said to have curative properties.

Jewels of the coast

Down to the coast now to **Looe Bay**, where East and West Looe are linked by a bridge. The former is the larger and more prosperous, dependent on tourism and the revived fishing industry.

Go west a few miles to **Polperro** ㉒, which lives up to its reputation as one of Cornwall's most picturesque fishing villages. Clinging to the steep hillside, colour-washed cottages bedecked with flowers crowd the narrow alleys, many of them inhabited by artists who come here seeking inspiration. The paths winding up the hill offer splendid views over the harbour.

Briefly inland now to **Lostwithiel** ㉓, once Cornwall's capital, a serene, rather French-looking place beside the Fowey. There are many attractive 18th-century buildings in the town, and the 14th-century **Duchy Palace** stands in Quay Street. **Lostwithiel Museum** (open Easter–Sept, Mon–Sat 10.30am–12.30pm, 2.30–4.30pm; entrance charge), housed in the old prison, has an excellent collection of local photographs.

Fowey ㉔ (pronounced Foy), at the mouth of the river of the same name, is a lovely place, its houses huddled daintily above a deep-water harbour, one of

Map on page 236

TIP

In a disused clay pit near St Austell the biggest greenhouse in the world is being built. The Eden Project aims to recreate the tropical rainforest and other climates in a "green world".

BELOW: the church and quay at Fowey.

A local fisherman.

BELOW: Cornwall's gardens glow with rich colour.

the south coast's best sailing areas. Fowey has a proud past: it sent 47 ships and 700 men to the Siege of Calais during the Hundred Years' War (1337–1453). The following century, above **Readymoney Cove**, Henry VIII built a fort, **St Catherine's Castle**, which contains the mausoleum of the locally powerful Rashleigh family: their town house is now the Ship Hotel.

The **Fowey Town Museum** (open Easter and Whitsun–Oct, Mon–Fri 10.30am–12.30pm, 2–4.30pm), housed in a building that once served as a prison, commemorates the town's maritime past.

From Truro to Land's End

Leaving Fowey, take the A3082 which joins the A390 to **St Austell** and on to **Truro ㉕** – every inch a city, although the ring road has separated its heart from its maritime heritage. The triple towers of the neo-Gothic **Cathedral** soar above the the the rooftops of 18th-century houses. **Lemon Street** is one of the most homogenous Georgian streets in England. The City Hall hosts regular flea markets and the Pannier Market offers a glimpse of bygone days. The past is well documented in the **Royal Cornwall Museum** (open Mon–Sat 10am–5pm; entrance charge) which has a superb collection of archaeological finds, local and natural history, ceramics and costume.

Turn off the A39 onto the B3289 to reach **St Mawes ㉖**, on the Roseland Peninsula. Ferries bustle in and out of the harbour, and yacht owners fill the Victory Inn. Pretty thatched cottages line the seafront road to the three huge circular bastions of **St Mawes Castle** (open Easter–Sept, daily 10am–6pm, Oct–Easter, Fri–Tues 10am–4pm; English Heritage), built by Henry VIII in 1543 as defence against a French attack from the sea. The garden of **Lamorran**

CORNISH GARDENS

Cornwall's mild climate has produced some beautiful gardens. Among the best are:

Glendurgan, which is set in a wooded valley near Falmouth. Rare and exotic sub-tropical plants and an unusual 19th-century laurel maze; plants for sale; National Trust; tel: 01872 862090.

Trebah, Falmouth. Hydrangeas, rhododendrons and azaleas plus a water garden and cascades; colour all year round; tel: 01326 250781.

Lost Gardens of Heligan, Pentewan, St Austell. These "lost" Victorian gardens have recently been renovated. The Italian garden, kitchen garden, walled garden and "jungle" area have been returned to their former glory; tel: 01726 845101.

Trelissick, near Truro. This is a plantsman's garden, famous for its tender exotic plants and shrubs, as well as its delightful setting; National Trust; tel: 01872 862090

Trewithen, Truro. Internationally known for its camellias, rhododendrons, magnolias, plus many rare trees and shrubs; tel: 01726 883647.

Caerhays Castle, Gorran, St Austell. An informal woodland garden overlooking the sea. Camellias, magnolias and rhododendrons; tel: 01872 501144.

House (open April–Oct, Wed and Fri 10am–5pm; entrance charge) in Upper Castle Road has a Mediterranean feel, with palms and sub-tropical plants flourishing on the hillside (*see below left for more Cornish gardens*). Level with the top of the tower below, the lich-gate of the church of **St Just-in-Roseland** frames what may be the most perfect view in Cornwall. The 13th-century church itself, reflected in St Just Pool, is almost as pleasing.

On the other side of the estuary called the Carrick Roads lies **Falmouth** ② (there's a ferry in summer; otherwise return to Truro and continue on the A39). The town developed after Sir Walter Raleigh (1552–1618) decided it would make a good harbour. Henry VIII built **Pendennis Castle** (open April–Sept, daily 10am–6pm, Oct–Mar, till 4pm; English Heritage) at the same time as the one at St Mawes, but the expected French attack never came. The castle today has a good museum and discovery centre, and access to formerly secret installations. The town received a charter in 1661 and the church of King Charles the Martyr was built the following year.

The **Cornwall Maritime Museum** (open April–Oct, Mon–Sat 10am–5pm, Nov–Mar, till 3pm; entrance charge) has exhibits on the Royal Mail packet ships, oyster fisheries and other maritime artefacts. The Customs House is imposing, with its Doric columns, and the **Falmouth Art Gallery** (open Mon–Fri 10am–5pm, Sat 10am–1pm; admission free) has frequently changing exhibitions of paintings, sculpture, photographs and textiles.

Helston ② is the next important port of call. It really comes alive on 8 May, the celebration of Flora Day, a pagan ritual to welcome spring. The **Helston Folk Museum** (tel: 01326 564027 for opening hours) has interesting displays on life in the region in days gone by, and **Flambards Victorian Village and**

Map on page 236

On the way to Falmouth you'll see the sign for Come-to-Good, a thatched Quaker meeting house built in 1710 after the Tolerance Act ended their persecution. (For good, read God.)

LEFT: Falmouth Bay.
BELOW: shiny machines at Helston Folk Museum.

St Michael's Mount.

Gardens (open Easter–Oct, daily 10am–5pm; entrance charge) is an authentic life-sized re-creation of a turn-of-the-century village. The thatched **Blue Anchor Inn** is a good place to stop if you're keen on real ale – they brew theirs on the premises.

The A394 takes you west to the rocky island of **St Michael's Mount** (open April–Oct, Mon–Fri 10.30am–5.30pm, Nov–Mar, guided tours as tide and weather permit; National Trust). A Benedictine monastery was founded here in the 12th century (the Priory Church crowns the summit), then fortified by Henry VIII after the Dissolution as part of his string of coastal defences.

Across **Mount's Bay** lies **Penzance** ㉚, the star of the Cornish resorts and the warmest place in the British Isles, with palm trees and sub-tropical plants flourishing in **Morrab Gardens**, off Morrab Road near the **Penlees House Gallery and Museum** (open Mon–Sat 10.30am–4.30pm, Jul–Aug, also Sun from noon; entrance charge). This is West Cornwall's centre for arts and heritage, and displays paintings from the Newlyn School. In Wharf Road, the **National Lighthouse Museum** (open April–Oct, daily 10.30am–4.30pm; entrance charge) is a hands-on museum documenting every aspect of lighthouse life.

Take the A30 now to **Land's End** ㉛, the most westerly point in England. The **Land's End Centre** (open daily 10am–dusk) allows you to explore a discovery trail and underground exhibitions; there's also a beached trawler, a theatre and lots of shops and restaurants.

Mines, legends and artists

BELOW: serene Padstow at twilight.

On the road to St Ives (the B3306 which hugs the coast) you'll pass **St Just**, where Cornish miracle plays are performed in a grassy amphitheatre called the

Playing Place; and **Botallack**, which has the most picturesque of the ruined mine buildings. The **Levant Steam Engine** (National Trust) is the oldest working beam engine in Cornwall. Along the cliff is the **Geevor Tin Mine Museum** (open April–Oct, Sun–Fri 10am–5pm; tel: 01736 786059 for winter times; entrance charge). A little further up the coast is **Zennor**, a place of magic and legends. The **Wayside Folk Museum** (open May–Sept, daily 10am–6pm; tel: 01736 796945 for winter hours; entrance charge) is an unusual, privately owned collection of local history and lore.

Exhibits in the Tate Gallery St Ives.

But our goal is **St Ives** ❸❷, the liveliest and most interesting of the resorts. Its most distinguishing point is the "island" which divides the Atlantic surfing beach of Porthmeor from the harbour and beach of Porthminster, with the little granite chapel of St Nicholas on its topmost point. St Ives grew prosperous on pilchards and tin mining, and the houses of the pilchard fishermen still crowd the tangled streets of Downalong, while the tin miners lived in Upalong. Both industries collapsed, but the town was saved by its scenic beauty and the quality of its light, which attracted artists here.

The **Tate Gallery St Ives** (open Tues–Sun 10.30am–5.30pm and Mon in July–Aug; entrance charge) has excellent permanent and temporary exhibitions, concentrating on works by artists connected with the region, prominent among whom is Alfred Wallis, who took up painting at the age of 70, was discovered by Ben Nicholson and achieved (largely posthumous) fame.

The **Barbara Hepworth Museum** (hours as above) displays her work in a museum and sub-tropical garden. For more paintings, go to the Wills Lane Gallery, to the St Ives Society of Artists, and the Penwith Society of Arts (tel: 01736 796297 for opening hours for all three).

BELOW: the Old Post Office at Tintagel.

Continue up the north coast, beautiful despite the plethora of seaside bungalows and caravan sites, to **Newquay**, a fishing town with a pleasant harbour, and a beach popular with windsurfers. Inland, at Kestle Mill, is **Trerice** (open April–Oct, daily except Tues and Sat 11am–5.30pm; National Trust), an exquisitely decorated and furnished Elizabethan manor house.

Padstow and Tintagel

Our route continues inland (A392/A39) to reach **Padstow** ❸❸ on the River Camel estuary, a picturesque little place with a small harbour and cobbled streets. If you're here on 1 May you'll see the famous **Padstow Hobby Horse** and his colourful entourage in a procession celebrating the coming of summer. **Prideaux Place** (open April–Oct, Sun–Thurs 1.30–5pm; entrance charge), which overlooks the town and deer park, is one of the stops on the procession's route, and one of the nicest of Cornwall's stately homes.

Pick up the A39 at Wadebridge and turn left at Camelford for **Tintagel** ❸❹, where the **Old Post Office** (open April–Oct, daily 11am–5.30pm; National Trust), a 14th-century manor house, has been delightfully restored. It's amazing that so much remains of **Tintagel Castle** (open April–Oct, daily 10am–6pm, Nov–Mar, till 4pm; English Heritage), ravaged by time and the elements on a windswept headland of black craggy cliffs, accessible only by footbridge.

Map on page 236

TIP

The Tarka Trail (*see page 251*) is centred around Barnstaple. To hire bikes for this 21-mile/33-km level, traffic-free cycle route, starting from the railway station, tel: 01271 24202.

BELOW:
going home from the beach at Bude.

Once a Celtic stronghold, then home to the earls of Cornwall, it's best known as the legendary birthplace of King Arthur, and home to Merlin the magician. Carry on north to **Bude**, where wharf buildings converted into shops, galleries and cafés make an attractive canal waterfront.

Westward Ho!

Here we cross back into Devon to visit **Clovelly** ❸ a perfectly preserved fishing village, still privately owned, where steep cobbled streets lined with brightly-painted houses lead up from the harbour. It was made famous by Charles Kingsley (1819–75) in *Westward Ho!* The resort of this name, a 19th-century development, lies nearby.

Follow the road round Barnstaple Bay to **Bideford** ❸, also closely associated with Kingsley. There's an impressive medieval bridge, and the quay is the main-line station for **Lundy Island**, a peaceful sliver of land 11 miles (18 km) off-shore, home to 35 puffins and a wealth of other bird and marine life.

Nearby **Barnstaple** ❸, on the Taw estuary, is best known for its glass-roofed 19th-century **Pannier Market**, the finest in Devon, where fresh produce is on sale. The major resort on Devon's north coast is **Ilfracombe** ❸, although its beach is not remarkable. (For the finest beach in Devon, turn off on the B3343 and wind down to the sands and dunes of **Woolacombe**.) But Ilfracombe has a port full of character, and a highly eccentric **Museum** (open April–Sept, 10am–5.30pm, Oct–Mar, 10am–12.30pm; entrance charge).

The road out plunges down to Watermouth Cove, then round **Combe Martin Bay**. At the top of the valley is the **Wildlife and Dinosaur Park** (open April–Oct 10am–4pm; entrance charge) a huge favourite with children. ❑

EXMOOR NATIONAL PARK

Exmoor ❸ contains a great variety of landscape and wildlife; parts are open heather-covered moor, but it also includes some of Britain's most dramatic and beautiful coastline. It is not as high as Dartmoor and is more extensively farmed, with habitation more widely spread; many of its hills are topped with Iron Age forts. Among many highlights (starting from Combe Martin on the moor's western edge) are:

The Great Hangman, with breathtaking cliff scenery.
The Cliff Railway (daily 8am–7pm) linking Lynton and the pleasant seaside town of Lynmouth.
Valley of the Rocks, a dramatic land formation.
Doone Valley, made famous by R. D. Blackmore's novel.
Culbone Church, said to be England's smallest parish church.
Selworthy, a picture-book pretty village.
Dunster, with a castle and circular Yarn Market.
Dunkery Beacon, the highest spot (1,740ft/511 metres).
Landacre Bridge a medieval structure on the River Barle.
Tarr Steps, a clapper bridge near Withypool.
For information, or details of guided walks or routes for independent walkers, contact the Visitors' Centre, 7/9 Fore Street, Dulverton, TA22 9EX, tel: 01398 323841.

WEST COUNTRY WRITERS

Whether crafting poetry or thrillers, family sagas or anthropomorphic tales, writers find the West Country inspirational

The West Country is a region that has both produced and inspired numerous writers, some of whose works have been immortalised in place names. R. D. Blackmore's *Lorna Doone* (1869), set in the 17th century, gave its name to the Upper East Lyn, which became the Doone Valley. Much of mid-Devon has been christened Tarka Country, after *Tarka the Otter*, written by Henry Williamson (1895–1977).

Charles Kingsley (1819–75), whose father was vicar of Clovelly, wrote *Westward Ho!* while living in nearby Bideford, and the name was borrowed for the resort.

Other writers associated with Devon are Sir Arthur Conan Doyle (1859–1930), who used Dartmoor as the location for *The Hound of the Baskervilles* in 1902; and John Galsworthy (1867–1933) who wrote *The Forsyte Saga* while living in Manaton on the east side of the moor. Two centuries earlier, John Gay (1685–1732), author of *The Beggars' Opera*, was born and educated in Barnstaple.

Perhaps the most famous of Devon's writers is Agatha Christie (1890–1976), Britain's most prolific author, whose thrillers still sell about 4 million copies a year. She was born in Torquay and wrote two of her books while staying at the Art Deco hotel on Burgh Island. Her daughter still lives in her home on the Dart, which is very occasionally opened to the public.

Cornwall, too, has its share of literary figures. D. H. Lawrence (1885–1930) wrote *Women in Love* at Zennor where he set up a small and short-lived group of like-minded people during World War I, intent on isolating themselves both from London and from the conflict. Virginia Woolf (1882–1941) used early memories of Godrevy Lighthouse in her 1927 novel *To The Lighthouse*. Sir John Betjeman (1906–84) also spent childhood holidays in Cornwall, in Trebetherick at the mouth of the Camel estuary. His early poems, such as *Summoned by Bells*, reflect bicycle trips to churches, and he described travelling by rail to Padstow as "the best train journey I know".

More recently, Winston Graham, in his immensely popular Poldark novels, has drawn on the 19th-century mining industry around Perranporth.

Most inextricably associated with Cornwall, however, is Daphne du Maurier (1907–89). She wrote several of her early works at Bodinnick, near Fowey, and later ones at Menabilly. She used Jamaica Inn on Bodmin Moor as the setting for the eponymous novel, and gave evocative Cornish settings to *Frenchman's Creek* and *Rebecca*, the latter published in 1938 and later memorably filmed by Alfred Hitchcock. ❑

ABOVE: Daphne du Maurier as a young woman.
RIGHT: Conan Doyle; Agatha Christie.

ÆSTHETICS.

1 Pope Pius IX, 1792-1878, enamel colours and gold, title **His Holiness the Pope** The potter must have used only a half portrait as his source, since the Pope wears trousers/ Paired with Cardinal Manning 5).

...By Sampson Smith, Longton, 1870.

...collection

Ridley, 1500-1555 and Latimer, 1485-1555, ...hops and printed title. Both Bishops took ...art in the Reformation and were ...t at the stake.

5 Henry Edward Manning, 1808-1892, enamel colours and gold, title **Cardinal Manning** He was a convert to the Roman Catholic faith. He became Archbishop of Westminster and was named Cardinal in 1875. Paired with Pope Pius IX (no. 1).

Made by Sampson, Smith, Longton, about 1875

Ex Pugh collection

6 Giuseppe Garibaldi...

9 Napoleon I, bone china, enamel colours and gold. The smallest Staffordshire portrait figure.

Made in Staffordshire, 1840s

Ex Pugh collection

10 N...

13 James Cook, 1728-1779, enamel col... Explorer who travelled... was mur...

HEREFORD AND THE WELSH BORDERS

The border counties play host to literary and arts festivals, produce world-famous pottery, and lay claim to some splendid castles and cathedrals and the world's first iron bridge

T he great border castles of Herefordshire are a legacy of the time when this green and pleasant region was a fiercely disputed frontier between England and Wales, where the Norman lords established the Marches. This chapter explores the castles and valleys, the pretty towns of the Wye valley and takes in the world's first iron bridge at Telford, and the pottery town of Stoke-on-Trent.

We start with a visit to **Ross-on-Wye ❶**, which stands on a red sandstone cliff above a bend in the River Wye. The slender spire of **St Mary's Church** which tops the cliff can be seen for miles around. The church is known for its hedge-hogs: stone ones, wooden ones, painted and embroidered ones. The area of parkland that surrounds the church is known as The Prospect, and it does indeed offer a wonderful prospect across the river. Ross is a busy market town centred on a 17th-century arcaded **Market Hall** (housing a heritage centre) which is set in a square where markets are still held.

The **Ross International Festival** in the last two weeks of August is a feast of high-quality theatre, music and film which is well worth visiting, but the town gets very busy so accommodation should be organised in advance.

PRECEDING PAGES: the Wye from Symond's Yat. **LEFT:** Staffordshire figurines in Stoke. **BELOW:** Ross-on-Wye Market Hall.

FACT FILE

Location The area follows the Welsh border from south to north, taking in parts of Herefordshire, Shropshire and Cheshire.
By car Via the M4/M5/M50 from London to Ross-on-Wye; M5 from Birmingham; M56 from Manchester to Chester
By coach tel: 0990 808080.
By rail London Paddington to Hereford, journey time approx. 2 hours 45 minutes; tel: 0345 484950.
Top attractions Hereford Cathedral and the Mappa Mundi Centre; Ironbridge Gorge Museum; Ludlow Castle; Royal Doulton, Spode and Wedgwood potteries.
Main events Hay Festival of Literature and the Arts, Ross-on-Wye International Arts Festival, Hereford Three Choirs Festival.
For children Alton Towers Theme Park, tel: 01538 703344; Gladstone Working Pottery Museum, tel: 01782 319232.
Most famous sons Industrial pioneer Abraham Darby (1678–1717); naturalist Charles Darwin (1809–82); poet Wilfrid Owen (1893–1918).
Tourist information Hay-on-Wye, tel: 01497 820144; Hereford, tel: 01432 268430; Ross-on-Wye, tel: 01989 562768; Stoke-on-Trent, tel: 01782 236000.

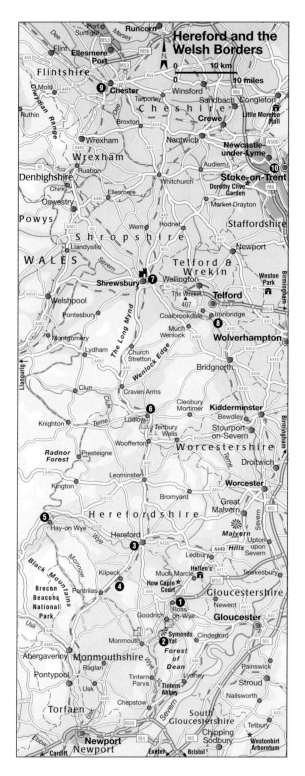

Amazing diversions

From Ross, make a diversion some 8 miles (13 km) southwest to a spot that should not be missed: **Symonds Yat ❷**, a rocky outcrop offering stunning views over the Wye. The ferry that links Symonds Yat East and West across the river runs on an overhead chain and is operated by hand. The **Jubilee Maze** (open April–Sept, daily 11am–5pm; entrance charge; tel: 01600 890360 for school holiday and winter times) is an intriguing puzzle and the adjoining Museum of Mazes allows you to test theories and discover the mysteries of maze-making.

On your way back to Ross, take a look at **Goodrich Castle** (open April–Sept, daily 10am–6pm, Oct–Mar, 10am–4pm; English Heritage), the best-preserved and most intact of the border fortresses.

From Ross, take the A449/B4224 through the valley towards Hereford. There are numerous opportunities to get off the beaten track for riverside and woodland walks. To the left of the road is **How Caple Court** (open daily 9am–5pm; entrance charge) where you'll find 11 acres (4.5 hectares) of beautiful gardens (including a Florentine sunken garden) with great views, interesting walks, a plant shop and a little café.

To the right of the road, at **Much Marcle**, is **Hellens** (open April–Oct, Wed, Sat–Sun, guided tours at 2pm, 3pm and 4pm; entrance charge), a virtually untouched Tudor house set in extensive grounds with fish ponds and coppices. There's also a ridge-top picnic spot near Much Marcle which has stunning views.

Hereford

Ignoring all other tempting diversions, make your way now to **Hereford ❸**, the pleasant cathedral city that is capital of the Wye Valley. Its greatest treasure is the 12th-century **Cathedral** (open daily 7.30am–6.30pm; tours at 11.30am and 2pm in summer; donations welcomed), with a lovely early-English Lady Chapel and the restored Shrine of St Thomas of Hereford. The **Mappa Mundi Centre** (open April–Oct, Mon–Sat 10am–

Map on page 256

4.15pm, Sun 11am–3.15pm, Oct–Mar, Mon– Sat 11am–3.15pm; entrance charge), displays the largest and finest medieval map of the world, as well as the famous **Chained Library**, in a brand new building.

Evey three years the Cathedral plays host to the world's oldest music festival, the **Three Choirs Festival** (August 2000, 2003, and so on).

The new **Courtyard Centre for the Arts** is a state-of-the-art venue for theatre, music and dance, which also comprises an art gallery and restaurant. The **Hereford Museum and Art Gallery** (open Tues–Sat 10am–5pm; admission free) offers a good introduction to the city and area, plus changing art exhibitions. There are several other museums, too – on cider making and waterworks, for example – but you may just want to wander through the streets, shop in medieval courtyards, or sit and watch the river flow by. Or you could take to the water on one of the **Cathedral Cruises** (April–Oct, daily on the hour from 11am, weather permitting), informative 40-minute trips which start from the Old Wye Bridge.

The village of **Kilpeck** ❹ involves a slight detour (about 8 miles/13km south on the Abergavenny road) but it's worth making. It has the most wonderfully ornate Norman church in England. **St Mary and St David** (open daylight hours; admission free), was built in 1142 and is very well preserved, with unusual carvings on the south door, chancel arch and the semi-circular apse.

Richard Booth, who changed the face of Hay-on-Wye.

Secondhand book centre

Backtracking a little on the A465, take a left turn on to the B4348 for the trip to the border town of **Hay-on-Wye** ❺ (most of the town is in Wales). Hay became a major book centre in the 1970s when an eccentric businessman, Richard Booth, seeing how many shops and cinemas were losing business to the bigger towns,

BELOW:
Hereford Cathedral.

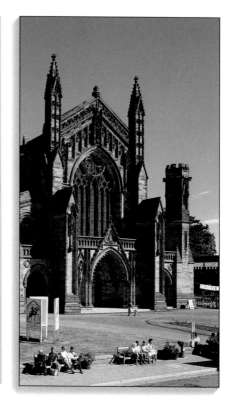

HEREFORD CIDER

Herefordshire is the place to go for cider. If you are there in spring you will see orchards of trees loaded with pale pink apple blossom, in late summer with rosy cider apples. Numerous cider breweries open their doors to visitors, providing instructive guided tours of their premises, demonstrations of cider making, tastings and opportunities to buy.

Among the most interesting are Lyne Down Cider (tel: 01531 660691) where demonstrations of small-scale traditional cider making are given during the season; and Dunkerton Cider Mill (tel: 01544 388653) where there is also a good restaurant, the Cider House. Franklin's Cider Farm Shop (tel: 01584 810488) also makes perry from locally grown pears which, like the cider apples, are milled and pressed on the farm and left to ferment naturally. The Barrels in Hereford (tel: 01432 342546) is an 18th-century inn with its own brewery attached. At Bulmer Visitors' Centre (tel: 01432 352000) there are tours of England's best-known commercial cider makers. If you want to explore the history of the industry in more detail, visit the Cider Museum and King Offa Distillery (tel: 01432 354207) in Hereford. All these distilleries suggest that you check availability in advance if you would like a tour.

To the left and right of the A4112 lie what are known as the black and white villages – clusters of black and white cottages, shops and inns, clustered around village churches. Weobley, Eardisland and Pembridge are among the most picturesque.

began converting the empty premises into bookshops. Financial difficulties foiled his plan to rule the town unchallenged, and other booksellers moved in. Today, Hay is a book enthusiast's paradise, and each June the **Festival of Literature and the Arts** attracts thousands of readers and writers to the little town.

Into Shropshire

The A438/A4112 leads via Leominster to **Ludlow** ❻, a lovely town where lie the ashes of A. E. Housman (1859–1936), the poet who immortalised the dreamy slopes of his home county in *A Shropshire Lad*. It's an architecturally pleasing town, with 13th-century taverns and Tudor market buildings. **Ludlow Castle** was the seat of the presidents of the council of the Marcher lords, and it was here that John Milton's play, *Comus*, was first performed in 1634. West of Ludlow (and just over the Welsh border) is Knighton, a good centre for exploring **Offa's Dyke**. This 8th-century earthwork built by the Saxon King Offa to protect England from the marauding Welsh now carries a long-distance footpath.

North of Ludlow on the A49 lies **Shrewsbury** ❼, beautifully situated on a meander in the River Severn, crossed by the English bridge and the Welsh bridge. It has 15th-century houses, some quaint half-timbered shopfronts, and some fine parks and gardens. The pink sandstone castle near the station was converted into a museum by Thomas Telford (*see next page*) and now incorporates the **Shropshire Regimental Museum** (open Tues–Sat 10am–5pm; entrance charge). The solid and unassuming **Cathedral** is built of the same reddish stone as the castle.

Shrewsbury is the birthplace of scientist Charles Darwin (1809–82), whose *Origin of the Species* changed Victorian ways of thinking. The World War I poet Wilfrid Owen (1893–1918) was also born here.

BELOW:
Ludlow Castle.

Ironbridge to Chester

East of Shrewsbury on the A5/M54 is **Telford**, a new town named after the 18th-century engineer Thomas Telford. Initiated in the 1960s, the ambitious project takes in **Coalbrookdale** and **Ironbridge ❽** on the River Severn, where the world's first iron bridge was built by Telford in 1773. It was in Coalbrookdale, a region rich in natural resources which had been a mining centre since the time of Henry VIII, that Bristol brassmaker Abraham Darby pioneered the use of coke to smelt iron, thus making the process much cheaper while retaining high quality, and turning the area into the busiest industrial centre in the world.

Nine different museums, which include original furnaces, foundries, brick works, the Coalport china works and a recreated Victorian town, are incorporated in the splendid **Ironbridge Gorge Museum** (open daily 10am–5pm; a passport ticket with no expiry date allows entrance to all museums).

Our next port of call (north on the A442/A41) is **Chester ❾**, the most northerly and the most exciting of the timbered Tudor towns of the Welsh Marches. Its particular architectural character can be seen in the so-called **Rows** of double-tiered and covered walkways as you walk down Eastgate, Westgate or Bridge Street. The oldest of the Rows dates from 1486, and most of them from the 16th century.

Potter at work in Coalport Museum

In Roman times Chester was an important stronghold called Deva; part of an amphitheatre can be seen just outside the city walls, by St John's Street. The **Grosvenor Museum** (open Mon–Sat 10am–5pm, Sun 1–5pm; entrance charge) records the Roman legacy with models of the ancient fortress city. Under the Normans, Chester became a near-independent state governed by a succession of earls. The tidal estuary of the River Dee allowed the city to flourish as a port

BELOW: the world's first iron bridge.

Chester Cathedral's refectory ceiling.

until the 15th century, when the estuary began to silt up. After that, shipping was transferrred to the natural port of Liverpool.

The 2-mile (3-km) walk around the city walls will help you to get oriented. This is one of the few British cities with its medieval walls still intact, with those on the north and east sides following the original Roman plan. The **Cathedral** was a Benedictine abbey until the Dissolution of the Monasteries under Henry VIII. An unusually square building, it has a massive south transept featuring a grand Victorian stained-glass window.

Due east of the city, via the A54/34 is **Little Moreton Hall** (open April–Oct, Wed–Sun 1–5pm, Nov–Dec, Sat–Sun 1–5pm; entrance charge), an ornately decorated, half-timbered and moated manor house, built in the late 15th century, which is worth an expedition if you have time.

The Potteries

Stoke-on-Trent ❿ was made famous by Arnold Bennett (1867–1931) in his novels of the "Five Towns", in which he described provincial life with a discernment and attention to detail that has rarely been matched. But the city is now six towns in one, as Fenton has been added to Tunstall, Burslem, Hanley (the city centre), Stoke and Longton to form the metropolitan area.

Thousands of people come here simply to pick up a bargain at one of 40 factory shops, selling everything from dinner services to ceramic jewellery, and with "seconds" on sale at reduced prices. But Stoke is also a progressive town with a lively centre and the newly opened **Cultural Quarter** where the Victoria Hall stages classical and rock music, comedy and children's shows and the Regent Theatre hosts touring productions of opera, ballet and musicals.

BELOW:
Chester City Hall.

All the big names in pottery are represented here. **Royal Doulton** (tel: 01782 292434), **Spode** (tel: 01782 744011) and **Wedgwood** (tel: 01782 204218) have visitor centres which – in an imaginative and entertaining way – allow you to explore the history and craft of ceramics, to have a go at throwing or painting a pot and, of course, to visit their factory shops. Factory tours must be booked in advance. The Tourist Office (tel: 01782 236000) provides full details on the numerous other factory tours and shops in the area. The Wedgwood Express (tel: 01782 415206) and the China Dayrider (tel: 01782 747000) connect with incoming trains at Stoke railway station and take you to many of the factories, shops and museums on a single-price ticket.

When you've had enough of pottery, there are a number of places to visit in the vicinity. About 7 miles (12 km) north of Stoke-on-Trent is **Biddulph Grange Garden** (open April–Oct, Wed–Fri noon–5.30pm, Sat–Sun 11am–6pm; National Trust), an unusual Victorian garden in which visitors are taken on a miniature tour, from an Egyptian Court to a mini-Great Wall of China, as well as a pinetum and a fernery. Or there's the **Dorothy Clive Garden** (open April–Oct, daily 10am–5pm; entrance charge) near Market Drayton, which is glorious in early summer when the rhododendrons are in full bloom and has pleasant woodlands at any time of the year; and the **Shugborough Estate** (open April–Sept, daily 11am–5pm; National Trust), the magnificent ancestral seat of the Earls of Lichfield which is being restored as a 19th-century working estate. The stable block houses the original 18th-century kitchens.

When the children have tired of all this, cart them off on the short trip to **Alton Towers** (open Mar–Nov, daily; entrance charge), the country's leading theme park, which is constantly updating its thrills and spills. ❑

Map on page 256

BELOW: pottery gilding in Stoke-on-Trent.

DERBY TO THE EAST COAST

Map on page 266

The Pilgrim Fathers, Robin Hood and D. H. Lawrence all have links with this region, which spans the Midlands, incorporating bulb fields and family-friendly beaches

Settled snugly in the centre of England, **Derby ❶** is a useful jumping-off point for the Peak District (*see page 275*) but it's also a lively city in its own right, with plenty to see and do, and with good public transport making a car unnecessary. In Irongate, the oldest part of town, there's the **Cathedral** (open daily 8.30am–6pm; donations welcomed) with a fine wrought-iron screen. The **Derby Heritage Centre** (open Mon–Sat 9am–5pm; admission free; tel: 01332 299321) is housed in the former grammar school, whose pupils included the Rev. John Cotton, founder of Boston, Massachusetts, and which gives a good run-down on the city's history, as well as organising ghost walks at night.

The **Royal Crown Derby Visitor Centre** (open Mon–Sat 9.30am–5pm, Sun 10am–4pm) runs tours and demonstrations and, of course, there's a shop where you can buy the famous china. The city's lively in the evening, too, with plenty of restaurants, bars and cinemas, and a variety of entertainment at the **Derby Playhouse** (tel: 01332 363275), one of England's leading repertory theatres which won an award in 1999 for being the most welcoming theatre in England.

Kedleston Hall (house open April–Oct, Sat–Wed 1–5.30pm; park daily 11am–6pm; National Trust), 5 miles (8 km) from the city centre, is a splendid 18th-century Palladian mansion complete with Robert Adams interiors, a huge

PRECEDING PAGES: National Fishing Heritage Centre, Grimsby. **LEFT:** Robin Hood and friend, Nottingham. **BELOW:** Lincoln Cathedral.

FACT FILE

Location Lying just to the south of the Peak District (for which Derby and Nottingham are good jumping-off points) and covering a swathe of middle England between The Wash and the mouth of the River Humber.
By car The M1 to Derby or Nottingham (Exit 25) takes about 2 hours from London.
By coach National Express coach service from London Victoria, about 2 hours 30 minutes, tel: 0990 808080.
By train About 1 hour 40 minutes to both Derby and Nottingham from London St Pancras, tel: 0345 484950.
Major attractions Burghley House, Stamford; Clumber Park "Dukery"; Magna Carta at Lincoln Castle; Pilgrim Fathers' Memorial, Boston; The Tales of Robin Hood, Nottingham; Spalding Tropical Forest; Usher Gallery, Lincoln.
For children Butterfly and Wildlife Park, Spalding; the beaches of Skegness, Cleethorpes and Mablethorpe; Skegness Seal Sanctuary.
Best theatres Derby Playhouse; Nottingham Playhouse.
Famous sons (and daughter) Alfred, Lord Tennyson; D.H. Lawrence; Sir Isaac Newton; Lady Margaret Thatcher.
Tourist information Derby, tel: 01332 255802; Lincoln, tel: 01522 529828; Nottingham, tel: 0115 9773558.

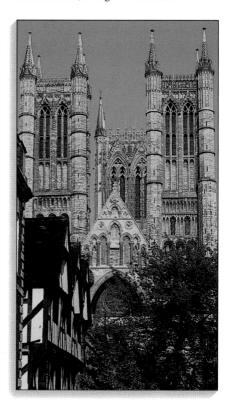

collection of paintings, and an **Indian Museum**, housing objects collected by Lord Curzon, the owner, when Viceroy of India (1899–1905).

A town without a sheriff

TIP

In late October there's a floodlit Robin Hood Pageant at the Castle (tel: 0115 9155330) and in August the Robin Hood Festival takes place at nearby Sherwood Forest (tel: 01623 824490). The forest is now a country park, to which year-round access is free (tel: 01623 823202).

Return to Derby (or skirt it to the south) and take the A52 to **Nottingham ❷**, a place still associated in popular imagination with Sherwood Forest, Robin Hood and, of course, the evil sheriff. The Norman gatehouse of **Nottingham Castle** remains intact, set in impressive grounds, and houses the **Castle Museum & Art Gallery** (castle open daily 10am–5pm; museum 1–5pm; admission free on weekdays). A short distance away, in Maid Marion Way, you can visit **The Tales of Robin Hood** (open daily 10am–6pm; entrance charge), where the life and times of the outlaw are enacted.

Nottingham is also famous as the birthplace of the writer D. H. Lawrence (*see page 267*), and for its lace making, an industry which is well documented in the **Museum of Nottingham Lace** (open daily 10am–5pm; admission free) in the Lace Market. But although Nottingham is an historic city, it also has a modern face, with a plethora of good restaurants, bars, shops, cinemas and clubs catering for the students of its two popular universities.

We go to the northern outskirts now to visit **Newstead Abbey**, the home of Lord Byron (1788–1824), a beautifully furnished house surrounded by lakes, terraces and Japanese and Spanish gardens. A little further north is **Clumber Park** (park open daily during daylight hours; walled garden April–Sept, Sat–Sun 11am–5pm; National Trust), one of Nottingham's famous "Dukeries" or large hunting estates, consisting of park-, farm- and woodland, a serpentine lake, and a walled garden enclosing a Victorian apiary, fig house and vineries.

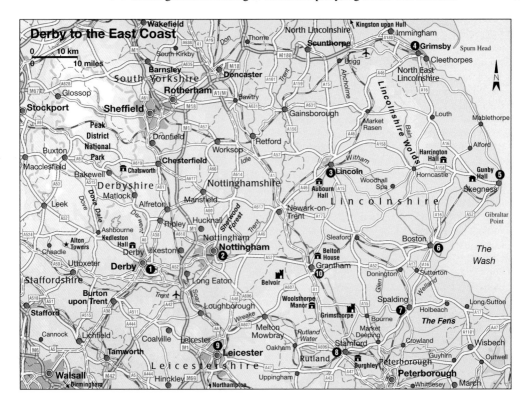

Derby to the East Coast

Lincoln

Take the A57 now towards **Lincoln ❸**, which towers impressively over its flat Fenland setting. It's a city with Roman, Norman, medieval and Georgian influences, with a well-preserved historic area at the top of the hill, and the modern town below. The three towers of its magnificent **Cathedral** (open Mon–Sat 7.15am–6pm, Sun till 5pm; donations welcomed), dominate the skyline from afar. The building is an attractive blend of Norman and Gothic, and has some fascinating misericords in the choir stalls. Concerts and mystery plays are staged here (tel: 01522 535599 for details).

Lincoln Castle (open April–Oct, Mon–Sat 9.30am–5.30pm, Sun 11am–5.30pm; Nov–Mar till 4pm; entrance charge) is also Norman in origin, although there have been many later additions. For 900 years it served as the town prison. It contains a copy of the Magna Carta, signed and sealed by King John at Runnymede in 1215.

Among the city's many fine Norman and medieval buildings is the **Jew's House** in The Strait, dating from the 1170s, when a large Jewish community flourished here, and believed to be the oldest surviving example of domestic architecture in the country.

If you have time for only one museum or gallery, make it the **Usher Gallery** (open Mon–Sat 10am–5.30pm, Sun 2.30–5pm; entrance charge) in Lindum Road where there are works by Peter de Wint, J. M. W. Turner, L. S. Lowry and Walter Sickert, as well as memorabilia relating to the Lincolnshire-born Poet Laureate Alfred, Lord Tennyson (1809–92) whose statue stands in the Cathedral grounds. However, if you have children, the lively **Toy Museum** (open April–Sept, Tues–Sat 11am–5pm, Sun noon–4pm, Oct–Christmas, Sat and

The entrance gate at Lincoln Castle.

BELOW: England's oldest pub.

D. H. LAWRENCE

The first thing that most people associate with D. H. Lawrence is *Lady Chatterley's Lover*, which was eventually published in 1963 after an unsuccessful prosecution for obscenity, and changed English attitudes towards censorship. But this was his last novel, finished in 1929 when he was dying of tuberculosis, and was the culmination of a prolific writing career which included collections of short stories and poems as well as novels.

Born in Nottingham in 1885, Lawrence was the son of a miner, and a product of the Victorian era's concern to make education available to the poor. But while far more working-class children were reading books, very few were writing them. His mother, an ex-teacher, was determined that he should not follow his father down the pit, and encouraged him to continue his education – he eventually won a scholarship to Nottingham University College. The passionately strong bond between mother and son was recreated in the autobiographical novel, *Sons and Lovers* (1931). In 1912 he met his future wife, Frieda (already married to one of his professors); their life together was to be turbulent, penurious and peripatetic, as they travelled in Australia, America and Mexico. His last years, when in failing health, were spent in Italy and the south of France.

school holidays 11am–5pm, Sun noon–4pm; entrance charge) will be a sure fire success. There are even old-fashioned penny in the slot machines to amuse nostalgic adults.

The Lincolnshire coast

Grimsby (about 50 minutes' drive northeast of Lincoln on the A46) is situated on the east coast at the mouth of the River Humber, with access to miles of safe and sandy beaches. Sadly, the fishing industry which brought prosperity to the town in the 19th century has dwindled to almost nothing in recent years, but the ethos and atmosphere remain.

At the **National Fishing Heritage Centre** (open daily 10am–6pm; entrance charge) some superior interactive displays take you on a credible trip through old Grimsby and its port, and allow you to roam around a restored 1950s trawler. Afterwards, you can buy good smoked fish from **Alfred Enderby Traditional Fish Smokers** in Fish Dock Road (tel: 01472 342984).

Popular family resorts on this coast include Cleethorpes (closest to Grimsby), Mablethorpe and, best known of all, **Skegness** ❺, with 6 miles (10 km) of safe and sandy beaches. Here, accommodated in one of the many small hotels or bed-and-breakfast establishments, children can build sandcastles and enjoy donkey rides, and parents can take advantage of gardens and bowling greens as they did in the days before the Costa Brava beckoned.

The **Magic World of Fantasy Island** (open Easter week and May–Nov, daily 10am, closing times vary, tel: 01754 872030; admission free) offers entertainment when the beach palls or the weather is bad; and the **Skegness Natureland Seal Sanctuary** (open April–Oct 10am–5pm; entrance charge) in North Parade

TIP

Cleethorpes has a diverting Deep Sea Experience (tel: 01472 290220) with walkways through a vast fish tank, and specimens from the tropical reefs of Australia and Florida.

BELOW: Skegness Beach gets busy in summer.

aims to combine education and conservation with entertainment. Four miles north, just off the A52, **Hardy's Animal Farm** is a good townies' introduction to the workings of a modern farm, and there's an adventure playground, too.

American connections

From Skegness the A52 parallels the coast, then turns inland a short way to **Boston ❻** on the banks of the River Witham. It's an attractive little town, and has one of the finest produce markets in Lincolnshire, held each Wednesday and Saturday. On Wednesday, produce is auctioned in Bargate Green, an entertaining event even if you don't intend to buy. Boston also has the tallest working windmill in England – the Maud Foster Windmill – and a church tower, known locally as the Boston Stump, which soars to 272 ft (83 metres).

Modern artists are much in evidence here: murals are created all over town to disguise empty or neglected properties; the Memorial Gardens Archway is a modern piece in forged steel; and gracefully poised welded steel sculptures of human figures by artist Rick Kirby are displayed in Friary Court.

Most of all, Boston is known for its American connections. It was here that the Pilgrim Fathers were imprisoned in 1607, for trying to leave the country. Their cells can be visited in the **Guildhall Museum** (open Mon–Sat 10am–5pm; entrance charge) and the **Pilgrim Fathers' Memorial** stands on the river bank near the sea, on the spot where they were arrested.

Spalding to Stamford

From Boston we are heading southwest on the A16 to **Spalding ❼**, the heart of the Lincolnshire bulb industry. If you come here in spring you will see acres of

Map on page 266

TIP

Lincolnshire is well known for its markets which are held throughout the county. If you enjoy the bustle of a market and the chance to buy fresh produce, contact the local tourist offices for times and venues.

LEFT: Boston town centre.
BELOW: St Botolph's Church.

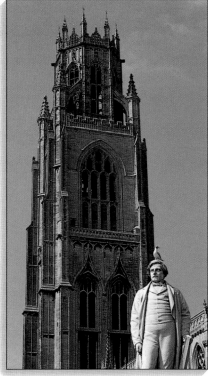

Stamford High Street in the rain.

tulips, hyacinths and daffodils, and all summer long you can visit the **Bulb Museum** (open Mar–Oct, daily 10am–4pm; admission free) which depicts the industry from 1880 to the present. **Spalding Tropical Forest** (open daily 10am–5.30pm; entrance charge) offers more exotic delights, with rain forests, oriental gardens, waterfalls, orchids and sweet-scented climbing flowers; while the **Butterfly and Wildlife Park** (open Mar–Oct, daily 10am–5pm; entrance charge) keeps its butterflies in a free-flying environment and stages falconry displays twice daily (usually at noon and 3pm).

Keep to the A16 to reach **Stamford ❽**, a mellow stone-built town with no fewer than five medieval churches, and some streets and squares in which all the buildings pre-date the Victorian era. The **Stamford Museum** (open Mon–Sat 10am–5pm, plus Sun 2–5pm in summer; entrance charge) gives a good historical background to the town, but its best-loved exhibits, with adults and children alike, are the wax models of Daniel Lambert, England's fattest man (who collapsed and died at Stamford Races in 1809) and Tom Thumb, the smallest. The museum also produces useful Town Trails, to make sure you don't miss anything, from the peaceful water meadows to the 12th-century priory.

Just to the south of Stamford is **Burghley House** (open April–Oct, daily 11am–4.30pm; entrance charge), one of the most glorious Elizabethan mansions in the country. Built in the late 16th century for William Cecil, the first Lord Burghley and treasurer to Elizabeth I, this has been a family home ever since, which gives it a special atmosphere lacking in many stately homes. The state rooms hold a wonderful collection of paintings, furniture, porcelain and tapestries; and the deer park, landscaped by "Capability" Brown, is delightful. A newly planted sculpture garden is open on the same days as the house.

BELOW: splendid Burghley House.

Leicester and Grantham

Due west on the A47 lies **Leicester 9**, a busy modern city with ancient origins. **Castle Park** is the historic heart: the castle gardens and riverside are tranquil spots for walking, and the city's Saxon, Roman and medieval forebears are all represented. Visit the **New Walk Museum** (open Mon–Sat 10am–5.30pm, Sun 2–5.30pm; entrance charge) for a wonderfully eclectic display, ranging from Ancient Egyptian artefacts to dinosaurs and German Expressionism.

Leicester's markets are also worth seeing: the great food hall in the **Market Centre** (open Tues–Sat 7.30am–6pm) and the outdoor **Retail Market** (open Mon–Sat 7.30am–6pm) both offer a vast selection of fresh food as well as clothing and other goods.

From here you can return to Nottingham or head south to London on the M1, but if you have time, pay a visit to **Grantham 10**, a pleasant old town of red-brick and half-timbered houses with a steepled parish church. It used to be famous for its connections with Sir Isaac Newton (1642–1727) who propounded the theory of gravitation, and who was born at nearby Woolsthorpe Manor, but these days it is better known as the birthplace of Margaret Thatcher, the Conservative prime minister who dominated British politics in the 1980s; she was brought up here above her father's grocer shop. Friendly little **Grantham Museum** (open Mon–Sat 10am–5pm; entrance charge) in St Peter's Hill explores the town's links with both of them, and much more.

Just north of the town on the A607 is the elegant 17th-century **Belton House** (open April–Oct, Wed–Sun 10am–5pm; entrance charge) with a formal topiaried walk. For those too young to be interested in such things as houses and gardens, there's an adventure playground and an activity room. ❑

Map on page 266

Leicester's historic heart.

LEFT: a tranquil spot in Castle Park.
BELOW: Leicester's Concert Hall.

THE PEAK DISTRICT

Map on page 276

Bleak and challenging in parts, but threaded with pure rivers and dotted with idyllic villages and some splendid stately homes, the Peaks are a walker's paradise

T he Peak District is a region of outstanding beauty lying at the southern end of the Pennines. It's the last knobbly vertebrae on "the backbone of England" and the first real hill country encountered by travellers heading north from London. Over the years, as a centre of lead-mining, then of silk and cotton production, it has been much changed by man, but retains some wild and wonderful walking country. Today, it is highly acccessible, and much visited: surrounded by the conurbations of the North and the Midlands, it has over 100 roads running through the area. It is the nearest National Park to London (and also the first, founded in 1950) and easily reached by the M1 motorway.

Our tour will begin in Matlock, in the southern Peaks, the largest town and the administrative centre of the district. Modern **Matlock ❶** was created by John Smedley, a 19th-century industrialist who watched over its development from the fairy-tale mock-Gothic and now ruined folly of **Riber Castle**, which overlooks the town from its commanding hilltop to the south. The castle is now the centre of the **Riber Wildlife Park** (daily 10am; entrance charge), which runs a breeding programme for European lynx and other rare and endangered species.

From here, take the A6, crossing the bridge over the River Derwent and passing into the Derwent Gorge, where high limestone crags crowd in on the left.

PRECEDING PAGES:
mill stones at
Stanage Edge.
LEFT: a climber on
High Tor.
BELOW: Riber
Wildlife Park.

FACT FILE

By car About 2 hours on the M1 motorway from London; leave at Exit 28 (Matlock) for the southern dales, Exit 29 (Chesterfield) for the central and northern areas.
By coach National Express daily coach services from London and Manchester. A good coach service also links the main Peak District towns, tel: 0990 808080.
By train About 2 hours from London St Pancras to Derby, Nottingham, Chesterfield and Sheffield. Local services link with the main Peak District towns, tel: 0345 484950.
Main towns Matlock, Buxton, Bakewell.
Major attractions Castleton Caves; Chatsworth House; Dove Dale; Haddon Hall; Lyme Park; Pennine Way.
Special events Buxton International Festival of Music and the Arts (late July); well-dressing ceremonies throughout the summer.
For children Chatsworth Farm and Children's Adventure Playground; Gulliver's Kingdom Theme Park; the Ranger Service runs children's fun days and activities throughout the summer, tel: 01629 815185.
Local specialities Bakewell puddings; Stilton cheese
Tourist information Bakewell 01629 813227; Buxton tel: 01298 25106; Chesterfield tel: 01246 207777; Matlock tel: 01629 580580.

*Cable cars to the
Heights of Abraham.*

Soon the biggest of the lot, the 300-ft (90-metre) **High Tor** appears, almost overhanging the road, with rock climbers clinging to the rock face like flies on a wall. Just beyond High Tor the swinging gondolas of the **Heights of Abraham Cable Cars** (open daily 10am–4.30pm, Feb–Mar, weekends only) can be seen.

The Heights of Abraham, named after General Wolfe's 1759 victory in Quebec, are reached by turning left as you enter Matlock Bath. They include the **Rutland and Great Masson Show Caverns** (times as above), former lead mines that now provide exciting underground tours, picnic sites and nature trails up to the **Victoria Prospect Tower**, built in 1844 and commanding stupendous views across the gorge.

Mines, mills and Stilton cheese

Matlock Bath ❷ became popular as a holiday spot in Victorian times when the railways arrived. Today, it is well-known as a weekend destination for bikers and for its illuminations over the Lovers' Walks along the Derwent from late August

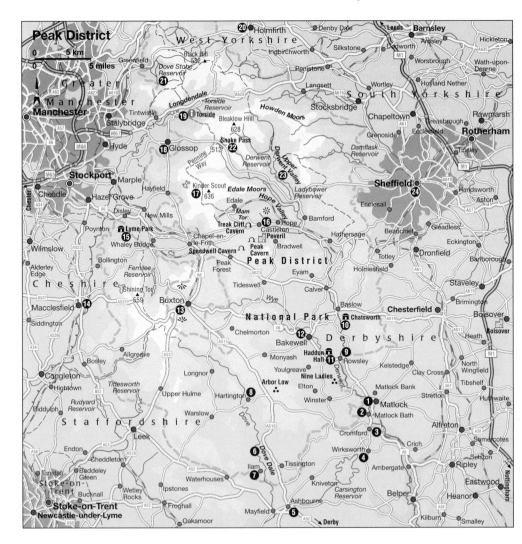

Map
on page
276

to early October. Among its modern attractions is the **Peak District Mining Museum** (open daily 11am–4pm; entrance charge) in the Pavilion, a fascinating introduction to the world of the lead miner, with tunnels through which children can crawl. **Gulliver's Kingdom Theme Park** (open April–Sept, daily 10.30am–5pm, Mar and Oct, Sat–Sun; entrance charge) is set high on a hillside above Matlock Bath and has river rides and a mine train.

Follow the A6 through Matlock Bath to **Cromford ❸**. Richard Arkwright, one of the architects of the Industrial Revolution, came here in 1771 to build the world's first water-powered cotton mill and create an industrial village that was a wonder of the age. It was poor communications that stopped the Derwent Valley becoming one of the principal centres of that world-shattering revolution. The **Arkwright Mill** (open Mon–Fri 9am–5pm; entrance charge), an international heritage site, is clearly signposted. Tours around the village are arranged from the Arkwright Mill. Workers' cottages in North Street off the Wirksworth road, completed in 1776, show how Arkwright wanted his workers to live.

A little further on is Cromford Wharf and the **High Peak Junction Workshops** (open April–Sept, daily 10.30am–5pm, Oct–Mar, Sat–Sun; entrance charge) of the **Cromford Canal**, which runs for 5 miles (8 km) to Ambergate. Turn right at Scarthin Nick crossroads and left up a steep hill, passing the outstanding viewpoint of the **Black Rocks of Cromford**. Here there's a picnic site and access to the **High Peak Trail**, a route that follows the line of the former Cromford and High Peak Railway, completed in 1831 as an extension of the Cromford Canal. As the road enters quarry-scarred **Wirksworth ❹**, signs indicate the **National Stone Centre** (open April–Sept, daily 10am–5pm, winter till 4pm; entrance charge), an exciting new attraction with treasure trails, audiovisual shows and exhibitions, set in a former limestone quarry by the High Peak Trail.

Roam the narrow streets to appreciate the atmosphere of Wirksworth, which has been a lead-mining centre for centuries. Its story is graphically told in the **Wirksworth Heritage Centre** (open summer, daily 10am–5pm; check tourist office for winter times; entrance charge). Created in a former silk and velvet mill, this award-winning centre has three floors of interpretive displays and exhibits, including a replica quarryman's house from the early 20th century.

Wirksworth's sloping **Market Place** has many fine 18th- and 19th-century buildings, including the Moot Hall (not open to the public). The **Parish Church of St Mary** is mainly 13th century, and contains a wonderful 7th-century carved coffin lid.

Continue along the B5035 to **Ashbourne ❺**, "the gateway to Dove Dale". The cathedral-like **Parish Church of St Oswald** is one of the finest in the Peak District, and its soaring 14th-century spire is an elegant landmark. Nearby, in Church Street, is the beautiful gabled and mullioned Elizabethan Old Grammar School (private). On the way to the cobbled Market Place, you will come to the restored timber-framed **Gingerbread Shop**, which still makes the local delicacy on the premises. The **Tourist Information Centre** (open April–Sept, daily 9.30am–5pm, Oct–Mar, Mon–Sat 10am–4pm) is in the Market Place.

Richard Arkwright invented a horse-driven spinning frame before the water-powered one at Cromford. He was knighted in 1786 and became high sheriff of Derbyshire the following year.

BELOW: Ashbourne's Gingerbread Shop.

Planning the route.

Take the A515 Buxton road up a steep hill to the north, then turn left on a minor road signposted to Thorpe and Dove Dale. Thorpe is an unpretentious limestone village standing at the foot of **Thorpe Cloud** (942 ft/287 metres), one of the sentinels of **Dove Dale** , probably the most famous and certainly the most popular and over-used of the White Peak dales (National Trust; car park). Over a million people visit it every year, and the National Park and footpath authorities run a continuous programme of repairs to the 7-mile (11-km) path that runs north through the dale to Hartington. Go beyond the famous **Stepping Stones** beneath Thorpe Cloud and Bunster Hill (many people don't) to the famous series of rock pinnacles and caves such as Tissington Spires, Ilam Rock, Pickering Tor and Reynard's Cave, with its natural archway.

Just beyond the Dove Dale turn is the quaint estate village of **Ilam** , largely rebuilt by 19th-century shipping magnate Jesse Watts Russell in Neo-Gothic style. Russell lived at mock-Gothic **Ilam Hall** (grounds and park open daily during daylight hours; hall private; National Trust). In the grounds stands the beautiful **Church of the Holy Cross**, a mixture of Saxon, Norman and Early English.

Make your way back to the A515 and head north to **Hartington** . You'll cross the line of the Tissington Trail at the **Hartington Station National Park Visitor Centre**, housed in a railway-signal box – children love it because they can operate the signals. Hartington has a wonderful youth hostel in a Jacobean hall, and is the home of the **Stilton Cheese Factory**, one of only a few in the country. Return to the main road and take the A5012 back towards Matlock.

BELOW: honey for sale in Hartington. **RIGHT:** the mock-Gothic Ilam Hall.

Some 10 miles (16 km) up the A6 from Matlock is **Rowsley** , with the splendid 17th-century Peacock Hotel. Opposite it, a road leads to **Caudwell's Mill and Craft Centre** (open Mar–Oct, daily 10am–6pm, Nov–Feb, Sat–Sun

Map on page 276

only; entrance charge). This 19th-century mill on the Wye, one of few working water-powered roller mills, was lovingly restored by a group of enthusiasts and still produces and sells flour. Local craftspeople work in the former stableyard.

Stately homes

From here, the B6012 takes you to **Chatsworth House ❿** (open mid-Mar–Oct, daily 11am–5.30pm; entrance charge). Home of the Dukes of Devonshire for some 400 years, and known as "the Palace of the Peaks", this is one of the finest houses in England, and contains one of the most important private art collections in the country. The **Sketch Galleries** and the **Sculpture Gallery** show the Duke's continuing interest in art.

Highlights of the tour include the magnificent **Painted Hall** by Louis Laguerre, which shows scenes from the life of Julius Caesar, and is the setting for the annual Chatsworth Children's Christmas Party. The **State Rooms** are stunning in their opulence. Note the superb 17th-century English tapestries in the Drawing Room, the wonderful painted ceiling, again by Laguerre, in the State Bedroom, and Jan Vandervaart's famous *trompe l'oeil* violin "hanging" behind a door. The **Great Dining Room** is where the young Princess Victoria had her first dinner with the grown-ups in 1832. It has recently been redecorated in lovely ruby silk panelling, and is notable for its gold-encrusted barrel ceiling and fine collection of paintings. On a different scale, but also impressive, is the series of small rooms known as the **Queen of Scots Rooms**, where the unfortunate monarch lodged during several stays between 1570 and 1581.

The house as we see it today is largely the creation of the 4th Earl and the Dutch architect William Talman, and it was built in the Palladian style between

In 1998 Amanda Foreman won the prestigious Whitbread prize for her biography of Georgiana, the 18th-century Duchess of Devonshire .

BELOW: Chatsworth House, the "Palace of the Peaks".

Enjoying Chatsworth Playground.

Haddon Hall is familiar to many because it has featured in a number of cinema and television films.

BELOW: one man and his dog at Chatsworth.

1678 and 1707. The only part of the original 16th-century Tudor house that remains is the **Hunting Tower** (private), up through the trees of Stand Wood behind the house.

Also in Stand Wood is the **Chatsworth Farm and Children's Adventure Playground** (open mid-Mar–Oct, daily 10.30am–4.30pm; entrance charge). In the farmyard the realities of farm life are shown and explained; while the playground has a sand and water play area for younger children and commando-style obstacles for older ones.

About a mile up the A6 from Rowsley is another famous stately home, **Haddon Hall** ⑪ (open April–Oct, daily 11am–5.45pm, closed Sun July–Aug; entrance charge), home of the Duke of Rutland and known as "the most romantic medieval manor house in England", a description that is hard to dispute. Haddon is remarkably unrestored: most of what you see from the sloping **Lower Courtyard** dates from the 14th and 15th centuries. The time-worn steps and oak-panelled rooms breathe history. Among the highlights are the wonderful **Banqueting Hall**, the very essence of a medieval manor house, complete with minstrels' gallery and massive 13th-century oak refectory table. The **Long Gallery**, with elaborate oak panelling featuring the boar's head and the peacock of the founding families, is wonderfully light and airy. But many people's favourite area is the **Kitchen**, stone-flagged and walled with massive oak tables, chopping blocks and mixing bowls almost worn through with centuries of use.

The **Chapel of St Nicholas**, one of the oldest parts of the house, originally served the now-disappeared village of Nether Haddon. It contains some of the finest 14th- and 15th-century wall paintings in Britain. The tour ends with the famous terraced gardens: a riot of roses, clematis and other blossoms in summer.

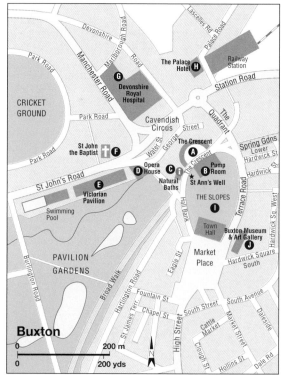

Beyond Haddon Hall you come to **Bakewell** ⓬ whose history goes back to the Saxons, as a visit to the parish church of **All Saints** will reveal: although heavily restored in Victorian times, the cruciform church still has fragments of Saxon and Norman work, and two of the finest Saxon preaching crosses in the Peak District are in the churchyard.

Just behind the church is the **Old House Museum** (open April–Sept, daily 2–5pm; entrance charge), one of the finest local museums in the country. It is housed in a 1534 Tudor building, which was used in the 19th century by Richard Arkwright as accommodation for workers employed at his mill on the Wye. There are collections of memorabilia, costumes, lace, samplers and toys, and the Victorian kitchen is retained, along with recreated craftsmen's workshops.

Back in the centre of town, visit the **Old Market Hall National Park and Tourist Information Centre** (open April–Sept, 9.30am–5.30pm, Oct–Mar, till 5pm, Thurs till 1pm; entrance charge) in Bridge Street. The arcaded building dates from the 17th century, and was for many years used as a market hall. Displays tell the story of the town and the Peak District, and regular audio-visual shows and talks are presented upstairs in the half-timbered roof space. There is a well-stocked shop where maps and guides are on sale.

Try the original Bakewell puddings.

Outside the Visitor Centre is the **Old Original Bakewell Pudding Shop**, one of three in the town that claim to hold the original recipe to this much-loved almond and puff pastry confection. The story is that it was created when a flustered cook at the 17th-century Rutland Arms Hotel in nearby Rutland Square poured her pastry mix over the jam instead of the other way around. Whether this is true or not, the pudding (or tart, as it is known outside the region) has become synonymous with Bakewell.

BELOW: a Bakewell Carnival float.

The northern spa

Leaving Bakewell, follow the A6 through the pretty Wye Valley to **Buxton** ⓭. Start by admiring the elegant Corinthian-styled buildings of the **Crescent Ⓐ**, now beautifully restored after many years of neglect. Designed by York architect John Carr in the 1780s, it was part of the master plan of the 5th Duke of Devonshire to make Buxton a fashionable spa town. The **Assembly Rooms**, once used for church services, have been restored as part of the public library. The **Thermal Baths** have become the Cavendish Shopping Arcade, but they retain a plunge pool complete with bosun's chair-type seat showing how some patients were encouraged to "take the waters".

Opposite the Crescent is the low classical structure built in 1894 and known as **The Pump Room Ⓑ**. The building is now closed to the public, but you can still use the drinking fountain outside, known locally as **St Ann's Well** – the scene during July of one of the town's well-dressing ceremonies. There are often queues of people waiting to fill containers with the warm, blue, slightly effervescent water. Buxton's Tourist Information Centre is housed in **The Natural Baths Ⓒ**, left of the Crescent, where there is an interpretive display showing the origins of the thermal waters. Appropriately, it is sponsored by the Buxton Mineral Water company.

Maps:
Area 276
Town 280

Walk past the Natural Baths and up to the corner of The Square, where massive gritstone "cloisters" face the attractive Pavilion Gardens. Turn right at the corner and you'll see the ornate, twin-domed frontage of the **Opera House** , designed and built in the grand Edwardian style by the eminent theatrical architect Frank Matcham in 1905 and sensitively restored in 1979, after serving for many years as a cinema. It seats 1,000 people in a magnificently decorated auditorium lit by a massive gas-fired crystal chandelier. The theatre stages a varied programme of comedy, drama, ballet and concerts, as well as opera, and is the home of the widely acclaimed **Buxton International Festival of Music and the Arts**, held annually at the end of July.

Beside the theatre is the splendid **Victorian Pavilion** ❺ (1871), well supplied with restaurants and bars. Its **Conservatory** houses a variety of tropical and native plants, and a small aviary. In the centre of the Pavilion is the superb **Octagon**, or Concert Hall, which soars above the Pavilion Gardens. Just beyond the Octagon is a large modern swimming pool, filled with warm spa water.

The **Pavilion Gardens** provide 23 acres (9 hectares) of pleasantly landscaped space by the banks of the River Wye. Although the gardens continue beyond Burlington Road, turn right into St John's Road to the parish church of **St John the Baptist** ❻, a beautiful example of Italianate Georgian architecture standing in an oasis of green. Designed by Sir Jeffrey Wyatville, who worked closely with the 6th Duke of Devonshire at Chatsworth, it is built in a Tuscan style and contains some fine mosaics and stained glass behind a massive portico under an elegant tower rising to a copper dome.

Beyond the parish church is the great dome of the **Devonshire Royal Hospital** ❼ (closed to the public), formerly the Great Stables, built in 1790 to

It was the Romans who first put Buxton on the map. They called it "Aquae Arnemetiae", which means the Spa of the Goddess of the Grove. There are Roman remains to be seen in the town museum.

BELOW: tropical plants in the Victorian Pavilion Conservatory.
RIGHT: the Buxton Opera House.

house the horses of spa visitors. The great dome that so dominates Buxton was begun in 1880, when, with the widest unsupported iron-framed dome in the world, spanning 152ft (46 metres), it was an architectural wonder. Across Devonshire Road stands the imposing facade of the **Palace Hotel** , Buxton's largest and most prestigious, built at the height of the resort's popularity in 1868. It stands close to the **London and North Western Railway Station**, of which, unfortunately, only the facade remains, with its great semi-circular fan window.

From the station, walk down The Quadrant back to The Crescent and the steep paths that wind up **The Slopes** ❶, designed to provided graded paths for exercise. At the top of The Slopes, which offer fine views across the town, is the **Town Hall**, designed by William Pollard and opened in 1889. Hall Bank leads steeply up from The Slopes to the Market Place and the area known as Higher Buxton, where the weekly street market is held. Turn left down Terrace Road to **Buxton Museum and Art Gallery** ❶ halfway down on the right (open Tues–Fri 9.30am–5.30pm; Sat till 5pm, April–Sept, also Sun and bank holidays, 10.30am–5pm; entrance charge). This is an excellent little museum with an award-winning display entitled "The Wonders of the Peak", which takes you back in a time tunnel complete with sounds and smells.

Macclesfield and Lyme Park

Macclesfield ⓮ was granted a charter by Edward I to establish a free borough in 1261, but the town's modern prosperity rests on the silk industry that began in 1742. Three excellent museums tell the story of the town's rise to fame as a silk producer, and the best place to start is the **Macclesfield Heritage Centre** (open Mon–Sat 11am–5pm, Sun 1pm–5pm; entrance charge) in Roe Street,

**Maps:
Area 276
Town 280**

TIP

Buxton has a market on Saturday, and a smaller one on Tuesday. Many of its shops close on Wednesday afternoon. Half-day closing is a custom that is dying out in England, but is retained in a number of small towns.

BELOW:
a well-dressing tableau at Buxton.

WELL DRESSING

Nothing to do with fashion, well dressing is a Peak District custom that takes place in many villages – about 20 in all – throughout the summer months. Pagan in origin – it was probably an act of thanksgiving for the spring well-water on the high, dry limestone plateau – the ceremony was gradually taken over by the Christian religion, which absorbed what it could not suppress, and is now usually linked to the day that honours the patron saint of the local church, at the beginning of what is sometimes known as Wakes Week.

Designs, usually on biblical themes, are etched into malleable clay on a wooden background, then brought to life, like a natural mosaic, with leaves, berries, bark and grass. The tableau is carried in a procession and placed over the local well, where it is blessed by the village priest in a ceremony that generally coincides with the local summer fête.

Well dressing can be seen in Wirksworth and Ashford in May; Rowsley, Bakewell and the Hope Valley at the end of June; in Bamford and Buxton in July; in Eyam in August; and in numerous other villages. Consult the local tourist office or the informative *Peakland Post* (available free from tourist offices) for details of dates and places.

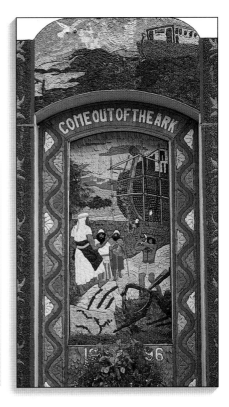

Working on a Jacquard handloom at Paradise Mill.

BELOW: walking the Peaks is a popular weekend activity.

which also houses the **Silk Museum** – the only museum in the country dedicated to the silk industry. The last handloom weaver in Macclesfield retired in 1981, but you can see 25 working Jacquard handlooms at the **Paradise Mill Working Silk Museum** (open April–Sept, Tues–Sat 1–5pm, Oct–Mar, till 4pm; entrance charge), which is a few minutes' walk away. An interesting way of exploring the past is to follow the Silk Trail (details from the Tourist Information Centre at the Town Hall, open Mon–Thurs 8.45am–5pm, Fri tll 4.30pm).

From Macclesfield take the B5470 to **Lyme Park** ⓑ (house open April–Oct, Sat–Wed 1.30–5pm; park all year, daily at 8am; National Trust with Stockport Borough Council). Lyme is one of the Peak District's most impressive stately homes. Originally Tudor, the present Palladian mansion was designed by Leone Leoni in 1720, and its three-storey Ionic portico on the south front is reflected by a peaceful lake. The interior is famous for its intricate carvings by Grinling Gibbons, its clock collection and its beautiful orangery, but Lyme Park's latest claim to fame has been as a location for the BBC's 1995 television adaptation of Jane Austen's *Pride and Prejudice*. The extensive 1,320-acre (534-hectare) park is famous for its red deer, the largest herd in the Peak District, and it backs on to the moorland of Park Moor, where the hunting tower known as the Cage is a prominent landmark.

Castleton and the caves

From Lyme Park, get on the A6 as far as **Whaley Bridge**, a pleasant little town where colourful canal boats are moored in the canal basin. From here you can follow a minor and at times extremely steep road to the **Goyt Valley** where there is good rock climbing for the intrepid and, for the rest, lovely views over

WALKING THE PEAKS

If you are a seasoned and adventurous walker you will have a fair idea of where you want to go and what kind of terrain to expect in the Peak District, but for those who would like to ramble but are a bit hesitant there is an extensive scheme of Park Ranger-led walks. Some 200 walks cater for differing interests (some specialise in archaeology or botany, for example) and different levels of experience. There are gentle walks that are suitable for children and wheelchair-accessible, and tougher hikes for experienced hill walkers.

You can do a rugged 12-mile (20-km) moorland walk to Kinder's waterfall, learn about wildlife in the Goyt Valley, walk the hills above Dove Valley, or gently discover the Upper Derwent. The starting point of most walks can be reached by public transport – use it whenever you can, to help cut down on traffic.

All walks are free, but for some you need to book in advance. For more information, ring the Walks Information Line (tel: 01629 815185, Wed 10–11am, Thurs 2–3pm) or ask a local tourist office for the (free) *Peakland Post*, which gives full details. Don't forget you need sturdy shoes, waterproofs and a packed lunch for the longer walks.

the Fernilee and Errwood Reservoirs, and a forest trail to what is left of Errwood Hall, demolished when the valley was flooded to provide water for Stockport.

After this detour, take the A6 again for about 5 miles (8 km) then turn right towards **Castleton** ⑯, the "capital" of the **Hope Valley**. Prominent in the village is the parish church of **St Edmund** with some lovely 17th-century box pews. It plays an important part in Castleton's **Garland Ceremony** on Oak Apple Day (29 May), when the Garland King and Queen, on white horses, lead a procession, the King encased from head to waist in the "garland", a wooden cage covered in flowers. The procession stops at all the village pubs, where a special tune is played and children dance, then ends up at the church, where the garland is strung from the top of the tower and left to wither. The custom is thought to have its origins in a pagan ceremony to welcome the return of spring.

Castleton owes its fortune to its strategic importance and its geography. Ever since the Celtic Brigantes tribe built their massive hill fort on the windswept 1,698-ft (517-metre) summit of **Mam Tor** (National Trust) this has been a military and administrative centre, although the modern village only came into existence when William Peveril, William the Conqueror's illegitimate son, built **Peveril Castle** (open April–Sept, daily 10am–6pm, Oct–Mar, till 4pm; closed 1–2pm; English Heritage). Situated on a limestone spur between the precipitous slopes of Cave Dale and the huge chasm of Peak Cavern, the castle is as impregnable as a castle could be. Not much remains of Peveril's early structure but the views from the ramparts are magnificent.

The Garland King at the Castleton Garland Ceremony.

But most people come to Castleton to visit the famous show caves which display the unique semi-precious mineral known as Blue John. The oldest of the caves is **Peak Cavern** (open April–Sept, daily 10am–5pm, Oct–Mar, till 4.30pm). Its entrance is said to be the largest in Britain, under a 300-ft (90-metre) cliff of limestone over which towers Peveril Castle. Inside, the spacious entrance area was once home to a community of rope-makers, whose equipment still survives. The roof is still blackened with the soot from their sunless homes.

BELOW: National Park Study Centre at Castleton.

In the **Speedwell Cavern** (open April–Sept, daily 9.30am–5.30pm, Oct–Mar, till 4.30pm) at the foot of the **Winnats Pass** (National Trust), you are transported to the Bottomless Pit by a boat that is legged along a flooded lead mine drainage level like a barge in a canal tunnel. The Winnats Pass is a spectacular limestone gorge formed after the last Ice Age. The scene of the tragic murder of a pair of lovers in the 18th century, it is now the only road out of the Hope Valley to the west, since constant landslips from the crumbling slopes of Mam Tor led to the closure of the former A625 turnpike road in the early 1970s.

Treak Cliff Cavern (open April–Sept, daily 9.30am–5.30pm, Oct–Mar, 10am–4pm) probably has the most spectacular formations, and it is one of the few sources of the semi-precious banded fluorspar known as Blue John. Ornaments made from this brilliant brittle mineral are sold here and in the village.

The fourth of Castleton's caves, the **Blue John Cavern** (open daily 9.30am–6pm, or dusk if earlier), is reached by turning right and right again at the top of the Winnats Pass. This cavern was discovered 300

Map on page 276

A mass trespass took place on Kinder Scout in 1932 when five ramblers were arrested for riotous behaviour. Their actions sparked the National Parks and Access to the Countryside movement.

The five great Victorian reservoirs that fill Longdendale valley supply Manchester with 24 million gallons (110 million litres) of water a day.

BELOW:
market in Glossop.

years ago when miners in search of Blue John broke into the previously unknown range of caves.

The Pennine Way

From Winnats Pass you can take the steep, narrow road between Mam Tor and Rushup Edge which drops steeply down into the Vale of Edale, with magnificent views of **Kinder Scout** ⑰, the district's reigning summit (2,088 ft/636 metres). At **Edale** is a **National Park Visitor Centre** (open daily 9am–5pm), for this is the southern point of the great long-distance path, the 250-mile (400-km) **Pennine Way**, which marches along Britain's backbone between the Peaks and the Scottish border. This is serious walking country, and weather forecasts are available at the centre, which doubles as a mountain rescue point.

Serious walkers might also want to head up to the northern moors; high, wild country of desolate moorland and long valleys, where the trans-Pennine roads are often closed by snow in winter. To do so, get back on the A6, then the A624 to **Glossop** ⑱, a small industrial town with a surprisingly elegant main square. Glossop's wealth was founded on textiles: there were nearly 60 cotton mills here in the 19th century. **Old Glossop** still has a pleasing pre-industrial air and a range of 17th-century gritstone houses. The history of the region is well told in the **Glossop Heritage Centre** (open Mon–Sat 10.30am–4.30pm) just off Norfolk Square (the 11th Duke of Norfolk was a patron of Glossop).

From Glossop head for the A628. Passing through the hamlet of Tintwistle (pronounced "Tinsel"), you enter the dramatic cross-Pennine valley of **Longdendale**, an important packhorse route for centuries. The Woodhead Railway ran through the valley in 1847; it included the Woodhead Tunnel, then the longest in the world, and was built at the cost of many lives. The line is closed now and redesignated the **Longdendale Trail**, part of the **Trans-Pennine Trail** which links the Irish and the North seas. It is served by a **Peak National Park Information Centre** at **Torside** ⑲ (open summer weekends and bank holidays) near the sailing club on Torside Reservoir.

At nearby **Crowden**, you again cross the line of the Pennine Way, which drops from the peaty heights of **Bleaklow** (2,060 ft/628 metres) to the south to climb the boggy wastes of **Black Hill** (1,908 ft/582 metres) to the north, on one of the toughest sections of the pennine path. **Crowden Youth Hostel**, to the left of the road, converted from a row of cottages by the National Park authority in 1965, creates a vital first overnight stopping place for northbound walkers.

Risqué cards and risky roads

From Crowden, take the A6024 to **Holmfirth** ⑳, a town with three claims to fame: it has a fascinating collection of saucy postcards at the **Holmfirth Postcard Museum** (open Mon–Sat 10am–4pm, Sun till 4pm; entrance charge); some of the earliest silent films were produced here (by the postcard company); and the long-running BBC Television comedy series *Last of the Summer Wine* is set here.

Head back now across **Wessenden Head Moor**, recrossing the line of the Pennine Way again, then take a sharp turn just before Greenfield to beautiful **Dove Stone Reservoir** ㉑, with good surrounding walks and a thriving sailing club. Head back to Glossop through Stalybridge (in the eastern suburbs of Greater Manchester), then get on the A57 which will take you across the Snake Pass to Sheffield. Best not to try it in winter: the **Snake Pass** ㉒ is one of the highest and most exposed roads in Britain – it reaches 1,680ft (512 metres) at the summit – and is always one of the first to be closed in winter, and the last to reopen. Even a light scattering of snow on either side of the pass can mean the road will be closed on top.

Map on page 276

The road runs above Holden Clough, passing the peat banks of **Featherbed Moss**. It levels out at the summit where the unmistakable line of the Pennine Way is crossed. Such is the erosion on this popular wilderness route that sections have been paved with gritstone slabs recycled from demolished local mills. This crossing is on one of the toughest sections of Britain's hardest long-distance path. From the summit, the road swings down in a series of sharp bends to **Lady Clough** then to the isolated **Snake Pass Inn**, a welcome landmark, and sometimes a life-saving one, for walkers or stranded motorists.

The Snake Pass Inn is a welcome sight for walkers.

As the A57 continues towards Sheffield you pass, on the right, the western arm of the **Ladybower Reservoir** (the largest in the Upper Derwent), and on the left, the **Upper Derwent Valley** ㉓, a man-made landscape, from its reservoirs and dams to the surrounding conifer woods, which has proved so popular that minibus and cycle-hire services are provided at weekends to keep traffic from choking the entrance road. The main road continues over the Ashopton Viaduct to the western suburbs of **Sheffield** ㉔. Once the steel capital of Britain, the city is recovering from the industry's decline, and while many see it simply as a convenient base for visiting the Peaks, it does have its own attractions. ❑

BELOW: Sheffield's Orchard Square Shopping Centre.

THINGS TO DO IN SHEFFIELD

An enlightened attitude to public transport makes Sheffield easy to get around. The Supertram, a glossy modern tramcar, is a pleasure to ride. A popular university also ensures a lively atmosphere and plenty of bars, clubs and cheap-ish restaurants. Try visiting:

The National Centre for Popular Music (open daily 10am–6pm; entrance charge) a brand new museum of rock music, housed in huge steel drums

Sheffield City Museum and Mappin Art Gallery, Weston Park (open Tues–Sat 10am–5pm, Sun/bank holidays 11am–5pm; entrance charge) holds most of the important archaeological finds in the Peak District. The art gallery has a fine collection of works by local artists.

The Ruskin Gallery, Norfolk Street (open Mon–Sat 10am–5pm; entrance charge) houses the collection of the Guild of St George, the movement started by the pre-Raphaelite John Ruskin (1819–1900) to bring the finest in art and nature to the attention of working-class people.

Abbeydale Industrial Hamlet (open Tues–Sat/bank holidays 10am–5pm, Sun 11am–5pm; entrance charge) a museum of the industrial past. Craftsmen demonstrate their skills in this restored steelworks, with a crucible steel furnace and working waterwheels, set by the River Sheaf.

THE NORTHWEST

Liverpool, home of the Beatles, also has a great waterfront and excellent galleries, while Manchester has emerged as a thriving metropolis, and Blackpool remains a seaside institution

The Northwest is not one of England's prime holiday destinations, but with two vibrant and exciting cities – Liverpool and Manchester – and the smaller historical city of Lancaster, as well as Blackpool, one of the country's best-known seaside resorts, plus miles of sands at Morecambe Bay, and the lovely Ribble Valley, the region has lots to offer.

City on the Mersey

It is possible to visit **Liverpool** ❶ and avoid references to the Beatles, but it's not easy. The group are still the main reason many people come here, and there is plenty to see on the Beatles trail. **The Beatles Story** (open daily 10am–5pm; entrance charge) in Albert Dock will take you through their whole career; the **Cavern Club**, a new building on the old site, is open every day except Sunday; Paul McCartney's childhood home now belongs to the National Trust and is open to the public (20 Forthlin Road, tel: 0870 9000256; advance booking essential); and **Magical Mystery Tours** run daily (tel: 0151 7093285 for reservations) to all sites of interest to Beatles fans and 1960s enthusiasts.

Albert Dock is a busy development with a variety of shops, bars, restaurants, museums and galleries. The **Merseyside Maritime Museum** (open daily

PRECEDING PAGES: Liverpool's Albert Docks. **LEFT:** the Rochdale Canal, Manchester. **BELOW:** the Beatles.

FACT FILE

By car Connections to Merseyside via the M6, M56, M58 and M62, about 4 hours from London; to Manchester via the M6, M62, M56, about 3 hours 30 minutes.
By train InterCity services from London to Liverpool, about 2 hours 30 minutes; about 3 hours to Manchester; tel: 0345 484950.
By coach National Express services from London, Birmingham and many other cities to Liverpool, Manchester, Lancaster and Blackpool; tel: 0990 808080.
By air Manchester Airport, 10 miles (16 km) south of the city centre, tel: 0161 4893000.
Liverpool Waterfront Pass Tel: 0151 7088574; entry to five sites on one ticket.
Bridgewater Packet Boat Service Tel: 0161 7482680 for trips around Manchester's canals.
Manchester United Football Club Museum Tel: 0161 8774002 for tours of the Old Trafford grounds and a museum visit.
Liverpool Football Club Museum and Tour Centre Tel: 0151 2606677.
Tourist Information Centres Liverpool, tel: 0151 7098631/7088854; Manchester, tel: 0161 2343157/0891 715533; Blackpool, tel: 01253 478222/343434.

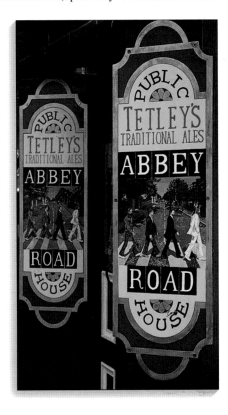

Hands-on at the Maritime Museum.

10am–5pm; entrance charge) documents the history of the port, and the **Museum of Liverpool Life** (open daily 10am–5pm; entrance charge) explores the city's contribution to national life. Among the fine galleries are the **Tate Gallery Liverpool** (open Tues–Sun 10am–6pm; admission free) with a national collection of modern art; and the **Walker Art Gallery** (open Mon–Sat 10am–5pm, Sun noon–5pm; entrance charge) displaying outstanding examples of European art from the 14th century to the present.

Music of all kinds is a vital part of the Liverpool scene: the **Philharmonic Hall** is home to the prestigious Royal Liverpool Philharmonic Orchestra; and **Cream** is considered by many to be the best dance club in the country. While we are on the subject of biggest and best, the Neo-Gothic **Liverpool Cathedral** (open daily 8am–6pm; donations welcomed) is the largest Anglican cathedral in England; and **Aintree** is the ground on which the **Grand National**, one of the best-known horse races in the world, is held every April.

The changing face of Manchester

Manchester ❷ is changing so fast it's hard to keep up with it. The city came to prominence during the 19th century when it was at the forefront of the Industrial Revolution. Its "dark satanic mills" sprang up when cotton production was revolutionised by Richard Arkwright's steam-powered spinning machines in the late 18th century. When a railway line linked the city with Liverpool in 1830, and the Manchester Ship Canal was completed in 1894, Manchester's prosperity was sealed, and the huge Victorian civic buildings we can see today are evidence of a city that believed in its own destiny. The tenements in which the mill workers lived were razed by slum-clearance projects in the 1950s.

BELOW: gateway to Mancester's Chinatown.

But Manchester's docks went the way of many others, and for years the city centre was drab, under-used and under-populated, before a huge revitalisation process began. Now the centre throbs with life. There's a shiny new shopping centre; a colourful Chinatown; a Gay Village, spanning out from a canal-side promenade; and three universities which ensure a lively young scene.

Some things to include on a visit are a tour of **Granada Studios** (times vary; tel: 0161 8324999), where for a fairly hefty charge you can take a look behind the scenes of leading television programmes; the extensive **Museum of Science and Industry** (open daily 10am–5pm; entrance charge) an award-winning museum with full working machinery; the **City Art Gallery** (open Mon–Sat 10am–5.30pm, Sun 2–5.30pm; admission free); and the **Manchester Jewish Museum** (open Mon–Thurs 10.30am–4.30pm, Sun till 5pm; entrance charge) where a record of the city's Jewish history is housed in a restored synagogue. If you have time, try to book for a performance by the resident Hallé Orchestra at the splendid new **Bridgewater Hall** (tel: 0161 9079000).

Down in the valley

To reach the **Ribble Valley**, take the A666 north, past Blackburn, and head for **Clitheroe ❸,** a pleasant little town for an overnight stop if you want to explore the area. From the remains of its ancient castle, perched on a limestone crag, there are splendid views of the valley. Nearby stands the remains of the 13th-century Cistercian **Whalley Abbey**, and a parish church with Saxon crosses outside. To the west, **Ribchester**, a pretty little village with a 17th-century bridge over the river, has the remains of a huge Roman fort, part of which has been excavated to reveal the foundations of two granaries.

Map
on page
292

TIP

Manchester is proud of its new café society: try Mick Hucknall's Spanish Barça Bar (tel: 0161 8397099), overlooking the Bridgewater Canal, or Bill Wyman's Sticky Fingers (tel: 0161 8354141), housed in a restored church.

BELOW: in the pretty Ribble Valley.

Beside the seaside

Leaving the peaceful valley, the B5269 joins the M55 motorway for the short trip (about 12 miles/20 km) to **Blackpool** 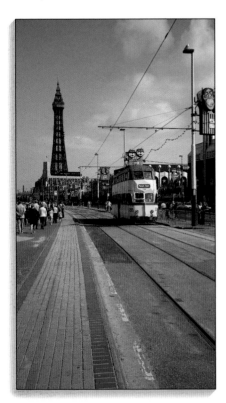, which became a popular seaside resort when the arrival of the railways in the mid-19th century enabled Lancashire cotton workers to enjoy a day beside the sea. Up until the time of easily-accessible package holidays to the Mediterranean in the 1970s, it remained the north's premier resort: loud, brash and cheerfully vulgar. It's not quite the same now, but it still packs in the visitors and knows how to keep them amused.

The main political parties take it in turns to hold their annual autumn conferences in Blackpool.

Fast-food stalls, and restaurants, bingo halls and amusement arcades line the **Golden Mile**, which parallels long, wide stretches of sand, where sand-surfers and kite flyers have the time of their lives. Trams trundle along the prom, three piers offer traditional summer entertainment, and the **Pleasure Beach** has every ride imaginable. The famous 518-ft (158-metre) **Blackpool Tower** looms above it all: in September and October it is outlined in coloured lights as the centrepiece of the spectacular **Blackpool Illuminations**. There's also indoor and outdoor go-karting, a Sea Life Centre, 10-pin bowling, indoor swimming pools, a waxworks and a zoo, so children are well catered for.

City of the red rose

Head north now on the A588 to **Lancaster** , the county town of Lancashire, founded by the Romans. In 1322 Robert Bruce razed the castle and much of the town to the ground but they were rebuilt by John of Gaunt, and his Gateway Tower is a fine specimen. During the 15th-century so-called Wars of the Roses, the House of Lancaster was symbolised by the red rose, the House of York by the white. Part of the **Castle** is used as a Crown Court (open April–Oct when

BELOW: the famous Blackpool Tower.

court not in session; entrance charge) and the Shire Hall can be visited at the same times. There's also a priory church, **St Mary's**, with a fine Saxon doorway and beautiful choir stalls. As a university town, Lancaster has plenty of social life: no shortage of bars and restaurants, and an interesting little arty cinema.

Shrimps and sands

Morecambe Bay ⑥ is known for its shrimps and its sands. The shrimps are small, brown and tasty and are gathered in nets taken across the sand by horse and cart. The sands, a vast spread of tidal flats that are home to thousands of sea birds, can be very dangerous: the tide sweeps across the bay and performs a pincer movement around the sandbars, then spreads over the flats, and in no time at all a peaceful expanse of sand becomes a choppy sea. There are guides who will lead you, when the tide is right, all the way round the bay. The best way to see the sands and their bird population is by train on a track that trundles over viaducts from Ulverston (*see page 302*) to Arnside.

Morecambe is a pleasant holiday resort on the bay, which claims to have originated the idea of illuminations in order to lengthen the summer season, but somehow it didn't catch on here the way it did in Blackpool.

Carnforth ⑦ is the last stop on our route, a small town just north of Morecambe, whose main claims to fame are the **Railway Museum** (open daily; entrance charge) where a large collection of locomotives, including the *Flying Scotsman*, have been restored to gleaming working order; and **Leighton Hall** (open May–Sept, Tues–Fri and Sun 2–5pm; entrance charge), home of the Gillow furniture family, many of whose superb products can be seen here. In the extensive grounds there are eagle and falconry displays most afternoons. ❑

Map on page 292

BELOW: the Cross Bay Walk, Morecambe.

THE LAKE DISTRICT

The landscape that inspired the Lakeland poets continues to exert its spell on visitors, who come to walk the fells, to sail the waters, or simply to enjoy the breathtaking scenery

Map on page 300

London

The **Lake District**, in northwest England, is a small area, but extremely beautiful, with the varied delights of soft hills and woodland, the panoramas of the great lakes, the unexpected discoveries of the smaller waters or tarns, the bare contours of the fells and high ground and the awe-inspiring power of the more remote mountains and mountain passes. The poet William Wordsworth, who was born here at Cockermouth in 1770 and spent most of his life here, rightly remarked: "I do not know any tract of country in which, within so narrow a compass, may be found an equal variety in the influences of light and shadow upon the sublime or beautiful features of landscape."

The Lake District is more frequently visited, both by day tourists and holiday-makers, than any other region of outstanding natural beauty in the British Isles. On the whole it copes remarkably well with the vast numbers of visitors, but traffic congestion can be a big problem in summer.

The two routes that were popularised by the first tourists in the 1760s and 1770s still carry the greatest share of summer traffic. One is from Penrith to Ambleside by the west shore of Ullswater and over the Kirkstone Pass, now the A592; the other is from Keswick to Windermere by the side of Thirlmere, Grasmere, Rydal Water and Windermere, now the A591.

PRECEDING PAGES: Coniston Water. **LEFT:** fell walkers take a welcome break. **BELOW:** wooden sculpture in Grizedale Forest.

FACT FILE

Location 250 miles (400 km) from London, 75 miles (120 km) north of Manchester, the Lake District covers 30 miles (48 km) north–south, and 20 miles (32 km) east–west.
By train London King's Cross or Euston to Penrith or to Oxenholme (with a connecting service to Windermere); journey time about 4 hours 30 minutes. From Edinburgh to Carlisle, about 1hours 30 minutes; tel: 0345 484950.
By coach National Express from London Victoria to Kendal; journey time about 6 hours 30 minutes; tel: 0990 808080.
By car about 5 hours from London via the M40/M6.
By air Manchester Airport, near the M6, is approximately 80 miles (130 km) south of Windermere.
Most famous sons (and daughters) Children's writer Beatrix Potter (1866–1943); the poet William Wordsworth (1770–1850).
For children The World of Beatrix Potter; Lowther Leisure and Wildlife Park; Grizedale Forest Sculpture Playground.
Festivals Appleby Horse Fair (June); Ambleside Rush-bearing Festival (July); Lowther Horse Country Fair.
Tourist information Coniston, tel: 015394 41533; Hawkshead, tel: 01539 436525; Kendal, tel: 01539 725758; Keswick, tel: 017687 72645; Ullswater, tel: 01768 482414; Windermere, tel: 015394 46499.

Lake District

Solway Firth

Gretna

Brampton

Glasson
Cardurnock
Houghton
Milton

Burgh
by Sands
Linstock

Newton
Arlosh
Kirkbride
Carlisle
Scotby
Castle
Carrock

Silloth
Calvo
Kirkbampton
Cumwhinton

Blitterlees
Abbeytown
Micklethwaite
Croglin

Beckfoot
Pelutho
Thursby
Wreay

Allonby
Waverton
Wigton
Rosley
Welton
Southwaite
Kirkoswald

Allonby Bay
Aspatria
Arkleby
Mealsgate
Boltongate
Caldbeck
Sebergham
Lazonby
Little
Salkeld

Crosscanonby
Bothel
Ireby
Parkend
Plumpton
Langwathby

Maryport
Dearham
Sunderland
Bewaldeth
Hutton-in-the-Forest
Unthank

Flimby
Blindcrake
Mosedale
Laithes
Greystoke
Dalemain
Penrith

Broughton Moor
Great
Broughton
Cockermouth
Bassenthwaite
Skiddaw
931
Mungrisdale
Scales
Stainton
Dacre
Tirril
Brougham

Workington
Bridgefoot
Bassenthwaite
Lake
Mirehouse
Applethwaite
Threlkeld
Hutton
Wreay
Hackthorpe

Moss
Bay
Branthwaite
Pardshaw
Thornthwaite
Keswick
Castlerigg
Stone Circle
Dockray
Watermillock
Aira
Force
Ullswater

Distington
Gilgarran
Mockerkin
Braithwaite
Stair
Great Dodd
856
Sandwick
Bampton

Parton
Pica
Loweswater
Loweswater
Derwent
Water
Thirlmere
Glenridding
Rosgill
Shap

Whitehaven
Asby
Frizington
Crummock
Water
Grange
Watendlath
Helvellyn
950
Patterdale
Bridgend
Hartsop
Haweswater
Reservoir

Hensingham
Mirehouse
Sandwith
Cleator Moor
Buttermere
Rosthwaite
Wytburn
Harter Fell
765

St Bees
Head
Egremont
Cleator
Ennerdale
Water
Pillar
892
Seatoller
Seathwaite
Stonethwaite
Kirkstone Pass
454

St Bees
Haile
Nether
Wasdale
Scafell
Pike
977
Lake District
National Park
Grasmere
Rydal Mount
Cumbria
Tebay

Beckermet
Wast
Water
Chapel Stile
Ambleside
Kentmere
A6

Sellafield
Wellington
Eskdale
Green
Hardknott
Roman
Fort
390
Wrynose Pass
Troutbeck
Forest Hall

Seascale
Gosforth
Boot
Cockley Beck
Hawkshead
Windermere
Staveley
Watchgate

Holmrook
Beckfoot
Hardknott
Pass
The Old Man
of Coniston
803
Coniston
Bowness-on-
Windermere
Burneside

Ravenglass
Muncaster
Seathwaite
Grizedale
Forest Park
Hill
Top
Winster
Kendal

Ulpha
Hoses
Coniston
Water
Satterthwaite
Winster
Sizergh
Oxenholme

Broughton-
in-Furness
Blawith
Force
Rusland
Levens
Sedgwick

Bootle
Foxfield
Lowick
Bouth
Cartmel
Fell
Row
Levens Hall

Broadgate
Haverthwaite
Ayside
Grange-
over-Sands
Woodhouse
Milnthorpe

Irish
Sea
Selker
Bay
Silecroft
Greenodd
Arnside
Burton-in-Kendal

Kirkby in
Furness
Millom
Arrad Foot
Cartmel
Priory
Lindale
Kents Bank
Silverdale
Whittington

Haverigg
Ulverston
Pennington
Cartmel
Holker
Hall
Humphrey
Head Point
Warton
Arkholme

Bardsey
Flookburgh
Carnforth
Hornby

Furness
Abbey
Dalton-in-Furness
Scales
Newton
Morecambe
Bay
Hest Bank
Halton

North Scale
Leece
Rampside
Morecambe
Lancashire

Barrow-in-Furness
Isle of
Walney
Foulney Island
Heysham
Lancaster

South End
Hilpsford
Point
Scotforth
Forest of
Bowland

Sunderland
Point Glasson
Preston

N

| 0 | 10 km |
| 0 | 10 miles |

Away from these routes you can find quiet areas of great beauty – particularly if you avoid the high summer – and experience the sense of solitude and oneness with nature that was valued so highly by the 19th-century Romantic poets (*see page 306*).The central area of mountains was never much affected by industry or quarrying, and the 19th-century shipbuilding, iron manufacturing and coal mining that once flourished by the coast have now almost entirely disappeared. Sheep farming was the traditional way of life of the hill folk, and it continues today throughout the area covered by the Lake District National Park, often on farms owned and leased by the National Trust.

A map on page 300

Gardens, halls and abbeys

Approaching from the south along the M6, turn off at Junction 36 to Levens. **Levens Hall ❶** (open Apr–Sept, Sun–Thurs, house: noon–5pm, garden 10am–5pm; entrance charge) is an Elizabethan house furnished in Jacobean style, and built around a 14th-century pele tower. The famous topiary garden is little changed since its trees were first shaped in the 17th century.

A Cumbrian sheep farmer.

The A590 south from Levens leads to **Cartmel Priory ❷** (open Mon–Fri 11am–5pm by prior arrangement; tel: 01539 536874), near the resort of Grange-over-Sands on a finger of land pointing down into Morecambe Bay. It was founded in 1188 by the Baron of Cartmel and was saved from destruction at the time of Henry VIII's Dissolution of the Monasteries by the quick-wittedness of local people who claimed that it was their parish church. Only the gatehouse and the church remain. Inside the latter there is good medieval carving and old glass; the lovely east window dates from the 15th century, as does the tower. The village is delightful, too.

LEFT: Levens Hall topiary garden.
BELOW: Cartmel village square.

Nearby **Holker Hall** (open April–Oct, Sun–Fri 10am–6pm; entrance charge), the splendid home of the powerful Cavendish family, is set in an attractive garden. The architect Sir Joseph Paxton (1801–65) planted the monkey puzzle tree (Chile pine) which has reached an enormous height.

The Furness Peninsula, the southern tip of Lakeland, was in medieval times the heart of a great Cistercian estate farmed by the monks of **Furness Abbey** ❸ (open Easter–Oct, daily Nov–Mar, Wed–Sun; entrance charge; tel: 01229 823420 for details). The abbey, which lies in a lovely setting, was the second-richest Cistercian establishment in England at the time of its suppression in 1537. Its red sandstone buildings, standing out against green lawns, date from the 12th and 15th centuries. The abbey lies to the north of **Barrow-in-Furness**, the peninsula's main town, and once a major shipbuilding centre. Head north now on the A590 to the historic town of **Ulverston** ❹ on an old ship canal, where you can visit the **Laurel and Hardy Museum** (open daily 10am–5pm; entrance charge). Sounds incongruous, but Stan Laurel was born here in 1890.

Back on the A591 near Levens, where we began, you will come to **Sizergh Castle** (open April–Oct, Sun–Thurs 1.30–5.30pm; National Trust) whose medieval defensive appearance is softened by attractive gardens. About 3 miles (5 km) on you reach **Kendal** ❺, which is a good centre for exploring the Lakes. It is still a working town, not just a holiday centre, carrying on its daily life in the midst of fine 17th- and 18th-century buildings. The church is a Perpendicular structure, and the lively Brewery Arts Centre is worth a look. Beside the church stands 18th-century **Abbot Hall Art Gallery and Museum of Lakeland Life and Industry** (open Mar–Oct, daily 10.30am–5pm; tel: 01539 722464 for winter hours; entrance charge). The former has paintings by John Ruskin and

The area in which Furness Abbey stands is known as the Vale of Deadly Nightshade because these sinister plants once grew here in such profusion.

BELOW: the Abbot Hall Museum.
RIGHT: Finckle Street, Kendal.

J. M. W. Turner and by local artist George Romney; the latter concentrates on local trades and crafts, and has a room devoted to *Swallows and Amazons* author Arthur Ransome (1884–1967) whose books have a Coniston Water setting.

Map on page 300

The Southern Lakes

The A591 runs from Kendal to the town of **Windermere ⑥** and the lake of the same name. It's a Victorian town, which really came into being when the railway arrived. In a pretty setting on the lakeside is the **Windermere Steamboat Museum** (open April–Oct, daily 10am–5pm; entrance charge), where mementos from the age of steam (including the 1850 steam-launch *Dolly*, said to be the oldest mechanically powered boat in the world) can be seen. Windermere is closely associated with the children's writer Beatrix Potter (1866–1943), and **The World of Beatrix Potter** (open daily; entrance charge; tel: 01539 488444) in the Old Laundry at Crag Brow recreates her characters in a lively exhibition. You can walk down Lakes Road to **Bowness-on-Windermere ⑦**, the most popular resort, which has a very attractive centre but is almost always too crowded for comfort.

Cruising the lake is a popular pastime.

You can also take a car ferry to Near Sawrey and **Hill Top**, Potter's home (open April–Nov, Sat–Wed 11am–5pm; National Trust), a fine example of a 17th-century Lakeland farmhouse, with a traditional cottage garden, but, like Bowness, it is always crowded at peak periods.

In nearby **Hawkshead ⑧** on the west side of the lake, is the **Beatrix Potter Gallery** (open April–Oct, Sun–Thurs 10.30am–4.30pm; National Trust) housed in the office of her solicitor husband and little changed since his day. It has changing displays of many of her original drawings and watercolours.

BELOW: sailing on Lake Windermere.

TAKING TO THE WATER

Looking at lakes, in scenery such as this, is wonderful, but at some point most people actually want to get on the water, whether to get from one point to another, to view the fells from a different perspective or simply to feel at one with the water.

Ullswater Steamers are the best way to enjoy the lake and the mountains around it. In the summer season there are three scheduled services every day between Glenridding, Howtown and Pooley Bridge, and five one-hour cruises. You can take a one-way trip and walk back if you prefer that option. Tel: 01539 721626 or 017684 82229 (Glenridding Pier).

Windermere Lake Cruises operate a fleet of launches and steamers all year round between Ambleside, Bowness and Lakeside, with connections for the Lakeside and Haverthwaite Steam Railway, the Brockhole Visitor Centre and the Aquarium of the Lakes. Steamers have licensed bars and coffee shops and are heated in the winter. Tel: 015395 31188 (Lakeside), 015394 43360 (Bowness) or 015394 32225 (Ambleside).

Coniston Water has the National Trust steam yacht, the *Gondola*, launched in 1859 and now renovated, which takes visitors on memorable cruises, tel: 01539 441288.

The school that Wordsworth attended in Hawkshead.

William Wordsworth (1770–1850) (*see page 306*) attended the **Grammar School** at Hawkshead (open April–Oct, Mon–Fri 10am–12.30pm, 1.30–5pm, Sun 1–5pm; entrance charge). Upstairs is a superb library with books dating from the foundation of the ancient school by Archbishop Sandys in 1585. **St Michael's Church** preserves wall paintings of scriptural texts. From beneath its east window you can take in the view of this tiny, whitewashed town.

West of Hawkshead stands the medieval arched **Courthouse**, all that remains of a group of 15th-century manorial buildings constructed when the Cistercian monks from Cartmel ruled much of the area. Further west, on the B5285, is **Tarn Hows**, which may be the prettiest lake in the district. There are adequate National Trust car parks (including one close to the lake for disabled people) and a good footpath right round the tarn, which was created in the 19th century by building a dam and merging three smaller tarns.

You can continue on the west side of the lake towards Ambleside, but if you take the A591 from Windermere you will also be able to visit **Troutbeck**, a delightful village which has several roadside wells dedicated to various saints; a church with a Pre-Raphaelite east window (the combined work of Edward Burne-Jones, William Morris and Ford Maddox Brown); an old inn called the Mortal Man; and a 17th-century farmhouse, **Townend** (open April–Nov, Tues–Fri and Sun 1–5pm; National Trust), built by a yeoman, which has a wonderful collection of carved woodwork and domestic implements.

Ambleside ❾ is a Victorian town of splendid slate buildings. The tiny **House on the Bridge** spanning the beck beside Rydal Road, houses a National Trust information centre. There is also a glass-blowing workshop and an old corn mill, complete with water wheel.

BELOW: Hawkshead village centre.

Old Man and eminent men

Instead of continuing north from here you could make a diversion on the A593 to **Coniston Water**  where the **Old Man of Coniston** (2,635 ft/ 803 metres) can be climbed via a well-marked route from the village. In St Andrew's Church, John Ruskin (1819–1900), the art historian and critic, is buried. The **Ruskin Museum** (open Easter–Oct, Sun–Fri 11am–5pm; entrance charge) is a few minutes' walk from the church. Ruskin lived at **Brantwood** (open Mar–Nov, daily 11am–5.30pm, winter, Wed–Sun; entrance charge), on the northeast shore of Coniston Water. Many of his paintings are preserved, and the house remains much as he left it. It's accessible by road (B5285) or by the newly-renovated Victorian steam yacht *Gondola* from Coniston Pier, which is operating once more after lying wrecked in Nibthwaite Bay for many years.

To the east of Coniston lies **Grizedale Forest Park** ⓫, a large tract of land the Forestry Commission has imaginatively given over to nature trails, modern sculptures and a small theatre.

Get back on the A593 now to Ambleside, then pick up the road towards Keswick. You'll soon come to **Rydal Mount** (open Mar–Oct, daily 9.30am–5pm, Nov–Feb, 10am–4pm; entrance charge), which was the home of the Wordsworth family from 1813 until William's death in 1850. The house (still owned by a descendant) contains portraits and family mementos; the grounds were landscaped by Wordsworth and retain their original form.

Rydal Water is a small reedy lake with a population of waterfowl, and red squirrels in the larches round the edge.

Two miles (3 km) north lies **Grasmere** ⓬, a pleasant village on the lake of the same name "the prettiest spot that man has ever found" according to

Map on page 300

John Ruskin

BELOW: the *Gondola* has returned to Coniston Water.

*Dove Cottage
in Grasmere.*

Wordsworth. **St Oswald's Church** with its ancient timber roof is worth a visit in its own right, not just to see the Wordsworthian graves. The display of manuscripts and portraits of the poet's family and friends in the **Wordsworth Museum** (open mid-Feb–Dec, daily 9.30am–5.30pm; entrance charge) brings home the magnitude of the poetry that was written here and the importance that Wordsworth and his friend Samuel Coleridge (*see below*) held in the cultural life of their day. Entrance to the museum also gives access to whitewashed **Dove Cottage** from which William, his wife Mary, and sister Dorothy, had a view over Grasmere to the fells, although it's now hemmed in by later buildings.

Pencils for poets

The 17-mile (28-km) journey to Keswick on the A591 passes **Thirlmere** ⑬, a reservoir created from two smaller lakes in 1890 to supply the needs of Manchester. **Helvellyn**, the third-highest mountain in England (3,118 ft/950 metres), rises steeply to the right. Close to Keswick you could turn off to **Castlerigg Stone Circle**, an ancient monument which Victorian tourists associated with the Druids. The views from here are tremendous.

BELOW: Castlerigg
Stone Circle –
views from here
inspired the poets.

Keswick ⑭ is a Victorian town with a much older centre, which has been popular with visitors since the 1760s. It has a **Moot Hall** (market hall), grand as a church, which now houses a helpful information centre. The town came to prominence through the manufacture of pencils, using graphite mined in Borrowdale. The factory is now the **Cumberland Pencil Museum** (open daily 9.30am–4pm; entrance charge). Keswick's **Museum and Art Gallery** (open Easter–Oct, Tues–Sun 10am–noon, 1–4pm) has mementos and manuscripts of Samuel Coleridge, Robert Southey and Hugh Walpole, who all lived nearby.

THE LAKE POETS

There's no getting away from the Lake Poets – not that anyone really wants to. They were the first generation of English Romantics, united by their love of poetry, free thought, progressive causes and natural beauty.

William Wordsworth (1770–1850) was the focus. Born in Cockermouth, he lived most of his adult life in the district, accompanied by his wife Mary and sister Dorothy (1771–1855), whose journals provided inspiration for her brother's work. His line "I wandered lonely as a cloud..." must be one of the few that every English person knows. Samuel Coleridge (1772–1834) joined them in 1800, living in Greta Hall, Keswick, and continuing the intense friendship begun a few years earlier. It ended in an irrevocable quarrel 10 years later, by which time he was addicted to opium. Robert Southey (1774–1843) joined the group shortly afterwards; he took over Greta Hall and lived there for 40 years. He was appointed Poet Laureate in 1813. Thomas de Quincey (1775–1859), was more of a journalist than a poet, but closely associated with the group. He settled for a while in Grasmere, at Dove Cottage, previously occupied by the Wordsworths, and made his name in 1822 with *The Confessions of an English Opium Eater* – a subject on which he was well qualified to write.

Map
on page
300

Lovely **Borrowdale Valley** has long been a favourite with both artists and walkers. The B5289 from Keswick skirts **Derwent Water** ⑮, which mirrors a range of splendid fells. To the left of the road are the **Lodore Falls** "receding and speeding, And shocking and rocking..." as Robert Southey wrote. Where the valley narrows to form the Jaws of Borrowdale (best seen from Friars Crag on the right as you leave Keswick) lies the pretty village of Grange, reached over a narrow bridge. A mile to the west is **Brackenburn** (private), the home of Hugh Walpole, who set *The Herries Chronicle* (1930–33) in the region. From Grange you can walk beside the waters of the Derwent and through the oak woods.

Stay on the B5289 and you'll pass Rosthwaite and Seatoller. Between the two is **Johnny Wood**, with a nature trail. The road continues through **Honister Pass**, where fell walkers park their cars and make the relatively easy climb to the summit of **Great Gable** (2,949 ft/899 metres). From here the road drops down to **Buttermere** ⑯ at the foot of Fleetwith Pike (2,126 ft/648 metres). You can walk round Buttermere (which is quieter than the other lakes), then stop at the **Fish Inn** in the village, where the strength of the ale was recommended back in the 18th century. In **Buttermere Church** there's a plaque to Alfred Wainwright (1907–91), most famous of the fell walkers. Through the window (on a clear day) you can see **Haystacks Fell**, where his ashes were scattered.

Lodore Falls.

Back on the road, and turning left when it joins the B5292, you come to **Cockermouth** ⑰, a pleasant market town of red sandstone buildings which is mostly visited by those keen to see the **Wordsworth House** (open April–Oct, Mon–Fri 11am–5pm and Sat in high summer; National Trust), where the poet was born in 1770. From the extensive gardens a terraced walk leads down to the River Derwent.

LEFT:
hikers at Langdale.
BELOW: walking builds up a hearty appetite for the local food.

The A595 leads straight to Carlisle from here, but our tour takes the A66 which skirts **Bassenthwaite Lake** for a while then passes Keswick, with Skiddaw Forest to the left. **Skiddaw** (3,054 ft/931 metres) and **Blencathra**, also known as Saddleback (2,847 ft/868 metres), are the dominant fells. At the foot of Skiddaw lies **Mirehouse**, the home of scholar James Spedding 1808–81 (open Apr–Nov, house Sun and Wed 2–4.30pm, grounds daily 10am–5pm; entrance charge).

John Ruskin, who climbed Blencathra in 1867, thought it "the finest thing I've yet seen... there being a fine view at the top... fresh wind blowing and plenty of crows".

From Ullswater to Carlisle

It's only a 15-mile (24-km) drive from Keswick to the old town of Penrith, but there are a few interesting diversions to be made en route. You could incorporate a visit to **Dacre**, a few miles before the town on the right. It has a largely Norman church, even earlier carvings and views of 14th-century **Dacre Castle**. Nearby is **Dalemain** (open Easter–mid Oct, Sun–Thurs; tel: 01768 486450 for opening hours), an old house unaltered since 1750, with fine interiors (including a Chinese drawing room), paintings and a pleasant garden.

Dalemain lies just off the A592, which leads past **Ullswater** ⓲ and over the Kirkstone Pass to Ambleside. Ullswater is the second-largest lake after Windermere, and it was here that the Wordsworths saw the dancing daffodils. There are steamers on the lake (*see page 303*) from which one can enjoy magnificent views of Helvellyn and other surrounding mountains. **Aira Force** (National Trust), on the north shore beneath **Gowbarrow Fell**, is one of the most impressive waterfalls in the Lake District, tumbling 60 ft (18 metres) in a gorge flanked by trees. The fell, a former deer park, is a good place to wander, enjoying magnificent views without too much strenuous effort.

BELOW: a dog's a good companion on a fell walk.

WALKING THE FELLS

Walking is the most popular activity in the Lake District. The travel shelves of local bookshops are crammed with books, most of which describe circular and not-too-arduous routes. The Lake District National Park organises walks, and details are given in their free newspaper, which is available at any Information Centre. The Cumbria Tourist Board also produces a booklet called *Short Walks Good for Families*.

For more experienced walkers – those who believe there is no substitute for the fell walking books written and illustrated by Alfred Wainwright – there are some great challenges: a circuit taking in the Langdale Pikes, beginning and ending at the Dungeon Ghyll car park at the head of Great Langdale, is one of the most popular. In the east of the region, the summit of Helvellyn can be approached from either Thirlmere or Ullswater – one route from the latter being up the magnificent Striding Edge. In Central Lakeland, Great Gable can be climbed from Honister Pass, while Wasdale Head is the most popular starting point for those wishing to conquer Scafell Pike. The southern fells are dominated by the Old Man of Coniston, while Skiddaw looms 3,354 ft (931 metres) above Bassenthwaite Lake.

After this diversion, it's on to **Penrith** ⓳ a sturdy working town of red sandstone buildings, where the 14th-century castle is a picturesque stump in a park near the station, and a collection of ancient stones, known as the Giant's Grave, stand in the churchyard of 18th-century St Andrews. **Brougham Castle**, just southeast of Penrith, is a Norman structure built on the foundations of a Roman fort. The ruins here are impressive: the top gallery of the keep has fine views and is worth the effort of climbing. A few miles further south, off the A6, the **Lowther Leisure and Wildlife Park** offers a variety of activities in 150 acres (60 hectares) of parkland, and the **Lakeland Bird of Prey Centre** (open Mar–Oct daily, with falconry displays at 12.30pm, 2pm and 4pm).

Just north of the town, at Little Salkeld, stands an impressive Bronze Age stone circle known as **Long Meg and her Daughters**. On the B5305 is a stately home worth a visit: **Hutton-in-the-Forest** (open May–Sept, Thurs, Fri, Sun; entrance charge; tel: 017684 84449 for details). It's a gracious building, with a 13th-century tower and a splendid 17th-century Long Gallery, a walled garden and pleasant woodlands.

Carlisle ⓴, 21 miles (34 km) north of Penrith on the M6, is our last stop. It's also the last city before the Scottish border on the northwestern side of the country. Now the capital of Cumbria, it has suffered numerous attacks over the centuries, and the Norman **Castle** obtained its unusual outline when its roof was strengthened to carry cannons. The **Tullie House Museum and Art Gallery** (open daily; entrance charge; tel: 01228 34781 for details) houses an eclectic collection of Roman artefacts, wildlife displays and Pre-Raphaelite paintings. Carlisle is a good starting point for Hadrian's Wall (*see page 346*). A special bus operates daily in summer from the town centre (tel: 01228 625600). ❑

Map on page 300

There's lots for children to do at Lowther Leisure and Wildlife Park.

BELOW: falconry display at the Lakeland Bird of Prey Centre.

PLAY UP, PLAY UP AND PLAY THE GAME!

England's special gift to the world is cricket.
Most countries don't want it, and the ones that do
have proved to be much better at it

A Frenchman reporting on the state of cricket in England in 1728 wrote: "Everyone plays it, the common people and also men of rank. They go into a large open field and knock a ball about with a piece of wood. I will not attempt to describe this game." Apart from a lack of sensitivity to the music of leather balls on willow bats, this foreigner was sensible in not attempting a description of a game which involves two teams of 11 players, two wickets, two umpires, tea and sandwiches and, in county and international Test matches, takes five days to play. It has been said that the English, not being spiritual people, invented the game to give themselves some conception of eternity.

BATTING FOR A BETTER WORLD

Many see cricket as a civilising influence. Writing on the French Revolution, the historian G.M. Trevelyan reflected, "If the French noblesse had been capable of playing cricket with their peasants, their châteaux would not have been burnt." In this idealised pursuit the village blacksmith had the opportunity to hurl balls down at the Lord of the Manor. And with such sporting spirit, in which one did one's best, never cheated, and played with a "straight bat", the British Empire was made.

△ **CRAZY GAME, CRAZY GUYS**
One delight of the game is seeing in what bizarre circumstances it might be played. The players pictured here in the Solent on the south coast meet for a 90-minute match once a year, the only time when the Brambles Sandbar is revealed by an abnormal tide.

▷ **SMALL BUT PERFECT**
The leather balls are small and hard. Bowlers use the sewn seams to make the ball do as they want.

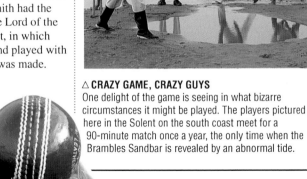

◁ THE IDYLL

Cricket is still played on village greens. Games last all afternoon, with a break for tea, and there's beer when stumps are pulled.

▽ HOWZAT!

If a batsman is thought to be out, a cry goes up for the umpires to adjudicate. The headgear shows it can be a dangerous game.

W. G. GRACE, HERO AT THE WICKET

The colossus of cricket was William Gilbert "W.G." Grace, depicted here in by *Vanity Fair* magazine in 1877. He was a giant on the field, knocking up runs with consummate ease. Born in Bristol, he played for a Gloucester team of Gentleman *v* Players at the age of 16. He twice captained England and toured the US and Canada. At home crowds flocked to see him wherever he appeared. He had a doctor's practice, and remained a gentlemen player, though this amateur status did not prevent him making money from the game where he could. His reputation for fairness and a straight bat overshadowed the odd occasion when he would replace bails claiming that the wind had blown them off. He went on playing until he was 66 and Sir Arthur Conan Doyle watched him old age, recording, "At the end of a century he had not turned a hair."

◁ OLD SCHOOL TIES

Lords cricket ground (left) in London is home to the Marylebone Cricket Club, its members identified by garish ties (above). The MCC is the game's governing body, and international Test matches are played at the grounds.

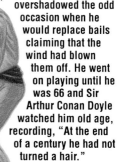

YORK

*This venerable city of the north, easily explored on foot,
has a vast Minster and strong links with the Romans,
Vikings and the golden age of railways*

Engl's most ancient northern city lies on the River Ouse in the centre of the Vale of York between the Yorkshire Dales and the North York Moors. It was once the principal town of Yorkshire, and it remains the see of the Archbishop of York, Primate of England, second to the Archbishop of Canterbury in the hierarchy of the Church of England. Its streets, walls and buildings mark the pageant of its history, from Roman and Viking ancestry, medieval heart and Georgian elegance. A child-friendly city, its Viking, Castle and Railway Museums have plenty to engage young people as well as adults.

The starting point of any visit is **York Minster ❹**, England's largest medieval church (*see next page*), which dominates the town. The **Minster's Visitor's Centre** is beside it in St William's College, founded in 1461 as the home of the chantry priests who sang Masses for the souls of the founder. In Dean's Park on the north side of the Minster is the **Minster Library**. The Archbishop's Palace once covered this area and the library, which is the largest cathedral library in the country, is in its former chapel. To the right of the chapel is the **Treasurer's House** (open Mar–Oct, 10.30am–5pm; National Trust). Built in 1419, it was fully restored at the end of the 19th century, but ghosts of Roman legionnaires continue to march through its cellar. The Roman city was walled but the walls

Maps:
City 317
Area 324

PRECEDING PAGES:
York Minster.
LEFT: The National
Railway Museum.
BELOW: street
busker.

FACT FILE

Location 207 miles (333 km) from London, 195 miles (392 km) from Edinburgh
By car M1 motorway from London to Leeds, the last 36 miles (60 km) on the A1 and A64. Allow 3 hours
By train from London's King's Cross every 30 minutes. Journey time 1 hour 50 minutes to 2 hours 20 minutes
Nearest airport Leeds/Bradford
Boat trips cruises on the Ouse include one-hour trips downstream to the Archbishop's Palace at Bishopthorpe.
Most famous site The Minster, with the greatest collection of medieval stained glass in Britain
Best for Yorkshire high teas Betty's Tea Room, St Helen's Square – cinnamon toasts and laden tea trolleys
Festivals Jorvik Viking Festival with ceremonial boat burning (January), three-day Ebor Festival at Knavesmire horse-race track – "the Ascot of the North" (August)
National symbol a white rose: the Wars of the Roses, immortalised in Shakespeare's *Richard III*, were fought between the House of York (white Rose) and the House of Lancaster (red rose)
Royal connection the second male son of a monarch is traditionally given the title Duke of York
Tourist information tel: 01904 621756

THE MAGNIFICENT MINSTER

With fine medieval stained glass, this is the most elegant buildings in the north. For a detailed floor plan see page 398

The Minster is the largest Gothic cathedral north of the Alps and is both a cathedral – because of its archbishop's throne – and a minster because it has been served since Saxon times by a team of clergy. It has the widest nave in England, stands 196 ft (60 metres) high, is 525 ft (160 metres) long and 250 ft (76 metres) wide across the transept. The finest stained-glass in the country give an immediate impression of airy lightness. The first church was founded in 627, followed by two Norman cathedrals and the present Gothic one, completed in 1472. Major restoration was needed after two 19th-century fires, and one

in 1984, caused by lightning, destroyed the south transept roof.

The Nave is Decorated Gothic in style and was completed in the 1350s. The pulpit on the left has a brass lectern, in use since 1686. The 14th-century West Window, painted in 1338. is known as the "heart of Yorkshire" because of the shape of the ornate tracery. Shields in the Nave arches are the arms of nobles who fought against the Scots in the 14th century. The Dragon's Head peeping out from the upper gallery is a crane used to lift a font cover. To the right of the nave is the Jesse Window of 1310. The North Transept is dominated by the Five Sisters' Window from 1260, the oldest complete window in the Minster

The Chapter House (admission

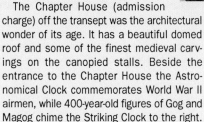

charge) off the transept was the architectural wonder of its age. It has a beautiful domed roof and some of the finest medieval carvings on the canopied stalls. Beside the entrance to the Chapter House the Astronomical Clock commemorates World War II airmen, while 400-year-old figures of Gog and Magog chime the Striking Clock to the right.

The Screen in the crossing is decorated with the statues of 15 kings of England from William I to Henry VI. Daily services are held behind it in the Choir. The Great East Window at the east end of the church has the world's largest area of medieval stained glass, with scenes from the Bible. On the south side of the Choir St Cuthbert's Window (1435) shows scenes from the life of the saint. The Norman Crypt contains the coffin of the minster's founder, St William.

The South Transept, restored after the 1984 fire, has mirrored tables to see the new carvings, six designed by children. The Rose Window, which commemorates the end of the Wars of the Roses in 1486, escaped destruction in the fire. Walls of the Norman churches and remains of the Roman forum lie beneath the Central Tower in the Foundations Museum and Treasury. ❏

CLOCKWISE FROM LEFT: The Minster's exterior; the Archbishop's throne; the Screen; and the Astronomical Clock.

that can be seen today date largely from the 14th century and are the longest remaining medieval walls in Britain. **Monk Bar B**, which lies on the north side of the Minster, gives access up on to the Bar Walls. Walking round the wall to the left and encircling the former Archbishop's Palace brings you to **Bootham Bar C**, which once led out to the Forest of Galtres. Armed guards used to wait to act as guides to protect travellers from wolves in the forest.

From here descend to Exhibition Square where there is a fountain and statue of the local artist William Etty whose work can be seen in the nearby **City Art Gallery** (open Mon–Sat 10am–5pm, Sun 2.30–5pm; entrance charge), which has a modest collection of old masters. Behind the gallery is Museum Gardens and the **Yorkshire Museum D** (open Mon–Sat 10am–5pm, Sun 1–5pm; entrance charge). The region's most important archaeological, geological and natural finds are housed here. There is a reconstruction of a Roman kitchen and a marble head of Constantine the Great who was proclaimed Roman Emperor when he was quartered in this city in 306.

Into the old town

Cross the street in front of the museum and head straight into the old town to arrive at **Stonegate E**, the finest street in York, which follows the Roman Via Praetoria. Elegant shops now use the 15th and 16th-century houses: No 52A is the 1180 **Norman House**, the oldest surviving house in the city. Another historic site is Coffee Yard where coffee houses were once meeting places described by the 19th-century author Laurence Sterne as "chit chat" clubs.

Stonegate leads down towards the River Ouse where the **Guildhall F** and **Mansion House** lie. The Mansion House is the residence of the city's Lord

Parliament Street pals.

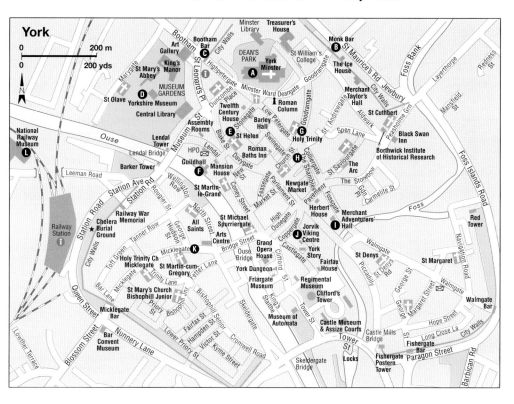

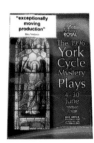

The medieval York mystery plays, revived in 1951, are performed every three years: 2002, 2005, and so on.

Mayor, the only one outside London to be accorded the title of The Right Honorable; the building was completed in 1730, 10 years before London's Mansion House. The arched passageway alongside this pretty building leads to the **Guildhall** (open Mon–Thur 9am–5pm, Fri 9am–4.30pm; May–Oct, also Sat 10am–5pm, Sun 2–5pm; entrance charge). First mentioned in 1256, it was rebuilt in the 15th century, and since 1810 the city's business has been conducted from the council chamber rich with Victorian carved desks and chairs, and with a view over the river. Hooks on the ceiling were used for hanging meat. Committee Room No. 1 is where the Scots received payment in silver from the Parliamentarians in 1646 for handing over Charles I who had fled to Scotland. The cash was counted out on the table. The impressive, oak-beamed Common Hall is a replica: the original was destroyed by German bombs. The contemporary stained-glass window is by York artist Harry Harvey.

Petergate, at the opposite end of Stonegate, leads to **Goodramgate** where boutique and antique shops occupy Tudor buildings. Eleven tenements from the 11th century are known as Lady's Row; opposite is a 1960s error, an eyesore of concrete arches which brought strict controls on subsequent developments. Halfway down the street is **Holy Trinity Ⓖ**, one of the most delightful of the city's churches. Built between 1250 and 1500, it has a two-tiered pulpit (1785) and a reredos with the Ten Commandments, Creed and Lord's Prayer.

Heart of the old town

Goodramgate leads down to **King's Square** and Colliergate where the shortest street in York has the longest name: Whipmawhopmagate. A plaque suggests this is 16th-century dialect for "What a gate!". King's Square is the place to be in summer: buskers, jugglers and street artists provide some of the best free entertainment in the north of the England. Leading off the square is **The Shambles Ⓗ**, York's most famous street and one of the best-preserved medieval streets in all Europe. Once called Fleshammels (the street of the butchers), its broad windowsills served as shelves to display meat. The half-timbered houses lean inwards and neighbours can shake hands across the street. Three narrow alleyways lead to **Newgate Market**, open daily with stalls selling everything from fish to fashions. The original main market area was on **Pavement,** on the other side of the Newgate Market. This was the first paved street in the city, a place of punishment (whipping, pillorying) and execution.

Fossgate, which leads from Pavement down to the River Foss, is where the richest of the city's medieval merchants used to live. Just before the river on the right is a stone portal leading to the **Merchant Adventurers' Hall Ⓘ** (open daily 8.30am–5pm, Nov–Mar, closed Sun; entrance charge). Still the home of the most powerful of the York guilds, the hall has a massive, timber-framed roof and a 14th-century undercroft used for receptions.

The other end of the Pavement leads to Coppergate and the **Jorvik Viking Centre Ⓙ** (open April–Oct, daily 9am–7pm, Nov–Mar, 9am–5.30pm; entrance charge). The museum is based on an archaeological

BELOW: The Shambles.

dig at Coppergate in the 1970s which revealed wicker houses and shoulder-high walls, the best-preserved Viking settlement in Britain. Visitors are whisked back to a reconstructed settlement in "time cars". Background chatter of the ancient Norse language and evocative smells of middens and latrines give a convincing atmosphere. Craftsmen are at work and a sailing ship lies at a wharf. The museum is popular, so be prepared to queue at weekends and in summer.

Map on page 317

The age of horse and steam

Castlegate behind the Viking Centre ends in a great earth mound topped by **Clifford's Tower**, thrown up by the Normans in their conquest of England. The **Castle Museum** (open Mon–Sat 9.30am–5.30pm, Sun 10am–5.30pm; entrance charge), housed in what was a female and a debtors' prisons, is a folk museum with reconstruction of a complete Yorkshire street and a glimpse of lost ways of life. There is still evidence of the former prison: the cell of the highway robber Dick Turpin is preserved; in 1735 he was sentenced next door in the Assize Court and hanged on St George's Field.

On the south side of the River Ouse is **Micklegate** , once York's most important street, as it was the road into the city from London. Many fine Georgian houses were built along it. But for a century and a half, visitors have been arriving by rail: York is famous for its railways, personified in George Hudson, the 19th-century "Railway King". **The National Railway Museum** (open Mon–Sat 10am–6pm, Sun 11am–6pm; entrance charge) is one of the greatest in the world. Exhibits range from George Stephenson's tiny *Agenoria* of 1829 to the *Mallard*, which broke the world steam speed record 99 years later, reaching 126 mph (203 kph), and Queen Victoria's favourite travelling "home". ❏

George Hudson, three times Lord Mayor of York, was York's "Railway King", obsessed with "makin' all t'railways coom to York". But by 1847 his speculations had ruined him.

LEFT: the Jorvik Viking Centre.
BELOW: National Railway Museum.

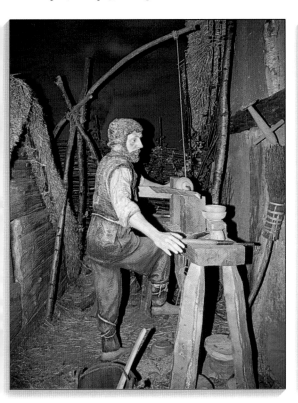

YORKSHIRE

The Dales and Moors of Yorkshire are as rugged and resolute as their inhabitants. Beyond York are the great former abbeys of Whitby, Fountains and Rievaulx

Map on page 324

Yorkshire is England's Big Country. Until 1974 this region north of the River Humber was divided into three Yorkshire "Ridings", from the Old Norse *trithing*, meaning three administrative parts. North Riding (now largely North Yorkshire) was larger than any other county in England. Characterised by miles of moorland, the three modern counties of Yorkshire extend from the Pennines to the North Sea, and includes two national parks – the Yorkshire Dales to the west of York and the North York Moors to the north – separated by the Vale of York, where the A1 follows the old Roman Road heading for Hadrian's Wall.

Limestone, shale and sandstone of the Carboniferous Age shaped the Yorkshire Dales, which are cut through by fast-flowing rivers and douched with waterfalls. The Jurassic limestone of the North York Moors has been used for houses, castles and spectacular abbeys such as Fountains and Rievaulx. To the south the Yorkshire Wolds are chalk hills rising to 800 ft (240 metres), reaching the sea at Flamborough Head. Grouse are the prize of the moors; trout fill the short, fast rivers and streams of the Pennines and Dales.

Yorkshire is traditionally a sheep-rearing region, and incessant grazing means there is no true wilderness. An overall pattern of drystone walls links the farms,

PRECEDING PAGES: *Wuthering Heights* setting on the Yorkshire Moors. **LEFT:** Danby Dale. **BELOW:** Litton in the Yorkshire Dales.

FACT FILE

Main town Leeds, York (*pages 315–19*)
Main attraction Yorkshire Dales and North York Moors National Parks
By car the A1 goes through the Vale of York, the Dales on the west, the Moors to the north east
By bus the North York Moors National Park Authority operates a Moorsbus, timetables at tourist offices
By train two quaint trains serve the area: the North Yorkshire Moors Railway, from Pickering to Grosmont, and the Settle–Carlisle line
National characteristic stubbornness
National obsession cricket
National anthem *On Ilkla Moor baht 'at*
Local words dale (valley), fell (hill), force (waterfall), gill (wooded ravine), scar (deep rock face)
Most impressive monuments Fountains Abbey, Rievaulx Abbey
Best stately home Castle Howard
Most famous family the Brontës
Eat and drink bilberry pie, Wensleydale cheese, Sam Smith's beer
Tourist information Harrogate, tel: 01423 525666; The Moors Centre, Danby, tel: 01287 660654

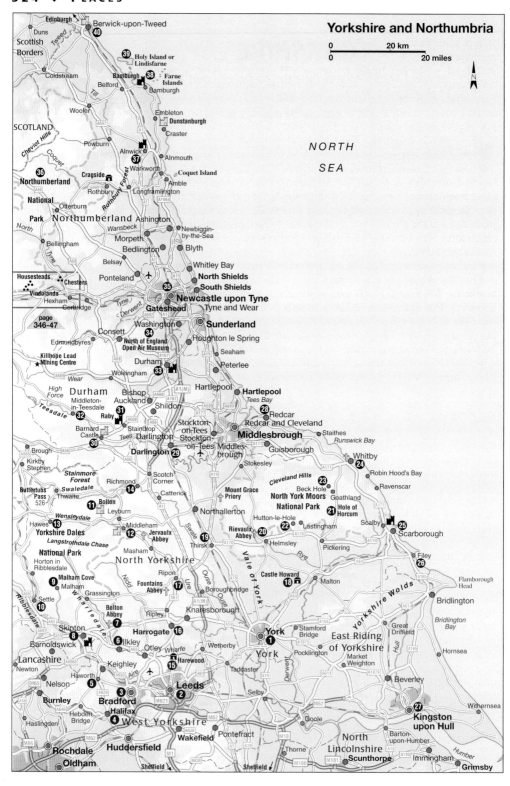

Yorkshire and Northumbria

villages and market towns. The buildings, constructed in local slate and stone, are unpretentious in style but perfectly suited to the needs of a pastoral community, from the farmhouse with its big, flagged, ground-floor rooms, to the field barns with just enough space to accommodate young cattle. The farmers' way of life, evolving in isolation, bred a sturdy, independent type of person, the sort about whom James Herriot, the celebrated Dales vet (whose real name was Alf Wight), wrote in his best-selling books.

Map on page 324

The wool towns

Yorkshire sheep produced a wool trade which enriched the monasteries and the town of **York ❶** (*see pages 315–19*). After the Industrial Revolution, however, cloth manufacturer was centred on the towns to the south of the Dales. England's third-largest and Yorkshire's main city, **Leeds ❷** (population 450,000), is one place to go to see the region's industrial heritage. **The Armley Mills Museum** (open Mon–Sat 10am–4pm, Sun 12.30–4pm; entrance charge), on the northwest side of this lively university city, is a woollen mill equipped with all the machinery and equipment that once helped to make Britain the richest nation.

The **Royal Armories Museum** (open daily 10am–5pm; entrance charge) beside the River Aire at Clarence Dock contains an impressive collection of weaponry, from an elephant's suit of armour to Saddam Hussein's supergun. The museum was moved here from the Tower of London but has so far failed to attract enough visitors to justify the move. **The City Art Gallery** (open Mon–Sat 10am–5pm, Wed till 8pm, Sun 1–5pm; admission free) has works by Courbet and Sisley as well as Atkinson Grimshaw (1836–93), a local artist and one of the best painters of Victorian towns, and the great landscape painter John Sell Cotman

Among the chic shops in Leeds is Harvy Nichols' only provincial store. Marks & Spencer, the high street clothing giant, started life in a market in this one-time "ready-to-wear capital of England".

BELOW: moorland sheep that made the wool towns rich.

THE BRONTËS OF HAWORTH

The reputation of Yorkshire's most talented literary family brings thousands of visitors to their moorland home every year

With their Celtic background, it was inevitable that the writing of the Brontë girls —Charlotte, Emily and Anne— would be strong and imaginative. Their father, Patrick (1777–1861), was a poor Irish boy from Emdale in County Down who made good, changing his name from Brunty to Brontë after his hero Lord Nelson, who had been given the dukedom of Bronte by King Ferdinand of the Two Sicilies in 1799.

Patrick married Maria Branwell, from Cornwall. She bore him six children in quick succession, but died of cancer in 1821 when they were all still young, leaving them in the care of their distraught father.

Patrick was to outlive all of his children, whose short, sad lives give the Brontë story a particular poignancy. The family moved to Haworth in 1829 after Patrick was appointed curate for life. His two oldest children, Maria and Elizabeth, died in 1825. The other four, often left to their own devices, created a fantasy world, writing tiny books with minuscule script. In 1846, using pseudonyms, the three girls wrote and published a book of poems, which sold just two copies.

Success came the following year with the publication of Charlotte's *Jane Eyre*, now regarded as a classic feminist novel. Ferndean Manor, described in the book was probably the 16th-century home of the Cunliffes in Wycoller, reached by a 9-mile (15-km) footpath from Haworth called the Brontë Way.

Charlotte's success was followed by Emily's *Wuthering Heights* and Anne's *Agnes Grey*. Charlotte had written: "Speak of the North – a lonely moor, silent and still and trackless lies." But it was Emily who most vividly described the atmosphere of Haworth's moors, which she saw as wild and savage. She used the landscape when portraying Heathcliffe in *Wuthering Heights*; he was described by Catherine, the object of his passion, as "an unreclaimed creature, without refinement, without cultivation; an arid wilderness of furze and whinstone".

Charlotte became a literary celebrity. In 1852 she married the Rev. Arthur Bell Nicholls. Both Emily and her brother Branwell died in 1848, aged 30 and 31. Anne died a year later, aged 29, and Charlotte in 1855, aged 38 and pregnant. Patrick, last of the Brontës, died in 1861, aged 64. The parson's body was lowered into the vault within the altar rails and placed beside the coffin of Charlotte.

All the Brontës except Anne, who was buried in Scarborough, lie in the family vault near the Brontë's pew in the old church of St Michael and All Angels. ❏

CLOCKWISE FROM TOP LEFT: the Brontës' homemade books; Charlotte; Emily; the Black Bull, Haworth, where their brother Branwell drank.

Map on page 324

(1782–1842). The sculptor Henry Moore, who was born not far away in Castleford in 1898, studied in Leeds and the Henry Moore Institute, with sculpture galleries, was added in 1995. His work is also to be seen at the **Yorkshire Sculpture Park**, south of Leeds near Wakefield, where the sculptor Barbara Hepworth was born in 1903. It has a programme of temporary exhibitions.

Bradford's ❸ famous artistic son is David Hockney, who was born in this mill town in 1935. Some of his paintings are on the walls of the **1853 Gallery** (open daily 10am–6pm; admission free) in **Salts Mill**, Saltaire. Founded by Titus Salt, one of the local 19th-century textile barons who built solid dependability and vigour into every brick of the city's Italianate Town Hall and Gothic Wool Exchange. His model village of Saltaire enshrined his ideals in a mill, hospital, school, library, church and almshouses, but religiously excluded pubs.

Two other famous sons are the composer Frederick Delius (1862–1934) who inspires regular festivals, and the writer J. B. Priestley (1894–1984) who wrote prolifically and with an acute eye for Yorkshire characters. Bradford's claim to fame otherwise lies in the **National Museum of Photography, Film and Television**, which has one of the best photographic collections in the country, as well as hands-on film fun (open Tues–Sun 10am–6pm; admission free). In the 1950s immigrants from the Indian subcontinent were encouraged to work in Bradford's mills, and today 20 per cent of city's population is Muslim. There is no shortage of balti and other Indian restaurants in town.

Halifax ❹, west of Bradford, was another important wool town, noted for its carpets and yarns. Its 18th-century Piece Hall is the only remaining cloth hall in Yorkshire. Cottage weavers sold their "pieces" in 315 small rooms in the collonaded galleries that provide an attractive shopping area today, and a market is still held here. To the south west of Halifax lie the attractive Pennine woollen mill towns of **Hebden Bridge** and **Heptonstall**, both good bases for Pennine walks. A little further north is another Pennine mill village, **Haworth** ❺, the second most popular literary shrine in England after Shakespeare's Stratford. The Brontës moved to Haworth in 1820 (*see left*) and today more than a million visitors arrive to see the fine Georgian **Parsonage** (open Easter–Oct, daily 10am–5pm, winter 11am–4.30pm; entrance charge), restored to look as it did when it was the writers' home. The main street of this hillside village was surfaced with stone setts, to provide horses with a good grip as they drew laden carts. The flanking gritstone houses were built right up to the edge of the street, with no allowance for gardens. Houses with a third storey and long, narrow windows were both the home and workplace of hand-loom weavers – in the time of the Brontës more than 1,200 looms were chattering in the village. The Parish church has a Brontë memorial chapel and an American admirer paid for the stained-glass window on which Charlotte is commemorated. The walk to Top Withens, the inspiration for *Wuthering Heights*, is about 5 miles (8 km). Haworth station is the headquarters of the working steam railway, **Keighley and Worth Valley Railway Preservation Society** (open July–Aug, daily, Sept–Jun, weekends and public holidays only).

TIP

A great place for children is Eureka! in Discovery Road, Halifax, England's first "hands-on" museum designed especially for children. It's open every day.

BELOW: preserving the valley railway.

A dozen miles north of Haworth is **Ilkley** ❻, a Victorian inland spa for the prosperous burghers of Leeds and Bradford. The 16th–17th-century Manor House behind the church was built on the site of a Roman fort and now houses a small local history museum. Ilkley has immortalised its rugged climate in the Yorkshire anthem *On Ilkla Moor baht 'at* which, translated, tells you that it is not prudent to venture forth on Ilkley Moor without a hat.

The Dales

The head of a Swaledale tup (a male sheep of the local breed) appears on the emblem of the Yorkshire Dales National Park. He has been nicknamed Rastus the Ram.

To the north of Ilkley lies the expanse of the 680-sq. mile (1,770-sq. km) **Yorkshire Dales National Park**, characterised by drystone walls, bustling market towns, lonely farmhouses and cathedral-like caverns. Dales are merely valleys, and they take their name from the rivers that created them — Ribblesdale, Wensleydale, Swaledale. The motorist can do worse than abandon a fixed itinerary and explore at will. The easiest excursion from Ilkley takes you into surrounding Wharfedale, an alluring mix of water, wood, crag and castle. **Bolton Abbey** ❼ 5 miles (8 km) northwest of Ilkley dates from the 12th century. Its stunning location by the River Wharf has long made it a major attraction.

West of Ilkley is the market town of **Skipton** ❽, "the gateway to the Dales". Its position on the Leeds–Liverpool canal brought it great prosperity during the Industrial Revolution. Many of the warehouses still stand, and so does the much older **Skipton Castle** (open Mon–Sat 10am–5pm, Sun 1–5pm; entrance charge), home of the powerful Clifford family from the 14th to 18th centuries . Skipton provides easy access to **Malham Cove** ❾, one of the great wonders of the Yorkshire Dales. This immense limestone cliff has been eroded by the stream which once poured from the lip of the cove and it now flows underground.

BELOW:
Bolton Abbey.

Knee-cracking steps lead to the tip where limestone pavement, with clints (blocks of worn limestone with crevices known as "grykes") form a pattern like the whorls of a brain. The view from here is magnificent. It is possible to continue walking north along the Pennine Way. **Gordale Scar**, 1½ miles (2 km) east of Malham, has 16-ft (50-metre) overhanging cliffs described by the poet William Wordsworth as a lair "where young lions crouch".

To the west of Malham is the small market town of **Settle ⑩**, separated from **Giggleswick** by the River Ribble. Beside Market Place, which comes alive on Tuesday, are The Shambles, which, like York's, were once a butchers' domain. Ye Olde Naked Man Café got its name when it was an inn and fashion was deemed to be needlessly flamboyant. Settle is an excellent point from which to explore Ribblesdale or begin a circular tour of the flat-topped Ingleborough Hill, taking in the magnificent Ribblehead Viaduct, built from 1869 to 1876 to carry the Settle–Carlisle railway across Batty Moss. This trans-Pennine line has the highest mainline station in England, 1,150 ft (350 metres) up, at **Dent**.

To the north **Wensleydale** is broad and wooded and seems serene until the eye catches the forbidding **Bolton Castle ⑪** (open Easter–Nov, daily 10am–5pm; entrance charge), perched on a hillside. Tradition has it that the mortar was mixed with ox blood to strengthen the building. Wander through the stables area into the open courtyard which was once the Great Hall and you can easily imagine yourself transported back to 1568 when Mary, Queen of Scots was imprisoned here. The building was fortified in the 14th century by Richard le Scrope, chancellor to Richard II. He was a friend of Chaucer and the poet used him as the model for his *Knight's Tale*. Nearby are the impressive Aysgarth Falls. Here, beside an enormous single-arched bridge, is a 200-year-old mill,

Map on page 324

Wensleydale, the best-known cheese in Yorkshire

BELOW: the Moors at Sutton Bank.

now a museum holding a splendid collection of 19th-century coaches. At the bottom of the Dale is the town of **Middleham** ⑫, famous for it race-horse stables and **castle** (open April–Oct, daily, Nov–Mar, Wed–Sun; entrance charge), owned briefly by Richard III. As Duke of Gloucester, he came to Middleham to be tutored by the Earl of Warwick, and he married the earl's daughter, Anne. His death in 1485 at Bosworth (near Leicester), the final battle in the Wars of the Roses, ended the 24-year reign of the House of York. The castle remains include a 12th-century keep, 13th-century chapel and 14th-century gatehouse.

Near the head of the Dale and in the heart of the Yorkshire Dales National Park is the excellent **Dales Countryside Museum** (open April–Oct, daily 10am–5pm; entrance charge) at **Hawes** ⑬, from *haus*, a mountain pass. With exhibits based on a remarkable collection of Dales bygones donated by Marie Hartley and Joan Ingilby, authors of many Dales books, this is becoming a cultural focus of upland life in the Dales. On view is a traditional dales kitchen and displays relating to dairy farming, industry, local crafts and community life. Nearby is Hardraw Scar or Falls, where water cascades 100 ft (30 metres) over a cliff, approached through the Green Dragon Inn.

On neighbouring Gayle is the **Wensleydale Creamery Visitors' Centre** (open Mon–Sat 9am–5pm, Sun 10am–4.30pm; admission free) where visitors can watch the production of Wensleydale cheese and taste the results.

Buttertubs Pass, 1,726 ft (526 metres), links Wensleydale with **Swaledale** to the northeast ("buttertubs" are deep limestone shafts). Swaledale is steep and rocky, noted for its intricate patterns of drystone walls and field barns. It also has **Richmond** ⑭, a market town with a cobbled square, impressive **castle** (open daily10am–5pm; entrance charge) and splendidly restored Georgian theatre.

The Georgian Theatre Royal in Richmond is England's oldest surviving theatre in its original form. It has a collection of playbills and painted scenery dating back to 1836.

BELOW: Swaledale near Keld.

Splendour and sulphur

There are other ways to leave Leeds than via Ilkley. Strike north on the A61 and, after 9 miles (14 km), you reach the ornate **Harewood House ⑮** (open Mar–Oct, daily 10am–5pm; entrance charge). Its interiors are by Robert Adam, furniture by Thomas Chippendale and gardens by "Capability" Brown and it has a remarkable bird park. It was built in the 1760s by Edwin Lascelles and is now the home of the Earl and Countess of Harewood.

Eight miles (13 km) further along the A61 is **Harrogate ⑯**, where the **Royal Pump Room Museum** (open daily 10am–5pm; entrance charge) on Royal parade illustrates the development of the town as the Queen of Inland Spas. Harrogate, say some Yorkshire folk, can take credit for one great invention: respectability. It has lavish lawns, abundant flowers and the controversial Conference Centre, a fortress-like brick complex with a 2,000-seat auditorium. Being on a hilltop and a late starter among Yorkshire towns, Harrogate was able to develop gracefully. Many 19th-century buildings have their original cast-iron canopies. The protected 200-acre (90-hectare) Stray gives the town a spacious appearance, added to by a number of gardens. **Harlow Car Botanical Gardens** (open daily 10am–4pm; entrance charge), sustained by the Northern Horticultural Society, has a plant centre, museum of gardening and plant collections. Harrogate promotes a spring flower show and has the permanent ground for the three-day Great Yorkshire Show in July, the largest agricultural show in the north of England. The Northern Antiques fair is held in the autumn.

Neighbouring **Knaresborough**, where the River Nidd flows down a spectacular limestone gorge, is celebrated for the cave of Mother Shipton, a prophetess born here in 1488, who is said to have foretold, among other things, the

Map on page 324

TIP

Betty's Café Tea Rooms is the best place for cakes and pastries in Harrogate. It was founded in 1919 by Frederick Belmont, a young Swiss confectioner.

LEFT: Betty's Café, Harrogate.
BELOW: boats on the River Nidd at Knaresborough.

WILDLIFE ON MOOR AND DALE

The wildness of the Yorkshire landscape attracts a variety of birds and encourages carpets of springtime flowers

Among the region's varied wildlife, the red grouse, target of the sporting shooters, must hold pride of place. The only bird exclusive to Britain, it is also the only bird that remains on the open moor in winter. Its coarse yet cheerful call, uttered as it flies over the heather and often written as "go-back, go-back, go-back", is the archetypal sound of the North York Moors.

In spring the grouse is joined by snipe, plover and golden plover. The moors are also home to England's largest, though modest, populations of merlins. The Swainby moors are one of the strongholds of this small, darting hawk. Also seen on occasion is the hen

harrier, a truly magnificent bird with enormous wingspan, that hunts by flying low over the heather and suddenly swooping sideways. Upland waders – curlews, redshanks, dunlins – fare best on the well-maintained grouse moors.

The Dales support a good population of dippers, with some kingfishers and, in spring and summer, grey wagtails and sandpipers. Mature woodland is home to green and greater spotted woodpeckers and flycatchers, while in the forest plantations of the moors are crossbills and nightjars

Roe deer and, to a lesser extent, red and fallow deer can be found where there is woodland cover, and there are sika deear in Studley Royal, part of Fountains Abbey estate. Mink, introduced via Lancashire fur farms, have spread through the area, but in the rivers, otters are scarce.

Several flower species reach their northern or southern limit on the moors. On Levisham Moor are two arctic-alpine species at the edge of their range – chickweed wintergreen and dwarf cornel, a kind of miniature dogwood. The early purple orchid shows up against the limestone of the Dales and the yellow mountain pansy is found in many areas. In the moist wooded ravines, such as Gunnerside Gill, are the star-shaped flowers of the spring sandwort.

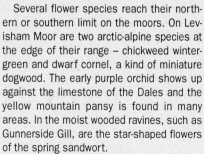

In Kirkdale the rare May lily blossoms on its only native site in Britain. But while other common species, such as globeflower and bird's eye primrose, are also found, it is perhaps the more familiar flowers that give most delight. The Farndale daffodils are famous, and there are carpets of bluebells at Glaisdale, Hasty Bank near Stokesley and other places. Nowhere are snowdrops prettier than on the banks of Mulgrave Old Castle, Sandsend. And on early-spring walks in the Forge Valley, or through the woods at Sunnington, popular flowers such as wood anemone, wood sorrel, violet and primrose, as well as shier species like early purple orchid, brush the boots at almost every step. ❑

CLOCKWISE FROM LEFT: red grouse, wood sorrel, merlin, yellow mountain pansy.

Map on page 324

Spanish Armada and the coming of the motor car. In Castle Grounds are The Old Court House Museum and **Knaresborough Castle** (open Easter and May–Sept, daily 10.30am–5pm; entrance charge). The museum is in a 14th-century building and its local history exhibits include memorablia from the Civil War.

Four miles (6.5 km) to the north, **Ripley** is a village conceived in the style of Alsace in France and a town hall labelled Hôtel de Ville; Sir William Amcotts Ingilby and his wife, who were largely responsible for rebuilding the town in the 1820s, were great Francophiles. **Ripley Castle** (open April, May, Oct, Sat–Sun, June and Sept, Thurs–Sun, July–Aug, daily; entrance charge) has collections of armour and paintings; it has been the home of the Ingleby family for 600 years.

Ripon ⓱, further along the A61, developed around the sombre Saxon cathedral founded by St Wilfrid in the 7th century. The massive seven-light east window, 51 ft (16 metres) high and half as wide, dates from the 14th century, but the most special feature is the crypt under the central tower, dating from 672, which is redolent of Saxon times. Horse racing has been part of Ripon's social life for more than 300 years, and the town has an unusual **Prison and Police Museum** (open Easter–Oct, daily 11am–5pm; entrance charge). Nearby is **Newby Hall**, an Adam house set in 25 acres (10 hectares) of splendid garden.

Three miles (5 km) to the southwest are the atmospheric remains of *Sancta Maria Fonctibus*, **Fountains Abbey** (open April–Sept, daily 10am–7pm, Oct–Mar, till 5pm, Nov–Jan, closed Fri; guided tours; National Trust), once Britain's richest Cistercian monastery. In 1132 monks first arrived in Skelldale "thick-set with thorns, fit rather to be the lair of wild beasts than the home of human beings". They came under the Cistercian rule and Fountains grew powerful and affluent. Kitchens and dormitories survive, a tribute to old craftsmanship, giving today's visitor an unusually clear idea of medieval monastic life. Hubb's Tower reaches 160 ft (50 metres) and the Cellarium, which has its roof, is where wool was stored. The Abbey was pulled down during the 16th-century Reformation. In the 18th century the estate was preserved and landscaped with the 400-acre (160-hectare) deer park, Studley Royal. In 1967 Fountains became a World Heritage site.

Friar Tuck, Robin Hood's fellow outlaw, is said to have been a monk at Fountains Abbey.

North York Moors

The North York Moors are a place apart. The most sharply defined of Britain's 11 national parks, they are bounded on two sides by steeply plunging escarpments and on a third by towering cliffs that defy the North Sea. Only where neighbouring farmland slopes up gradually from the Vale of Pickering do the Moors lack an obvious frontier. Within their 553 sq. miles (1,380 sq. km), they embrace the largest unbroken expanse of heather moorland in England. In summer the heather flings a coat of regal purple across the full 40-mile (60-km) width of the Moors, from the Vale of York to the sea. Other seasons have colours, too: the bright green of bilberries in spring, russet bracken in autumn, and in winter subdued greys and brown.

The Moors can be approached directly from York or from the A1. On the eastern side of the Vale of York on the A64, is **Castle Howard** ⓲ (open Mar–Oct, daily 11am–4.30pm; entrance charge). The first build-

BELOW: heather moors, Hoo Hole.

"Relapse" or "Virtue in Danger" and "The Provoked Wife" were the best-known works by John Vanburgh before he designed Castle Howard. This sudden change of occupation, from playwright to architect at the age of 35, led to fame and fortune: he went on to design Blenheim Palace.

ing to be designed by Sir John Vanburgh (1664–1726), it inspired 20th-century poet John Betjeman to write: "Hail Castle Howard! Hail Vanburgh's noble dome, Where Yorkshire in her splendour rivals Rome!" The centrepiece of the entire house is the marble-floored Hall which rises up to the magnificent 70-ft (21-metre) dome, across which charge great "Horses of the Sun". The principal rooms contain paintings by Gainsborough, Reynolds and Rubens and furniture by Sheraton and Chippendale. The Pre-Raphaelite chapel has stained glass by Edward Burne-Jones. The west wing, a Palladian addition, has a magnificent Long Gallery. In the parkland a lovely walk along the terrace leads to the elegant Chapel of the Four Winds, returning by the south lake.

Just off the A1 is the thriving market town of **Thirsk** ⓭, now famous as the "Darrowby" of James Herriot's vet books, which translated into the successful 1980s television series, *All Creatures Great and Small*. Herriot's former surgery (open daily) is now a visitor centre devoted to the author.

Rievaulx Abbey

Approaching the Moors from this westerly or southerly direction, most visitors will arrive in **Helmsley**, whose quaint shops give it a distinctly "Cotswolds" feel. Nearby, tucked amid hanging woods and placid pastures deep in the Rye Valley, are the breathtaking ruins of **Rievaulx Abbey** ⓴ (open daily Easter–Nov, 10am–6pm, winter till 4pm; English Heritage), an extensive Cistercian monastery founded in the 12th century. The now supremely beautiful setting was viewed as "a place of horror and waste" by the abbey's 12 founder monks who arrived direct from France in 1132. Larger than Fountain's Abbey (*see page 333*), Rievaulx was both the first and biggest Cistercian abbey in the north of

BELOW:
Rievaulx Abbey.

THE END OF THE MONASTERIES

When Henry VIII issued the Suppression Act in April 1536 there were 800 monasteries, nunneries and friaries in England and Wales populated by 10,000 monks, canons, nuns and friars. The Act was ostensibly in response to a six-month survey by a team of royal visitors which found "manifest sin, vicious, carnal and abominable living daily used and committed amongst the little and small abbeys". But this was a smokescreen: Henry wanted the religious houses' wealth. Most had agreed to acknowledge Henry as head of the new Church of England after his acrimonious break with the Catholic Church of Rome over his divorce arrangements. Only the smaller establishments were at first dissolved but the manner of their repression led to a rebellion, known as The Pilgrimage of Grace, as the dissolved houses were defiantly reinhabited, often with the support of the larger houses. The king retaliated, forcing the surrender of the larger monasteries. Four years after the Act was passed not a single monastery, nunnery or friary remained.

By the end of Henry's reign, two-thirds had been sold off, saving the king from bankruptcy. Their grandeur and wealth can be glimpsed at Fountains and Rievaulx, which are among the best preserved of Henry's ruins.

England. At its 13th-century peak it housed 150 monks and 500 lay brothers "so that the church swarmed with them, like a hive with bees". By the time of its dissolution in 1538 only 22 monks remained, and the huge dormitory was being used as a grain store. Because of the abbey's narrow site, between steep banks of the Rye, the church was aligned north–south. Its greatest glory is its chancel, from around 1230. Standing to its full height, with two tiers of lancet windows above cluster-column arches, it is a majestic example of the Early English style.

Northwest of Rievaulx, by the A19, is another romantic ruin, **Mount Grace Priory** (open April–Oct, daily 10am–5pm, Nov–Mar, Wed–Sun; National Trust and English Heritage). This is the best preserved of Britain's nine Carthusian monasteries. A monk's cell has been restored and an exhibition is housed in a handsome Jacobean mansion converted from the priory's gatehouse.

Ryedale is just one among a network of Dales penetrating the great dome of moorland. In some places they create dramatic natural features, such as the **Hole of Horcum ㉑** above the Vale of Pickering; elsewhere they enfold villages and farmhouses built mainly of warm, honey-coloured sandstone. The prettiest villages include **Hutton-le-Hole ㉒** in Farndale, with a broad green, and 17th- and 18th-century limestone cottages built by Quaker weavers. The **Ryedale Folk Museum** here (open Easter–Oct, 10am–5.30pm; entrance charge) is the premier museum of moorland life. There are a number of vernacular buildings in the grounds and traditional craft making can be seen. In November the museum stages the world championships of Merills, an ancient peg-board game once popular on the moors. Nearby Lastingham has a splendid Norman crypt.

On the northern flanks, above Eskdale, are **Goathland** and **Beck Hole ㉓**, the former the setting for the TV series *Heartbeat*, the latter a delightful hamlet

Map on page 324

Ryedale Folk Museum.

BELOW: around the Ryedale Folk Museum in Hutton le Hole.

Captain Cook, the Pacific explorer and Whitby's famous son.

with an arc of cottages facing a green. Quoits is played here, inquests afterwards being conducted in the Birch Hall Inn where beer is served through a hatch in a flag-stone bar adorned with quoiting pictures. **The Moors Centre** (open April–Nov, daily 10am–5pm, Nov–Mar, Mon–Fri 11am–4pm; entrance charge), a showcase for the **National Park** and starting point for waymarked walks, is at **Danby** 12 miles (18 km) east.

Heading north across the Moors to the sea, from **Pickering** to **Grosmont**, is the steam-powered **North Yorkshire Moors Railway** (Easter–Nov). A stop in Pickering should include a visit to the Beck Isle Museum of Rural Life where the photography of Sydney Smith (1884–1956) is a beautiful record of rural England in the first half of the 20th century. The most dramatic section of the railway journey is Newton Dale, with sheer cliffs 400 ft (120 metres) high. For the more energetic, there is the 42-mile (68-km) Lyke Wake Walk, which crosses the Moors between Osmotherley and Robin Hood's Bay.

Coastal highlights

The Moors end at the east coast, where breaks in the precipitous cliffs provide space for pretty villages and the occasional town. **Whitby** ㉔ is a picturesque fishing port with a jumble of pantiled cottages climbing from the harbour. On East Cliff are the 13th-century remains of **Whitby Abbey** (open daily 10am–6pm, Nov–Easter till 4pm; English Heritage) on which site a 7th-century monk wrote the *Song of Creation*, considered to mark the start of English literature. The Sutcliffe Gallery in Flowergate exhibits and sells the evocative Victorian photographs of Whitby and its hinterland by Frank Sutcliffe (1853–1941). The Antarctic and Pacific explorer Captain Cook (1728–79) lived in this former whaling port – a whale's jawbone still acts as an arch to remind people of the town's former trade. **Captain Cook Memorial Museum** (open April–Nov, daily 10am–5pm; entrance charge) in Grape Street is the focal point of a heritage trail tracing his life throughout the region. To the north of Whitby, steep roads lead down to **Runswick Bay**, a self-consciously pretty assortment of fishermen's cottages, and Staithes, where the young Cook was briefly and unhappily apprenticed to a grocer. To the south, seekers after solitude can divert from the coastal road to find **Ravenscar** – "the resort that never was". It has fine walks, but never developed economically beyond one rather imposing clifftop hotel.

BELOW: the seafront, Whitby.

Robin Hood's Bay, a popular resort close by, once offered sanctuary to the benign outlaw and was a haunt of smugglers. Off its main street run the snickets and narrow lanes that, together with the diminutive Dock, give Robin Hood's Bay its Toytown character. Time should be spent exploring the intimate network, full of odd corners and sunny squares.

Further south lies **Scarborough** ㉕, whose eclipse as a posh watering hole is exemplified by the fate of the Grand Hotel, among the handsomest in Europe when it opened in 1867 and now run by holiday-camp cheerleaders. The 12th-century **castle** (open Easter–Nov, daily, Dec–Easter, Wed–Sun; entrance charge) is worth seeing. Anne Brontë – who, like so many

Map
on page
324

invalids, came for the bracing air – is buried in the graveyard of St Mary's. The town also has an enviable theatrical reputation built around Alan Ayckbourn, the local-born playwright, who premiers all his plays at the Stephen Joseph Theatre.

Filey ㉖ offers unpretentious delights, with amusement arcades, a splendid beach and Filey Brig, the breakwater at the north end of the bay. Off the dramatic 400-ft (130-metre) cliff at nearby Flamborough Head, John Paul Jones, commodore of a French squadron showing American colours, captured two British men-of-war in 1779.

The Yorkshire Wolds

Flamborough Head is where the chalk ridge of the Yorkshire Wolds meets the sea. Just to the south is **Beverley**, a picture-postcard mix of medieval and Georgian streets, but its main attractions are the Gothic Minster and its former chapel, St Mary's, which between them contain one of the largest collections of carvings in the world. The Minster dates from 1220 and among its wood and stone carvings are 68 misericords and the elegant tomb of Lady Idoine Percy who died in 1365.

Kingston upon Hull ㉗, usually referred to simply as Hull, is the principal town on the River Humber. This once great fishing port was badly bombed in World War II, but the dock area has been restored and there is a museum of the town's maritime history. Surviving merchant houses in the High Street are best seen at the house where William Wilberforce was born in 1758: relics of the slave trade he helped to outlaw are among the mementos on display. From Hull the river runs down to the bleak birdlands of Spurn Head, where a small community keeps a lifeboat manned. ❏

A rabbit carved on a portal in the chapel of St Mary's in Beverley Minster is said to have been the inspiration for Lewis Carroll's White Rabbit in "Alice in Wonderland".

LEFT: Whitby pub.
BELOW: the harbour at Staithes.

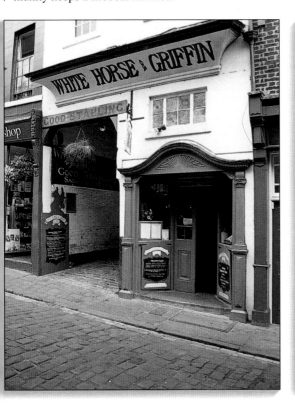

NORTHUMBRIA

*This is the land of the Geordies. Newcastle is its capital,
Durham its finest city. It is one of the most ancient Christian
enclaves in England. Hadrian's Wall kept out the wild Scots*

Map
on page
324

History is everywhere in these bleak northern hills – the last flourish of the Pennines before they cross the borders into Scotland. It was a grim posting for Roman soldiers stationed along Hadrian's Wall, but it appealed to the Christians, who chose lonely Lindisfarne on the wild, sandy Northumbrian shore as a bastion and exemplar of the early church. Incursions came from the Vikings, who left their language in such local dialect names as *stell* (sheepfold) and *beck* (stream). Still the local "Geordie" dialect is the strongest in England.

The Normans came next, ravaging Northumbria in their pitiless "harrying of the North"; but they were builders, too, and they raised the mighty cathedral at Durham, mainly as a defence against the Scots. The Scottish border was always a volatile place and, for some 300 years until the early 17th century, rustic gangsters called reivers ruled the roost.

Coal mining put the area in the forefront of the Industrial Revolution and in the 20th century Britain's major shipbuilding yards grew up along the Tyne and Wear rivers, but these times are now passed. The farming community, raising both sheep and cattle, is finding life as hard as anywhere in Britain. A tourism campaign has dubbed the north Pennines "England's last wilderness" and at Kielder the largest man-made forest has proved a great attraction.

PRECEDING PAGES:
Lindisfarne Castle,
Holy Island.
LEFT: Central
Arcade, Newcastle.
BELOW: the Tyne
Bridge, Newcastle.

FACT FILE

Main towns Newcastle, (London 278 miles/450 km), Durham 14 miles (23 km) south of Newcastle.
Railway Intercity from London King's Cross, about 3 hours.
Road A1 and M1 from London, about 4 hours.
Ferry connections From North Shields to Norway (20 hours), Germany (23 hours), Netherlands (14 hours).
Airports Newcastle, Teesside.
Locals "Geordies", can be hard to understand, have a reputation for hard drinking and a black sense of humour.
Big attractions Open spaces, castles, vast sandy beaches, the biggest waterfall in Britain.
Best wildlife The Farne Islands.
Most historic place Holy Island (Lindisfarne), sea-swept monastery home of St Cuthbert.
Finest building Durham Cathedral.
Best for children North of England Open Air Museum at Beamish.
Food and drink Newcastle Brown ale, Craster kippers, stottie cakes (don't get too excited).
Best night out The club scene in Newcastle.
Most scenic route Tyne Valley Regional railway, running coast to coast along Hadrian's Wall, tel: 0345 484950.
Tourist information Durham, tel: 0191 3843720.

Teesdale and the Pennines

The first beach resort in Northumbria is **Redcar**  ❷❽, a lively playground with a sandy beach which serves the decaying industrial centres of **Middlesbrough**, **Stockton-on-Tees** and **Darlington** ❷❾. The region boomed in the 19th century as coal and iron were discovered and the railways pioneered an undreamed-of prosperity. George Stephenson's *Locomotion No. 1* built in 1825 is displayed at Darlington's **Railway Museum** (open daily 10am–5pm; entrance charge). It ran on the world's first railway line, from Darlington to Stockton.

Sixteen miles (25 km) to the west on the River Tees is "Barney"– **Barnard Castle**, ❸⓿ capital of Teesdale. On Wednesdays, market day, the town is crowded with farmers the length of the Upper Tees, bringing their stock to be sold and to shop from the stalls in Butter Market. There are many 18th-century buildings in the town, but the oldest, the delightful, leaning Blagroves House, now a restaurant, dates from the 16th century. The **castle** (open April–Sep, daily 10am–6pm, Oct–Mar, Wed–Sun 10am–4pm; English Heritage) stands on a bluff above the River Tees, with two standing towers and the remains of a 15th-century great chamber. Follow Newgate out of Barnard Castle to reach the extraordinary **Josephine and John Bowes Museum** (open Mon–Sat 10am– 5.30pm, Sun 2–5pm; entrance charge). Looking like a grand French château, its outstanding collection of French and Spanish paintings include El Grecos and Goyas.

Just outside Barnard Castle is **Raby Castle** ❸❶ (open Easter, May–June, Wed and Sun 1–5pm, Jul–Sep, Sun–Fri; gardens 11am–5pm; entrance charge), a fine medieval fortification set in a 200-acre (80-hectare) deer park. It has decorated period rooms, a 600-year-old kitchen and stables full of period carriages. **Cotherstone**, a famous cheese-making village just west of Barnard Castle is is

BELOW: Bowes Museum, Barnard Castle.
RIGHT: High Force.

many people's favourite Teesdale village, but **Middleton-in-Teesdale ⚡** is the real centre for Upper Teesdale. A staging post on the Pennine Way, here the Moors start to crowd in on the river, making it a superb centre for exploring such sites as **High Force**, a few miles to the west. This is the greatest waterfall in England, which crashes 70 ft (21 metres). For a further scenic trip along the river, continue on the B6277 to **Alston** in the valley of the River South Tyne where the **South Tynedale Railway** runs regular steam and diesel-hauled passenger trips beside the river. Another local experience is the **Killhope Lead Mining Centre** (open April–Oct, daily 10am–5pm; entrance charge) to the east along the A689, where visitors can see the workings of the lead mines and go underground.

Between Barnard Castle and Durham is **Bishop Auckland** (open May, Jun and Sept, Fri and Sun, 2–5pm; July, Thur, Fri and Sun 2–5pm, Aug, Thurs–Sun 2–5pm; entrance charge), residence of the Durham's bishops since Norman times, Its throne room, state rooms, medieval kitchen and chapel, said to be the largest private chapel in Europe, are open to the public.

Maps:
Area 324
Town 344

The Quakers who ran the London Lead Company built the model town of Nenthead where they introduced compulsory schooling for their employees and inaugurated the country's first free library.

A Tour of Durham

The cathedral and castle of **Durham ⚡**, caught in a loop in the River Wear, are a UNESCO World Heritage site. To tour this compact and friendly university town, start in the Market Place and the Tourist Information Centre. Nearby are **St Nicholas' Church ⓐ**, once part of the city walls and **Guildhall ⓑ** (open Mon–Fri 10am–5pm; entrance charge) with a Tudor doorway and balconies, rebuilt in 1851. South of the square is Saddler Street, with Tudor gables, a former street of butchers, which eventually leads to **Palace Green ⓒ**. From here

BELOW: Durham Cathedral on the River Wear.

there is a grand view of the the city's finest buildings, including the cathedral and legacies of a 17th-century benefactor, Bishop Cosin. On the left is the elegant 17th-century red-brick **Bishop Cosin's Hall D** next to Bishop Cosin's Almouse (1666), now an tea room. Just beyond is **Bishop Cosin's Library E**, a favourite backdrop for photographs of students who have just graduated. A gateway to the right leads to University College in **Durham Castle F** (guided tours only; July–end Sept, Mon–Sat 10–noon, 2–4.30pm; otherwise Mon, Wed and Sat 2–4.30pm. Tours may be cancelled if university events are taking place). One of the finest Norman palaces in Britain, with an impressive Great Hall and Chapel, it was the domain of the powerful Prince Bishops of Durham, who had their own parliament, laws, coinage and army, privileges first granted by William the Conqueror to quell the Scots and not relinquished until 1836.

Across the Green is the **Cathedral G** (open May–Aug, 7.15am–8pm, Sept–April, 7.15am–6pm; donations welcomed). Inside, massive columns stride down the nave like a petrified forest; boldly incised with spirals, lozenges, zigzags and flutings, their impact is stunning. Largely completed by 1189, it was the first major English church to be covered entirely by stone vaulting and is the finest example of early Norman architecture. Its outstanding features include the Galilee Chapel, with a tomb of England's first great historian, the Venerable Bede (died 735) and the Chapel of the Nine Alters, which contains the remains of St Cuthbert (*see page 351*) for which the cathedral was built. **The Treasury Museum** (open Mon–Sat 10am–4.30pm, Sun 2–4.30pm; entrance charge) contains other relics of the saintly Bishop of Lindisfarne.

Turn right outside the Cathedral down Dun Cow Lane to the **Durham Heritage Centre H** (open April–May, Mon–Fri 2–4.30pm, June and Sept, 2–4.30pm,

BELOW:
the city of Durham.

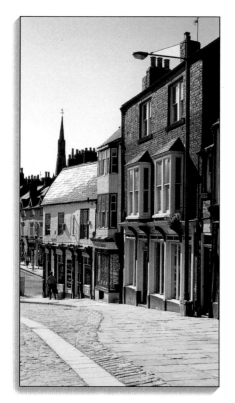

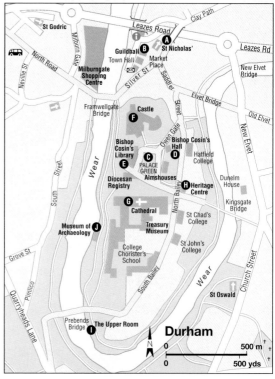

July–Aug, 11am–4.30pm) which has exhibitions and audio-visual displays of the city. From here descend to the Riverside Walk, a pleasant path beside the Wear which leads to **The Upper Room** , a sculpture of The Last Supper carved from 11 elm trees by Colin Wilbourn in 1987. Cross Prebends Bridge (1778) for a classic view of the cathedral. Otherwise, continue round to the Old Fulling Mill, home of the **Museum of Archaeology** ❶ (open April-Oct, daily 11am–4pm, Nov–Mar, Wed–Sun 12.30–3pm), which displays local finds.

County Durham and the North Pennines

Durham's proud industrial legacy can be seen at the award-winning **North of England Open Air Museum** ❷ at **Beamish** between Chester le Street and Stanley on the A693 on the north side of Durham (open April-Oct, Tues–Thurs, Sat–Sun 10am–5pm, last admission 3pm; entrance charge). One of the leading attractions in the Northeast, it vividly re-creates the industrial and social past with reconstructed buildings and attendants in period dress. There is a Victorian town, with cobbled streets, shops, pub, stables, park and railway station with a replica of George Stephenson's *Locomotion*. There is a farm with rare breeds and a colliery and engine house with the steam winder built in 1855 for the Beamish colliery. Nearby is the Mine and Pitt Cottages where the miners of nearby Hetton-le-Hole originally lived. Set aside at least half a day for a visit.

Newcastle upon Tyne

Nine miles (15 km) from the mouth of the Tyne, **Newcastle upon Tyne** ❸ is at the hub of a sprawling conurbation which engulfs Tynemouth, South Shields, Wallsend, Jarrow and Gateshead. A centre of coal mining and shipbuilding,

Maps:
Area 324
Town 344

TIP

To the southeast of Newcastle is the Old Hall in Washington village, home of George Washington, now run by the National Trust. Special events celebrate Independence Day, Thanksgiving and Washington's birthday (24 February).

BELOW:
Anthony Gormley's *Angel of the North.*

"He crossed to Britain where he set many things to rights and built a wall 80 miles long to separate the Romans from the barbarians," wrote Spartianus, nearly 200 years after the event. Hadrian arrived in the Tyne in 122, five years after he had been made Roman Emperor. He enjoyed touring his vast Empire, and on his journeys he would live as an ordinary legionnaire, in full uniform, but often bare headed, and marching 20 miles (32 km) a day.

industrial England never got grittier than this: Catherine Cookson Country in South Shields offers tours, but the grim working-class conditions which the popular novelist described can no longer be seen in this lively university town which has a bright nightlife and well-supported football club.

The town spans the river across famous bridges: the High Level Bridge built by George Stephenson who inaugurated the railway industry here, the Swing Bridge where the Roman bridge stood and the Tyne Bridge, which has the largest arch (531 ft/162 metres) of any bridge in Britain. The old town, known as the Chares, is a small area of narrow streets and steep lanes on the north side of the river; around here are the **Custom House** (1766), **Guildhall** (1658) and **New Castle** (open Tues–Sun 10am–5pm; entrance charge). Built in 1177 for Henry II on the site of a Roman fort, the castle has a well-preserved keep with royal apartments, Great Hall and chapel. The railway cuts it off from the Black Gate (1247) which houses traditional local instruments in the Bagpipe Museum. The **cathedral** of St Nicholas is just beyond, identified by a crown spire. Dating mainly from the 14th–15th centuries, it has a fine altar screen depicting Northumbria's many saints. Several museums are worth seeking out. The Laing Art Gallery in Higham Place has a good collection of British art and some antiquities. Local history, period furnishing and militaria are on shows at the John George Joicey Museum in City Road.

Hadrian's Wall: a tour of Rome's last outpost

Built by order of the Emperor Hadrian in 130 to separate the Romans from the unconquered Picts and Scots, Hadrian's Wall was 16 ft (5 metres) high and ran 73 miles (117 km), coast-to-coast, from the Solway to the Tyne. Thriving civilian settlements, known as *vici*, spread out to the south behind the protection of the wall, with houses, temples, shops and theatres, serving the needs of both the local tribespeople and the 10,000 auxiliary soldiers from all over the Empire who were stationed at this last northern outpost of Rome. In 1987 the Hadrian's Wall Military Zone was designated a World Heritage Site by UNESCO. This 70-mile (100-km) circular route visits most of the important military sites along the

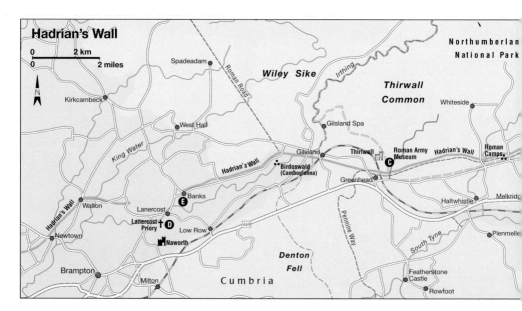

Map below

way. A full day should be put aside for this journey, which starts at the historic market town of **Hexham** and ends at **Chesters A** just 3 miles (5 km) to the north. **Hexham Abbey** has one of the finest crypts in England and **The Border History Museum** (open Easter–Nov, daily 10am–4.30pm, winter Wed–Sun; entrance charge) is housed in what is claimed to be the first purpose-built prison in England, from 1330. From Hexham join the A69 main road to **Haydon Bridge B** and Haltwhistle to the **Roman Army Museum C** (open Feb–Nov, daily 10am–5pm; times vary out of season; entrance charge) near **Greenhead**. The museum is adjacent to the unexcavated Roman fort of Magnis at Carvoran and is devoted to the life of Roman soldiers stationed on the wall.

The A69 continues towards the busy little market town of Brampton, and 1 mile (2 km) beforehand a minor road leads to the 12th-century Augustinian **Lanercost Priory D** (open Easter–Nov, daily 10am–6pm; English Heritage). Continue down this road to cross the *vallum* of the wall at **Banks E**. Follow it eastwards through Gisland to the 14th-century Thirwall Castle built with masonry from the wall. This is a good palace to explore the wall on foot.

From here the B6318 follows the lie of the Stanegate, the military road which served the south side of the wall. After about 7 miles (11 km) signs to the right indicate Chester Roman Fort at **Vindolanda F** (open Feb–Nov, daily 10am–5pm; entrance charge). This has a full-sized reconstruction of the wall and a turret, showing the sheer scale of the enterprise. There is a replica Roman temple, house and shop, with writing tablets and other artefacts. Only a short distance further on is the **Housesteads Fort and Museum** (open May–Sept, daily 10am–6pm, Oct–April, 10am–4pm; English Heritage/National Trust/Northumberland National Park). Housesteads (*Vercovicium*) is the most impressive Roman fort on the Wall, built around 128 and covering 5 acres (2 hectares). Around 1,000 infantry soldiers were garrisoned here, as well as cavalry. There are extensive remains of barracks, plus a bath-house, hospital and granary.

Continuing on the B6318, the road passes the fort of **Carrawburgh G** to **Chesters Roman Fort H**, formerly *Cilurnum* (open Easter–Nov, 9.30am–6pm or dusk, winter 10am–4pm; English Heritage). This housed 500 cavalrymen

Excavations along Hadrian's Wall

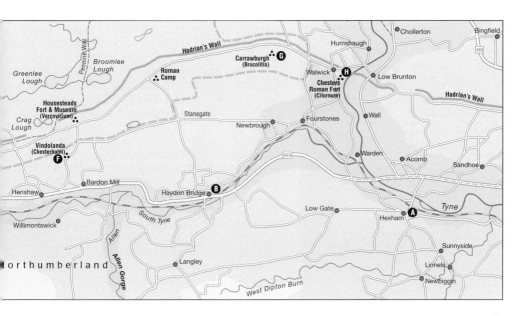

and the site museum includes several important Roman sculptures, altars and inscriptions. The remains also include the finest military bath-house in Britain.

Between the fort and the road are the remains of a civil settlement and away to the right is the barn which serves as joint **Visitor Centre** for the National Trust and the Northumberland National Park. The wall to the west is one of the finest stretches for walking.

National Park and the Cheviots

The **Cheviot Hills**, shared by England and Scotland, are quite distinct from the Durham Dales and the North Pennines. Rounded and covered in frosted-coloured rough grass, they reach 2,000 ft (610 metres) and their cloying blanket of peat is notorious to exhausted Pennine Wayfarers on the final leg of their 270-mile (435-km) marathon from Edale in Derbyshire. **The Northumberland National Park** ❸ covers 405 sq. miles (1,049 sq. km) between Hadrian's Wall and the Cheviots. There is a Visitor Centre for the park in Church House in Main Street in the pretty market town of **Rothbury**, the capital of Coquetdale, on the east side of the region and the town offers many opportunities for good walks. Just outside the town is **Cragside House** (open Easter–Oct, Tues–Sun 1–5.30pm, Nov–14 Dec, Tues, Sat, Sun, 10.30am–4pm; National Trust), a fantastic mock-Tudor, mock-medieval building created by the inventor and arms manufacturer Lord Armstrong, standing in 900 acres (300 hectares) of gardens famous for rhododendrons and azaleas.

The **Simonside Fells** lie to the west, stretching in a wide arc of steep crags. The views north towards the Cheviots are among the finest in Northumberland. There is an important Iron-Age hillfort at **Lordenshaws**, built around 350BC and

BELOW:
Kielder Water

KIELDER, MAN-MADE WILDERNESS

Kielder, in its own, totally artificial way, is a unique landscape. Situated between Hadrian's Wall and the Scottish border on the west of the Northumberland National Park, it has the largest man-made forest in Europe, covering 300 sq. miles (777 sq. km), complemented by Kielder Water, Europe's largest man-made lake, opened in 1982, with a 27-mile (43-km) shoreline.

This artificial landscape, crisscrossed by 500 miles (800 km) of track, has proved immensely popular, with walkers, horse riders, cyclists and leisure seekers, especially for visitors from nearby Tyneside. Bellingham (pronounced Bellin-jam), the chief town of north Tynedale, serves as the "Gateway to Kielder". Otherwise the Tower Knowe Visitor Centre near Falstone is the best starting point.

There are fishing and water-sports facilities at Leaplish Waterside Park as well as cycle hire, sauna, solarium and restaurant. Kielder Water Cruises in the bay of Whickhope offer 75-minute trips around the reservoir. Kielder Village is a 1950s forestry community which is now the headquarters of the Forestry Commission's Border Forest operations, based in Kielder Castle, the late 18th-century castellated shooting lodge of the Duke of Northumberland which today has a Visitor Centre.

there are good walks along the Simonside Ridge from here. To the northwest is the delightful village of **Holystone** and the **Lady's** or **St Ninian's Well**. Set in a copse, a short walk north of the village, it is a tranquil rectangular pool of clear water fed by a never-failing sparkling spring. A Celtic cross in the pool is a reminder that, on Easter Day in 627, 3,000 pagan Northumbrians were apparently baptised here by St Paulinus, a Roman missionary from Kent.

Map on page 324

The coast, Lindisfarne and the Farne Islands

The Northumbrian coast has some of Britain's finest and least-spoilt beaches, and the 40 miles (65km) from the salmon and boatbuilding town of **Amble** and the Scottish border has been designated an area of outstanding natural beauty. Just inland from Alnmouth is the ancient town of **Alnwick** ❽ (pronounced Annick) and the stupendous **Alnwick Castle** (open Easter–Oct, 11am–5pm; entrance charge), home from 1309 to 1670 of the Percys, the powerful earls of Northumberland. Just beyond Alnmouth is **Warkworth** (Easter–Nov, 10am–6pm, winter 10am–1pm, 2–4pm; English Heritage) with a fortified house dating from the 11th century and also belonging to the Percys.

Craster kippers.

The picturesque fishing village of **Craster** is famous for its kippers (oak-smoked herrings) which you can enjoy in Robson's Restaurant here they have been curing herrings for four generations. A 30-minute coastal path leads to **Dunstanburgh Castle**, one of the most romantically sited ruins in Britain. Beyond the magnificent dune-backed sweep of **Embleton Bay** is **Beadneall** and the busy little harbour town of **Seahouses**, where boats take visitors to the **Farne Islands**. These are some 30 small islets lying between 1½ and 5 miles (2.5–8 km) offshore. Rich wildlife includes 21 species of seabirds and a large

BELOW: Seahouses.

Map
on page
324

TIP

Try the mead from
St Aiden's Winery in
Lindisfarne village.
This traditional local
ale of the Holy Island
monks is made
with honey.

BELOW: the Farne
Islands make a fine
bird sanctuary.

colony of seals. Ferries at Easter and throughout August and September take visitors to Inner Farne, St Cuthbert's retreat and Staple Island, owned by the National Trust, where they are allowed ashore.

Beyond Seahouses is **Bamburgh Castle** (open Apr–Nov, daily 11am–5pm; entrance charge), the most impressive of the coastal castles, often used as a backdrop in films. It has a Norman keep, but was largely remodelled in the 19th and 20th centuries. The fine armoury collection has been transferred from the Tower of London.

To reach **Holy Island** or **Lindisfarne** , it is necessary to turn inland and take the A1 for 6 miles (9 km) to Beal. Before crossing the causeway, check the tide tables. The 4-sq. mile (10-sq. km) island is a nature reserve, and the romantic remains of **Lindisfarne Priory** (open Easter–Nov, daily 10am–6pm, 10am–4pm in winter; English Heritage) date from 1083. The adjacent museum displays Saxon carvings from the site and the adjoining church of St Mary's contains copies of the famous Lindisfarne Gospels, beautiful illuminated manuscripts which may have been written to honour the canonisation of St Cuthbert (*see right*); the originals are in the British Museum. At St Aidan's Winery in Lindisfarne village you can buy traditional mead (ale made with honey). Lindisfarne Castle on the southeast side of the island was built in romantic medieval styles by Sir Edwin Lutyens, in 1903.

Berwick-upon-Tweed , the last town in England, has changed allegiance between England and Scotland 11 times. Its most impressive feature is its perfectly intact Elizabethan walls and ramparts, built in 1569, and a walk around them might include visits to the 18th-century barracks, designed by John Vanburgh, the Georgian guardhouse and the ruins of the 12th-century castle. ❑

ST CUTHBERT, THE "FIRE OF THE NORTH"

From the Holy Island of Lindisfarne, this
legendary local monk and animal lover
inspired the spiritual life of the northeast

Cuthbert, greatest of the northern saints, was born in the Scottish borders in 635. While tending sheep in the Lammermuir Hills he saw a vision of a great light and angels in the sky, and, taking this as a sign that he should spread the Christian message, he became a monk.

In the same year as his birth, the Northumbrian King Oswald won a famous victory over Welsh and Mercian invaders near Hexham. In thanks, he sent for St Aiden from the holy island of Iona in Scotland to spread the Christian message through his kingdom. Aiden and 12 companions founded the first monastery at Lindisfarne, a tiny rocky island, cut off by the tides from the mainland twice each day. This was to become the cradle of Christianity in northeast England and for the rest of Europe. Aiden was succeeded by Cuthbert in 664.

Cuthbert, "the Fire of the North", ignited the Christian flame in the region. News of his gift for healing spread far and wide and he was frequently called to other monasteries throughout the north to preach and heal. But Cuthbert preferred solitude and he often withdrew to live the life of a hermit in a tiny cell on the rocky island of Inner Farne.

There are many legends associated with St Cuthbert, mostly related by the Venerable Bede, who wrote the invaluable first history of the English people (*Historia Ecclesiastica Gentis Anglorum*) up to the time of his death in 731 from his monk's cell in the monastery of Jarrow, near Newcastle. Among these is the tale of the sea otters drying Cuthbert's feet and warming him with their breath after he had spent a night praying in the cold North Sea. His love of animals was characteristic,

and the eider ducks still found around the Farne Islands are known as St Cuthbert's ducks, or Cuddy's, because he had managed to tame them.

Cuthbert died in 687 and was buried on Lindisfarne. Shortly afterwards, an unknown monk began work on the famous Lindisfarne Gospels, a beautifully illuminated manuscript now in the British Museum. Cuthbert's body was not destined to stay on his beloved Lindisfarne. After a series of Viking raids on the coast, monks removed it, first to Chester-le-Street and later to Ripon, before it eventually arrived, in 995, on a peninsula on the River Wear known as Dunholme (which became today's city of Durham).

Today the remains of the famous Celtic saint reside in the Lady Chapel behind the altar of the great Norman cathedral (*see page 336*) while those of his great chronicler, Bede, are at the opposite end of the cathedral, in the Galilee Chapel. ❏

ABOVE: Lindisfarne Gospels. **ABOVE RIGHT:** a "Cuddy" duck. **RIGHT:** A 12th-century wall painting of St Cuthbert in Durham Cathedral.

INSIGHT GUIDES 👁

TRAVEL TIPS

Insight Guides portray destinations in depth, providing the complete picture and the top photography

Insight Pocket Guides focus on the best choices for places to see and things to do and include large fold-out maps

Insight Compact Guides' portability makes them the perfect books to carry with you for on-the-spot reference

Three types of guide for all types of travel

INSIGHT GUIDES Different people need different kinds of information. Some want *background information* to help them prepare for the trip. Others seek *personal recommendations* from someone who knows the destination well. And others look for *compactly presented data* for on-the-spot reference. With three carefully designed series, Insight Guides offer readers the perfect choice. Insight Guides will turn your visit into an experience.

The world's largest collection of visual travel guides

CONTENTS

Getting Acquainted

The Place

Area 50,056 sq miles (129,645 sq km).
Capital London.
Population 48.9 million.
Language English.
Religion Protestant (Church of England): the monarch is the titular head of the church; the primate is the Archbishop of Canterbury.
Time Zone Greenwich Mean Time (GMT), 1 hour behind Continental European Time, 5 hours ahead of Eastern Seaboard Time. British Summer Time (+ one hour) runs from late March to September.
Currency The pound (£) divided into 100 pence (p).
Weights and Measures Officially metric but imperial measures are widely used, notably for distances (miles) and beer in pubs (pints).
Electricity 240 volts, square, three-pin plugs; two-pin shaver plugs.
Direct Dialling country code: 44.

Climate

Temperate, generally mild and always unpredictable. It is unusual for any area to have a dry spell for more than two or three weeks, even in summer (June to August). However, it rains most often in the north and west where temperatures are also cooler than in the south.

In summer, the average maximum temperature in the south is in the 70s Fahrenheit (23–25°C), although over 80°F (27°C) is not unusual. During the winter (November to February), the majority of England is cold and damp rather than snowy.

For recorded weather information, tel: (0891) 500401.

Economy

England is a trading country, with much of its economic wealth derived from the export of goods and services, particularly financial services and communications. With over half the land farmland, cereal crops and vegetables are important both for the home and export market.

Although heavy industry is no longer a major earner, manufacturing remains crucial to the economy. England produces a wide range of goods, from food and drinks, to pharmaceuticals, textiles and machinery. Following devaluation of the pound against other European countries in the early 1990s and determined fiscal budgeting by the Labour government, the English economy is gradually improving. Both the public and businesses continue to be financially cautious, however, and some major high-street names are feeling the pinch. But this is being counteracted by improved property sales and lower interest rates. Plus more new businesses are emerging and fewer failing, and unemployment remains consistently low compared with during the bust-and-boom 1980s. One encouraging aspect is that Britain is now attracting major investment (dominated by the car industry) from elsewhere, particularly the US and Japan.

Government

England is a constitutional monarchy with a parliamentary democracy. Although Queen Elizabeth II is head of state, she has no real power. England is governed centrally from Parliament at Westminster in London. Parliament consists of two bodies, the House of Commons (consisting of 659 Members of Parliament or MPs) and the House of Lords. The Commons has supreme control of national policy, finance and legislation. The House of Lords is known as the Revising Chamber, which ratifies, fine-tunes and

Customs Regulations

For information on the import and export of goods to England contact:
HM Customs and Excise,
New Kings Beam House,
22 Upper Ground,
London SE1 9PJ
Tel: 020-7620 1313.

sometimes overturns Commons legislation. After centuries of being predominantly made up of unelected hereditary peers, the Lords is in the process of radical upheaval. In November 1999, in its bid to create a meritocratic democracy, the Labour Party annulled the voting rights of most hereditary peers, but it remains to be seen how this will affect the legislative process.

Governments stay in power for a maximum term of five years. Voting is voluntary, and MPs are elected if they win the majority of votes in their constituency. The two main political parties are the Labour Party, which was formed at the end of the 19th century and the Conservative Party (Tories), which dates back to the 18th century. Other opposition comes from the Liberal Democratic Party.

The public can watch Parliament in session in the Public Galleries of the House of Commons and House of Lords. The Commons is in session Monday to Thursday from 2.30pm until around 10pm, Wednesday from 9.30am until around 10pm, Thursday 11.30am until early evening and Friday 9.30am–3pm. For information, tel: 020-7219 4272 (Commons) or 020-7219 3107 (Lords).

For tours of the Houses of Parliament, English residents should contact their MP.

Business Hours

Town centre shops generally open Monday to Saturday 9am–5.30pm, although a few smaller shops may close for lunch. Some small towns and villages have half-day closing one day in the week. Shopping centres in towns and cities are likely to have at least one evening of late-night shopping, with many more in the run-up to Christmas.

Supermarkets tend to be open 8.30am–8pm Monday to Saturday and 10am–4pm on Sunday, and some branches of the larger stores have all-night opening on certain days of the week (most often Thursday or Friday night). Some local corner shops and off-licences stay open until 10pm.

Offices usually operate Monday to Friday 9am–5.30pm with an hour for lunch.

Pubs are permitted to open between 11am and 11pm Monday to Saturday and noon–10.30pm on Sunday. However, some may close for periods during the day, and pubs can apply for a licence for extended opening hours for special events or nights like New Year's Eve.

Public Holidays

- **January** New Year's Day (1)
- **March/April** Good Friday, Easter Monday
- **May** May Day (first Monday), Spring Bank Holiday (last Monday)
- **August** Summer Bank Holiday (Last Monday)
- **December** Christmas Day (25), Boxing Day (26)

Planning the Trip

Clothing

Temperatures can fluctuate considerably from day to day so come prepared with suitable warm and wet-weather clothing. Generally, short sleeves and a jacket are recommended for summer and a warm coat and woollens for winter.

On the whole the English tend to dress casually and with a few exceptions formal dress is not essential for evening events, although a jacket and tie are required by smart hotels, restaurants and clubs.

Visas and Passports

To enter Britain you need a valid passport (or any form of official identification if you are an EU citizen). Visas are not needed if you are an American, Commonwealth citizen or EU national (or come from most other European or South American countries). Health certificates are not required unless you have arrived from Asia, Africa or South America. If you wish to stay for a protracted period or apply to work, contact:

Immigration and Nationality Directorate
Block C, Whitgift Centre
Wellsey Road, Croydon CR9 1AT.
Tel: 0870 6067766.

Health

Treatment If you fall ill and are a national of the EU, you are entitled to free medical treatment for illnesses arising while in England. Many other countries also have reciprocal arrangements for free treatment. But most visitors have to pay for any medical and dental treatment and they should ensure that they have adequate health insurance.

Accidents In the case of minor accidents, your hotel will know the location of the nearest hospital with a casualty department. Self-catering accommodation should have this information, as well as the number of the local GP (general practitioner), posted on a notice in the house.

Chemists/pharmacies Boots is the largest chain of pharmacies, with numerous branches around the country. In larger towns there is often a rota of late-opening chemists.

Money Matters

Most banks are open Monday to Friday 9.30am–4.30pm, with Saturday banking common in shopping areas. The majority of branches have at least one automatic machine (ATM) where credit or cashpoint cards can be used to withdraw cash.

The major English banks tend to offer similar exchange rates, so it's worth shopping around only if you have large amounts of money to change. Banks charge no commission on traveller's cheques presented in sterling. If a bank is affiliated to your own bank at home, it will make no charge for cheques in other currencies either. But there is a charge for changing cash into British currency.

Some high-street travel agents, such as Thomas Cook, operate *bureaux de change* at comparable rates. There are also many privately run *bureaux de change* (some of which are open 24 hours a day) where exchange rates can be low but commissions high.

Credit cards International credit cards are accepted in most shops, hotels and restaurants. John Lewis department store in London is a notable exception.

Eurocheques are widely accepted by hotels and some larger restaurants; though these are gradually being phased out.

Getting There

By Air

England's two major international airports are Heathrow (mainly scheduled flights), 15 miles (24km) from London, and Gatwick (scheduled and charter flights), 24 miles (40km) from the capital. An increasing number of international flights now arrive at the airports of Birmingham, Manchester and Glasgow (in Scotland) and London's smaller airports, Stansted and Luton. There is also the tiny London City Airport, a few miles from the City (financial heart of the capital), used by small aircraft only to fly to European capitals.

London Airports

Heathrow Airport There is a fast rail link between Heathrow and Paddington station. Called the Heathrow Express, it runs every 15 minutes from 5.10am to 11.40pm and takes 15 minutes. Fares are £12 single and £24 return. On some flights it is now possible to check in at Paddington, depositing your luggage with the airline there; you must do this at least two hours before your flight.

The cheapest way from Heathrow into central London is by the Underground (known as the Tube),
which takes about 45 minutes. The single fare is £3.40. Heathrow is on the Piccadilly Line, which goes directly to central areas such as Kensington, Piccadilly and Covent Garden. Paddington is on the District, Circle, Bakerloo and Hammersmith & City Line. For information about the Tube, tel: 020-7222 1234.

London Regional Transport (LRT) runs an Airbus service with red double-decker and single-decker buses picking up from terminals 1, 2 and 3. The A1 goes to Victoria, via Earl's Court and Knightsbridge, while the A2 goes to Euston via Marble Arch. Buses leave at half-hourly intervals from 6.30am to 10.15pm, take about an hour and stop at major hotels. Tickets can be purchased from the driver. For information, tel: 020-7222 1234.

Heathrow is also well served by taxis. A ride into town in a familiar London black cab will cost around £45, depending on your destination. To book a black cab, tel: 020-7272 0272. A cheaper option is to find a local minicab firm (for numbers see the *Yellow Pages* phone book, or ask at your hotel).

Gatwick Airport isn't on the Underground network, but has sophisticated train and coach services into London and to other
large cities. The Gatwick Express train to London leaves every 15 minutes from 5am until midnight, and there is an hourly service during the night. The journey into Victoria station takes just under half an hour. For information, tel: 0990 301530.

Green Line's Flightline 777 coaches to London leave from both the North and South terminals and take about 70 minutes to reach Victoria. Tickets can be bought from the driver. Tel: 0990 747777 for times and prices.

Hotelink runs a coach service to hotels in central areas of London. Booking is essential, however, tel: (01293) 532244.

Luton Airport has a regular train service to St Pancras station in London, taking 45 minutes. Alternatively, there are Green Line 757 coaches and Luton and District buses to London's Victoria Station, which take about 90 minutes (tel: 0345 788788).

Stansted Airport has a direct train service to London's Liverpool Street station, which runs every half hour on the half hour, taking about 40 minutes.

For those heading elsewhere in England other than London, there are regular Railair bus links to nearby rail stations.

Tourist Information Worldwide

The British Tourist Authority has offices worldwide. Any requests for information should be sent in writing.

● **Australia**
Level 16
Gateway
1 Macquarie Place
Sydney, NSW 2000
Tel: 02–9377 4400
Fax: 02–9377 4499.

● **Canada**
Suite 120
5915 Airport Road
Mississauga
Ontario
L4V1T1
Tel: (905) 405 1840
Fax: (905) 405 1835.

● **New Zealand**
17th Floor
151 Queen/Windham Street
Auckland 1
Tel: 9–303 1446
Fax: 9–377 6965.

● **Singapore**
Cecil Court
138 Cecil Street
Singapore 069 538
Tel: 65–27 5400
Fax: 65–227 5411.

● **South Africa**
Lancaster Gate
Hyde Lane
Hyde Park
Sandton 2196
Tel: 11–325 0342
Fax: 11–325 0344.

● **USA – Chicago**
625 N. Michigan Ave, Suite 1510
Chicago
IL 60611
Tel: (312) 787–464
Fax: (312) 787–9641.

● **USA – Los Angeles**
11661 San Vicentre Blvd
Los Angeles
CA 90049
Tel: (310) 820–4206
Fax: (310) 820–4406.

● **USA – New York**
7th Floor
551 Fifth Avenue/45th Street
New York
NY 10176–0799
Tel: (212) 986–2266
Fax: (212) 986–1188.

Coach Connections

National Express runs a coach service connecting Heathrow, Gatwick, Stansted and Luton airports with one another and the first three airports with Victoria coach station, central London. Tel: 0990 808080.

London City Airport is poorly served by public transport, despite its proximity to the City (6 miles/10 km). There is a mainline train from Silvertown station (about 5 minutes' walk from the airport) which connects with the Underground at Stratford or West Ham. Or there is a frequent Shuttlebus service that goes to Liverpool Street station (25 minutes) and Canary Wharf (10 minutes). Connections to the Underground and overground rails services can be made at both these stations. For enquiries, tel: (020) 7646 0000.

Regional Airports

Manchester Airport is 10 miles (16km) south of the city of Manchester. Frequent rail services run into Piccadilly station (taking 20 minutes) in the centre of Manchester, from which there are regular Intercity trains to London and other major cities. Alternatives are local buses or a taxi (approximately £12).

Birmingham Airport is 8 miles (13km) southeast of Birmingham. A courtesy bus links the airport directly with Birmingham International station. From there trains run every 15 minutes to New Street station in the centre of the city, taking about 15 minutes. Intercity trains from New Street to London Euston run on the hour every hour and take about 80 minutes.

Channel Tunnel

By train

Eurostar provides regular passenger-only trains linking England with France and Brussels. Services run from London's Waterloo station to Paris Nord (3 hours) and Brussels Midi (2 hours 40 minutes), with many trains stopping in Ashford, Kent. Or there are trains from Manchester and Birmingham to the Continent.

Booking is not essential, but it is worth watching out for offers on tickets bought in advance.

For UK bookings, tel: 0990 186186. From the US, tel: 1-800-eurostar, or elsewhere tel: (44) 1233 617575.

By car

"Le Shuttle" trains travel through the tunnel from Folkestone in Kent to Nord-Pas de Calais in France. Services are every hour in each direction from 7am to 11pm and every two hours through the night. Booking is not essential. Tel: 0990 353535.

Sea Transport

Sea services operate between a dozen British ports and more than 20 Continental ones. The major ferries have full eating, sleeping and entertainment facilities. The shortest route to the Continent is to France from Dover in southeast England to Calais, which takes about 90 minutes by ferry and half an hour by Hovercraft.

Brittany Ferries, UK
Tel: 0990 360360
Sails to Portsmouth from St Malo (33-99 82 80 80) and Caen (33-33 22 38 98) in France; to Poole in Dorset from Cherbourg, France (33-33 32 22 38 98); and to Portsmouth or Plymouth, depending on the season, from Santander in Spain (34-42 214 5000).

Hoverspeed, UK
Tel: 0990 240241
Runs a hovercraft service to Dover from Calais, France (33-21 46 12 14).

P&O European Ferries, UK
Tel: 0990 980980
Sails to Dover from Calais in France (33-21 46 04 40), and to Portsmouth from Cherbourg (33-33 88 65 70) and Le Havre in France (33-35 19 78 50).

Hoverspeed Seacat, UK
Tel: (08705) 240241
Operates the fast hovercraft service to Folkestone from Boulogne, France (33-21 30 27 26).

Stena Line, UK
Tel: (0990) 707070
Sails to Dover from Calais, France (33-21 46 78 30); to Newhaven from Dieppe, France (33-50 63 90 03); and to Southampton from Cherbourg in France (33-33 20 43 38).

If you plan to bring a vehicle by ferry it is advisable to book in advance, particularly during holidays. If travelling by night on a long journey it is also recommended that you book a sleeping cabin.

Flight Information

● **Birmingham Airport**
   Tel: (0121) 767 5511
● **Gatwick Airport**
   Tel: (01293) 535353
● **Heathrow Airport**
   Tel: (020) 8759 4321
● **London City Airport**
   Tel: (020) 7646 0000
● **Luton Airport**
   Tel: (01582) 405100
● **Manchester Airport**
   Tel: (0161) 489 3000
● **Stansted Airport**
   Tel: (01279) 680500

Disabled Travellers

Many Tourist Information Centres (TICs, *see over the page*) have leaflets giving information on access and facilities for the disabled at places of interest.

Free holiday information is available from:

Holiday Care Service
2nd Floor
Imperial Buildings
Victoria Road
Horley RH6 7PZ
Tel: (01293) 774535.

The Royal Association for Disability and Rehabilitation (RADAR),
Unit 12, City Forum,
250 City Road,
London EC1V 8AS.
Tel: 020-7250 3222
Provides an information service and free list of publications with travel details for the disabled.

Information Centres

There are over 800 Tourist Information Centres (TICs) throughout Britain. Most are open office hours, which are extended to include weekends and evenings in high season or in areas where there is a high volume of visitors all year round. Some close between October and March. TICs are signposted with the distinctive "i" symbol.

For general information about the whole of the country, contact (by phone or fax only):
The English Tourist Board/British Tourist Authority
Thames Tower
Black's Road
London W6 9EL
Tel: 020-8846 9000
Fax: 020-8563 0302.

For local information, write to or telephone the following:
East of England Tourist Board
Toppesfield Hall
Hadleigh
Suffolk IP7 5DN
Tel: (01473) 822922
Fax: (01473) 823063.
Heart of England Tourist Board
Larkhill Road
Worcester WR5 2EZ
Tel: (01905) 761100
Fax: (01905) 763450.
London Tourist Board and Convention Bureau
6th Floor
Glen House
Stag Place
London SW1E 5LT

Tel: (020) 7932 2000
Credit card reservations
Tel: 020-7604 2890
Fax: 020-7932 0222.
South East England Tourist Board
The Old Brew House
Warwick Park
Tunbridge Wells TN2 5TU
Tel: (01892) 540766
Fax: (01892) 511008.
Southern Tourist Board
40 Chamberlayne Road
Eastleigh SO50 5JH
Tel: (023) 8062 0555
Fax: (023) 8062 0010.
West Country Tourist Board
60 St David's Hill
Exeter EX4 4SY
Tel: (01392) 425426
Fax: (01392) 420891.
Yorkshire Tourist Board
312 Tadcaster Road
York YO24 1GS
Tel: (01904) 707961
Fax: (01904) 701414.
Northumbria Tourist Board
Aykley Heads
Durham DH1 5UX
Tel: (0191) 375 3000
Fax: (0191) 386 0899.
North West Tourist Board
Swan House
Swan Meadow Road
Wigan Pier
Wigan WN3 5BB
Tel: (01942) 821222
Fax: (01942) 820002.

Tourist Information in London

● **British Travel Centre**
Britain Visitor Centre
Lower Regent Street
London SW1Y 4NS.
Personal callers only. Offers tourist information, plus a booking service for rail, air and sea travel, sightseeing tours, theatre tickets and accommodation. There is also a currency exchange bureau. Open Monday to Friday 9am–6.30pm and 10am–4pm at weekends.

● **The London Visitor and Convention Bureau** (LVCB) provides general information and booking services for hotels, theatres and sightseeing tours at the following centres: Victoria Station, Liverpool Street tube station, Waterloo International terminal (arrivals hall), Heathrow terminals 1, 2, 3 (underground station concourse) and Selfridges (Oxford Street, W1).

Practical Tips

Lost Property

If you have lost your passport, you must get in touch as quickly as possible with your embassy.

For possessions lost on trains contact the station where the train ended its journey. The same applies should you leave something on a coach.

For anything lost on public transport in London, contact the London Transport Lost Property Office, 200 Baker Street, NW1 5RZ, tel: 020-7486 2496 between 9.30am and 2pm Monday to Friday, or fill in an enquiry form, available from any London Underground station or bus garage. Leave at least two full working days before making a visit to the lost property office.

Tipping

Most hotels and restaurants add a 10–15 percent service charge to your meal bill. It's your right to deduct this amount if you are not happy with the service provided. Sometimes when service has been added, the final total on a credit card slip is still left blank, the implication being that a further tip is expected: don't pay it. It is customary to give hairdressers, sightseeing guides, railway porters and cab drivers an extra 10 percent.

Media

Newspapers
With over 100 daily and Sunday newspapers nationwide, there's no lack of choice. Of the quality dailies *The Times* and *The Daily Telegraph* are on the right politically, *The*

Guardian on the left and *The Independent* in the middle. On Sunday *The Observer* leans slightly left of centre, while the *Independent on Sunday* stands in the middle and the *Sunday Times* and *Sunday Telegraph* are both on the right.

The Financial Times is renowned for the clearest, most unbiased headlines, plus exhaustive financial coverage.

The tabloids are half the size, and a less formal easy read. *The Sun, The Star* and *News of the World* (out on Sunday) are on the right. *The Mirror, Sunday Mirror* and *Sunday People* are slightly left. The *Daily Mail* and *Mail on Sunday* are slightly more upmarket equivalents of the *Express* and *Sunday Express*.

Listings Magazines

Listings magazines are published in the larger cities and sold in newsagents. In London, the long-established weekly *Time Out* (out on Wednesdays) is supreme. But the London-only *Evening Standard* includes a good free magazine, *Hot Tickets*, on Thursdays.

Local papers publish details of events around the country and the quality daily newspapers have a limited listings section. But out of London your best port of call is a Tourist Information Centre *(see page 360)*. Many local papers have a listings section on Fridays.

Foreign Newspapers

These can usually be found in large newsagents, rail stations and

branches of John Menzies and W H Smith nationwide.

Television

There are five national terrestial channels: BBC1, BBC2, ITV, Channel 4 (C4) and Channel 5 (C5). Both the BBC (British Broadcasting Corporation) and ITV (Independent Television) have regional stations that broadcast local news and varying programme schedules in between links with the national networks based in London (daily and local newspapers publish listings).

BBC1, ITV and C5 broadcast programmes aimed at mainstream audiences, while BBC2 and C4 cater more for arts, cultural and minority interests. However, the advent of cable and satellite channels has forced terrestial stations to fight for audiences with a higher incidence of programmes such as soap operas, game shows and situation comedies, and the overlap can make channels seem similar.

There are more than 60 cable and satellite channels on offer, ranging from sport and movies to cartoons and golden oldies. Pricier hotel rooms often offer a choice of cable stations, including CNN and NBC's Super Channel.

Postal Services

Post offices are open 9am–5.30pm Monday to Friday, and 9am–12.30pm on Saturday. London's main post office is in Trafalgar Square, behind the church of St Martin-in-the-Fields, and it stays open until 8pm Monday to Saturday.

Stamps are sold at post offices, selected shops and newsagents, many supermarkets and from machines outside larger post offices. Mail posted first class should reach British destination the next day, and second class takes a day longer. The rate to Europe for letters is the same as first-class post within Britain.

Mail can be forwarded to you at any post office in England if it is addressed c/o Poste Restante.

Radio Stations

● **Classic FM** 100.9 FM
24-hour classical music unpompously presented.
● **Jazz FM** 102.2FM
Jazz alone failed to provide big enough audiences, so the station was broadened to include soul and blues.
● **Kiss FM** 100FM
24-hour dance.
● **1FM** 98.8FM
Britain's most popular radio station, which broadcasts mainstream pop.
● **Radio 2** 89.2FM
Easy-listening music and chat shows.
● **Radio 3** 91.3FM
24-hour classical music, plus some drama.
● **Radio 4** 93.5FM
News, current affairs, plays.
● **Radio Five Live** 909MW
Rolling news and sport.
● **BBC World Service** 648kHz
International news.

Telephones

It is usually cheaper to use public phones rather than those in hotel rooms as hotels make high profits out of this service.

British Telecom (BT) is the main telephone operating company. Its public telephones are by far the most plentiful, though a number of other telephone companies also have kiosks. Some public phones take coins only, some plastic phone cards and/or credit cards, and some all three. Phone cards can be purchased from post offices and newsagents in varying amounts between £1 and £20.

The most expensive time to use the telephone is 8am–6pm weekdays, while the cheapest is after 6pm on weekdays and all weekend. Calls are charged according to distance.

Embassies

Most countries have diplomatic representation in London (a

Useful Numbers

● **Emergencies** 999
For fire, ambulance or the police in emergencies only. Telephone 192 for numbers of a local police station or your embassy otherwise.
● **Operator** (for difficulties in getting through) 100
● **Directory Enquiries (UK)** 192
● **International Directory Enquiries** 153
● **International Operator** 155
● **Telemessages** 0800 190190

Telephone Codes

On 1 June 1999 new dialling codes were introduced for the following cities: London, Portsmouth, Southampton and Coventry.
London 0171– will change to: 020-7
London 0181– will change to: 020-8
Portsmouth (01705) will change to: (023) 92
Southampton (01703) will change to: (023) 80
Coventry (01203) will change to: (024) 76
The old numbers will continue to work until October 2000.

selection is given below), others can be found through the *Yellow Pages* or via Directory Enquiries, tel: 192
Australia
Australia House
Strand
London WC2B 4LA.
Tel: (020) 7379 4334.
United States
24 Grosvenor Square
London W1A 1AE.
Tel: (020) 7499 9000.

Medical Services

In a medical emergency, either call an ambulance (999) or make your way to the nearest Accident and Emergency department (in most large hospitals). Your hotel will give details. For emergency dental care go to the nearest hospital casualty ward. Otherwise, call Directory Enquiries (192) or consult the *Yellow Pages* phone directory for local dentists.

Getting Around

Driving

You should drive on the left-hand side of the road and observe speed limits. It is illegal to drink and drive, and penalties are severe. Drivers and passengers, in both front and back seats, must wear seat belts where fitted. Failure to do so can result in a fine. For further information on driving in Britain consult a copy of the *Highway Code*, widely available in bookshops.

If you are bringing your own car you will need a valid driving licence or International Driving Permit, plus insurance coverage, vehicle registration and a nationality sticker.

Parking

Road congestion is a problem in most town and city centres, and parking is often restricted. Never leave your car on a double yellow line, in a place marked for *permit holders only,* within a white zig-zag line close to a pedestrian crossing, or in a control zone. Also, don't park on a single yellow line when restrictions are in force, usually 8.30am to 6.30pm weekdays (consult signs on the curb). These are offences for which you can face a fine. Either use a meter or a car park (distinguished by a white P on a blue background).

Pay particular attention if leaving your car in central London. In many areas illegal parking may result in wheel clamping. This means your car is immobilised with a clamp until you pay to have it released, which can take several hours. Or your car may be towed away to a pound. Retrieving it costs more than £100, plus the £30 parking

fine. If you want to find out if your car has been towed away, tel: (020) 7747 4747.

Breakdown

The following motoring organisations operate 24-hour breakdown assistance. They have reciprocal arrangements with other national motoring clubs. All calls are free.
AA 0800 887766.
Britannia Rescue 0800 591563.
Green Flag 0800 400600.
RAC 0800 828282.

Car Rental

You must be over 21 years old (over 25 for some companies) and have held a valid full driving licence for more than one year. The cost will usually include insurance and unlimited mileage and road tax. It does not incorporate insurance cover for accidental damage to the interior of the car, wheels and tyres or insurance for other drivers.

Some companies offer special weekend and holiday rates, so shop around. International companies (such as those listed below) may offer holiday packages with discounts of as much as 40 percent on advance bookings through travel agents or branches in your own country. Many rental firms provide child seats and luggage racks.
Avis 0990 900500.
Hertz 0990 996699.
Budget 0800 181181.
Europcar (0870) 6075000.

Speed Limits

- Unless otherwise stated, **30 mph (50 kph)** in built-up areas.
- **60 mph (100 kph)** on normal roads away from built-up areas.
- **70 mph (112 kph)** on motorways and dual carriageways (divided highways).
- **Camping vans** or **cars towing a caravan** are restricted to 50 mph (80 kph) on normal roads and 60 mph (96 kph) on dual carriageways.

Rover Tickets

Coach
National Express
Tel: 0990 808080)
Offers a Tourist Trail Pass, which entitles you to unlimited travel on National Express coaches for specified periods.
Green Line
Tel: (020) 8668 7261)
Supplies a Diamond Rover ticket for a day's unlimited travel on Green Line coaches and buses.

Train
For UK residents there are several passes, including a Family, Senior Citizen's and Young Person's Railcard, which are valid for one year. They reduce the price of a long-distance InterCity trip and allow you an unlimited number of journeys on off-peak trains. The BritRail ticket (available from European travel agents only) also gives you unlimited travel in Great Britain for specified periods.

Public Transport

Domestic Flights
From the major international airports there are frequent shuttle services to England's many domestic airports.
Airlines providing domestic services are:
● **KLM UK**. Tel: 01279 660400.
● **British Airways** (the country's largest airline), Heathrow and Great Britain flight information, tel: 0990 444000.
Reservations, tel: 0345 222111.
● **British Midland Airways**
Tel: 0870 6070555.

Major Domestic Airports
Bristol
Tel: (01275) 474441.
East Midlands
Tel: (01332) 852852.
Leeds-Bradford
Tel: (0113) 250 9696.
Liverpool
Tel: (0151) 288 4000.

Newcastle upon Tyne
Tel: (0191) 286 0966.
Norwich
Tel: (01603) 411923.
Southampton
Tel: (023) 8062 9600.

Trains
A total of 25 private operating companies run trains in regions around the country. There are many money-saving deals, such as cheap-day returns, and generally tickets bought at least two weeks in advance are vastly cheaper than standard rates. Some saver tickets are available if bought abroad before arriving.
For most journeys it is not necessary to purchase tickets until the day you travel, or make seat reservations, except over Christmas when InterCity trains are booked well in advance.
Trains are divided into first and second-class carriages, with first-class accommodation up to twice the price of second. It is sometimes possible to upgrade your ticket to first-class on InterCity trains for a small extra payment after boarding.
On long distances overnight, it may be worth having a sleeping compartment. Available on InterCity trains, these are basic but comfortable and must be booked in advance.

Coaches
National Express operates a comprehensive network of coach services with fast and comfortable coaches running on long journeys,

Train Enquiries

● **National Rail Enquiry Service**
For train times, cancellations and advance credit card bookings tel: 0345 484950 (24 hours a day).
● **British Nationwide Train, Bus & Coach Hotline**
For timetable information tel: 0006 5500000.
● **International Rail Enquiry Service** For services from Britain tel: 0990 848848.

London Transport

● **London Regional Transport** (LRT) publishes a map and guide for visitors which is available from information centres at the following Underground stations: Piccadilly Circus, Oxford Circus, Heathrow and at major train stations in the capital.
● **The Off-Peak One Day Travelcard** is a one-day pass that allows unlimited travel on the Tube, buses, Docklands Light Railway and services to stations in Greater London. It is valid after 9.30am on weekdays or all day at weekends and bank holidays.
● **Other Travelcards** are valid for a week or a month and can be used at any time. To buy a pass you will need a passport-sized photograph.
For further information, tel: (020) 7222 1234.

equipped with washrooms and stewards. Fares are considerably cheaper than the equivalent journey by train, although you must book your seat in advance. For enquiries and bookings, tel: 0990 808080.
From April to November National Express provides scheduled day trips to cities of interest such as Bath and Stratford-upon-Avon, museums such as Madame Tussaud's and the Natural History Museum in London and theme parks such as Alton Towers (with entrance fees included). **Green Line** (tel: (020) 8668 7261) has similar services.

Taxis
Outside London and large cities and away from taxi ranks at stations, ports and airports you will usually have to telephone for a cab rather than expect to hail one in the street. By law cabs must be licensed and display charges on a meter. Add at least 10 percent for a tip.
London "black cab" drivers are famous for their extensive

Sightseeing Tours

- All English cities of historical interest have double-decker buses that tour the sites. Some are open-topped so, weather permitting, you can enjoy fresh air and uninterrupted camera angles. Many have a commentary in several languages.
- For guided tours of the capital, London Coaches (tel: 020-8877 1722) operates a hop-on, hop-off service so you take in the sites at your pace over a 24-hour period.
- Golden Tours (tel: 020-7233 7030) and Frames Rickards (tel: 020-7837 6311) offer sightseeing day trips from London to places like Oxford, Bath, Canterbury and Windsor with commentary from a Blue Badge Guide (the elite of guides) and, in some cases, lunch.

knowledge of the city's streets. Minicabs (unlicensed taxis, which look like private cars) are not allowed to compete with black cabs on the street and have to be hired by telephone or from a kiosk. If hiring a minicab, agree to a fee beforehand.

If you have a complaint, make a note of the driver's licence number and contact the Carriage Office, tel: 020-7230 1631.

Travelling Around London

If you are staying in London for a while it is worth investing in an *A–Z Map* which gives detailed information of the capital's complex of streets.

The Underground (also known as the Tube) is the quickest way to get across London. Services start at 5.30am and run until around midnight. Tubes get packed in the rush hours (8–9.30am and 5–6.30pm). Make sure that you have a valid ticket as it is illegal to travel without one. Smoking is prohibited. Fares are based upon a zone system with a flat fare in the central zone. Tickets may be purchased from a ticket office or machine. A daily travel card is worth buying if you are making more than two journeys.

The Docklands Light Railway has two branches connecting up with the Underground network. It operates in the same way as the Tube, with similar fares.

London buses provide a comprehensive service throughout Greater London and have their route and number clearly displayed on the front. Buses carry on running hourly throughout the night, with services to most parts of London departing from Trafalgar Square. Smoking is prohibited.

Waterways

Britain has over 2,000 miles (3,200km) of rivers and canals, with a wide choice of boats and places from which to hire them. Possibilities include exploring England's many canals, or taking a pleasure cruiser along the Thames, Avon or the Severn, or around the Norfolk Broads.

For information:
British Waterways Board
The Toll House
Delemere Terrace
Little Venice
London W2 6ND
Tel: 020-7286 6101.

Where to Stay

Choosing a Hotel

By international standards, hotels in Britain are expensive, so if you are holidaying on a tight budget you should consider staying in bed-and-breakfast accommodation. Alternatively there are plenty of youth hostels throughout the country, which take people of all ages (*see page 372 for details*).

Not all hotels include breakfast in their rates and they are also likely to add a service charge of 10–15 percent. However, all charges should be clearly displayed on the tariff.

It is advisable to book in advance, particularly at Christmas, Easter and throughout the summer, although during the rest of the year there is generally little difficulty in finding somewhere suitable to stay. You can book a room through a travel agent, directly with a hotel or via the Tourist Board.

Booking Services Tourist Information Centres (*see page 360*) displaying a Local Bed Booking Service sticker will book (free or for a small fee) for personal callers, whereas those involved in the Book-A-Bed-Ahead scheme will reserve you somewhere to stay in any area where there is another TIC involved in the scheme. A small fee is required, and this is added to the hotel's bill. All TICs have free lists of local accommodation.

The Britain Visitor Centre in Lower Regent Street, London, provides a booking service for the whole of the country (*see page 360*).

The **English Tourist Board** (020-8846 9000) produces a series of useful *Where To Stay* guides dealing with every type of accommodation, from farms to self-catering boating holidays. To be listed, an establishment has to pay to be inspected and then pay to be included, so leaflets are not impartial. A series of books covering B&B and self-catering accommodation is also produced by the ETB.

Hotel Listings

Many hotels offer special weekend and low-season breaks between October and April. Details can be obtained from individual hotels, chains of hotels or from the English Tourist Board (tel: 020-8846 9000) which publishes a brochure, *Let's Go: Short Breaks in England*, with details of reduced rates at hundreds of hotels.

London

The London Tourist Board provides a bed booking service that is available through information centres or by telephone (credit cards only). Tel: 020-7932 2020.

Higher prices do not always mean quality, so look out for the LVCB membership sticker indicating that certain standards have been met.

Many moderately priced hotels are small and don't have restaurant facilities, although they may provide room service. Some hotels offer babysitting and booking services for theatres and restaurants, while smarter establishments cater fully for business travellers.

Top Class
Berkeley Hotel
Wilton Place, SW1X 7RL.
Tel: 020-7235 6000.
Fax: 020-7235 4330.
Many rate the Berkeley as the best in London. It's low key, seldom advertised, with a country house atmosphere. Not a business hotel. Swimming pool. Attracts many English customers. **££££**
Claridge's
Brook Street, W1A 2JQ.
Tel: 020-629 8860.
Fax: 020-7499 2210.

Price Guide

Prices quoted are for a double room including breakfast and VAT at high season.
££££ over £250
£££ £150–250
££ £80–£150
£ under £80

Has long had a reputation for dignity and graciousness. **££££**
The Dorchester
53 Park Lane, W1A 2HJ.
Tel: 020-7629 8888.
Fax: 020-7495 7342.
One of the most expensive in London. Views over Hyde Park.
££££
Durley House
115 Sloane Street, SW1X 9PJ.
Tel: 020-7235 5537.
Fax: 020-7259 6977.
Seriously luxurious, with all mod cons and a Michelin award. **££££**
The Savoy
Strand, WC2R 0EU.
Tel: 020-7836 4343.
Fax: 020-7240 6040.
One of London's legends, with a solid reputation for comfort (its 600 rooms are excellent) and personal service (if a little over-formal). Conveniently central. **££££**

Luxury
Blakes Hotel
33 Roland Gardens, SW7 3PF.
Tel: 020-7370 6701.
Fax: 020-7373 0442.
Very trendy and popular with theatrical and media folk. Cosmopolitan. Has 52 rooms. **££££**
Brown's Hotel
Albemarle Street, W1X 4BP.
Tel: 020-7493 6020.
Fax: 0171-493 9381.
A distinguished, very British, Victorian-style hotel. Smart Mayfair location. Has 116 rooms. **££££**
Capital Hotel
22–24 Basil Street, SW3 1AT.
Tel: 020-7589 5171.
Fax: 020-7225 0011.
Luxurious small hotel (56 rooms) in Knightsbridge. Restrained with tasteful decor. Friendly service. Restaurant has Michelin star. **££££**

Goring Hotel
15 Beeston Place,
Grosvenor Gardens,
SW1W 0JW.
Tel: 020-7396 9000.
Fax: 020-7834 4393.
Family-owned traditional hotel near Buckingham Palace. Relaxed. Homemade food. **£££–££££**
The Halkin
5 Halkin Street, SW1X 7DJ.
Tel: 020-73331000.
Fax: 020-7333 1100.
Top-class and ultra-modern. Every room has its own sitting room. Michelin rated. **££££**
Landmark London
222 Marylebone Road, NW1 61Q.
Tel: 020-7631 8000.
Fax: 020-7631 8080.
Modern eight-storey building with large rooms and all facilities.
£££–££££
The Ritz
150 Piccadilly, W1V 9DG.
Tel: 020-7493 8181
Fax: 020-7493 2687.
One of the most famous hotels in the world, not quite what it was. Refined English cuisine, legendary high-teas. Formal dress essential. Has 130 rooms. **££££**
Tower Thistle Hotel
St Katharine's Way, E1 9LD.
Tel: 020-7481 2575.
Fax: 020-7488 4106.
A big modern hotel, handy for the City. Has 826 rooms, all with private bath. Meals. **£££–££££**
22 Jermyn Street
22 Jermyn Street, SW1Y 6HL.
Tel: 020-7734 2353.
Fax: 020-7734 0750.
Peaceful townhouse. Rooms with two phone lines and fax/modem.
££££

Moderate
Academy Hotel
17–25 Gower Street, WC1E 6HG.
Tel: 020-731 4115
Fax: 020-7636 3442.
A small and welcoming Bloomsbury hotel. Licensed bar; evening meal available. Has 35 rooms, 5 with private bath. **£££**
Basil Street Hotel
Basil Street, SW3 1AH.
Tel: 020-7581 3311.

Fax: 020-7581 3693.
Tremendous reputation, and lots of old-fashioned charm. Has 95 rooms, 82 with private bath. **£££**

Elizabeth Hotel
37 Eccleston Square,
SW1V 1PB.
Tel: 020-7828 6812.
Fax: 020-7828 6814.
Friendly hotel set in an elegant period square, only two minutes' walk from Victoria station. Has 40 rooms, 22 with bath. **££**

Tophams
28 Ebury Street,
SW1W 1SD.
Tel: 020-7730 8147.
Fax: 020-7823 5966.
Old style with faded charm. Very popular, one of the best-value hotels in London. Friendly. **££**

Inexpensive

Clearlake Hotel
18–19 Prince of Wales Terrace,
W8 9PQ.
Tel: 020-7937 3274.
Fax: 020-7376 0604.
Comfortable small west London hotel in a quiet location with views of Hyde Park. With 17 rooms. Good value. **£**

Lonsdale Hotel
9–10 Bedford Place,
WC1B 5JA.
Tel: 020-7636 1812.
Fax: 020-7580 9902.
Established B&B with real character in Bloomsbury. Has 34 rooms, 3 with private bath. **££**

Hotel Strand Continental
143 Strand, WC2R 1JA.
Tel: 020-7836 4880.
Fax: 020-7379 6105.
One of the cheapest hotels in

Step Back in History

For a taste of England past, it is possible to stay in a number of restored old buildings, from a medieval castle to a lighthouse.
The Landmark Trust Tel: (01628) 825925.
The National Trust Members only (*see page 379*). For details write to: The National Trust, 36 Queen Anne's Gate, London SW1H 9AS.

London. Very central. Has 22 rooms, no private bath. No credit cards. **£**

The Southeast

Alfriston

The George Inn
High Street, BN26 5SY.
Tel: (01323) 870319.
Fax: (01323) 871384.
15th-century pub and hotel in a popular village nor far from the sea. 4-poster beds. The restaurant specialises in fish. **£**

Arundel

Amberley Castle
nr Arundel, BN18 9ND.
Tel: (01798) 831992.
Fax: (01798) 831998.
Eleventh-century castle dripping with atmosphere. Opulently furbished with antiques and the odd suit of armour. Individually decorated rooms. Excellent service. Fine classic cuisine in baronial hall. **£££–££££**

Swan Hotel
27–29 High Street,
BN18 9AG.
Tel: (01903) 882314.
Fax: (01903) 883759.
A listed building at the heart of a delightful village, very popular with tourists. Good restaurant. **£**

Brighton

The Old Ship Hotel
King's Road, BN1 1NR.
Tel: (01273) 329001.
Fax: (01273) 820718.
One of the oldest Brighton hotels. Elegant, traditional but not too grand. **££**

The New Madeira Hotel
19–23 Marine Parade, BN2 1TL.
Tel: (01273) 698331.
Fax: (01273) 606193.
Ask for a room at the front, with a bay window, to have a view of the bright lights of the pier. **£**

Canterbury

Falstaff
8–10 St Dunstan's Street,
Westgate CT2 8AF.
Tel: (01227) 462138.
Fax: (01227) 463525.

Inn within easy reach of both the cathedral and the shops, with 24 rooms. **££**

Chichester

The Millstream Hotel and Restaurant
Bosham, nr Chichester, PO18 8HL.
Tel: (01243) 573234.
Fax: (01243) 573459.
Quiet country hotel near Bosham harbour with various rosettes for its food and hospitality. **££**

Suffolk House Hotel
3 East Row, PO19 1PD.
Tel: (01243) 778899.
Fax: (01243) 787282.
Privately-run hotel in a Georgian house not far from the cathedral. Restaurant and garden. **££**

Midhurst

Angel Hotel
North Street, GU29 9DN.
Tel: (01730) 812421.
Fax: (01730) 815928
Dates back to 1420. Hilaire Belloc called it "the most revered of all prime inns". Many original features. With 28 rooms. **££**

New Romney

Romney Bay House
Coast Road, Littlestone, TN28 8QY.
Tel: (01797) 364747.
Fax: (01797) 367156.
This quirky 1920s house by the sea was built by Portmeirion architect Sir Clough Williams-Ellis. Very welcoming. Beautiful decor. Good food, and excellent Sunday teas. Has 10 rooms. **£–££**

Rye

The Mermaid Inn
Mermaid Street, TN31 7EY.
Tel: (01797) 223065.
Fax: (01797) 225069.
Popular 15th-century inn and well known for honeymooners. Excellent restaurant. Has 28 rooms (15 with 4-poster beds). **£**

The West Country

Barwick

Little Barwick House
Barwick, nr Yeovil, BA22 9TD.
Tel: (01935) 423902.

Fax: (01935) 420908.
Unpretentious Georgian dower house with gardens. Has 6 rooms and an excellent restaurant. **££**

Bath
Bath Spa Hotel
Sydney Road, BA2 6JF.
Tel: (01225) 444424.
Fax: (01225) 444006.
Set in extensive grounds. All comforts, excellent restaurant. **£££**
Priory Hotel
Weston Road, BA1 2XT.
Tel: (01225) 331922.
Fax: (01225) 448276.
Gothic-style 19th-century house near park. Comfortable, individual and quiet. **£££**
The Royal Crescent Hotel
15–16 The Royal Crescent, BA1 2LS.
Tel: (01225) 739955.
Fax: (01225) 339401.
The ultimate address in Bath. Antiques, paintings, individually decorated rooms. Noted food and secluded garden. Has 45 rooms. **£££**
The Queensberry Hotel
Russel Street, BA1 2QF.
Tel: (01225) 447928.
Fax: (01225) 446065.
Comfortable and characterful Georgian hotel. Renowned for its Olive Tree restaurant serving British fare with French, Italian and Moroccan influences. **££**
Bloomfield House
146 Bloomfield Road, BA2 2AS.
Tel: (01225) 420105.
Fax: (01225) 481958.
Upmarket B&B in large 19th-century neoclassical house. Some rooms with 4-poster or half-tester beds. No smoking. **£**
Eagle House
Church Street, Bathford, BA1 7RS.
Tel: (01225) 859946.
Fax: (01225) 859430.
B&B in a pretty conservation village just outside Bath. Friendly and homely but smart. **£**
Somerset House Hotel and Restaurant
35 Bathwick Hill, BA2 6LD.

Price Guide
Prices quoted are for a double room including breakfast and VAT at high season.
££££ over £250
£££ £150–250
££ £80–£150
£ under £80

Tel: (01225) 466451.
Fax: (01225) 317188.
Attractive Georgian house, which is family run and noted for its fine food. Dinner included. **£**

Bigbury-on-Sea
Burgh Island Hotel
TQ7 4BG.
Tel: (01548) 810514.
Fax: (01548) 810243.
Art Deco hotel, with access by sea tractor. Agatha Christie wrote two of her books here. Has 15 suites. **££**

Bradford-on-Avon
Old Manor Hotel
Trow, Trowbridge, BA14 9BL.
Tel: (01225) 777393.
Fax: (01225) 765443.
Sixteenth-century manor farmhouse. Restaurant. **£–££**

Castle Combe
Manor House
Castle Combe, nr Chippenham, SN14 7HR.
Tel: (01249) 782206.
Fax: (01249) 782159.
Old manor with clubby feel. Best rooms in the main house have beams, exposed stone walls and quality furnishings. **££**

Chagford
Mill End Hotel
Sandy Park, TQ13 8JN.
Tel: (01647) 432282.
Fax: (01647) 433106.
Old mill, with wheel in operation, in a peaceful setting on the River Teign. Excellent for families, with good children's menu. **£**

Dartmouth
Nonsuch House
Church Hill, Kingswear, TQ6 0BX.

Tel/fax: 01803 752829.
Edwardian manor with stunning views over Dartmouth harbour. Has 3 rooms and a small garden. **£**
The Royal Castle
11 The Quay, TQ6 9PS.
Tel: (01803) 833033.
Fax: (01803) 835445.
Originally a 17th-century coaching inn on Dartmouth's quayside. Good food and award-winning breakfasts. Has 25 rooms. **£**

Freshford
Homewood Park
Hinton Charterhouse, Freshford, BA3 6BB.
Tel: (01225) 723731.
Fax: (01225) 723820.
Quintessentially English country house hotel with outdoor pool, gardens and cosy bar. Has 19 rooms. **££**

Gillan
Tregildry
Gillan, Manaccan, nr Helston, TR12 6HG.
Tel: (01326) 231378.
Fax: (01326) 231561.
Small, friendly hotel with stunning views over Gillan Bay. **£**

Monkton Combe
The Manor House
BA2 7HD.
Tel: (01225) 723128.
Fax: (01225) 722972.
Attractive, very reasonably priced 16th-century manor. Breakfast served until noon. **£**

Penzance
Abbey Hotel
Abbey Street, TR18 4AR.
Tel: (01736) 366906.
Fax: (01736) 351163.
Delightful period stuccoed building overlooking harbour. Tastefully decorated. Restaurant. **££**

Saltford
Brunel's Tunnel House Hotel
High Street, BS31 3BF.
Tel: (01225) 873873.
Fax: (01225) 874875.
One-time home of Isambard Kingdom Brunel. Rooms individually furnished. Ensuite. **£**

Ston Easton
Ston Easton Park
Nr Bath, BA3 4DF.
Tel: (01761) 241631.
Fax: (01761) 241377.
Most notable for its gardens, this fine Palladian manor provides country house splendour and service. Some rooms with Chippendale 4-posters. No children under 7. **£££**

The Southwest

Brockenhurst
New Park Manor
Lyndhurst Road, SO42 7QH.
Tel: (01590) 623467.
Fax: (01590) 622268.
Excellent country retreat set in 6 acres (2.4 hectares) of grounds in New Forest. Fine restaurant, stables, heated pool and tennis court. With 25 rooms. **££**
Careys Manor
SO42 7RH.
Tel: (01590) 623551.
Fax: (01590) 622799.
This fine Arts and Crafts mansion of 1888 will appeal to the active: mountain bikes are available, and there is a pool, gym, sauna and playground. **££**
Whitley Ridge Hotel
Beaulieu Road, SO42 7QL.
Tel: (01590) 622354.
Fax: (01590) 622856.
A friendly small hotel in a secluded Georgian house set amid parkland, with 13 rooms. **£**

Evershot
Summer Lodge
Summer Lane DT2 0JR.
Tel: (01935) 83424.

Hotel Chains

Hotels belonging to big chains offer a reliable, if at times impersonal, service. Many incorporate conference rooms, health and leisure facilities and secretarial services.

Forte
Tel: 0345 404040 in the UK; and 1 (800) 225-5843 in the US.

Fax: (01935) 83005.
Former Georgian dower house set in mature gardens. Tastefully furnished and noted for its excellent service and hospitality. **££££**

Lyme Regis
The Alexandra
Pound Street,
DT7 3HZ.
Tel: (01297) 442010.
Fax: (01297) 443229.
Large 18th-century house (26 rooms) set in grounds overlooking bay. Comfortable, welcoming. **£££**

Lymington
Stanwell House
High Street, SO41 9AA
Tel: (01590) 677123.
Brightly decorated Georgian coaching house, with yacht for charter. Good food. Has 29 rooms. **££**

Sparsholt
Lainston House Hotel
nr Winchester, SO21 2LT.
Tel: (01962) 863588.
Fax: (01962) 776248.
Beautiful country house in extensive grounds with a good restaurant. Has 38 rooms. **££**

The Thames Valley

Aylesbury
Hartwell House
Oxford Road, nr Aylesbury,
HP17 8NL.
Tel: (01296) 747444.
Fax: (01296) 747450.
Country house hotel set in 90 acres of grounds. Plush baroque-style public rooms, antiques and

Intercontinental Hotels & Resorts
Tel: 020-7495 2500
Fax: 020-7495 2769.
Hilton International
Tel: 0800 8568003
Fax: (01923) 218548.
Ibis Hotels
Tel: 020-8759 4888
Fax: 020-8564 7894.

excellent leisure facilities. Has 45 rooms. No children under 8. **£££–££££**

Henley-on-Thames
Red Lion
Hart Street, RG9 2AR.
Tel: (01491) 572161.
Fax: (01491) 410039.
Overlooks the finishing post of the regatta on the River Thames. With 26 comfortable rooms. **££**

Windsor
Oakley Court
Water Oakley, SL4 5UR.
Tel: (01753) 609988.
Fax: (01628) 637011.
A charming Victorian house with grounds leading down to the Thames. Lovely, mostly big, rooms. **£££**

Oxford to Stratford

Bibury
Bibury Court
Cirencester, GL7 5NT.
Tel: (01285) 740337.
Fax: (01285) 740660.
This glorious Jacobean house fulfils everyone's idea of the perfect Cotswold manor. Very good value. **££**

Buckland
Buckland Manor
Nr Broadway, WR12 7LY.
Tel: (01386) 852626.
Fax: (01386) 853557.
Thirteenth-century manor in extensive gardens. Michelin rated. **£££**

Cheltenham
On the Park
Evesham Road, GL52 2AH.
Tel: (01242) 518898.
Fax: (01242) 511526.
Pretty townhouse with tasteful, individually-decorated bedrooms and luxurious bathrooms. No children under 8. **££**

Lower Slaughter
Lower Slaughter Manor
Lower Slaughter,
nr Bourton-on-the-Water, GL54 2HP.
Tel: (01451) 820456.

Fax: (01451) 822150.
Luxurious Georgian manor in its own grounds, with grand public rooms, antiques, chintzy fabrics and bathrooms with his and hers washbasins. Superb breakfast. **£££–££££**

Oxford
Old Parsonage Hotel
1 Banbury Road, OX2 6NN.
Tel: (01865) 310210.
Fax: (01865) 311262.
A fine hotel in the renovated old parsonage, with 30 luxuriously appointed ensuite bedrooms. With Parsonage Bar restaurant. **£££**
Bath Place Hotel
4–5 Bath Place, OX1 3SU.
Tel: (01865) 791812.
Fax: (01865) 791834.
Family-run hotel in the heart of Oxford occupying a group of restored 17th-century cottages. Excellent restaurant. 12 rooms. **££**
Cotswold Lodge Hotel
66a Banbury Road, OX2 6JP.
Tel: (01865) 512121.
Fax: (01865) 512490.
Beautiful Victorian building, only a few minutes' walk from the city centre. 50 rooms. **££**
Cotswold House
363 Banbury Road, OX2 7PL.
Tel/fax: (01865) 310558.
Commended B&B. No smoking. **£**

Stow-on-the-Wold
The Grapevine
Sheep Street, GL54 1AU.
Tel: (01451) 830344.
Fax: (01451) 832278.
Immaculately maintained, hospitable hotel within an old stone building. With 23 rooms. **££**

Stratford-upon-Avon
The Shakespeare
Chapel Street, CV37 6QR.
Tel: 0870 4008182.
Fax: (01789) 415411.
This 17th-century half-timbered building is the best hotel in town. Central with a good restaurant. Has 63 rooms. **£££**
Caterham House
58–9 Rother Street, CV37 6LT.
Tel: (01789) 267309.
Fax: (01789) 414836.

Price Guide

Prices quoted are for a double room including breakfast and VAT at high season.

££££	over £250
£££	£150–250
££	£80–£150
£	under £80

Georgian house popular with theatre-goers. Quirky, special. **£**

Tetbury
The Snooty Fox
Market Place, GL8 8DD.
Tel: (01666) 502436.
Fax: (01666) 503479.
Old Cotswold stone coaching inn with fine restaurant. With 12 rooms. **££**

Upper Slaughter
Lords of the Manor
Upper Slaughter,
nr Bourton-on-the-Water, GL54 2JD.
Tel: (01451) 820243.
Fax: (01451) 820696.
Former rectory set in rolling Cotswold countryside, with fine views. A baronial atmosphere. First-class modern cuisine. **£££**

Weston on the Green
Weston Manor
OX6 8QL.
Tel: (01869) 350621.
Fax: (01869) 350901.
Sixteenth-century manor house set in beautiful gardens. Excellent cuisine in the Baronial Hall. **££**

Cambridge & E.Anglia

Aldbury, nr Tring
Stocks Hotel & Country Club
Stocks Road, HP23 5RX.
Tel: (01442) 851341.
Fax: (01442) 851253.
An elegant 18th-century manor house, in grounds. Has 18 rooms. **££**

Burnham Market
The Hoste Arms
The Green, PE31 8HD.
Tel: (01328) 738777.
Fax: (01328) 730103.

Characterful inn on the green. Restaurant. Live jazz. **£**

Cambridge
Cambridge Garden House
Granta Place,
Mill Lane,
CB2 IRT.
Tel: (01223) 259988.
Fax: (01223) 316605.
Modern Moat House by river, with own punts and rowing boats. Central location. **£££**
Quy Mill
Newmarket Road,
Stow-cum-Quy,
CB5 9AG.
Tel: (01223) 293383.
Fax: (01223) 293770.
Within a taxi ride of city centre, a 19th-century watermill in 11 acres with fishing. With 23 rooms. **££**
Arundel House Hotel
53 Chesterton Road,
CB4 3AN.
Tel: (01223) 367701.
Fax: (01223) 367721.
Privately-owned terraced hotel overlooking the River Cam. No room service. Has 105 rooms (79 with private baths). **£**

Ely
Lamb Hotel
2 Lynn Road.
Tel: (01353) 663574.
Fax: (01353) 662023.
This former coaching house is centrally located. **£**

Hintlesham, nr Ipswich
Hintlesham Hall
IP8 3NS.
Tel: (01473) 652268.
Fax: (01473) 652463.
Stylish hotel with Georgian facade set in parkland. Luxury rooms with en-suite bathrooms, plus library, garden room and parlour to retreat to. Has 33 rooms. High-quality British food. **££**

Morston, nr Holt
Morston Hall
NL25 7AA.
Tel: (01263) 741041.
Fax: (01263) 740419.
Flint manor on the Norfolk coast. Good food. **££**

Wells-next-the-Sea
Crown Hotel
The Buttlands, NR23 1EX.
Tel: (01328) 710209.
Fax: (01328) 711432.
A fine old coaching inn in a picturesque port. It has a popular bar and restaurant. **££**

The Lake District

Alston
Lovelady Shield
Nenthead Road, CA9 3LF.
Tel: (01434) 381203.
Fax: (01434) 381505.
Remote 19th-century house recently refurbished. Lavish breakfasts. With 12 rooms. **£**
Lowbyer Manor
CA9 3JX.
Tel: (01434) 381230.
Fax: (01434) 382937.
Characterful 17th-century manor house with exposed beams and inglenook fireplaces. With 8 rooms. **£**

Ambleside
Rothay Manor
Rothay Bridge.
Tel: (01539) 433605.
Fax: (01539) 433607.
Quintessential country house hotel with gardens. Friendly. **££**
Wateredge Hotel
Borrans Road, Waterhead, LA22 0EP.
Tel: (01539) 432332.
Fax: (01539) 431878.
Family-run hotel with views over Lake Windermere from most rooms. No children under 7. **£**

Cartmel, nr Grange-over-Sands
Aynsome Manor
LA11 6HH.
Tel: (01539) 536653.
Fax: (01539) 536016.
Sixteenth-century house in pictures-que lake village, off tourist track. **£**

Clappersgate, nr Ambleside
Nanny Brow Country House Hotel
LA22 9NF.
Tel: (015394) 32036.
Fax: (015394) 32450.
One of the best hotels in the Lakes, this Edwardian house is peacefully

Price Guide

Prices quoted are for a double room including breakfast and VAT at high season.
££££ over £250
£££ £150–250
££ £80–£150
£ under £80

situated in lovely grounds. Has 18 rooms. **£–££**

Keswick District
Stakis Keswick Lodore
Lodore Falls,
Borrowdale,
CA12 5UX.
Tel: (01768) 777285.
Fax: (01768) 777343.
Luxury hotel in 40 acres with excellent facilities. Some rooms overlook Derwent Water. **££**
Pheasant Inn
Bassenthwaite Lake,
nr Cockermouth,
CA13 9YE.
Tel: (01768) 776234.
Fax: (01768) 776002.
This heavily-beamed inn lies in a beautifully peaceful setting. **££**
The Mill
Mungrisdale, nr Penrith,
CA11 0XR.
Tel: (01768) 779659.
Fax: (01768) 779155.
Former mill cottage. Good food. **£**

Ullswater District
Barco House
Patterdale, CA11 0NW.
Tel: (01768) 482474.
Near lake. **£**
Waterside House
Watermillock, CA11 0JH.
Tel: (017684) 86038.
Fax: (017684) 86132.
Eighteenth-century house on lake shore. April to October only. **£**

Merseyside/ Shropshire

Chester
Queen Hotel
City Road, CH1 3AH.
Tel: (01244) 350100.
Fax: (01244) 318483.

Handy for the station, smart hotel with restaurant. With 90 rooms. **£**

Chaddesley Corbett
Brockencoate Hall
Chaddesley Corbett,
nr Kidderminster,
DY10 4PY.
Tel: (01562) 777876.
Fax: (01562) 777872.
Stylish hotel in 70 acres. Large bathrooms, conservatory lounge. **££**

Kings Norton
The Mill House
180 Lifford Lane, B30 3NT.
Tel: (0121) 459 5800.
Fax: (0121) 459 8553.
Award winner (including Michelin) for quality and service. Its 9 rooms have features like *trompes l'oeil* and stained-glass windows. Indoor pool. **££**

Shrewsbury
The Lion
Wyle Cop, SY1 1UY.
Tel: (01743) 353107.
Fax: (01743) 352744.
Attractive, heavily beamed 18th-century coaching inn. Has 59 rooms. **££**

Yorkshire & Northeast

Belford
The Blue Bell Hotel
Market Square, NE70 7NE.
Tel: (01668) 213543.
Fax: (01668) 213787.
Lovely hotel in a 17th-century coaching inn furnished in period style. Garden. With 15 rooms. **£**

Burnsall
Red Lion
Nr Skipton, BD23 6BU.
Tel: (01756) 720204.
Fax: (01756) 720292
Inn on River Wharfe. Great fresh fish, game and local produce. **£**

Harrogate
The Albany
22–3 Harlow Moor Drive,
HG2 0JY.
Tel/fax: (01423) 565890.
Small hotel overlooking the Valley Gardens. **£**

Skipton
Devonshire Arms Country House Hotel
BD23 6AJ.
Tel: (01756) 710441.
Fax: (01756) 710564.
On the Bolton Abbey Estate. Open fires, antiques and portraits from Chatsworth. Has 41 rooms and good classic cuisine. **£££**

York
Middlethorpe Hall
Bishopthorpe,
YO23 2GB.
Tel: (01904) 641241.
Fax: (01904) 620176.
Elegant country hotel in 17th-century house. With 30 rooms. **£££**
Dean Court
Duncombe Place,
YO1 7EF.
Tel: (01904) 625082.
Fax: (01904) 620305.
Comfortable, traditional hotel close to the Minster and in its own traffic-free zone. Has 40 rooms. **££**
Elmbank
The Mount, YO24 1GE.
Tel: (01904) 610653.
Fax: (01904) 627139.
Country-house atmosphere. **££**

Ashcroft
294 Bishopthorpe Road,
YO2 1LH.
Tel: (01904) 659286.
Fax: (01904) 640107.
Once a Victorian mansion, this hotel is set in wooded grounds sloping down to the River Ouse. **£**

Wensleydale
The Wheatsheaf
Carperby,
DL8 4DF.
Tel: (01969) 663216.
Fax: (01969) 663019.
Where the real-life James Herriot and his wife honeymooned. **£**

Peak District and East Midlands

Ashford in the Water
Riverside Country House Hotel
Bakewell,
DE45 1QF.
Tel: (01629) 814275.
Fax: (01629) 812873.
On the River Wye with 4-poster beds, fires and antiques. Has 15 rooms. High-class English dishes. **££**

Buxton
Old Hall Hotel
The Square, SK17 6BD.
Tel: (01298) 22841.
Fax: (01298) 72437.
A landmark since the 16th century, this dignified hotel is situated on the town handsome square. Has 37 rooms. **£**

Dovedale
Izaak Walton Hotel
Nr Ashbourne, DE6 2AY.
Tel: (01335) 350555.
Fax: (01335) 350539.
One of the Peak District's most stylish hotels, named after the author of The Compleat Angler. With 32 rooms. Fine English/French food. **££**

Hassop
Hassop Hall Hotel
Nr Bakewell,
DE45 1NF.
Tel: (01629) 640488.
Fax: (01629) 640577.
One of the Peak's most elegant venues. Classical Georgian house, set in spacious parkland. Has 13 rooms. Finest hotel menu in the area. Booking essential. **££**

Gourmet Hotels

Broadway, Cotswolds
The Lygon Arms
WR12 7DU.
Tel: (01386) 852255.
Fax: (01386) 858611.
Magnificent 16th-century inn, with antiques and log fires. **£££**

Chagford, Dartmoor
Gidleigh Park
TQ13 8HH.
Tel: (01647) 432367.
Fax: (01647) 432574.
Huge half-timbered, gabled house on the edge of Dartmoor, with babbling brook, all-year log fire and impeccable service. **££££**

Great Milton, nr Oxford
Le Manoir aux Quat'Saisons
Church Road, OX44 7PD.
Tel: (01844) 278881.
Fax: (01844) 278847.

Raymond Blanc's renowned restaurant and hotel with stunning gardens. Luxurious rooms, individually decorated and some with own terrace. **£££–££££**

London
The Connaught
Carlos Place, W1Y 6AL.
Tel: 020-7499 7070.
Fax: 020-7495 3262.
One of the best hotels in London. Discreet, immaculate service, superb decor. **££££**

New Milton, Hampshire
Chewton Glen
Christchurch Road, EH25 6QS.
Tel: (01425) 275341.
Fax: (01425) 272310.
One of England's best-known country house hotels in an elegant 18th-century mansion. The pool is

modelled on the bathhouses of ancient Rome. Rooms vary from country cottage to 4-poster antiquity. **££££**

Taplow, Thames Valley
Cliveden
Taplow, nr Maidenhead,
SL6 0JF.
Tel: (01628) 668561.
Fax: (01628) 661837.
Majestic, historic hotel in 350 acres (140 hectares) of parkland. The height of luxury. **££££**

Ullswater, Lake District
Sharrow Bay Hotel
Howton Road, CA10 2LZ.
Tel: (01768) 486301.
Fax: (01768) 486349.
Italianate luxury hotel in formal gardens overlooking Ullswater. **£££**

Hathersage
George Hotel
Main Road,
S32 1DB.
Tel: (01433) 650436.
Fax: (01433) 650099.
Former 16th-century coaching inn with fine garden. Traditional/Continental fare in the restaurant, great home-made pies in the bar. **££**

Millstone Inn
Sheffield Road,
S32 1DA.
Tel: (01433) 650258.
Fax: (01433) 651664.
Fine views down the Hope Valley to Kinder Scout. **£**

Matlock
Riber Hall Hotel
DE4 5JU.
Tel: (01629) 582795.
Fax: (01629) 580475.
Tudor mansion with wonderful views from mullioned windows. Has 11 rooms. **££**

Matlock Bath
Temple Hotel.
Tel: (01629) 583911.
Fax: (01629) 580851.
On a hilltop with splendid views, this hotel is owned by Austrians who feature their national dishes on the menu. Has 14 rooms. **££**

Rowsley
East Lodge Country House Hotel
DE4 2EF (just off the A6).
Tel: (01629) 734474.
Fax: (01629) 733949.

Pretty, tastefully-furnished country house in its own grounds. Fine restaurant. **££**

Peacock Hotel
DE4 2EB.
Tel: (01629) 733518.
Fax: (01629) 732671.
Fine old listed hotel. Famous in the world of angling for fishing in River Wye. Good restaurant. **£££**

Stapleford, nr Melton Mowbray
Stapleford Park
LE14 2EF.
Tel: (01572) 787522.
Fax: (01572) 787651.
Sumptuously appointed 17th-century country house hotel in gardens designed by "Capability" Brown. Deluxe rooms designed by eminent names, including Nina Campbell. Has 42 rooms. **££**

Inns and Pubs

Inns are cheaper and smaller than hotels but they may also offer charm, character and the opportunity of integrating with the local community. They often retain an old-world character with open fires, beams and a warm ambience (combined, of course, with modern comforts). Ask for recommendations, as many of the best are off the tourist track.

Staying at an inn or pub may not always be such a cosy experience, however, especially in urban areas where you are likely to find pubs with an institutional feel. Standards vary from basic to sophisticated,

with food facilities ranging from bar snacks to quality restaurants.

CAMRA, the Campaign for Real Ale, publishes a book listing the best pub accommodation.
CAMRA,
230 Hatfield Road,
St Albans AL1 4LW.
Tel: (01727) 86720.
Fax: (01727) 867670.

B&Bs and Guesthouses

These are generally private homes with a few rooms for rent. Standards vary, but you can usually expect friendly hospitality, which will include a hearty English breakfast and advice on where to visit and eat in the area. They are most abundant on the edge of towns and in prime tourist areas.

B&Bs tend to be exceptional value and it is always advisable to book in advance during peak seasons. B&B accommodation is also available in many farmhouses. Contact local tourist offices for lists.

Between a hotel and a B&B in terms of facilities, size and price, guesthouses are small and friendly, family-run businesses. Breakfast is usually included.

Companies that specialise in B&Bs include:
Bed and Breakfast Nationwide
Tel: (01255) 831235.
Fax: (01255) 831437.
The London Bed & Breakfast Agency
Tel: 020-7586 2768.
Fax: 020-7586 6567.

The AA publishes an annual guide to over 3,000 good B&Bs, from most good bookshops.

Youth Hostels

The national office of the Youth Hostal Association is just outside London at 8 St Stephen's Hill, St Albans, Hertfordshire, tel: 01727 855215.

For central bookings in London, tel: 020-7248 6547.

Self-Catering Agencies

Blakes Country Cottages
Tel: (01282) 445555.
Over 2,000 cottages sleeping 2–8 people in pleasant areas and villages.
Cornish Traditional Cottages
Tel: (01208) 821666.
About 400 cottages in Cornwall sleeping 2–12.
English Country Cottages
Tel: 0990 851155.
Wide variety of about 3,000 country properties including oast

houses, barns, castles and manor houses, which sleep up to 22 people.
Forest Holidays
Tel: (0131) 314 6100.
Truly rustic, 5 or 6-berth cabins or cottages owned by the Forestry Commission, in Yorkshire and Cornwall.
Service Suites
Tel: 020-7730 5766.
Serviced London flats and apartments for short lets.

Where to Eat

A generation of talented modern British chefs has injected new life into traditional recipes, combining them with French and international influences, to produce lighter, more delicately flavoured meals using the finest ingredients grown on British soil.

Meat Although beef is the nation's most traditional meat, game is now a favourite among restaurateurs.

Seafood White fish such as haddock, cod and plaice are most common on the English dinner plate, while oysters are a delicacy, eaten only during months with an *r* in them. Some of the best oysters come from North Farm, East Mersea in Colchester where tours of the oystery are given on the first Friday of each month.

Sunday lunch is a solid British tradition. Traditional weekly feasts are roast beef and Yorkshire pudding with horseradish sauce, and roast pork with stuffing and apple sauce. Many pubs serve hearty, good-value roasts.

Pies are an English staple. Among the nation's favourite savouries are steak and kidney, pork and game. Cornish pasties, a mix of lamb, potato and vegetables in a pastry packet, are well worth sampling in Cornwall. Apple pie is probably the best-loved of sweet pies, but egg-custard pie, lemon meringue and, at Christmas, mince pies are regulars on dessert lists.

Sausages are enjoying a resurgence in popularity. As well as old favourites, such as Cumberland and black pudding (best in the North), interesting new variants are being invented by the top chefs.

Pub grub International fast food chains proliferate in every town centre. Some of the more upmarket chains are Pizza Express, Café Rouge and Café Uno. But for a quick and inexpensive bite it is often more enjoyable and relaxing to go to a cosy café or pub serving homemade food. A typical bar snack menu offers wholesome food such as soups, steak-and-kidney and pork pies, lasagne, quiche, filled rolls and the ever-popular "ploughman's lunch" of bread, cheese, pickle and salad.

The following is a selection of Britain's finest restaurants. A much fuller list of the capital's top restaurants can be found in the *Insight Guide: London*.

Price Guide

Prices quoted are per person for a three-course meal with half a bottle of wine:

££££	over £75
£££	£40–75
££	£30–40
£	under £20

London

Top Notch

Chez Nico
90 Park Lane, W1.
Tel: 020-7409 1290.
Perfectionist Nico Ladenis serves classic French cuisine that's earned him three Michelin stars. Closed at weekends. **£££**

Le Gavroche
43 Upper Brook Street, W1.
Tel: 020-7408 0881.
Having confidently been one of England's top restaurants for many years, its high standards never waver. Two Michelin stars. Set lunch is best value. **££££**

Restaurant Marco Pierre White
21 Piccadilly, La Meridien Hotel, W1
Tel: 020-7259 5380.
Inventive cuisine. Fish especially fine. Three Michelin stars.
£££–££££

Traditional

Criterion Brasserie
224 Piccadilly, W1.
Tel: 020-7930 0488.

Worth a visit for the grand, Moorish decor, Marco Pierre White's latest venture, which is innovative and sophisticated. **££–£££**

The Ivy
1 West Street, W1.
Tel: 020-7836 4751.
High-quality decor, gallery-worthy art and good food. **£££**

Quaglino's
16 Bury St, SW1.
Tel: 020-7930 6767.
The buzz of 1930s London, with a wide menu. **££–£££**

Simpsons-in-the-Strand
100 Strand WC2.
Tel: (020) 7836 9112.
Edwardian dining room serving the best roast beef in London. Staunchly traditional. Informal dress not acceptable. **£££**

Tate Restaurant
Tate Britain Gallery, Millbank, SW1.
Tel: 020-7887 8877.
Beautiful decor, including a mural by Rex Whistler. Good for lunch. Renowned wine list. **££**

Contemporary

Joe Allen
13 Exeter Street, WC2.
Tel: 020-7836 0651.
One of London's best-loved American restaurants. Lively and great for actor-spotting. **££**

Hard Rock Café
150 Old Park Lane, W1
Tel: 020-7629 0382.
A shrine to rock music. Great hamburgers, long queues, high decibel level, good fun. **££**

Kensington Place
205 Kensington Church Street, W8.
Tel: 020-7727 3184.
Informal, bustling, New York-style restaurant. Modernist decor and adventurous food. **££–£££**

Maison Novelli
29 Clerkenwell Green, EC1.
Tel: 020-7251 6606.

Restaurant Call

Restaurant Services supplies up-to-date, impartial information on London's restaurants and a free booking service.
● Tel: 020-8888 8080.

Stunningly presented European dishes. An intimate brasserie, one of the capital's trendiest. **££–£££**

Mezzo
100 Wardour Street, W1.
Tel: 020-7314 4000.
Terence Conran's bright, modern, good value restaurants and café. **££–£££**

Zinc Bar and Grill
21 Heddon Street, W1.
Tel: 020-7255 8899.
Conran's latest venture, with 12metre (25ft) zinc bar, majoring on grills, salads and crustacea. **££**

Continental

Alastair Little (French)
49 Frith Street, W1.
Tel: 020-7734 5183.
Inventive food on a basic French mode. Delicious, fresh, nouvelle-style cooking. Very trendy. Rather stark retro-1980s decor. **££–£££**

Le Caprice (French)
Arlington House, Arlington St, SW1.
Tel: 020-7629 2239.
Fashionable café style. Pianist in the evenings. Excellent New York-style Sunday brunch. **££**

Orso (Italian)
27 Wellington Street, WC2.

Chinatown

Many of London's best Chinese restaurants are in Chinatown, which centres around Gerrard Street. If you are baffled by the choice, those well-patronised by the Chinese themselves are generally a good bet. Two of Chinatown's best-loved are:

Fung Shing
15 Lisle Street, WC2.
Tel: (020) 7437 1539.
Has long been regarded as one of the best restaurants in Chinatown and is consequently always packed. **££**

Wong Kei
41 Wardour Street, W1.
Tel: (020) 7437 8408.
Regulars aren't deterred by the rude service for which this restaurant is famed. Three floors serving good-value Cantonese food. Cash only. **£**

Tel: 020-7240 5269.
Basement Italian restaurant fashionable with theatre and media crowd. **££**

The River Café (Italian)
Thames Wharf, Rainville Road, W6.
Tel: 020-7381 8824.
Delightful northern Italian food and riverside tables. Book weeks in advance. **£££**

Other Nationalities

Bombay Brasserie
(Indian) Bailey's Hotel, Courtfield Close, SW7.
Tel: 020-7370 4040.
Stylish decor harking back to the days of the Raj. Well thought-out menu, with dishes from many regions. Great-value lunchtime buffet. **££**

Blue Elephant (Thai)
4–6 Fulham Broadway, SW6.
Tel: 020-7385 6595.
A tropical jungle in Fulham. Excellent food and charming service from waitresses in traditional costume. **££**

Brilliant (Indian)
72–4 Western Road,
Southall, Greater London.
Tel: 020-8574 1928.
One of the best Indian restaurants in the country. **£**

Nobu (Japanese)
19 Old Park Lane, W1.
Tel: 020-7447 4747.
New York's hottest brings a blend of South America and California to modern Japanese. **£££**

Rebato's (Spanish)
169 South Lambeth Road, SW8.
Tel: 020-7735 6388.
Worth a detour. Authentic tapas. **££**

The Red Fort (Indian)
77 Dean Street, W1.
Tel: 020-7437 2410.
Renowned Soho restaurant that offers good Mogul cooking in luxurious surroundings. **££**

Wagamama (Japanese)
10a Lexington Street, W1.
Tel: 020-7292 0990.
Cheap noodle bar. Good selection of Japanese beers. **£**

Modern European

Oxo Tower
Bankside SE1.

Tel: 020-7803 3888.
Brasserie and restaurant. Stunning river view. **£££**

L'Odéon
65 Regent Street, W1.
Tel: 020-7287 1400.
Superb globe-trotting menu from Bruno Loubet. **£–££**

The Pharmacy
150 Notting Hill Gate, W11.
Tel: (020) 221 2442.
Modern British cuisine. Design by Damian Hirst. **££**

The Southeast

Brighton

Terre à Terre
71 East Street.
Tel: (01273) 729051.
Bustling café with innovative vegetarian menu. Organic wine. **££**

Food for Friends in the Lanes
17–18 Prince Albert Street.
Tel: (01273) 202310.
A vegetarian favourite. **£**

Chilgrove, nr Chichester

White Horse Inn
1 High Street.
Tel: (01243) 535219.
Country pub and restaurant with a long-standing reputation. Al fresco meals in summer. **££**

East Grinstead

Gravetye Manor
Vowels Lane.
Tel: (01342) 810567.
Beautiful Elizabethan manor with fine gardens. Equally pleasing is the traditional and modern British cooking. Special. **£££**

Hastings

Röser's
64 Eversfield Place, St Leonard's.
Tel: (01424) 712218.
Unpretentious seafront restaurant offering simple food superbly prepared. Good wine list. **££**

Midhurst

Maxine's
Red Lion Street.
Tel: (01730) 816271.
An established restaurant that has won accolades without being pricey. Closed on Monday. **££**

Rye
Landgate Bistro
5–6 Landgate.
Tel: (01797) 222829.
Toni Ferguson-Lees has a local following for her blend of British and Mediterranean styles. Her speciality is seafood, but there's lots more at this popular bistro. **££**

Tunbridge Wells
Chi
26 London Road.
Tel: (01892) 513888.
Upmarket Chinese, the best for miles. Pleasant decor. **££**
The Hare
Langton Road, Langton Green, nr Tunbridge Wells.
Tel: (01892) 862419.
Drawing room-cum-library atmosphere. Large portions of upmarket food, with excellent desserts. Booking is essential. **££**
Thackeray's House
85 London Road.
Tel: (01892) 511921.
Excellent Anglo-French country cooking which consistently wins awards. The wine bar offers less expensive but equally good food. **££**

The West Country

Bath
The Hole in the Wall
16 George Street.
Tel: (01225) 425242.
Highly imaginative haute cuisine. **£££**
Lettonie
35 Kelston Road.
Tel: (01225) 446676
A popular haunt. Innovative food served with aplomb. **££**
The Moon and Sixpence
61 Broad Street.
Tel: (01225) 460962.
Old English favourites given an imaginative twist. Attractive feel. **££**
The Royal Crescent Hotel
Royal Crescent.
Tel: (01225) 739955.
Fine food, elegant surroundings. **£££**

Bristol
Markwick's
43 Corn Street.

Price Guide

Prices quoted are per person for a three-course meal with half a bottle of wine:

££££	over £75
£££	£40–75
££	£30–40
£	under £20

Tel: (0117) 926 2658.
Excellent reputation for flavoursome, trend-setting Anglo-Provençal cooking. **££**

Chagford
22 Mill Street.
Tel: (01647) 432244.
Ex-sous chef at Gidleigh Park Duncan Walker serves food in the Gidleigh tradition. **££**

Colerne
Lucknam Park.
Tel: (01225) 742777. Sophisticated classic British cuisine with a serious wine list in this Georgian manor. **£££**

Dartmouth
The Carved Angel
2 South Embankment.
Tel: (01803) 832465.
Accomplished modern British and European cuisine based on good local produce, overlooking Dartmouth harbour and the estuary. **£££**

Hunstrete, nr Chelwood
Hunstrete House
Tel: (01761) 490490.
Opulent surroundings and refined cuisine in a Georgian mansion set in a deer park. **£££**

Mousehole
The Lobster Pot Hotel
South Cliff.
Tel: (01736) 731251.
Seafood as it comes ashore. **££**

New Polzeath
Cornish Cottage Hotel
Tel: (01208) 862213.
Stunning location overlooking beach. Tim Rogers is a master in the modern British mode. **££**

Padstow
££ The Seafood Restaurant
Riverside.
Tel: (01841) 532485.
Fish enthusiast Rick Stein's showcase. One of the best seafood restaurants in England. Informal atmosphere in tasteful dining rooms. Booking essential
St Petroc's Bistro
4 New Street.
Tel: (01841) 532700.
Stein's bistro. Similar quality food to his restaurant but far cheaper. **££**

Plymouth
Chez Nous
13 Frankfurt Gate.
Tel: (01752) 266793.
Seriously good French bistro. Great list of inexpensive wines. **££**

St Ives
££ Alfresco Café-Bar
Wharf Road.
Tel: (01736) 793737.
Trendy harbour bar with excellent Mediterranean menu at lunch and stylish, mainly fish dinners.

Taunton
Castle Hotel
Castle Green.
Tel: (01823) 272671.
Classic British cuisine, first-class service, imposing setting. **££**

The Southwest

Beaulieu
Montagu Arms Hotel
Palace Lane.
Tel: (01590) 612324.
Hotel and restaurant serving excellent English food. **££**

Brockenhurst
Le Poussin
The Courtyard, 49–55 Brookley Road.
Tel: (01590) 623063.
First-rate French haute cuisine. Skilled use of organic local food. **££**

Hythe
Boathouse Brasserie
29 Shamrock Way, Hythe Marina Village.
Tel: (023) 8084 5594.

Baltis Nationwide

In London, good areas for cheap Indian food are Brick Lane in the East End and Southall, in west London. Drummond Street, near Euston station, has good vegetarian Indian restaurants. Leicester has some of Britain's finest Indian food along its "Golden Mile". But Birmingham is home of the popular balti. Its finest, say aficionados, are:

Adil
148 Stoney Lane, Sparkbrook.
Tel: (0121) 449 0335. **£**

Royal Naim
417–9 Stratford Road.
Tel: (0121) 766 7849. **£**

Shimla Pinks
214 Broad Street.
Tel: (0121) 633 0366. **£**

Ian McAndrew's waterside restaurant is strong on fish. Good-value 2-course set lunch. **££**

Hordle, nr Lymington
Gordelton Mill Hotel
Silver St.
Tel: (01590) 682219.
The extensive menu and superb French cuisine make this ivy-clad mill-cum-hotel a popular venue for local diners. Huge wine list. **££**

Stuckton
The Three Lions
Stuckton Road.
Tel: (01425) 652489.
Michael Womersley cooks like a dream. Admirably straightforward, technically consummate, tasty. **££**

Winchester
Hotel du Vin & Bistro
14 Southgate Street.
Tel: (01962) 841414.
A wine lover's heaven, with an attractive menu of top-notch modern food. **£££**

The Thames Valley

Bray
The Waterside Inn
Ferry Rd.
Tel: (01628) 620691.
In an idyllic spot overlooking the Thames, this is one of England's most exceptional restaurants. The genius of Michel Roux has earned him Michelin stars. **£££**

The Fat Duck
1 High St.
Tel: (01628) 580333.
Wooden tables, short menu and no-nonsense presentation, but Heston Blumenthal makes simplicity an art form. His tasty British fare is well respected. **££–£££**

Epsom Downs
Le Raj
211 Firtree Road.
Tel: (01737) 371064.
Stylish Bangladeshi cuisine with an excellent reputation. **£**

Goring
The Leatherne Bottle
Tel: (01491) 872667.
A characterful old riverside inn where the food is excellent. **££**

Shinfield
L'Ortolan
The Old Vicarage, Church Lane.
Tel: (0118) 988 3788.
Stunning flavours, innovative Anglo-French cuisine and an excellent cheeseboard. **£££**

Oxford to Stratford

Bibury
The Swan
Tel: (01285) 740695.
This charming stone hotel puts a stylish Mediterranean twist on modern British dishes. **££**

Birmingham
St Paul's Bar and Restaurant
50–54 St Paul's Square, Hockley.
Tel: (0121) 605 1001.
Trendy wine bar. **£**

Cheltenham
Le Champignon Sauvage
24–26 Suffolk Road.
Tel: (01242) 573449.
Interesting menu with a touch of class. David Everitt-Matthias wins awards for meat and desserts. **£££**

Malvern Wells
Croque-en-Bouche
221 Wells Road.
Tel: (01684) 565612.
Foodies' delight. Marion and Robin Jones grow their own veg, salad leaves and around 80 herbs, and Marion's use of them is masterly. Over 1,500 wines. **££–£££**

Nailsworth
William's Bistro
3 Fountain Street.
Tel: (01453) 835507.
Excellent light food from this deli-cum-restaurant. **££**

Old Minster Lovell
Lovells at Windrush Farm
Tel: (01993) 779802.
Dining is taken seriously and booking is essential. Dinner is seven courses with no choice, but the balance and finesse of cooking ensures that this is no marathon. Recommended. **££**

Olton
Rajnagar International
256 Lyndan Road, Olton, Solihull.
Tel: (0121) 742 8140.
Said to be the best Bangladeshi in the country. Pleasant decor. **££**

Oxford
Browns
5–11 Woodstock Road.
Tel: (01865) 511995.
This well-established restaurant offers breakfast, light lunches and three-course meals in a relaxed atmosphere. Open 11am–11.30pm. Expect queues. Children welcome. **££**

Chiang Mai Kitchen
130a High Street.
Tel: (01865) 202233.
Top-quality Thai cuisine at very reasonable prices in a fine 17th-century manor house, Kemp Hall. **££**

Gee's Brasserie
61a Banbury Road.
Tel: (01865) 558346.
Well-established restaurant in the Raymond Blanc tradition in a

beautiful, airy conservatory. **££**
Le Petit Blanc
71–2 Walton Street.
Tel: (01865) 510999.
Raymond Blanc's latest venture.
Light but traditional French dishes
in an airy atmosphere. Open all day
including breakfast. **££**
The Polash
25 Park End (opposite railway
station).
Tel: (01865) 250244.
Tandoori restaurant specialising in
the cuisine of Madras. **£**

Paulerspury, nr Northampton
Vine House
100 High Street.
Tel: (01327) 811267.
Old stone farmhouse with some
fine modern English dishes. **££**

Thame
The Old Trout
29–30 Lower High Street.
Tel: (01844) 212146.
Brasserie-style restaurant,
particularly good on fish. **££**

Winchcombe
Wesley House
High St.
Tel: (01242) 602366.
Heavily beamed 15th-century
former merchant's house. Stylish
range of modern European dishes
from the blackboard. **££**

Cambridge & E.Anglia

Cambridge
Three Horseshoes
High Street, Madingley.
Tel: (01954) 210221.
Thatched inn in pretty village 2
miles (3km) from Cambridge.
Reasonably priced modern
Mediterranean food and wine. **££**
Midsummer House
Midsummer Common.
Tel: (01223) 369299.
Elegant modern European cuisine in
stylish surroundings. **£££**

Holt
Yetman's
37 Norwich Road.
Tel: (01263) 713320.
Quirky and stylish, the daily menu

Price Guide

Prices quoted are per person for
a three-course meal with half a
bottle of wine:
££££ over £75
£££ £40–75
££ £30–40
£ under £20

centres on finest local produce
including organic meat, freshly-
caught fish and biodynamically
grown veg. **££**

King's Lynn
Rococo
11 Saturday Market Place.
Tel: (01553) 771483.
Light food imaginatively styled, with
fish and vegetarian dishes a
speciality. Good-value lunch. **££**

Melbourn
The Pink Geranium
Station Road.
Tel: (01763) 260215.
Highly sophisticated French cooking
in a 15th-century thatched cottage.
££–£££

Stanton
Leaping Hare Café
Wyken Vineyards.
Tel: (01359) 250287.
Elegant café-restaurant at one of
Britain's best vineyards. Californian-
style cooking. **££**

Sudbury
Red Onion Bistro
57 Ballingdon Street.
Tel: (01787) 376777.
Bustling bistro. Excellent value. **£**

Swaffam
Strattons
Stratton House,
4 Ash Close.
Tel: (01760) 723845.
Family-run hotel with a passion for
local ingredients. **££**

The Lake District

Ambleside
The Glass House Café Restaurant
Rydal Rd.

Tel: (015394) 32137.
A 16th-century wool mill serving
Mediterranean and modern British
food, plus teas served during the
day. **£**

Bowness-on-Windermere
Linthwaite House
Crook Road.
Tel: (01539) 488600.
English country-house cooking with
superb views over lake. **£££**
Porthole Eating House
3 Ash Street.
Tel: (01539) 442793.
A taste of the Mediterranean is the
inspiration behind this informal but
intimate setting. **££**

Crosthwaite, nr Kendal
Punch Bowl Inn
Tel: (01539) 568237.
Upmarket French-style pub grub at
very reasonable prices. **££**

Eskdale
The Woolpack Inn
Boots, Eskdale
Tel: (019467) 23230.
Well-known hostelry in western Lake
District. Good food with a selection
of real ales.

Keswick
Swinside Lodge
Newlands.
Tel: (01768) 772948.
Fantastic views from a fine Victorian
lodge serving a 5-course set menu.
Unlicensed. **££**

Leck, nr Cowan Bridge
Cobwebs
Tel: (01524) 272141.
Remote Victorian house offering
hearty 4-course, no-choice dinners.
Rooms available. **££**

Windermere
Miller Howe
Rayrigg Road
Tel: (015394) 42536.
John Tovey's well-known restaurant,
for gourmets who like immaculate
service. **££–£££**

Merseyside/ Shropshire

Altrincham
Juniper
21 The Downs.
Tel: (0161) 929 4008.
Seriously good food in a bistro-style setting. **££–£££**

Chester
Arkle Restaurant
Grosvenor Hotel, Eastgate Street.
Tel: (01244) 324024.
Traditional British dishes excellently presented, including one of the best bread boards in the land. An overly expensive wine list, though. **£££**

Langho
Northcote Manor
Northcote Road.
Tel: (01254) 240555.
Victorian country-house hotel with superb views of the Ribble Valley offering extensive menus of stylish traditional dishes. **££–£££**

Longridge, nr Preston
Paul Heathcote's Restaurant
204/8 Higher Road.
Tel: (01772) 784969.
The northwest's best restaurant. Paul Heathcote puts his own stamp on modern British cuisine while flying the flag for Lancashire with black pudding and excellent potato dishes. **££–£££**

Ludlow
Merchant House
Lower Corve Street.
Tel: (01584) 875438.
Imaginative cooking with top-quality ingredients and a no-nonsense approach from Shaun Hill. Booking is recommended as there's room for 20 only. **££**

Ramsbottom, nr Bury
Village Restaurant
16–18 Market Place.
Tel: (01706) 825070.
Informal bistro (drawing heavily on the deli in the basement, specialising in organic produce) serves upmarket food at great prices. **£**

Price Guide

Prices quoted are per person for a three-course meal with half a bottle of wine:

££££	over £75
£££	£40–75
££	£30–40
£	under £20

Waterhouses
Old Beams
Leek Road.
Tel: (01538) 308254.
Beams, open fires and Windsor chairs are the setting for consistently good French-style food. **£££**

Yorkshire/Northeast

Durham
Bistro 21
Aykley Heads House, Aykley Heads.
Tel: (0191) 384 4354.
Robust Anglo-French cooking in a 16th-century farmhouse. **££**

Grassington
Paul & Cheryl's Licensed Restaurant
Tel: (01756) 753333.
Bistro-style atmosphere, with light lunches and à la carte in the evenings. **£**

Heaton, nr Bradford
Restaurant Nineteen
North Park Road.
Tel: (01274) 492559.
Stylishly-decorated Victorian townhouse restaurant with B&B. Classic dishes, superbly prepared from a fixed-price 3-course menu. **££**

Hetton
Angel Inn
Tel: (01756) 730263.
Off the beaten track, but with long queues for bar meals. Fixed-price restaurant offers a wide range of excellently priced food and wine. **££**

Helmsley
Crown Hotel
Market Square.
Tel: (01439) 770297.
Serves a wide choice of country-style dishes. **£**

Huddersfield
Café Pacific
3 Viaduct Street.
Tel: (01484) 559055.
The highly individual, pan-global style of chef Scott Hessel is very popular. **£**

Ilkley
Box Tree
35–37 Church Street.
Tel: (01943) 608484.
Intimate restaurant serving classic French/modern British dishes without frills. **££–£££**

Malham
The Buck Inn
Tel: (01729) 830317.
Overlooking the village green. Home-cooked traditional fare in the bar. A la carte in the restaurant. **££**

Moulton
Black Bull Inn
Tel: (01325) 377289.
Inn popular for its fish bar (no reservations). A la carte in the Conservatory or Brighton Belle, a 1932 Pullman carriage. **££**

Northallerton
McCoy's
The Cleveland Tontine, Staddlebridge.
Tel: (01609) 882671.
English eccentricity at its best. Lavish period surroundings, laid-back atmosphere and some of the most interesting food England has to offer. Evenings only. **££**

West Witton
The Wensleydale Heifer
Tel: (01969) 622322.
Beside the A684 between Leyburn and Aysgarth, a 17th-century inn. Home cooking. **££**

Whitby
The Magpie Café
Pier Road.
Tel: (01947) 602058.
Legendary habourside restaurant. Though most famed for its fish and chips, it satisfies most other tastes with equal aplomb. Children's menu. **££**

Winteringham
Winteringham Fields
Tel: (01724) 733096.
A gem of a hotel with beams, panelling and open fireplaces. Expect surprises on the extensive menu ranging from game to gravadlax to goat. **£££**

York
Melton's
7 Scarcroft Road.
Tel: (01904) 634341.
Unassuming and child-friendly. Conventional and exotic English dishes. Good vegetarian range. **££**

Peak District and East Midlands

Baslow
Fischer's Baslow Hall
Calver Rd.
Tel: (01246) 583259.
Outstanding restaurant serving top-quality traditional British cuisine. The Café Max brasserie is a great way to sample Max Fischer's 5-star food cheaply. **££–£££**

Hambleton
Hambleton Hall
Hambleton, nr Oakham.
Tel: (01572) 756991.
Elegant dining room serving modern British cuisine in a fine country house hotel. **£££**

Leicester
Café Bruxelles
90–92 High Street.
Tel: (0116) 224 3013.
Trendy bar food, plus over 30 Belgian beers. **£**

Ridgeway, nr Sheffield
Old Vicarage
Tel: (0114) 247 5814.
Large Victorian house with a country house feel. A fixed-price menu of outstanding pedigree. **££**

Sites

English Heritage has more than 400 properties, including Stonehenge and Dover Castle. Membership is annual (with no shorter-term arrangements) and entitles you to free entry to all these sites, plus discounts off concerts held at them during the summer. Also available is an Overseas Visitor Pass, which lasts for two weeks. For details contact: English Heritage, 23 Saville Row, London W1X 1AB. Tel: 020-771-973 3000. Fax: 020-7973 3001.

The National Trust is a conservation charity with over 250 properties open to the public, from large country houses and abbeys to lighthouses. It also maintains over 150 gardens and protects over 600,000 acres (244,000 hectares) of countryside.

Membership is annual (with no shorter-term arrangements). It entitles you to free entry to properties and a copy of *The National Trust Handbook*. The annual fee can easily be recouped by a family taking a two-week holiday of leisurely sightseeing. Further information from: The National Trust, 36 Queen Anne's Gate, London SW1H 9AS. Tel: 020-7222 9251. Fax: (020) 7222 5097.

Both groups have reciprocal arrangements, generally giving members half-price entry for the first year, and free access to sites thereafter. The NT also has reciprocal arrangements with trusts overseas, including Australia, India, New Zealand, Jamaica, Malaysia, Malta, Ireland, the Netherlands and the US (Royalk Oak Foundation)..

The **Great Britain Heritage Pass** allows unlimited access to over 500 stately homes, castles, historic houses and abbeys in the UK. It is available from certain overseas offices of the BTA, and can be purchased on arrival from London's British Travel Centres at ports, airports and selected TICS.

National Parks

Dartmoor Dartmoor ponies roam freely across this expanse of moorland in Devon with exposed granite tors, heath and bogs.
Exmoor Straddling Somerset and Devon, with heathery moor and breathtaking coastline. Home to Exmoor ponies, sheep, red deer and cattle.
Lake District Stunningly beautiful countryside in Cumbria: 16 lakes are interspersed with high fells. A haven for fishing, boating, climbing and swimming.
Northumberland 398 sq miles (1,030 sq km) in the northeast. Characterised by rugged stretches of moorland, it includes some of the most spectacular coastline in England and Hadrian's Wall.
North York Moors A coastline of rugged cliffs, expanses of low moorland, deep valleys and heathered uplands, this national park covers 553 sq miles (1,430 sq km), including the 100-mile (160-km) Cleveland Way.
Peak District This well-preserved area of natural beauty at the tip of the Pennines between Sheffield, Derby and Manchester was England's first designated national park. It is characterised by high, bleak moors and low, gentle limestone countryside with dramatic wooded valleys and rivers.
Yorkshire Dales This wild expanse of great natural beauty covers 680 sq miles (1,760 sq km) in the Pennine Hills, featuring deep dales, waterfalls, caves and quarries.

Culture

Theatre

Britain's rich dramatic tradition is reflected in the quality of its theatre. Although London is the centre, most towns and cities have at least one theatre that hosts productions from their own theatre company or from touring companies that might include the Royal Shakespeare Company (RSC) and the National Theatre (NT).

Around half of London's theatres – totalling over 100, including fringe and suburban – are in the West End, centred around Shaftesbury Avenue and Covent Garden.

Tickets West End shows are popular so good tickets can be hard to obtain. If you cannot book a seat through the theatre box office, try Ticketmaster, 48 Leicester Square, WC2H 7LD (tel: 020-7344 4000; fax: 020-7915 0411) and First Call (tel: 020-7420 0000).

Avoid ticket touts unless you're prepared to pay several times a ticket's face value for a sold-out show. The SWET Ticket Booth in Leicester Square has unsold tickets available at half price on the day,

The Globe Theatre

The Globe Theatre (tel: (020) 7401 9919) is a reconstruction of Shakespeare's original Elizabethan theatre. It hosts a season of plays by the Bard, attempting to recreate the atmosphere of the original 16th-century performances. The Globe Exhibition (tel: (020) 7902 1500) tells the story of Elizabethan theatre and the reconstruction of the Globe. Open 10am–5pm daily, guided tours 9am–noon.

from noon for matinées and from 2pm for evening performances. Be prepared to pay cash only and for long queues. Some theatres, such as the National, keep back some tickets to sell at the box office from 10am on the day.

Fringe For fringe theatre there is usually no problem in buying a ticket on the door. Consult the listings in London's weekly *Time Out* magazine or quality newspapers for what's on in the West End and at London's many fringe theatres.

Open-air plays On a summer's evening Shakespeare's plays are performed (weather permitting) at the open-air theatre in Regent's Park. Check London tourist offices for listings.

Barbican Arts Centre
Barbican, Silk Street, London EC2Y 8DS. Box office tel: 020-7638 8891. Fax: 020-7382 7270.
Website: www.barbican.org.uk
Purpose-built concrete arts complex containing the Barbican Theatre, Concert Hall and The Pit which are well thought-out and comfortable with good acoustics. Tube: Barbican.

National Theatre
Upper Ground, South Bank, London SE1 9PX.
Tel: 020-7452 3333.
Fax: 020-7452 3344.
A wide range of modern and classical plays can be seen at three repertory theatres housed within this massive concrete structure: the Olivier, the Lyttelton and the Cottesloe. Tube: Waterloo.

Royal Court Theatre
Sloane Square, SW1.
Tel: 020-7565 5000.
Home to the English Stage Company, which produces plays by contemporary playwrights. Tube: Sloane Square.

The Royal Shakespeare Theatre
Stratford-upon-Avon.
Box office tel: (01789) 403403.
For 24-hour booking information, tel: (01789) 269191.
The world-famous Royal Shakespeare Company (RSC) performs a repertoire of plays by the Bard at the Royal Shakespeare Theatre, while works by his contemporaries are staged across

the river at the Swan Theatre (an Elizabethan-style playhouse). Nearby, at The Other Place, modern productions are performed. The RSC season at Stratford runs from March to September. The company also tours some of the year at the Barbican Centre in London.

In major cities it is always advisable to book tickets in advance, either from the box office or through commercial ticket agents. On weekdays, visitors may be able to tour behind the scenes.

Classical Music

Many English cities have their own professional orchestras and promote seasons of concerts. These include the Royal Liverpool Philharmonic, The Hallé in Manchester and the City of Birmingham Symphony Orchestra. In London there are the London Philharmonic and, at the Barbican Arts Centre, the London Symphony Orchestra.

In London the BBC sponsors the Henry Wood Promenade Concerts (usually known as the Proms) at the Royal Albert Hall. The BBC also funds several of its own orchestras, the BBC Symphony and the BBC Scottish Symphony Orchestra.

Chamber music has considerable support and there are several professional string and chamber orchestras such as English Chamber Orchestra and The Academy of Ancient Music.

Glyndebourne

For classical music lovers Glyndebourne is a highlight. Off the beaten track in Sussex, it is not the most obvious site for a major international opera festival. But ever since an ex-Eton schoolmaster inherited a mansion there and built an opera house, it has attracted top artists from around the world and become a major event. Performances are in the evening (bring your own Champagne and hampers) from May until October. Tel: (01273) 812321.

London Venues

Barbican Hall

Silk Street, London EC2 (tel: 020-7588 8211) is home to the London Symphony Orchestra and English Chamber Orchestra.

Royal Festival Hall

South Bank, London SE1 (tel: 020-7960 4242) is the premier classical music venue.
Also within the South Bank arts complex are the Queen Elizabeth Hall where chamber concerts and solos are performed, and the small Purcell Room.

Wigmore Hall

36 Wigmore Street, London W1 (tel: 020-7935 2141) is an intimate hall famous for lunch and Sunday chamber recitals.

Royal Albert Hall

Kensington Gore, London SW7 (tel: 020-7589 8212) comes alive in summer for the Proms.

Open-air concerts In summer, open-air evening concerts are held at the Kenwood Lakeside Theatre, Hampstead Lane, NW3 (tel: 020-8348 1286).

Opera

The Royal Opera and the English National Opera perform regular seasons in London.

Royal Opera House The Royal Opera resides at the Royal Opera House in Covent Garden, London WC2 (box office: 020-7304 4000). Magnificent theatre with worldwide reputation for lavish performances in their original language. Dress is formal. Expensive.

London Coliseum Not far away in St Martin's Lane, WC2, this elegant Edwardian theatre is where the English National Opera (ENO) puts on less traditional performances in English, and the tickets are cheaper. Tel: 020-7632 8300

Opera North Regional opera companies include Opera North, which is based in Leeds and tours the north of England.

Buxton The Opera House hosts a major opera festival in July and Gilbert and Sullivan festival from late-July to the end of August (tel: 01298 72190).

Ballet and Dance

The major venues are the Royal Opera House and the London Coliseum, home to the Royal Ballet and the Royal Festival Ballet respectively.

Sadler's Wells London's leading dance venue, in a flexible state-of-the-art theatre. Offers an innovative and exciting programme of dance and opera, contemporary and classical. Tel: (020) 7863 8000.

Birmingham Royal Ballet is based at the Hippodrome and tours nationwide. Tel: (0121) 622 2555.

Northern Ballet Company Based at the Dance House in Manchester, but tours all over England. Tel: (0161) 237 9753.

Jazz

There are many pubs and clubs that host live jazz, most notably in Camden, London; and Bracknell, Berkshire. Ronnie Scott's (tel: 020-7439 0747) in the heart of London's Soho is Britain's best-known jazz venue, with a great atmosphere and top international artists.

Diary of Events

The following are some of England's major festivals. For other events, contact tourist boards in the locality.

January

London International Boat Show Earl's Court.

February

Chinese New Year Colourful celebrations in London and Manchester Chinatowns.

Crufts Dog Show Earl's Court, London. Pedigree dogs compete for the world's most coveted canine prize.

Shrove Tuesday "Pancake Day", when the nation gorges on pancakes, originally the prelude to a fast until Easter.

March

Ideal Home Exhibition Earl's Court, London.

London Book Fair Centred around Bloomsbury

Sheffield Chamber Music Festival

April

April Fool's Day (1 April) The day when people play practical jokes (at least until noon). Most national newspapers include a spoof story or two (which can be hard to separate from the absurdity of the real news).

Harrogate Spring Flower Show

Queen's Birthday (21 April) Her real birthday (as opposed to the official birthday in June) is celebrated with a gun salute in Hyde Park and at the Tower of London.

Royal Shakespeare Theatre in Stratford-upon-Avon opens the new season.

May

Bath International Festival Choral and chamber music.

Brighton Arts Festival

Chelsea Flower Show Major horticultural show in the grounds of the Royal Hospital, Chelsea, London.

Glyndebourne Festival Opera season opens.

Newbury Spring Festival

Nottingham Festival

June

Aldeburgh Festival of Arts & Music

Beating Retreat in Horse Guards Parade, Whitehall, London. Military bands.

Biggin Hill International Air Fair Biggin Hill, Kent.

Bournemouth Music Festival

Dickens Festival Rochester, Kent

Glastonbury Pilgrimage Abbey Ruins, Glastonbury, Somerset.

Grosvenor House Antiques Fair Grosvenor House Hotel, Park Lane, London.

Royal Academy of Arts Summer Exhibition Burlington House, Piccadilly, London. Large exhibition of work by both professional and amateur artists running until August. All works for sale.

Trooping the Colour Horse Guards Parade, Whitehall, London. The Queen's official birthday celebrations.

July

Birmingham International Jazz Festival
Cambridge Festival
Cheltenham International Festival of Music
Royal Agricultural Show, Stoneleigh Park, Warwickshire.
Royal Tournament: Earl's Court, London. Military displays.
Proms Classical concerts at the Royal Albert Hall, London.

August

Great British Beer Festival Venues vary.
Notting Hill Carnival (bank holiday weekend) Ladbroke Grove, London. Colourful West Indian street carnival with exciting costumes, live bands, and thousands of revellers.

September

Farnborough Air Show Every two years.
Salisbury Festival

October

Birmingham International Film and TV Festival
Cheltenham Festival of Literature
Motor Show Earl's Court, London. Every two years.
Norwich Jazz Festival

November

Guy Fawkes Day (5th) Firework celebrations to commemorate the failure of Guy Fawkes to blow up the Houses of Parliament in 1605.
Christmas Lights In Oxford and Regent streets, London (mid-Nov).
London Film Festival: South Bank, London SE1 and other venues.
London to Brighton Veteran Car Run (1st Sunday) Hundreds of veteran cars and their proud owners start from Hyde Park and limp to Brighton.
Lord Mayor's Show Grand procession from the Guildhall in The City, London.
Military International Tattoo NEC, Birmingham.
State Opening of Parliament: House of Lords, Westminster, London.

December

New Year's Eve revels especially in Trafalgar Square, London.

Shopping

What to Buy

Cloth and wool Sweaters, dresses, caps, coats, scarves and other woollen goods are produced in all sheep rearing districts. The many mill shops around Bradford in Yorkshire are a bargain-hunter's paradise where lengths of fabric, fine yarns and fleeces from the Yorkshire Dales can be bought. Some mills give guided tours. Leeds, long a wool and cotton manufacturing town, is also a notable fashion centre. The British Wool Centre in Clayton has a historic display and items on sale from the British Wool Collection.

Shoes and lace Nottingham is the traditional manufacturing centre for these. At the Lace Hall, High Pavement, you can watch lace being made, learn about its history and buy gifts.

Suits The flagship of England's bespoke tailoring industry is Savile Row in London where gentlemen come from all over the world to have their suits crafted. Other outlets for traditional British attire are Burberry's (for raincoats), Aquascutum, Austin Reed and Jaeger which have branches in Piccadilly in London and department stores around the country.

Fashion Britain has a thriving fashion market, with its heart in London. Its top designers (including Caroline Charles, Jasper Conran, Katharine Hamnett, Bruce Oldfield, Paul Smith and Vivienne Westwood) are the height of haute couture and world famous. Many top international designers can also be found in London's Knightsbridge and Mayfair, and in department stores nationwide.

China and porcelain Stoke-on-Trent (in "the Potteries", Staffordshire) is the home of the great china and porcelain houses, including Wedgwood, Minton, Royal Doulton, Spode, Coalport and Royal Stafford. All these have visitor centres where you can often pick up some real bargains. You can findDartington Crystal at Great Torrington in Devon. Top-price china, glass and silver items can be found in Regent Street and Mayfair in London at exclusive shops such as Waterford, Wedgwood, Thomas Goode, Aspreys and Garrards.

Jewellery The centre for British jewellery production is in Hockley, Birmingham, where more than 200 jewellery manufacturers and 50 silversmiths are based.

Perfumes English flower perfumes make a delightful gift. The most exclusive come from Floris in Jermyn Street, and Penhaligons in Wellington Street, London. The Cotswold Perfumery in picturesque Bourton-on-the-Water makes its own perfumes.

Antiques A number of antique fairs are held nationwide throughout the year and many towns such as Bath, Harrogate and Brighton have antique centres and markets. Many old market towns, such as Petworth and Marlborough, thrive on the antiques trade.

The London and Provincial Antique Dealers' Association (LAPADA), 535 King's Road, London, SW10 0SZ, tel: 020-7823 3511, runs an up-to-date computer information service.

Consumables English delights that are easy to take home include Twinings or Jacksons tea, shortbread and numerous brands of chocolate. Benticks is famous for its after-dinner mints, Thornton's produces fine confectionery made from fresh ingredients while Cadbury's is a national favourite.

England is particularly proud of its conserves, jams, honeys, pickles and mustards (not least the famous anchovy spread, Gentleman's Relish). From delicatessens and farm shops.

Crafts Almost every town has a

street market once a week where cheap clothes and domestic ware can be bought and there may also be a good presence of local craft. There are many workshops in rural areas where potters, woodturners, leatherworkers, candlemakers and other craftsmen can be seen at work. A free map of these can be obtained from the Crafts Council, 44a Pentonville Road, London N1 9BY, tel: (020) 7930 4811.

Books University towns are the best source. Blackwells in Oxford and the many branches of Heffers in Cambridge are equally good for publications in English and most prominent foreign languages. Waterstones and Books Etc are in most large towns, and Foyles in London has several crammed floors. Serious book lovers should head for Hay-on-Wye, which has over 25 second-hand bookshops.

Gifts Some of the best places to seek out tasteful presents to take home are museum gift shops (especially the one at London's British Museum) and National Trust shops. Naturally British, 13 New Row, London WC2 supplies a wide selection of British goods in natural materials.

Export Procedures

VAT (value added tax) is a sales tax of 17.5 percent included in the price of virtually all goods except food and books. Most department stores and smaller gift shops operate a scheme to refund this tax to visitors, but often require that a minimum amount (usually £50) is spent. To get a refund you need to fill in a form from the store, have it stamped by Customs when you leave the country and then post it back to the store or hand it in to a cash refund booth at the airport. If you leave the country with the goods within three weeks you will be refunded the tax less an administration fee.

Sport

Tickets

Tickets for major sporting events can be purchased from commercial agents such as Ticketmaster (tel: 020-7344 4000) and First Call (tel: 020-7420 0000).

Spectator Sports

Football
The climax of the season is the English FA Cup at Wembley in London, which also plays host to many international games. Most league matches start at 3pm on Saturday or Sunday and 7pm midweek. For details of Premier League fixtures, tel: (020) 7976 7886. For other English games, tel: (01772) 325800.

Rugby
The Rugby Union season runs from September to May, with key matches played at Twickenham. One of the highlights is the Five Nations Championship, a knock-out between England, Ireland, Scotland, Wales and France.

Rugby League is played in summer and culminates in the Super League final at Old Trafford in Manchester (September).

For Rugby Union fixtures, tel: 020-8892 2000. For Rugby League, tel: (0113) 232 9111.

Cricket
Amateur cricket can be seen on village greens up and down the country throughout the summer. England's professional teams compete in 3 and 4-day matches all summer, plus one-day matches at weekends.

Every season England plays a 5-day Test Match against touring teams from Australia, India, New Zealand, Pakistan, Sri Lanka or the West Indies. These take place at half a dozen grounds in Britain including Lords and the Oval in London, Edgbaston in the Midlands and Headingly in Leeds. Tickets are sought-after and sell well in advance.

The Marylebone Cricket Club (MCC), based at Lords ground in St John's Wood, north London, is the governing body of the world game. Tel: 020-7289 1611.

Equestrian Sports
Flat racing
takes place between March and early November. The most important races are the Derby and Oaks at Epsom, the St Leger at Doncaster and the 1,000 and 2,000 Guineas held at Newmarket. The Royal Ascot meeting is quite a spectacle and a major social event. **Steeplechasing and hurdle racing** take place between September and

Wimbledon Tennis Championship

The Wimbledon fortnight is one of England's best-loved sporting highlights, attracting nearly 400,000 spectators. It takes place in June/July on the immaculate grass courts at the All England Club in Wimbledon, southwest London (train from Waterloo, or Southfields underground).

Most tickets are allocated by postal ballot (send a self-addressed envelope to The All England Lawn Tennis Club, PO Box 98, Wimbledon, London SW19 5AE by the end of the previous year). For details, tel: 020-8944 1066. A few tickets are kept back for some courts if you are prepared to camp out the night before, and spare seats are always to be had late-afternoon for some entertaining doubles matches.

early June. The National Hunt Festival meeting at Cheltenham in March is the most important event where the highlight is the Gold Cup. The most famous steeplechase, watched avidly and gambled on by millions, is the Grand National held at Aintree in Liverpool.

Major show jumping events
are the Royal International Horse Show at the NEC in Birmingham, the Horse of the Year Show at Wembley, London, and Olympia International Show Jumping Championships in London.

Polo matches
take place at Windsor Great Park or Cowdray Park, Midhurst, West Sussex on summer weekends. The governing body is the Hurlingham Polo Association (tel: 01869 350044).

Horse Trials
are held in spring and autumn nationwide. The major 3-day events (cross-country, show jumping and dressage) are held at Badminton, Windsor, Bramham, Burghley and Chatsworth.

The main equestrian body in Britain is The British Horse Society which governs the Pony Club and Riding Club. Tel: (01926) 707700.

Athletics
Athletics are governed by the Amateur Athletics Association (AAA), with the main national sports centre for athletics at Crystal Palace, south London (tel: 020-8778 0131).

Golf
The most important national event is the Open Championship every July. Other prestigious tournaments include the Ryder Cup for professionals and the Walker Cup for amateurs.

For dates and venues contact the Professional Golfer's Association (PGA), Centenary House, The Belfry, Sutton Coldfield B76 9PT, tel: (01675) 470333.

Motor Racing
The British Grand Prix, at Silver-stone in July, is the highlight of the Formula One calendar. But

England's race tracks (most notably Brands Hatch and Donnington) also host a range of races, from touring cars to Formula Ford to rallying. Details from the Royal Automobile Club, tel: (01753) 681736.

Participant Sports

Most towns have a sports centre and pool. There are also plenty of facilities for golf and tennis. For information on what's in each area you can contact the local council's leisure services department. Alternatively, get in touch with Sport England, 16 Upper Woburn Place, London WC1H 0QP (tel: 020-7273 1500).

Watersports
There are many opportunities to sail on the south coast and lakes in the north. There are excellent facilities for canoeing, windsurfing, jet skiing and boating on many inland waters.

Horse Riding
If you want to go out for a hack in the countryside, there are plenty of public riding stables in rural areas. However, most stables do not let riders out unaccompanied. Pony trekking is particularly popular on Dartmoor, Exmoor, in the New Forest and in Wales.

For information, contact The British Horse Society, Stoneleigh Deer Park, Kenilworth CV8 2XZ (tel: 01926 707700).

Golf
There are hundreds of courses around the country that welcome visitors. Courses close to London are generally heavily booked.

Further Reading

Other Insight Guides

Three types of Insight Guide are designed to meet the needs of every traveller.

The 190-title **Insight Guides** series includes books on *London, Oxford, Scotland, Wales, Glasgow, Edinburgh* and *The Channel Islands*.

The 120-title **Insight Pocket Guides** series offers personal recommendations and a pull-out map; titles include *South-East England, London* and *Scotland*.

The 120-title **Insight Compact Guides** series provides the ideal portable, fully illustrated guidebook to specific areas. Twenty titles cover every tourist area in the UK, from Cornwall to the Scottish Highlands *(see facing page)*.

Good Companions

Artist's London by David Piper, Fascinating images of London over the ages.
Cider with Rosie by Laurie Lee. Memories of an idyllic youth in Gloucestershire.
The Concise Pepys by Samuel Pepys. Read a first-hand account of the Great Fire of London and find out about daily life in 17th-century England.
A Guide through the District of the Lakes by William Wordsworth. Lyrical descriptions of the poet's beloved Lake District.
Hound of the Baskervilles by Sir Arthur Conan Doyle. Sherlock Holmes explores the mystery on the moors.
Jamaica Inn by Daphne du Maurier. A tale of Cornish "wreckers", who loot shipwrecks.
Jude the Obscure by Thomas Hardy. A sombre tale of love and loss with an evocative setting in southwest

England (known as "Hardy Country").

London: A Concise History by Geoffrey Trease. Good illustrated history.

Lorna Doone by R.D. Blackmore. The story of a tragic heroine and her lawless family brings Exmoor landscapes to life.

Mary, Queen of Scots by Antonia Fraser.

Mrs Dalloway by Virginia Woolf. A day-in-the-life of an Edwardian matron in London.

Oliver Twist by Charles Dickens. The classic tale of Victorian pickpockets in London's East End.

Pride and Prejudice by Jane Austen. Classic romance by one of England best-loved 18th-century novelists

A Shropshire Lad by A.E. Housman. Poems on the themes of Shropshire country life, and the life of a soldier.

Spectacle of Empire by James Morris. Popular history of the British Empire and its decline.

Tilly by Catherine Cookson. Set in Durham, the story of a girl born into a poor family in Victorian times.

Tour Through the Whole Island of Great Britain by Daniel Defoe.

Vanishing Cornwall by Daphne du Maurier. A perceptive view of the changing face of Cornwall.

Westward Ho! by Charles Kingsley. Heroic tale of West Country seafarers.

The Woodlanders by Thomas Hardy. Rural life and high emotions in the Wessex countryside.

Wuthering Heights by Emily Brontë. Passion and repression on the brooding Yorkshire Moors.

ART & PHOTO CREDITS

Picture Spreads

Cartographic Editor **Zoë Goodwin**
Production **Stuart A Everitt**
Design Consultants
Carlotta Junger, Graham Mitchener
Picture Research **Hilary Genin**

Map Production
Colourmap Scanning Ltd
© 2000 Apa Publications GmbH & Co.
Verlag KG (Singapore branch)

Index

Numbers in italics refer to photographs

66 I was first drawn to the Insight Guides by the excellent "Nepal" volume. I can think of no book which so effectively captures the essence of a country. Out of these pages leaped the Nepal I know – the captivating charm of a people and their culture. I've since discovered and enjoyed the entire Insight Guide series. Each volume deals with a country in the same sensitive depth, which is nowhere more evident than in the superb photography. 99

Sir Edmund Hillary

✳ INSIGHT GUIDES

The world's largest collection of visual travel guides

A range of guides and maps to meet every travel need

Insight Guides

This classic series gives you the complete picture of a destination through expert, well written and informative text and stunning photography. Each book is an ideal background information and travel planner, serves as an on-the-spot companion – and is a superb visual souvenir of a trip. Nearly 200 titles.

Insight Pocket Guides

focus on the best choices for places to see and things to do, picked by our local correspondents. They are ideal for visitors new to a destination. To help readers follow the routes easily, the books contain full-size pull-out maps. 120 titles.

Insight Maps

are designed to complement the guides. They provide full mapping of major cities, regions and countries, and their laminated finish makes them easy to fold and gives them durability. 60 titles.

Insight Compact Guides

are convenient, comprehensive reference books, modestly priced. The text, photographs and maps are all carefully cross-referenced, making the books ideal for on-the-spot use when in a destination. 120 titles.

Different travellers have different needs. Since 1970, Insight Guides has been meeting these needs with a range of practical and stimulating guidebooks and maps

Insight Guides – the Classic Series
that puts you in the picture

Alaska	China	Hong Kong	Morocco	Singapore
Alsace	Cologne	Hungary	Moscow	South Africa
Amazon Wildlife	Continental Europe		Munich	South America
American Southwest	Corsica	Iceland		South Tyrol
Amsterdam	Costa Rica	India	Namibia	Southeast Asia
Argentina	Crete	India's Western	Native America	Wildlife
Asia, East	Crossing America	Himalayas	Nepal	Spain
Asia, South	Cuba	India, South	Netherlands	Spain, Northern
Asia, Southeast	Cyprus	Indian Wildlife	New England	Spain, Southern
Athens	Czech & Slovak	Indonesia	New Orleans	Sri Lanka
Atlanta	Republic	Ireland	New York City	Sweden
Australia		Israel	New York State	Switzerland
Austria	Delhi, Jaipur & Agra	Istanbul	New Zealand	Sydney
	Denmark	Italy	Nile	Syria & Lebanon
Bahamas	Dominican Republic	Italy, Northern	Normandy	
Bali	Dresden		Norway	Taiwan
Baltic States	Dublin	Jamaica		Tenerife
Bangkok	Düsseldorf	Japan	Old South	Texas
Barbados		Java	Oman & The UAE	Thailand
Barcelona	East African Wildlife	Jerusalem	Oxford	Tokyo
Bay of Naples	Eastern Europe	Jordan		Trinidad & Tobago
Beijing	Ecuador		Pacific Northwest	Tunisia
Belgium	Edinburgh	Kathmandu	Pakistan	Turkey
Belize	Egypt	Kenya	Paris	Turkish Coast
Berlin	England	Korea	Peru	Tuscany
Bermuda			Philadelphia	
Boston	Finland	Laos & Cambodia	Philippines	Umbria
Brazil	Florence	Lisbon	Poland	USA: Eastern States
Brittany	Florida	Loire Valley	Portugal	USA: Western States
Brussels	France	London	Prague	US National Parks:
Budapest	Frankfurt	Los Angeles	Provence	East
Buenos Aires	French Riviera		Puerto Rico	US National Parks:
Burgundy		Madeira		West
Burma (Myanmar)	Gambia & Senegal	Madrid	Rajasthan	
	Germany	Malaysia	Rhine	Vancouver
Cairo	Glasgow	Mallorca & Ibiza	Rio de Janeiro	Venezuela
Calcutta	Gran Canaria	Malta	Rockies	Venice
California	Great Barrier Reef	Marine Life ot the	Rome	Vienna
California, Northern	Great Britain	South China Sea	Russia	Vietnam
California, Southern	Greece	Mauritius &		
Canada	Greek Islands	Seychelles	St. Petersburg	Wales
Caribbean	Guatemala, Belize &	Melbourne	San Francisco	Washington DC
Catalonia	Yucatán	Mexico City	Sardinia	Waterways of Europe
Channel Islands		Mexico	Scotland	Wild West
Chicago	Hamburg	Miami	Seattle	
Chile	Hawaii	Montreal	Sicily	Yemen

Complementing the above titles are 120 easy-to-carry Insight Compact Guides, 120 Insight Pocket
Guides with full-size pull-out maps and more than 60 laminated easy-fold Insight Maps

England's Cathedrals

Canterbury Cathedral

West Doorway (**A**); font (**B**);
pulpit (**C**); screen (**D**);
Library (**E**); Chapterhouse (**F**);
Lady Chapel (**G**); Choir (**H**);
St Michael's Chapel (**I**); pulpit (**J**);
Archbishop's throne (**K**);
Presbytery (**L**);
Site of Becket's shrine (**M**);
Trinity Chapel, with tombs of Black
Prince and Henry IV (**N**);
Corona (**O**); St Augustine's Chair (**P**);
Treasury (**Q**);
St Andrew's Chapel (**R**);
St Anselm's Chapel (**S**)

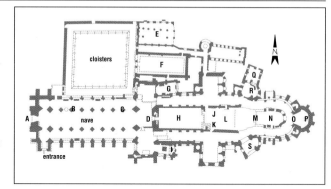

York Minster

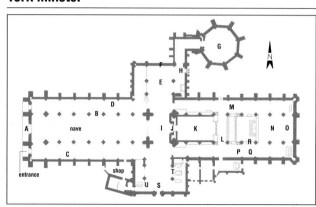

West Window, "The heart of
Yorkshire" (**A**); Dragon's Head (**B**);
Jesse Window (**C**); Bellfounders'
Window (**D**); North Transept (**E**);
Five Sisters' Window (**F**); Chapter
House (**G**); Astronomical Clock (**H**);
Central Tower Crossing (**I**); Screen
(**J**); Choir (**K**); Archbishop's Throne
(**L**); St William Window (**M**); Lady
Chapel (**N**); Great East Window (**O**);
St Cuthbert's Window (**P**); Norman
Crypt (**Q**); South Transept (**R**); Rose
Window (**S**); Archbishop Gray's tomb
(**T**); Foundations Museum (**U**)

Wells Cathedral

Sugar Chantry (**A**);
Saxon font (**B**);
St Calixtus Chapel (**C**);
St Martin's Chapel (**D**);
Choir (**E**);
South Choir Aisle (**F**);
St Catherine's Chapel (**G**);
St John the Baptist Chapel (**H**);
Lady Chapel (**I**);
Retrochoir (**J**);
St Stephen's Chapel (**K**);
Chapel of Corpus Christi (**L**);
North Choir Aisle (**M**);
Chapter House (**N**); Clock (**O**);
Bubwith's Chantry (**P**)

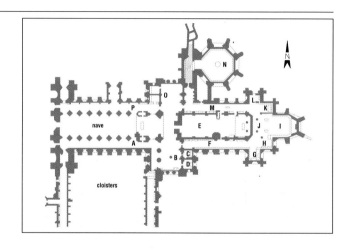

London's Top Sites

Westminster Abbey

Features: West Door (**A**); South Aisle (**C**); North Aisle (**D**); Choir (**E**); The Sanctuary (**F**); door to cloisters (**S**); Chapter House (**T**); Chamber of the Pyx (**U**); undercroft or crypt (**V**) **Chapels**: St Georges's (**B**); Abbot Islip (**H**); St John the Baptist (**I**); St Paul's (**J**); Henry V's chantry chapel (**K**); Henry V (**L**); Henry VII (**M**); St Nicholas's (**N**); St Edmund's (**O**); St Benedict's (**P**); St Faith's (**R**). **Tombs & Monuments**: British statesmen, in the North Transept (**G**). Poets' Corner, in the South Transept (**Q**)

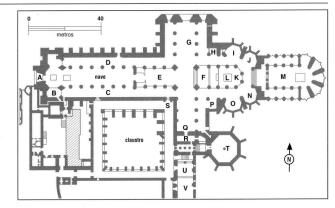

St Paul's Cathedral

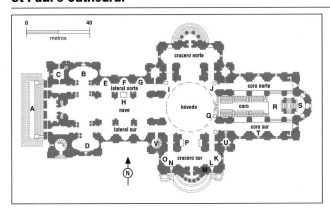

Features: marble steps (**A**); oak pulpit (**Q**); High Altar (**R**); Dean's pulpit and stairs to crypt (**U**); stairs to dome (**V**). **Chapels**: St Dunstan's (**B**); All Souls' (**C**); St Michael & St George's (**D**); American Chapel of Remembrance (**S**). **Tombs & Monuments**: Lord Leighton (**E**); General Gordon (**F**); Viscount Melbourne (**G**); Duke of Wellington (**H**); Joshua Reynolds (**I**); Dr Samuel Johnson (**J**); Admiral Earl Howe (**K**); Admiral Collingwood (**L**); JMW Turner (**M**); Sir John Moore (**N**); General Abercromby (**O**); Lord Nelson (**P**); John Donne (**T**)

Tower of London

Entrance (**A**); Lion Tower (**B**); Middle Tower (**C**); Byward Tower (**D**); The Bell Tower (**E**); St Thomas's Tower (**F**); Traitors' Gate (**G**); Bloody Tower (**H**); Wakefield Tower (**I**); King's House (**J**); Gaoler's House (**K**); Tower Green (**L**); Beauchamp Tower (**M**); Royal Chapel of St Peter ad Vincula (**N**); Jewel House (**O**); Regimental Museum (**P**); Hospital (**Q**); New Armouries (**R**); White Tower (**S**); Wardrobe Tower (**T**)

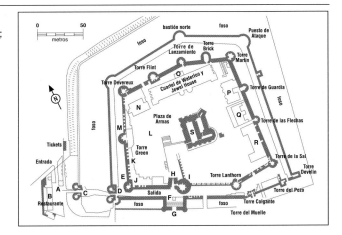

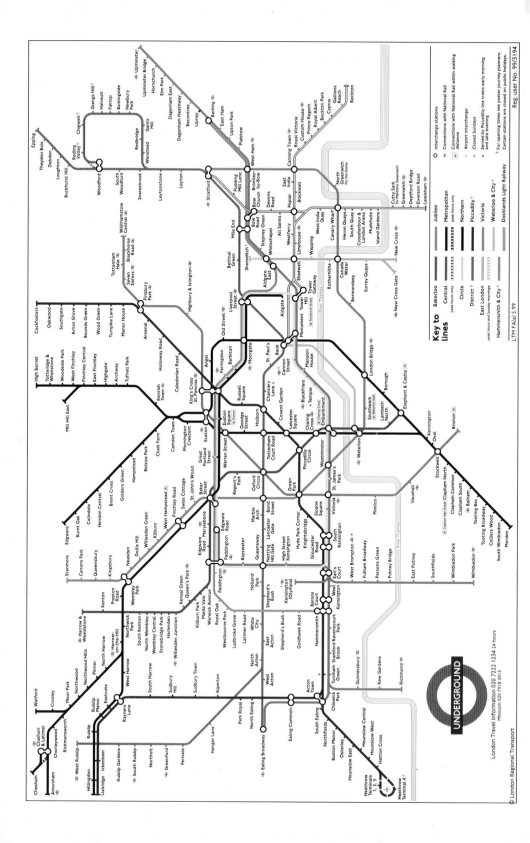